# Skills for Human Service Practice

*Working with Individuals, Groups, and Communities*

*Canadian Edition*

Agi O'Hara
Zita Weber
Kathy Levine

OXFORD
UNIVERSITY PRESS

# OXFORD

## UNIVERSITY PRESS

8 Sampson Mews, Suite 204, Don Mills, Ontario  M3C 0H5
www.oupcanada.com

Oxford University Press is a department of the University of Oxford.
It furthers the University's objective of excellence in research, scholarship,
and education by publishing worldwide in

Oxford   New York

Auckland   Cape Town   Dar es Salaam   Hong Kong   Karachi
Kuala Lumpur   Madrid   Melbourne   Mexico City   Nairobi
New Delhi   Shanghai   Taipei   Toronto

With offices in

Argentina   Austria   Brazil   Chile   Czech Republic   France   Greece
Guatemala   Hungary   Italy   Japan   Poland   Portugal   Singapore
South Korea   Switzerland   Thailand   Turkey   Ukraine   Vietnam
Oxford is a trade mark of Oxford University Press
in the UK and in certain other countries

Published in Canada
by Oxford University Press

Original edition published by Oxford University Press,
253 Normanby Road, South Melbourne, Victoria, 3205, Australia.
Copyright © 2006 Agi O'Hara and Zita Weber.

**Library and Archives Canada Cataloguing in Publication**

Skills for human service practice : working with individuals,
groups, and communities / [edited by] Agi O'Hara,
Zita Weber and Kathy Levine. —1st Canadian ed.

Includes bibliographical references and index.

ISBN 978-0-19-543010-3

1. Social service—Textbooks. I. O'Hara, Agi   II. Weber, Zita   III. Levine, Kathryn A. (Kathryn Ann)

HV40.S488 2010          361.3'2          C2009-906163-5

Cover image: Oliver Childs/iStockphoto

Oxford University Press is committed to our environment. This book is printed on
Forest Stewardship Council certified paper harvested from a responsibly managed forest.

**Mixed Sources**

Product group from well-managed forests
and other controlled sources
www.fsc.org   Cert no. SW-COC-000952
©1996 Forest Stewardship Council

**FSC**

Printed and bound in Canada.

1  2  3  4  -  13  12  11  10

# Brief Contents

# Expanded Contents

# Practice Skills

## CHAPTER 10

## CHAPTER 11

## CHAPTER 12

**CHAPTER 15**

**CHAPTER 16**

**CHAPTER 17**

There is an old Chinese adage that says, 'May you live in interesting times.' In terms of contemporary social service practice, it might well be said that this aphorism presents itself as a fact of life. Human services professionals are living in interesting times in which the workplace demands accountability, performance measurability, and evidence-based practice. The contemporary consumer-based workplace has generated a plethora of concepts and a language replete with terms such as trimming budgets, cost-effective practices, and externally-measurable procedures and effects. Current organizational and economic realities are challenging old and well-worn ways of working. Key structural and political influences have resulted in shifts from institutional to community-based care in many sectors, and greater regulation of organizations and professionals. New theoretical approaches are demanding a clearer articulation of the activities undertaken.

There are multiple influences on today's human services practitioner. Policy initiatives and demands for more flexible, participative, and collaborative ways of working are reported across many different contexts. Intellectual scrutiny and critique are now more evident than ever. At the same time, the difficulties experienced by individuals, families, and groups appear more intense than ever, challenging workers to respond to increased stress and trauma in the lives of the people with whom they work. This, in turn, calls for much better articulation of the knowledge, skills, and values of human services practice.

Living with both global and local uncertainty requires today's professionals to develop and nurture knowledge and skills that are transferable to a variety of settings. Professional identities are being reassessed and, sometimes, reshaped. Human services practitioners often work in multidisciplinary teams where 'multi-skilling' is expected and role diffusion is a necessary part of their professional life. Postmodernist thinking adds to this challenge by positing that certainty is inherently unattainable. Banging the drum of truth (or, what we considered to be 'truth') and precision is no longer good enough. Making grandiose claims about theory and practice will invite the deconstruction inherent in critical reflection.

The contributing authors to this book have individually and collectively lived through inevitable historical developments in theory and practice. Historical moments are significant. If it were not for the early theorists and their now seemingly simpler ways of constructing paradigms, we would not have had the building blocks that allowed later and contemporary theorists to develop more complex theoretical explanations. For instance, in 1917, Mary Richmond's recognition that social workers need to concern themselves with the social dimension of assessment (which was then termed 'diagnosis') was a radical idea. Her book, *Social Diagnosis*, was a guiding text for many years. It also marks one of the critical historical moments in the inexorable evolution towards the theoretical frameworks with which we are familiar today. Similarly, Jane Addams, another pioneer in social work, founded a settlement house, Hull House, in Chicago in 1889. She recognized the importance of the social context in determining people's lives and worked to build supportive communities. More recently, some authors have been intensely critical of earlier theories and theorists, perhaps forgetting that if they had not existed, current theorists would not have the luxury of such a revisionist position. Theories and strategies should only be judged in the context of their times. Not all that has gone before is narrow, uncritical, simplistic, or unenlightened.

This book was conceived and incubated in the belief that today's beginning human services practitioners can benefit from a practical, comprehensive resource book intended to help develop skills and encourage reflection on their practice. It is not a 'how to' manual that assures smooth practice in a context-free environment. Practice generally occurs in an organizational context and is governed by a set of agency policies and procedures that always need to be incorporated, as well as provincial and federal legislation. The main focus of the book is generic skill development in an applied context. There is recognition of the common elements in work across contexts and among various professions associated with the human services. Nevertheless, there is an acknowledgement that context shapes each piece of work in practice.

Although this is not primarily a theoretical book, the authors of the chapters endorse the time-honoured professional belief that theory is central to good practice. Essentially, the framework provided by any given theory—or, indeed, combination of theories—provides a lens that shapes what we think and how we put our thoughts into action. At all times, it is important to be conscious of the theories used in our work so that we can critically evaluate our assumptions and search for alternative views (Gambrill 1997; Napier & Fook 2000). The contributing authors adopt a critical practice perspective. Gibbs and Gambrill (1999) define critical thinking as '... the critical appraisal of beliefs, arguments, and claims in order to arrive at well-reasoned judgements' (Preface, p. xiii). They believe that critical thinking encourages practitioners to evaluate the soundness of beliefs, arguments, and claims across practice, research, policy, and administration contexts. Critical practice, utilizing appropriate skills, occurs in a theoretical context, often incorporating several interrelated theoretical traditions—for example, feminist theory with an anti-oppressive approach. Critical theory requires the practitioner to appreciate the political dimension of their work and to break down dualisms: the personal is political. For example, within social work, Ife suggests that critical theory, '... serves more as an affirmation of the critical and alternative spirit of social work, which can be traced back to Jane Addams ... and to many who came after her, who saw social work as an essentially critical practice to bring about a better, fairer and more just society, rather than merely providing professional interventions to individuals and families' (Ife 1997, p. 151). Such a critical approach requires that the practitioner (irrespective of their professional affiliations within the human services) be reflective and open-minded, taking into account different perspectives, assumptions, and experiences (Brechin

2000; Fook 2002; Healy 2000; Ife 1997). Embedded within a critical perspective is the notion that practitioners are not and cannot be 'all-seeing' and 'all-knowing' and that an open and critical approach allows for a process of evolving knowledge and skill development to occur.

Our practice grows and changes throughout our career, as we incorporate different constructions of the contexts and specific situations we face. Our skills evolve and are honed and revised as we encounter new and different practice situations. Our skills are potentially challenged whenever we reflect on our practice in familiar situations—when we revisit our once taken-for-granted assumptions and perspectives. Reflective practitioners are committed to examining what they are doing, why they are doing it, and what opportunities and barriers might exist to doing it differently. This involves paying attention to the situation at hand and the skills required for an appropriate response.

Determining what to include in a human services skills book is not easy. It is neither possible to cover all aspects of practice in every context, nor all related theories. Our choices are obviously guided by consideration of our target audience—the beginning practitioners and students associated with the human services. Creating the structure within which the chosen skills are to be presented is also challenging. It is essential that each of the skills are considered within the rubric of reflective and ethical practice, professional values, appropriate use of self, working within a legal framework, and an understanding of the diversity within the communities in which practice takes place. Although it is possible to include each of these perspectives in every chapter, the authors thought this would not only become repetitive but also create chapters that are excessively lengthy. Our preferred structure offers the first seven chapters, covering the above perspectives, as the necessary and constant foundational framework for the specific skills that follow.

Each chapter presents some aspect of practice for which certain skills are widely considered useful and appropriate. The text constitutes a comprehensive and practical treatment on practice skills across contexts. At all times, the notion of transferability of knowledge and skills is evident. Skills in assessment, for example, may vary a little from one context to another, but assessment will require some fundamental knowledge and reflection on the information that underpins it and the purpose for which it will be put to use. Skills are not bits of technology to be applied to any context without reference to theory. Skills are the means practitioners draw on to operationalize their thoughts and hypotheses about what to do in practice.

If we are asked to identify the key theoretical approach that underpins our work as practitioners, and, in turn, our writing in this book, it is clearly that of critical reflection. It is therefore fitting to begin the book with a chapter on reflective practice. In chapter 1, Lindsey Napier explains the sources of theoretical ideas underpinning critical reflection, provides arguments for the view that critical reflection is basic to professional practice and draws on two case studies to illustrate the processes involved. In chapter 2, Zita Weber looks at professional values and ethical practice, both of which are at the very core of human services work. She explores various ethical theories, principles, responsibilities, and codes of practice, offering numerous case scenarios to illustrate the application of the theoretical material and activities to reinforce the reader's understanding. In chapter 3, Jude

Irwin details the process of supervision, offering strategies to assist supervisees in being proactive, enabling them to take full advantage of the supervisory relationship. In chapter 4, Agi O'Hara develops the view that practitioner self-knowledge and -awareness is the foundation of effective work in the human services. She explores the appropriate use of self-disclosure, immediacy, and issues regarding practitioners' emotions, countertransference, and self-care. In chapter 5, Denise Lynch begins the discussion of cultural diversity in practice, focusing on the varied experiences of migrants and refugees in Australia. She offers strategies by which practitioners can incorporate values and ideas to direct their work in culturally-appropriate ways. Although grounded in the Australian experience, the strategies are transferable to many different contexts, including Canada. In chapter 6, Michelle Blanchard continues the discussion of cultural diversity, addressing issues of social justice for Indigenous people. Blanchard provides practical skills to enable professionals to develop cultural sensitivity and competence in their interactions with Indigenous workers, clients, and communities. She raises concerns about the issues that arise when conducting Indigenous research and offers practical skills to ensure that research is ethical and involves consultation, negotiation, and mutual understanding. In chapter 7, Fran Waugh focuses on the multi-dimensional context of practitioners' interventions with service users. She highlights various intersections between legislation; the agency's purpose, policies, and procedures; the theoretical perspectives informing practice; and the practitioner's experience, knowledge, and skills. In chapter 8, Zita Weber addresses the concerns of many practitioners regarding effective communication. She presents strategies and skills for speaking in and to groups, and offers guidelines for effective written communication. She highlights the many aspects of preparation and delivery of the spoken message, and details the specific roles and protocols of formal meetings. She offers practical guidelines for effective writing in various contexts, and includes a sample report to illustrate the application of these guidelines. In chapter 9, Agi O'Hara presents the microskills of interviewing, focusing on many of the skills associated with the various stages of the interview. She includes practice examples and activities to elaborate on the skills of welcoming and establishing the working relationship (beginning stage); attending, empathy, appropriate use of questions, paraphrasing, reflecting feelings, prompting, probing, summarizing, and self-disclosure (the middle stage); and considerations for appropriately ending interviews. In chapter 10, Zita Weber deals with the complex skills of assessment, emphasizing that whatever the practice context, assessment of the situation beforehand is the foundation of decision-making and planning for future action. Weber offers two theoretical frameworks—anti-oppressive and strength perspectives—through which she explores the assessment process, highlighting its stages and key elements. In chapter 11, Zita Weber looks at the role of advocacy, suggesting that most practitioners engage in it frequently, and that for some, such as social workers, it is believed to be a primary responsibility to their clients. She explores two types of advocacy (case and class) and a rights perspective, and the empowerment approach within which skills such as listening, questioning, recording, and providing feedback are practised. In chapter 12, Agi O'Hara explores the role of conflict in our lives, identifying the advantages and disadvantages of various responses we have to conflict. She discusses strategies by which we may better manage conflict and the role of the practitioner as a facilitator of their clients' conflict management and/or resolution. In chapter 13, Agi O'Hara offers the perspective that despite the variety of purposes for group formation, many processes and dynamics are common to all groups. The chapter details these frequently occurring group phenomena including group development, group leader tasks, styles of leadership, group goals and rules, use of structured exercises, and strategies for effective group closure. In chapter 14, Agi O'Hara continues the discussion of groupwork, focusing specifically on leader intervention. She develops guidelines for understanding group processes and offers the Critical Incident Model and Focal Conflict Model as the basis from which to develop appropriate and effective interventions. In chapter 15, Zita Weber offers another perspective on working in groups, this time with the focus on working in organizations, and the fact that many practitioners will inevitably be a member of several different types of teams. She discusses three models of teamwork and explores the many difficulties associated with working in teams, such as the myth of cooperation and issues associated with power, authority, and competence. She offers strategies to promote effective collaboration and numerous case examples to illustrate the suggestions made. In chapter 16, Karen Healy explores the nature of the relationship between human service professions and community work. Healy introduces the principles of asset-based community development and the skills associated with conducting an asset audit—a core technique of this approach—which identifies the strengths of the community, and assists in planning action with community members. She analyses the strengths and limits of asset-based community development and illustrates the practical application of the approach through the consideration of a detailed community case example. In chapter 17, Karen Healy continues her focus on community work, this time exploring the benefits of community education, which aims to both recognize and build the knowledge of a community, by engaging community members as peer learners and teachers. She offers the perspective that although community education strategies are generally only associated with community workers, the same practice principles can also be applied to a range of social service practices.

The material in this book is gathered from a wide range of sources and filtered through each contributor's insights and experiences. Their practice experiences are diverse, derived from numerous social work and psychology contexts, and their narratives are as unique as their authors. In the spirit of postmodernism, the reader can not expect a single pattern of presentation but, rather, a multiplicity of experiences and a crucible of narrative voices which reflect the essential differences and inherent subjectivity in practice. A variety of practice contexts and client populations are used in activities, case examples, and practice points to reinforce their applicability across the human services. These provide the reader the opportunity to tease out the salient features and key concepts in order to understand that effective practice involves the interplay of values, knowledge, and skills. The case examples are not actual case studies, but real situations re-worked for publication.

Throughout this book, the reader has the opportunity to learn by doing. Activities, case examples, and practice points have been created to be enjoyable as well as instructive, in the belief that learning should be fun.

Becoming a critical practitioner starts here. This book introduces you to the idea of using intellectual reflections and insights to meet the frustrations, obstacles, and difficulties along the practice path. Intellectual courage is needed to confront and not to accept uncritically the 'rightness' of long-held beliefs. Intellectual perseverance is needed to work with challenging issues over an extended period of time in order to achieve deeper understanding. Struggling with a sense of confusion, living with unsettling questions, and being confronted by discrepancies and inconsistencies in one's own thoughts and actions are part of our human experience. There might be individual differences, but, collectively, we all know that reflecting on premises, assumptions, and ideas, however difficult it may be, is a necessary part of being a practitioner. Critical practice questions taken-for-granted assumptions, deconstructs self-evident beliefs, and encourages open dialogue. Critical practice embraces reflection on opposing views, and the critical practitioner is ready and flexible enough to welcome the new discoveries that reflection brings.

Our aim in producing this book is to draw together ideas and information that provide practical skills in a variety of contexts—enabling the reader to use the book in accordance with their practice needs.

## References

Brechin, A. (2000). Introducing critical practice. In A. Brechin, H. Brown & M. A. Eby (eds), *Critical Practice in Health and Social Care*. London: Sage.

Fook, J. (2002). *Social Work: Critical Theory and Practice*. London: Sage.

Gambrill, E. (1997). *Social Work Practice: A Critical Thinker's Guide*. New York: Oxford University Press.

Gibbs, L., & Gambrill, E. (1999). *Critical Thinking for Social Workers*. Thousand Oaks, CA: Sage.

Healy, K. (2000). *Social Work Practices: Contemporary Perspective on Change*. London: Sage.

Ife, J. (1997). *Rethinking Social Work: Towards Critical Practice*. South Melbourne: Longman.

Napier, L., & Fook, J. (2000). *Breakthroughs in Practice: Theorising Critical Moments in Social Work*. London: Whiting and Birch.

Richmond, M. (1917). *Social Diagnosis*. New York: Russell Sage Foundation.

# Acknowledgements

We are grateful for the support, inspiration, and effort that made this book possible. We wish to thank colleagues, friends, and family who have stayed the distance with us in the journey from concept to final manuscript. Particular thanks go to Debra James from Oxford University Press, who believed in the idea from the beginning, Tim Fullerton, for his painstaking good work and humour during the editing process, and those colleagues who have shared their professional insights and aspects of their work in the form of scenarios for this book: Deborah Hart, Sheila Nicolson, Annette Riley, and Andrea Taylor.

# Contributors

**Michelle Blanchard** is an Indigenous woman from Minjeeribah (North Stradbroke Island), Australia, and a descendant of the Noonucal and Nugi clans. Her passion and interest is in writing and includes poetry, prose, and writing for performance. She is currently enrolled in a PhD program with the University of Technology, Sydney, where her research study encompasses Indigenous interpretation and representation in contemporary Indigenous theatre practices. Michelle currently holds the position of Deputy Director at the Koori Centre, University of Sydney, where she also lectures in Indigenous Australian Studies including history, culture, and health.

**Karen Healy** is Associate Professor in the School of Social Work and Applied Human Sciences at the University of Queensland, Australia. She has practised as a social worker in health, youth, and child protection services. She is author of two books on social work theories for practice, including *Social Work Theories in Context* (Palgrave Macmillan 2005), and she has written extensively on social work and policy studies.

**Jude Irwin** is Associate Professor in the Faculty of Education and Social Work at the University of Sydney. Jude's teaching, research, and practice interests span a number of areas including violence against women, children, and young people; discrimination against gay men and lesbians; and professional practice supervision. Jude has published widely, including four co-edited books, numerous journal articles, and several public reports.

**Kathryn Levine** is an Assistant Professor in the Faculty of Social Work at the University of Manitoba. Her practice and research interests focus on family violence issues, child and adolescent mental health, and the promotion of resilience in at-risk youth. She has extensive experience as a clinical social worker and has provided a wide range of therapeutic and clinical services to individuals, families, and groups within the child welfare, child and adolescent mental health, and public school systems. Her current research projects include an examination of the cumulative impact of violence exposure on adolescent girls; exploration of factors that promote family involvement in the career development processes for children; and homelessness and housing issues for persons with intellectual disabilities. Kathryn was a Fahs-Beck Scholar (recipient of a doctoral dissertation grant) in 2009.

**Denise Lynch** has a background in child protection, having worked in the New South Wales Department of Community Services at a front line and management level. She has been a private consultant and has been a lecturer in the School of Social Work and Policy Studies at the University of Sydney for ten years. Her teaching responsibilities include Practitioner Skills and Families and Violence. Her research interests are child protection, children as refugees in Australia, and children and justice. Her most recent conference presentation was on The Care, Protection and Adjustment of Refugee Children in Australia at the 15th International Conference on Child Abuse and Neglect.

**Lindsey Napier** teaches in the Faculty of Education and Social Work at the University of Sydney. With Jan Fook, she co-edited *Breakthroughs in Practice: Theorising Critical Moments in Social Work* (Whiting and Birch 2000). Her current research focuses on social work in dying, death, and bereavement; good practice in community care for people with dementia; and access to appropriate services for women experiencing both mental illness and domestic violence.

**Agi O'Hara** is a lecturer in Psychology in the School of Social Work and Policy Studies at the University of Sydney, specializing in the areas of counselling, child abuse, domestic violence, suicide prevention, grief, and practitioner skills. She has published in the areas of suicide prevention, professional practice, and online teaching. She is completing a PhD, focusing on mentoring programs with disadvantaged and at-risk children and youth. Agi is a registered psychologist with many years of experience working with individuals, couples, and groups, and has been a consultant to several government departments, and companies within the private sector, conducting groupwork training, and team-building courses and workshops.

**Fran Waugh** is a senior lecturer in the School of Social Work and Policy Studies at the University of Sydney. Fran teaches in the undergraduate and postgraduate Social Work program. Fran's practice research in areas of national priority, such as child emotional abuse, child protection, domestic violence, paediatric palliative care, and older people with dementia, is drawn from rigorous and often difficult engagement with these vulnerable and at-risk groups. Her PhD research focused on the work practices of statutory child protection workers in New South Wales in responding to emotional abuse notifications. Fran has an extensive practice background working in community health, family support, and child protection in both health and welfare settings.

**Zita Weber** is a lecturer in the School of Social Work and Policy Studies at the University of Sydney. Prior to entering academia, Zita worked in a number of mental health and rehabilitation settings. Zita teaches in both the undergraduate and graduate Social Work programs. Her research areas include mental health, loss and grief, migrant issues, and women's issues. In addition to published papers, Zita is the author of four books for the general public: *Back from the Blues, Out of the Blues, Good Grief*, and *The Best Years of a Woman's Life*.

# 1 Practising Critical Reflection
## Lindsey Napier

It is commonplace to hear that social workers must be 'reflective practitioners' and that 'reflective practice' is integral to good practice. This is occurring at a time when practitioners make frequent comment on the absence of time for pause to think. Rather, the requirement is to respond to continuous pressure to find quick fixes, sort out immediate problems, follow protocols, complete pre-categorized assessment forms, and perform tasks that require concentrated effort and stamina but may afford limited scope for discretion.

Practising in a *critically reflective* way focuses conscious attention on the 'whole self' of the practitioner: the thinking, feeling, believing, acting practitioner. A better understanding of the assumptions on which our actions are based and an awareness of our subjective position in our practice can lead to changes to our practice. Critical reflection is a developing project, informed by specific theoretical ideas about the meanings of 'critical'.

In this chapter, I provide a brief introduction to critical reflection. (For a fuller exposition of the theoretical underpinnings of critical reflection, see Fook 2002.) I explain the sources of theoretical ideas supporting critical reflection. I provide an argument for why critical reflection is basic to good social work, and especially crucial in these times. I illustrate the processes involved in reflecting critically on one's practice by way of an extended case example from my beginning social work practice. I describe a second incident, and ask readers to consider how they might step their way through the processes of critical reflection.

The skills of critical reflection are many. Critical reflection requires an ability to conceptualize, analyze, and examine the assumptions underpinning one's practice, in order to improve it. We must be able to become conscious of the ways in which language is employed to authorize particular perspectives; to make links between the personal, social, and political domains; to recognize and tolerate diversity; to invite and work with uncertainty; to examine the ways in which one exercises power and authority; and to imagine and consider unfamiliar and new ways of thinking and acting.

## Towards critical reflection

There are a number of strands to the development of critical reflection. It is important to understand them so that the specific meanings of critical reflection are clear.

The works of Argyris and Schön (1976) and Schön (1983, 1987) are often cited as the starting point for consideration of reflective approaches in professional education and practice. Schön questioned the traditional assumptions about knowledge generation. He queried the assumption that the only valid practice is the application of knowledge generalized from systematic, empirical research to specific situations. He pointed out that theory is also implicit in our actions, actions that may or may not be congruent with our espoused ideas and beliefs. He highlighted the difficulty of formal theory to 'inform' fully how to act in the constantly changing world of practice, in all its diversity, messiness, and unpredictability. Creativity, versatility, and judgment are essential. Reflection can promote a more effective practitioner, where the whole of knowledge is valued and uncritically embraced. Through reflection, the practitioner can also seek greater coherence in practice, by discovering the differences between *espoused* ideas and value commitments and one's *actual* practices.

The contributions of scholars in education, such as Mezirow and Brookfield, are crucial: they pointed to the distinguishing features of *critical* reflection in learning. Mezirow et al. (1991, p. 1) argued that critical reflection involves 'a critique of the presuppositions on which our beliefs have been built'. Rather than returning to prior learning to confirm that we have acted in line with our prior suppositions, he advocated 'challenging our established and habitual patterns of expectation, the meaning perspectives with which we have made sense out of our encounters with the world, others, and ourselves' (Mezirow et al. 1991, p. 12). He stressed that critical reflection is concerned with 'the why, the reasons for and consequences of what we do' (1991, p. 13). Brookfield, too, focuses on the recognition and analysis of assumptions—'the interpretive glue that binds the various meaning schemes comprising our structures of understanding' (1991, p. 177)—as central to the process of critical reflection.

Critical reflection is an approach and a process that is derived from adult education, one that focuses specifically on the personal experience of the practitioner. It is an ongoing and developing project in social work, informed variously by critical social theory (Agger 1991, 1998) and associated with developments in postmodern and critical social work. (To gain a fuller appreciation of these directions, I encourage you to read Hick et al. 2005; Fook 2002; Healy 2001; Fawcett et al. 2000; Healy 2000; Ife 1997; Rossiter 1996.)

Let us step back for a minute and remind ourselves of social work's core interests. They include understanding the social context of people's lives and highlighting the ways in which well-being is unequally socially distributed, and the ways in which social structures and social institutions oppress, sustain, and open up choices for people, in terms of thinking, beliefs, values, and action. Practitioners are no different: our understanding of ourselves is also embedded in the social structure.

Contemporary scholars in postmodern and critical social work emphasize the following implications of the current context for practitioners. They emphasize the need for social work to pursue its interests and work with the *uncertainties* characterizing information-rich but unstable social conditions. They highlight the need for a preparedness to relate to *diverse* interpretations of 'reality' and to people and situations in all their *diversity*. This reinforces social work's attention to *context*, including the specific institutional, policy, and agency context in which practice takes place. They impel us to be conscious of which dominant *discourses* (what gets said, by whom, and with what authority) are in place, and their attendants: how problems and issues are framed, the languages that express them, the practices arising, and the *power* relations promoted. How to invite and sustain *participatory* relationships with the people with whom we work, variously called clients, residents, stake-holders, fellow citizens, patients, consumers, or service users, is of central concern.

With these ideas in mind, critical reflection is directed to hunting out assumptions about the social relations of practice. It aims to assist us in uncovering the ways in which, in *specific contexts* of practice, we make meaning of people and situations, pursue particular perspectives, reveal those perspectives, and frame our actions through particular language, and, in so doing, make assumptions about power. Reflective processes are used to analyze and uncover the ways in which unacknowledged assumptions and discourses, of which we may not be conscious, construct power relations. In a critically reflective approach, the types of questions asked will direct us towards the political, and potentially emancipatory, aspect of situations which may be changed.

# The processes of critical reflection

From the range of ways to pursue critical reflection, I am choosing to illustrate the processes of critical reflection through a 'critical incident' approach. Based in the phenomenological research tradition, critical incidents are 'brief descriptions written by learners of significant events in their lives' (Brookfield 1991, p. 179). Ideally, such descriptions are sufficiently stark that readers are able to 'see' them clearly. The assumption is that while incidents are specific, the generic may well be embedded in them. As well, because they spring from the learner's (the practitioner's) pressing reality, the likelihood of motivation for creating change may be high.

I am going to relate two such incidents. My reasons for selecting them are as follows. The first incident was one that 'rocked' me at the time. It occurred during my first job as a social worker, and has stayed 'unfinished' for many years, waiting to be more fully understood. It was a situation I had not encountered before, perhaps therefore making it more memorable. The second incident occurred several years later. Again, the clarity of my response took me by surprise. At the time I understood neither the client's, the agency's, nor my own actions adequately.

## The first incident: A client's request

Recounting the incident in some detail enables me to pinpoint what I emphasized and failed to notice, and to discover what was critical about it for me.

The encounter took place in the home of the Carson family. (All names have been changed.) Their home was a spotlessly tidy, ground-floor flat (apartment) in a windswept public housing estate of London. Inside was bare of furniture and furnishings; outside was bare of life. Tenants kept to themselves. People came and went. I was one of them—the family caseworker—from a non-government family welfare agency, charged with providing support to hold together the family—Pat, Mick, and their four children, with a fifth 'on the way'. To the statutory authorities, they were 'trouble'. Mick was 'trouble' because he was 'work-shy', unable to hold down a job when he was required to accept one, and resistant to complying with official attempts to retrain or rehabilitate him. Pat was 'trouble' for several reasons: because she kept having babies, which they could ill afford; because frequent pregnancies were threatening her already precarious health; and because she refused to agree to medical pressure for termination and sterilization. Together, they were considered a 'drain' on the public purse. My agency, charged to work intensively with such 'problem families', downplayed its surveillance role and emphasized its support, friendship, and advocacy role. The family had no real choice about accepting our service. I had succeeded Maggie, whom both Pat and Mick had come to tolerate and rely on, in part to keep 'the authorities' at bay. Her departure had been a source of grief and anger, one more let-down in lives that were already empty of surrounding family, neighbourly relations, or friends.

I do not recall the immediate reason for my visit on this day, perhaps six months after I had taken over the family from Maggie. I recall that, typically, only Pat was at home. Mick usually went out, but not to paid employment. This time, I had not come to drive her to the agency's mothers' lunch group, or to sit and wait with her in the draughty corridors of the women's hospital where her pregnancy was being closely monitored, or to discuss her fears about allowing the older children to be taken on a holiday. We were simply talking, she about her disappointments in life—disappointments that would only to be relieved by the birth of a new child, by the attention that it would bring, and by the knowledge that she could give Mick babies. That rekindled their closeness. I remember thinking how, at that moment, the young, pretty, and carefree Pat had returned, flush with expectation.

Looking straight at me, she said, intently, 'What would you know about any of this? If you really cared about me, you would give me that new blouse you're wearing. Can I have it?' I knew immediately that I could not meet her request, and said something like 'I'm sorry, but I can't let you have this blouse.' I have no memory of saying anything about caring about her. I was shocked by the forthrightness of my response. For a minute, the tables were turned. 'The enemy' was not out there—the gas and electricity authorities enquiring about broken meters, housing authorities demanding payment arrears, Mick for being a broken man, for instance. I was it. The spectre of the agency's second-hand clothes store, so capably stocked and run by lady volunteers, haunted me: the clothes to which Pat had access were never new.

The basis of my refusal, which I did not disclose to Pat, was the judgment that to continue to do my job, some resources were essential for me. They included a car, which Pat enjoyed being driven in, and clothes, in which I could present myself 'respectably' to school principals, employment officials, hospital doctors, and moreover to other families on my diverse 'caseload'. The blouse had its own story, of course. I had bought the material and made the blouse to attend the wedding of a daughter of another of the families I worked with. I distinctly remember that it was the only new piece of clothing I possessed. I decided that sharing my perspective was irrelevant, for I assumed she had no intention of hearing it.

Pat's question cut across any pretence of equality. Her question showed me that while I was often there to support, advocate, troubleshoot, defend, and protect her, in the end, there were limits to what I would share of myself. The boundary clearly delineated the differences of economics, information-sharing, and privilege. It cleared the air between us.

Following Fook (2002), I am going to take the reader through the processes of critical reflection: deconstruction, resistance and challenge, and reconstruction. The focus is on me: my memories, perceptions, and actions. We must imagine the other perspectives to which we do not have access: in the first instance, those of Pat, Mick, and each of the four children.

# Deconstruction

To you, the reader, such an interchange may seem run-of-the-mill, and part of me is hesitant to write of it. But the fact that it has stayed intensely alive in my mind suggests otherwise. Engaging in critical reflection may not be comfortable, and an assurance of the reader's agreement to suspend judgment about behaviour will assist a person's exploration. As the reader, I invite you to play the role of 'critical friend', who will continuously be asking the question 'why?'.

In this initial account of deconstructing the situation, I am aiming to uncover the discourses that, from memory, dominated talk and action. I want to be aware of whose perspectives and interpretations of events were present and absent and whether some different perspectives and interpretation exist. To me, it is important to understand the roles that Pat and I occupied, as this encounter destabilized our implicitly established role relationship and the ways in which we both exercised power.

By any definition, the Carsons lived in extreme poverty. The social labels officially conferred on them were predominantly negative. They were labelled a **multi-problem** *family*. This constituted them as *the* problem, rather than as a family who *had* multiple problems. They were also labelled an *intractable* problem, as their behaviour had not changed over time. For instance, no number of official threats to withhold discretionary benefits for new floor or bed coverings changed Mick's attitude to paid employment. Problems were deemed the properties of such families, who were to be blamed, pulled into line, or minimally supported. Families were often referred to the agency that employed me as a last resort, when everyone else had washed their hands of them.

My family welfare agency had been founded on an ideal of service based in pacifist and communitarian ideals. It attracted workers like me, whose subjective position looked first to socio-economic structures—particularly the social class structure—to understand the sources of people's problems, rather than to the relative strength of people's moral fibre, their stage of maturity, or their preparedness to fulfill prescribed social roles, for example. Our espoused theory led us, in practice, to stick up for people on the basis that citizens had *rights* to basic social resources such as decent housing, regardless of social or employment status. We appealed to their strengths and the good intentions that they had to be 'good' parents. This practice often wore thin and we, too, slipped into endorsing a moral discourse, expressed in a language that exhorted parents to 'stand on their own feet', 'grow up', 'make do', 'get by', and 'manage'.

At the same time, the agency's espousal of a structural analysis of poverty often led it and me to deride officials who might be pursuing families for rent, electricity, or gas money, and to label families as innocents. We voiced our frustrations and agonies with each other. We did 'take sides', thus reinforcing our tendency, at least in public, to 'idealize the client' (and perhaps ourselves) and 'blame the system'. Such dichotomous thinking locks everyone into a fixed identity.

But the espoused language of the agency, a language of help, support, and belonging (expressed through addressing our clients on a first name basis, talking about 'our' families, etc.), was confused with the professional power we held and the statutory responsibilities we carried—to report suspected child abuse or call in the statutory mental health service, for example. We perceived at least the adult members of families as much more feisty, as subjects of their lives, caught up in an inequitable socio-economic system and rigid set of social norms that they could not meet. There is no doubt that we aimed at times to pressure them into social conformity, to nurture them into responsible parenthood, but we tried to do this in a spirit of alliance, a position that sprang from a clear structural analysis. These days, we would talk of the social rights of citizenship and of 'partnership' with families, in the face of calls for functional, resilient, or 'can-do' families.

Our clients and we were enmeshed in ideas about what constituted good women, wives, and mothers; mature adults (who took responsibility for reproduction); responsible men, good husbands and fathers (who produced a secure wage), and bad ones (who didn't provide).

Now, when I ask how particular discourses preserved power relations, I can offer different interpretations. Until this point, I had 'helped' in many practical ways. For her part, Pat had exercised power by keeping me at a distance from how she felt about life. To me, her 'opening up' may well have meant 'progress'. Building a relationship was probably thought to be valuable of itself. (This is the social work discourse about 'relationship'—it is an end in itself.) Pat was beginning to let me in. It is possible that for her, the encouragement to move closer may not *of itself* have been helpful. I recall Pat expressing bitterness and envy as she talked, but also a wistful hope that I would accede to her request and make a small personal sacrifice for her. It is possible that the more she shared of herself, the more she felt able to ask for herself, for things like a decent blouse. It is also possible that she wanted to make the terms of our relationship explicit. I recall that as she voiced her demand, it was the first time that she really came to life, flaring up with anger and claiming her power of speech. For once, I was the more vulnerable one, caught on the back foot, being required to explain myself. There was no fancy language spoken, no pretence of partnership between us. She challenged the terms on which offering and receiving help was based. The scope and limits to the kind of 'helping' that Pat valued, previously decided on my terms and kept implicit, were made explicit.

Our interchange also brought into the open the understanding that however well-intentioned I might be, however 'helpful' I wanted to be, and, importantly, however much she might 'open up' to me, we were not friends. Our life chances were poles apart. I was young, single, unencumbered, and could leave when I chose (and I did). She could not leave her situation. I must have represented what she did not have and might never have. She was now making the social distance between us explicit. We were not in the same boat.

It strikes me now how Pat and I were isolated together in this encounter. The common perspectives of other women and workers in similar situations to both Pat and I were missing. All of the other women in the families who received our service were struggling to keep their children from going into care: they had a lot in common. Their collective voice was interpreted through our daily negotiations on their behalf and regular forays into class advocacy and negotiation. And as workers, we were pretty much 'lone riders'.

## Resistance and challenge

I agree with Fook (2002, p. 95) that 'the very process of deconstruction is in itself an act of resistance'. The benefit is that I can then ponder the ways of thinking and acting to be reappraised and challenged. By considering diverse ways of interpreting events (deconstructing) and by identifying silences, omissions, biases, and the consequences of language, I already have a broader view of who I was in the situation described.

### Which ways of thinking and acting must I then challenge?

By refusing to agree to the terms on which help was offered, Pat showed me that damage can be wreaked by hiding behind an image (an identity, if you like) of the 'giving' worker. It can be inferred from this that I only give, that I do not withhold (practical help, support, and advocacy, for instance), that I do not wish to or need to 'receive'—that for all the friendly encounters, there is no reciprocity, in fact. Here are the binary oppositions. The primary identity enacted of 'giver' conceals the fact that I can also 'take away'—in Pat's case, I could instigate a process of removal of any or all of her children. I am all of those identities. Here, then, I am looking to challenge a way of thinking which allows the worker to remain concealed but expects the client to be more transparent. The contract between us was one primarily determined by the worker. Greater explicitness and authenticity was called for in my approach.

At the same time, the unfairness of the situation for both of us is now eminently clear. When I change my discussion of this incident from a language of caring and giving to one of entitlement and rights, it is clear that both of us had claims to an independent income that precluded our tussling over one blouse! While justice and fairness are often central to the language of social policy disputes, they are also played out in encounters like this. Inequality is both structurally sustained and interpersonally experienced. I doubt if it would have been appropriate for me to have said to Pat, 'It's not right or fair that though we both work hard, only I can afford a new blouse'; I think (though I'll never know) that that might only have added insult to injury. But thinking in terms of fairness and justness can at least relocate the entire locus of responsibility away from the two individuals to the broader social policy arrangements.

It seems right to challenge a language of giving, caring, and supporting for it can be oppressive. It can create two categories of persons—the giver and the receiver, the carer and the cared for, the supporter and the supported—and in so doing, deny the possibility that both parties exercise power, albeit in an unequal situation. It can lead to the strengths and abilities of both parties being overlooked and the relationship being characterized by deference. In fact, Pat's grim determination to maintain control and self-respect never ceased to amaze me.

## Reconstruction

How can I use this process of critical reflection to create and enact a new discourse? How can I exercise power humanely and justly within such a service context? (Healy 2005).

The ideas that informed my practices and those of the agency provided me with a clear analysis of the social sources of poverty; of the role of the welfare state in mitigating the worst effects of 'structural inequality' while at the same time maintaining a divided social order; and of the revolutionary political, social, and economic changes that would be necessary to change it. What it did not, and could not, prepare me for was how to recognize and manage my multiple identities with families like the Carsons. It could not, in part, because these moments in practice, such as I have just described, defy 'prescribed' responses. They bring the whole of us to them, our biographical, professional, personal selves. Perhaps the greater capacity one develops for 'social empathy', the more demanding it is to manage contradictory, multiple identities and the harder it is to keep acknowledging both the power one carries and the diverse ways in which it can be experienced. That is the task nevertheless.

There is also no prescription for authenticity and self-disclosure. How one plays them out is always contextual in relation to, for instance, agency purpose, statutory requirements, authority, and conflicting interests; and in relation to the availability of, attitude to, and relative confidence in using discretion. Being conscious of whose interests are being served by self-disclosure is central.

My agency took it for granted that its employees would and could use autonomous judgment, but I now think that a less permissive culture was necessary, one that gave permission and put in place structures to sort through how we worked with the challenges of our contradictory position. This might also have enabled a more explicit strategy for class advocacy and policy activism to be collectively and strategically developed, one where the collective voice of 'our families' and 'our selves' might have emerged.

## How critical reflection changed my practice

Through this process, I gained a different perspective on my contradictory role. I became better able to accept the limits of what one practitioner with scant resources can achieve. The contract with Pat became more explicit and I now see her more clearly in terms of her powerfulness in our encounters and in how she took on the world. Her very resistance was an act of strength. Above all, I wonder what might have ensued if we as colleagues had invested in collective critical reflection. I will never know what could have emerged from my colleagues and me, critically reflecting together on the relation between 'our personal', 'the professional', 'the social', and 'the political'. We did not need to be reminded to lift our gaze from 'the case' and consider 'the class': our critical analysis put us there. It was our participation in the lived experience that challenged us.

### Activity 1.1  Beginning the process of critical reflection

The process of critical reflection can occur at two levels. The first level of analysis focuses on how a specific situation or event changed your thinking and your practice in terms of your work, your role, your education, or your life circumstances. Think about a recent situation that challenged you in a particular way. Use the following questions to guide you in your process of critical reflection.

1. What ideas did you hold about the situation prior to the incident? Who or what most influenced or informed these ideas? How did these ideas affect your view of yourself

*continued*

as an individual, beginning social worker, or other role? How did these ideas affect your view of relationships with others? How did these ideas affect the way that others view you?

2. What happened? Describe your role in the incident. What did you do? How did you act? How did others react?

3. Analyze the incident. What is it about this event that sparked your particular reaction? Why did this event affect you? How did it change you? How did this event change your relationships with others?

4. What will you do differently because of this change? How will this change affect your work as a student, as a social worker, or other role?

5. What possibilities will this change open up for you in the future? What do you see as your next step?

The second level of critical reflection is intended to help you articulate your experiences in relation to social, cultural, gender, class, and other social group categories. Think about the incident again, and reflect upon how to connect this experience into the social and political aspects of our collective existence.

1. What is the setting of the agency for whom you work like? What ideas does it hold about the clients of the agency? What practices express these ideas? Where have you witnessed these practices? How are these practices/ideas supported in the larger culture?

2. How would you describe the people who work there and the people who use the services of the agency? What happens if there are conflicts when workers and clients are of a different race, gender, ethnicity, class, or sexual orientation? Do you ever find that there is a clash of ideas and practices? How do you explain this? How do you resolve this?

3. How might these differences affect your work as a social worker? Will they affect the amount of influence, power, or control you might have in the lives of clients, colleagues, or supervisors? What happens if the client, colleague, or supervisor is of a different race, gender, ethnicity, class, or sexual orientation than yourself? How might they experience you as a social worker? How would relationships between clients and workers, or workers and agencies, be altered if these differences did not exist?

Evidence from cumulative accounts of critical reflection suggests that not only can critical reflection encourage accountability, but it can also lead to a greater sense of coherence and clarity. Others have described a greater sense of self-affirmation and self-directedness. For me, a more coherent theory/practice of self emerged, grounded in 'real' connections between the personal, professional, and social. Fook (2005, personal communication) reports that the process has led practitioners to reframe power, in ways that are more complex, holistic, and self-affirming. A sense of liberation or freeing from restricted choices may ensue and, as in my case, a re-visioning of what is realistically attainable.

## A second incident: A gift from a client

This incident took place in an urban teaching hospital. I was a newly graduated social worker. The wife of a patient came looking for me. She and her husband were newly arrived immigrants from China with little command of English, now facing a particularly uncertain future following the husband suffering a stroke. With the help of interpreters, my main task had been to guide them through 'the system', ensuring they were informed and able to understand the admission, treatment, and discharge processes. One day, when I was not in my office, the wife left me a gift of sandalwood carvings, in the Chinese symbols for 'good luck'. I was surprised, as our contact had been brief, but I spontaneously accepted the gift. Later, I heard from others in the department that social workers do not ever accept gifts from patients or their families. I said nothing but knew that I would not follow this policy rigidly. I was certain my decision was the right one, not only because neither I nor the client knew 'the rules'. But I did not take the issue up with either my colleagues or supervisor. The critical question for me, and now for you, is why. (For another perspective on practitioners accepting gifts from clients, please see chapter 4, 'The Practitioner's Use of Self in the Professional Relationship'.)

## Activity 1.2  Deconstructing the second incident

To pursue the process of critical reflection, consider the second incident.

1. How would you assist the writer to deconstruct it? (See Fook 2002 for an extended list of questions.)
2. What are some of the perspectives revealed in this brief account of events, in relation to formal practice theories?
3. Whose perspectives are represented and whose are missing?
4. What might be the diverse perspectives of those who are missing?
5. Consider how diversely this incident could be interpreted.
6. How might the issue be framed differently?
7. Are particular ideas and assumptions evident?
8. What are the sources of the ideas and assumptions being played out?
9. Who is benefiting? Who is losing out?
10. Are particular practices, systems, or structures being upheld?
11. What can be learned about human services in this context?

*continued*

12. Have you been able to suspend judgment in starting to assist in deconstructing this incident?
13. If you have difficulty in doing so, identify where you are 'coming from' in terms of your ideas and assumptions, and consider their origins.
14. What, then, does it mean to resist, challenge, and reconstruct such an episode?

## Questions for Review

1. How does the process of critical reflection impact upon one's practice?
2. How can you integrate the process of critical reflection into your own practice?
3. What opportunities are created through the process of critical reflection? What are some limitations to this process?

## References

Agger, B. (1991). Critical theory, poststructuralism, postmodernism: Their sociological relevance, *Annual Review of Sociology*, 17, 105–31.

Agger, B. (1998). *Critical Social Theories*. Boulder, CO: Westview Press.

Argyris, C., & Schön, D. (1976). *Theory in Practice: Increasing Professional Effectiveness*. San Francisco: Jossey-Bass.

Brookfield, S. (1991). Using critical incidents to explore learners' assumptions. In J. Mezirow & Associates (eds), *Fostering Critical Reflection in Adulthood; A Guide to Transformative and Emancipatory Learning*. San Francisco: Jossey-Bass.

Fawcett, B., Featherstone, B., Fook, J., & Rossiter, A. (eds) (2000). *Practice and Research in Social Work*. London: Routledge.

Fook, J. (2002). *Social Work: Critical Theory and Practice*. London: Sage.

Healy, K. (2000). *Social Work Practices: Contemporary Perspectives on Change*. London: Sage.

Healy, K. (2001). Reinventing critical social work: Challenges from practice, context and post-modernism. *Critical Social Work*, 2(1). Retrieved 9 June 2005 from www.criticalsocialwork.com.

Healy, K. (2005). Under reconstruction: Renewing critical social work practices. In S. Hick, J. Fook, & R. Pozzuto, (eds) (2005). *Social Work: A Critical Turn*. Toronto: Thompson Educational.

Hick, S., Fook, J., & R. Pozzuto, (eds) (2005). *Social Work: A Critical Turn*. Toronto: Thompson Educational.

Ife, J. (1997). *Rethinking Social Work: Towards Critical Practice*. Melbourne: Longman.

Mezirow, J., & Associates (1991). *Fostering Critical Reflection in Adulthood; A Guide to Transformative and Emancipatory Learning*. San Francisco: Jossey-Bass.

Rossiter, A. (1996). A perspective on critical social work. *Journal of Progressive Human Services*, 7(2), 23–41.

Schön, D. (1983). *The Reflective Practitioner*. London: Temple Smith.

Schön, D. (1987). *Educating the Reflective Practitioner*. San Francisco: Jossey-Bass.

# 2 Professional Values and Ethical Practice

## Zita Weber

> **values n.** *the customs, standards of conduct, and principles considered desirable by a culture, a group of people, or an individual.*
>
> **ethics n.** *a system of moral principles and perceptions about right versus wrong and the resulting philosophy of conduct that is practiced by an individual, group, profession or culture.*
>
> Barker 1991, pp. 246, 77.

Professional values and ethical practice are at the very core of the work of human services practitioners. The practitioner has an obligation to be fully cognizant of the values, principles, and standards that guide their conduct. At any point, practitioners should be able to articulate their positions regarding the values that inform ethical practice. This is particularly crucial given the complexity and concerns of everyday practice. Critical reflection is called for when an array of potential perspectives present themselves to the practitioner. Taking a critical stance and engaging with varying perspectives, facing conflict, and working through the dilemmas makes for effective practice.

As Eby maintains, ethical practice is concerned with developing skills: 'the cognitive skills of reasoning, reflection, analysis and logic' (2000, p. 122). Developing these skills adds meaning to critical practice by embracing conscious questioning, reflection, and action in everyday practice. Tschudin and Marks-Maran (1993) stress this 'everyday' component of ethics. Ethics and ethical decision-making issues are not only the domain of philosophy and ethicists. Every day, social workers and other helping professionals are faced with the challenge of understanding how to make decisions in knotty, and sometimes seemingly unfathomable, situations.

As a critical practitioner, questions can crowd your mind. Do I experience conflicting pulls regarding courses of action? Is this the right decision? What are the alternative courses of action? Can a better choice be made? Is there another way of looking at this?

Practising critically means balancing the constraints and opportunities in practice. Critical practice means working with multiple perspectives, which can lead to challenging ways of thinking and encourage new ways of thinking.

## Values and ethics

Let's revise our understanding on values and ethics before moving on to the concerns of ethical practice. The term 'value' is derived from the Latin *valere*, meaning 'to be strong, to prevail, or to be of worth'. Values have several important attributes and perform several important functions. They are generalized, emotionally charged conceptions of what is desirable, historically created and derived from experience, and shared by a population or a group within it. They further provide the means for organizing and structuring patterns of behaviour.

To value something is to prefer it. It seems like a simple definition, yet reviewing reports and publications from many social service fields reveals no less than 180 different definitions for the term 'value' (Timms 1983). All values are historically constructed and historically relevant (Dominelli 2002). Dominelli also makes the distinction between personal and professional values. Furthermore, she maintains that critical practice contextualizes the individual: each person is a social being, operating in a social world within a particular social context and, it might be added, in a historical moment.

Values are translated into ethics to assist us in making difficult choices: 'Ethics are deduced from values and must be in consonance with them. The difference between them is that values are concerned with what is good and desirable, while ethics deals with what is right and correct' (Loewenberg & Dolgoff 1996, p. 21). Ethics, essentially, are practical rules or principles. Because most decisions in the human services sector are not clear-cut and there are many 'grey areas', we have to move beyond simplistic solutions. Ethics guide our professional behaviour.

An illustration of a social work ethical rule deduced from a value concerns the value of privacy and the ethic of informed consent. If we value the right to privacy of our clients, then it follows that a social worker would be obliged to obtain permission from clients—informed consent—before taping or recording an interview with them, or allowing observation by a third party. Privacy, then, is a desirable value and informed consent is the ethical rule and correct way of practice derived from this value.

## Activity 2.1  Value statements and values clarification

This activity provides an opportunity for you to explore some of your own values that shape and inform your decisions and actions.

1. Working alone, rate on a scale from 1 to 9 the following value statements.

   (1 = strongly disagree; 5 = Neutral; 9 = strongly agree. Numbers 1–4 are varied levels of disagreement. Numbers 6–9 are varied levels of agreement.)

   a)  All people have equal worth, no matter what.
   b)  Spanking children is a crime like any other assault.
   c)  Immigrants should be encouraged to establish their own cultural communities.
   d)  It does not matter what you do; some people just cannot change.
   e)  The best interests of the community or family are more important than those of the individual.

*continued*

2. Once you have responded to each statement, identify the values behind your positions.

# Personal and professional values

As identified in chapter 4, 'The Practitioner's Use of Self in the Professional Relationship'—your personal values—affect how you practise. Understanding your beliefs and attitudes ensures your appreciation of the dangers of imposing your values on your clients. Imposing personal values is antithetical to the client's right to self-determination. Although we might assume that there is general consensus about social work values, we might differ in assumptions regarding their implementation. Take, for example, the basic social work value of respecting human dignity and worth. One social worker might call on this generalized value to support a woman's decision to terminate her pregnancy. Another social worker might use the same generalized value to support a woman's decision to continue to full term in her pregnancy. Please see Table 2.1 for the fundamental social work values and principles.

**Table 2.1** Six core values and attendant principles

The Canadian Association of Social Workers (CASW) *Code of Ethics* (2005) identifies the following six core social work values and attendant principles (CASW 2005, pp. 4–8):

**Value 1:** Respect for Inherent Dignity and Worth of Persons
**Value 2:** Pursuit of Social Justice
**Value 3:** Service to Humanity
**Value 4:** Integrity of Professional Practice
**Value 5:** Confidentiality in Professional Practice
**Value 6:** Competence in Professional Practice

Many writers have reinforced the central role that values play in social work. A social work practitioner at a field educators' forum once asked: 'Does any other profession, with the exception perhaps of philosophy, concern itself as deeply with the matter of values as does the profession of social work?' Social work values are 'the fulcrum of practice' (Vigilante 1974, p. 114). The intersection between personal and professional values has also been noted. The following sentiment expressed by Perlman (1976, p. 389) remains relevant to contemporary practice: 'The need for conscious awareness of the values that influence our doing applies at every level of social work. Not only may subjective and unanalyzed values motivate the case- and group-worker, but community planners, researchers, indeed all of us are pushed and pulled by often unseen value assumptions and commitments. Only as we continuously raise these assumptions and commitments to full consciousness can we take possession of them.'

The question regarding how the abstract value can be expressed in action has also been addressed (Bloom 1975; Vigilante 1983). Are professional values that do not provide guidance and direction of limited use? Some might argue this. However, the counter-argument must be put: values are important because ethical principles and ethical rules can be derived from these values. Such principles and rules, when framed within a professional Code of Ethics, may provide social workers with the ethical criteria and starting point necessary for making difficult practice decisions. It should be noted that ethical principles are always derived from values. As Loewenberg and Dolgoff (1996, p. 20) maintain: 'A rule or principle that is not derived from values but from another source is not an ethical rule. Such a rule may be a bureaucratic rule, a principle derived from practice wisdom, or something else, but it is not an ethical rule.'

Several authors have elucidated on the range of ethical theories commonly used in social work and social welfare practice (Banks 2001; Eby 2000; O'Connor et al. 2003; Rhodes 1991). This literature is rich in its demonstration of the complexity and diversity of thought regarding ethics and ethical practice.

## Activity 2.2  Values exercise

Think of a time when you found your personal values challenged. Think of a time when your personal values changed. What did you learn about yourself and about others from these experiences?

Now think of a time when you felt forced to go along with values you did not respect. How might have you dealt with the situation differently?

# Theories and approaches to understanding ethics

Although an understanding of different theories can assuage our anxiety about our practice, a critical stance will always challenge and perhaps perplex the practitioner. 'Ethics is not only about giving the right *answer*, but also about seeking the right question, and seeking to understand what a person's world and meaning is (about)' (Tschudin & Marks-Maran 1993, p. 17). Six approaches to understanding ethics follow.

## Duty-based or Kantianist approach

The duty-based approach stems from the work of Immanuel Kant (1724–1804), whose philosophy, known as deontology, posits the concept of duty as being central to morality. This approach focuses on the fundamental respect and dignity owed to every individual and holds that the right act would always be guided by moral duties, responsibilities, and rights. Conversely, some actions will always be considered immoral, regardless of their positive benefits (Fowler & Levine-Ariff 1987). Although this approach does not give a clear moral basis for action, it makes us focus on the value of every individual person and the respect owed to a person and, therefore, it has strong appeal. 'It is reminiscent of other more familiar ethical sayings: "Do unto others as you would have them do unto you" or "What would happen if everyone did that?'" (Rhodes 1991, p. 32). Essentially, the duty-based approach emphasizes rationality and the importance of the will (Banks 2001). However, it might be argued that it is difficult to derive morality from reason alone and that not looking at the consequences of our actions might be dangerous. Because this approach highlights the worker–client relationship, there is necessarily an emphasis on individual rights and liberties at the expense of a focus on wider notions related to responsibility, welfare, and social justice inherent in organizational and wider societal contexts. Banks posits that these limitations can be redressed by adopting a framework that clearly positions varying principles in relation to each other and allows for reconciling conflicts between principles of ethical decision-making.

## Utilitarianism

Utilitarianism is associated with the philosophers and social reformers Jeremy Bentham (1748–1832) and John Stuart Mill (1806–73). Essentially, this approach identifies the goal of morality as the greatest happiness for the greatest number; consequentially, an action is deemed right insofar as it promotes that goal. Fowler and Levine-Ariff (1987) argue that consequentialism, of which utilitarianism is one form, puts forward the proposition that an action is right or wrong based on the consequences produced as measured against a specific end that is sought—for example, pleasure, utility, or dispassion. This approach focuses more on the overall happiness of the community at the expense of any particular individual. Utilitarianism can be attractive as a method for public decision-making because it is opposed to deontology, or the view that the worthiness of an action depends on its conformity with duty. Johnstone (1989) points out that deontologists complain that consequentialism carries the danger of confusing morality with expediency because consequentialism seems to allow that the good of one person may be sacrificed for the good of many. Nevertheless, the allocation of resources, based on principles of justice and fairness, often is based on the consequences approach. O'Connor, Wilson, and Setterlund (2003) claim that social workers have been influenced by both Kantian and utilitarian approaches in their work. Banks (2001) argues that both of these approaches are limited. Their limitations are based in their ethic of justice, individualized rights, impartiality, and rationality, all of which are not necessarily reflected in the reality of daily practice. Rhodes (1991, p. 29) challenges the efficacy of this perspective when she writes, 'when we explore the perspective, we find that it is not any real help in deciding particular cases and sometimes even runs counter to what we intuitively know to be moral'.

## Virtue-based approach

The virtues approach provides a familiar way of thinking about morality and the idea that if the virtues of people are encouraged, moral dilemmas would be solvable because each person would be acting from the goodness of their heart. This tradition can be traced back to the Greek philosophers, who extolled the cardinal virtues of courage, wisdom, temperance, and justice. To this list we might add virtues such as loyalty, truthfulness, generosity, humour, and compassion. However, this emphasis on virtues begs the question of social and political assumptions: Aristotle's concept of a good person might have been a rich Athenian gentleman. Today's concept, depending on your socio-political background, may be someone very different. The limitation of this approach is that it does not incorporate different concepts of human excellence or recognize the variations in society in its socio-political context. This approach does not make explicit the social and political assumptions inherent in different contexts. In addition, it might be dangerous to assume that the virtuous person will know the right action to take, given the complexity of the many ethical puzzles that can be faced. Virtue-based ethics might be criticized for not providing specific direction in ethical decision-making and for its assumption that virtues not only guide the individual towards the right action, but also specify what that right action ought to be (Pellegrino & Thomasma 1993). Typically, textbooks suggest that social workers should possess virtues such as compassion, detached caring, warmth, honesty, hopefulness, and humility (Rhodes 1991). Such virtues can be seen as a means of helping and are linked to the instrumental values of Biestek in *The Casework Relationship* (1957). Furthermore, codes of ethics contain such virtues and imply that these, along with ethical principles, are essential to practice (O'Connor et al. 2003). This is exemplified in the CASW *Code of Ethics* (2005) Value 4: *Integrity in Professional Practice* that compels social workers to 'demonstrate and promote the qualities of honesty, reliability, impartiality and diligence in their professional practice'.

## Principles-based approach

The principles-based approach relies on the tenet that principles are general guides that have become so fundamental in everyday thinking and living that they are no longer questioned. Eby (2000) gives the example of retribution established in the phrase 'an eye for an eye or tooth for a tooth', which originated in the Code of Hammurabi in 2100 BC. Ethics textbooks expound a number of principles fundamental to health care ethics in particular. However, these are applicable and transferable to social work and other helping professions in other contexts. The four basic principles are respect for autonomy, beneficence or doing good, non-maleficence or avoiding harm, and justice (Beauchamp & Childress 1994). These principles form the foundation of practice and help determine the course of action in any situation. The following unranked set of principles are proposed by Beauchamp and Childress (1994).

- Principle 1. Respect for autonomy asserts that individuals have a basic right to participate in and make decisions about and for themselves. This principle subsumes three elements: the ability to decide, the power to act upon choices and decisions, and respect for the individual autonomy of others.
- Principle 2. Beneficence asserts that helping professionals have a duty to pursue the welfare of others.
- Principle 3. Non-maleficence asserts the duty to do no harm to individuals.
- Principle 4. Justice asserts that available resources should be distributed equitably and fairly according to need, contribution, merit, ability, or some other means.

## Activity 2.3  Where do I stand on these principles?

Read the following case scenarios and reflect on the questions posed.

### Scenarios

A    A client requests that she be tested for Huntington's disease. The social worker has been told that the client's grandparent had the disease but her child, the client's parent, has not yet developed any symptoms. The parent has emphatically stated that she does not wish to know her genetic status. A positive result for the client automatically implies a positive status for the parent.

B    A client has a terminal illness and is seeking advice as well as practical strategies from the social worker regarding assisted suicide. She does not wish her family members to be informed of her plans as she knows they would attempt to stop her from carrying them out.

### Questions

1.  How important to me are the four principles (listed in the text above)?
2.  When they come into conflict, which one trumps the others?
3.  Is respecting a client's self-determination (autonomy) more important to me than either (a) doing good (beneficence) or (b) not doing harm (non-maleficence)?
4.  When the question of a client's welfare or safety conflicts with the client's autonomy, do I act paternalistically for the client's benefit but in violation of the client's autonomy?

## Feminist approach

This care-based approach identifies the limitations in those perspectives based on the duty and utility to understand the attitudes and insights of women. The feminist approach identifies the oppressive elements of society and renders the invisible visible. Feminist moral theorists (Gilligan 1982; Noddings 1984) advocate an approach that focuses on responsibility rather than duty, and relationships rather than principles. This feminist approach expands the boundaries of traditional ethics and, according to Rhodes (1991), is relevant to the helping professions in that ethical issues often relate to the nature of relationships and our responsibility in those relationships. The care-based approach to ethics aims to accommodate different voices, narratives, perspectives, and methods, and recognizes the multiplicity of languages of ethics. In essence, the feminist ethical approach acknowledges the importance and effect of power relationships, connectedness rather than individualistic autonomy, the lived human experience, communities and collectivities rather than individualism, different ways of knowing, and the importance of the everyday and the ordinary (Eby 2000). Accordingly, Banks (2001, p. 47) notes that care-based ethics are present in cultures that adopt a view of the self 'which stresses a sense of co-operation, interdependence and collective responsibility as opposed to the ethic of justice'. This care-based approach has been criticized as perpetuating common images and stereotyping and 'can lead to an absolute equation that woman = caring and man = instrumental' (Porter 1998, p. 192).

## Intuitionist ethical theories

According to Rhodes (1991), all ethical perspectives are based in intuition. It is a truism that we ultimately rely on our moral intuitions of what is right or good when formulating our goals. In so doing, we build practice wisdom which helps to shape and refine our moral intuitions in a rational way. Intuitive ethical theories or intuitionism, on the other hand, are particular perspectives that hold there is no rational system by which we can order conflicting moral factors and there is no general theory or set of rules by which each case can be decided. What we must do is consider and weigh the factors involved and to act on what we intuitively believe and decide is the best course. Those who advocate this approach claim there is no rational basis by which we can decide ethical issues. Ethics becomes a matter of individual intuitions. This begs the question: is there any point in thinking about ethics if there are no criteria we can use to prove that one approach is better than another? Basically, this perspective is antithetical to any professional Code of Ethics and 'it raises a number of questions for the practitioner: how to separate out prejudice or personal whim; and how to know which way to go if there are no criteria' (O'Connor et al. 1995, p. 222). However, this approach is appealing, for, as Rhodes (1991, p. 39) points out, 'it enables us to act flexibly without "sacrificing" a client to a moral principle. In some situations, we may have a "gut" feeling that we must, say, preserve confidentiality, even though we cannot find an adequate justification.'

From a critical practice perspective it is important to acknowledge that any articulation about ethics poses a particular ethical point of view. Reflect on the way questions are posed: what assumptions are being made about morality? What assumptions are being made about its proper domain and its limits? The central question might remain: 'How ought we to act in relation to others?' However, as critical practitioners, we might underline the importance of cultural understanding, an appreciation of historical precedents, and, indeed, the present historical moment, in making our ethical judgments. Ethical beliefs are part of the social, political, and historical context. Constructing an ethical decision-making model means being aware of the kinds of relationships, institutions, and laws that are grounded in a particular socio-political context in a particular culture at any particular point in time.

## Activity 2.4  Critique of assumptions of each ethics approach

Review the six approaches or theories to ethics: duty-based, utilitarianism, virtue-based, principles-based, feminist, and intuitionist, and offer two critiques of the assumptions of each approach. Before doing so, consider the following examples.

*continued*

1. Duty-based: fails to take account of the fact that the consequences of an action can have disastrous results.
2. Utilitarianism: it is difficult to know what all the consequences of an action will be.
3. Virtue-based: who decides what constitutes a virtue?
4. Principles-based: narrowing of life's complexity and potential conflicts into four or five principles is too rigid.
5. Feminist: glorifying care as normative for women only worsens the position of women.
6. Intuitionist: ethical decisions are arbitrary and subjective.

In the following skill-development activity, you will be challenged by reading the case scenario and reflecting on the questions that follow. Note: there is no right or wrong answer and the course of action is not cut and dried. Your challenge is to articulate why you have chosen a particular perspective in your response to this case.

## Activity 2.5  Ethical issues in action

You are forming a group for young people in a youth correctional facility. You know from past experience that young people sometimes exacerbate the severity of previous offences for which they have not been apprehended. You also know that they may talk about plans to run away from the institution or to commit other indiscretions while in the institution, such as smoking dope or stealing institutional supplies or property from peers and staff.

1. Do you experience conflicting pulls regarding your perspective and course of action?
2. What ethical approach or approaches might you consider in resolving the ethical issues raised? Why?

An understanding of the different theories and approaches to ethics will assist in deconstructing the complexity and multiple constructions and meanings in any specific situation. This understanding, however good, cannot stand alone. Knowledge of the different perspectives will not, by itself, help you to arrive at a decision. Your knowledge needs to be extended further by an understanding of, first, oneself 'ethically'; second, the theories and principles of ethics; third, the professional code; and fourth, ethical decision-making frameworks (Abramson 1996).

## Ethical principles and ethical responsibilities

Good practice presupposes that the practitioner understands the ethical base of their practice. This involves what Banks (2001, p. 54) has called 'a process of critical and responsible reflection' regarding the meaning and implications of ethical principles embedded in practice.

The application of ethical principles can only be judged within the context in which they are being considered. It is important to critically reflect on ethical principles and be guided by the tenet that behaving ethically in any given situation should satisfy not only you as the individual practitioner but also the judgment of professional peers. Dominelli (2002, p. 19) maintains that critical social workers acknowledge that 'they are in the business of making judgments and that these are often finely balanced ones'.

That these judgments are made in unique situations and particular contexts cannot be underscored enough. Responding to the particular, with its complexity and potential conflict, can be said to challenge the practitioner and confront any tendency to universalize rather than situate principles. The critical practitioner is aware that every ethical issue or dilemma is grounded in context and process.

## Activity 2.6  From societal values to ethical principles

Ethical principles are derived from societal values. Identify the relevant social work ethical rules for the following societal values:

1. equality
2. freedom
3. privacy
4. social justice

What are some of the ethical principles in social work and welfare practice? While it is impossible to universalize the range of ethical principles, some distillation of the basic universal positive principles is helpful.

Banks (2001) provides a framework comprising four basic ethical principles:

1. respect for and promotion of individuals' rights to self-determination
2. promotion of welfare or well-being
3. equality
4. distributive justice.

The ethical principle of self-determination will be elaborated. Self-determination is 'an ethical principle in social work, which recognizes the rights and needs of clients to make their own choices and decisions' (Barker 1991, p. 210). This is a straightforward definition, yet, in practice, the concept may be ambiguous. Is self-determination possible while the distribution of resources remains unfair and inadequate? Is the accepted definition a definition of negative self-determination, rather than that of positive self-determination? Positive self-determination holds that the task is that of creating an environment that allows people to be more self-determining. Freedberg (1989), who has reviewed self-determination within the history of social work, suggests that the practice implication of self-determination is that social workers confront a basic contradiction in their roles as client advocates and as agents of a society in which clients are disenfranchised. He maintains, 'Social workers need to recognize the political, ideological, and practice tensions inherent in self-determination to guide clients to true self-determination' (Freedberg 1989, p. 35).

The emphasis on self-determination and respect for diversity is woven throughout the *Code of Ethics* and the *Guidelines for Ethical Practice* (CASW 2005). It is important to note that the respect for diversity extends to both social work professionals—recognizing that 'a social worker's personal values, culture, religious beliefs, practices and/or other important distinctions, such as age, ability, gender or sexual orientation can affect his/her ethical choices' (CASW, p. 2)—as well as respect for clients' individualism.

As expressed by Value 5: *Confidentiality in professional practice*, confidentiality is arguably the best known precept of professional ethics. A client must feel free to communicate experiences, thoughts, and feelings without fear that they will be transmitted elsewhere. Generally, it is assumed that the client's reliance on confidentiality promotes trust in the social worker. Conversely, clients who have disclosed confidential information may feel betrayed by the professional, whom they trust, should this principle not be enshrined. Clark (2000) questions the seemingly absolute nature of confidentiality and Biestek (1957), its simplicity. Biestek wrote, 'The principle of confidentiality appears to be deceptively simple at first glance, but is actually very complex and difficult to apply to concrete casework situations' (Biestek 1957, p. 121).

The CASW *Code of Ethics* (CASW 2005, p. 10) recognizes that it is not always easy for a social worker to observe absolute confidentiality. 'In fact, the worker may be required to share acquired information with outside parties when "professional or legal obligations" exist to share information without client-informed consent'. Consequently, an ethical dilemma arises when a practitioner has to find the correct balance between (a) a client's right to privacy and (b) the right of other people and of society to certain information.

Facing issues around confidentiality and its limits highlights the complexity of everyday practice. As a concept, confidentiality is based on an oversimplified practice model that includes only the client and the social worker, and does not reflect the often challenging, potentially problematic, and multi-faceted issues faced by the practitioner. Essentially, confidentiality is more complex in practice, because often there are many participants in the situation and each of them can make conflicting demands for confidential information. These other players might include family members, other colleagues, other helping professionals, lawyers, police, the courts, and, in some cases of rehabilitation of injured workers, and insurance companies.

## Activity 2.7  Reflecting on choice

As a social worker, how would you go about making a decision, if you had to choose between a child's right to confidentiality and a parent's right to know things that affect the child.

*continued*

1. Why would you do as you have decided?
2. Do you have any 'clear and compelling reasons' to limit confidentiality?

# Professional codes

Professional codes of ethics are primarily a statement of the values and beliefs of a particular professional group, and are designed to serve the interests of that group and to protect the public. Codes offer practical guidance on behaviour. Codes delineate and identify professional boundaries. Codes remind practitioners that they possess particular knowledge and skills that are used to benefit vulnerable individuals and that 'they have a duty to inform governments and agencies of inequities, lack of resources or the need for policy changes' (Banks 2001, p. 92).

Eby (2000) points out that professional codes often look like a list of duties that need to be fulfilled. Most professional codes place emphasis on the duties approach to understanding ethical issues.

A code is not a document that can prescribe behaviour in all the complexities of contemporary practice (Shulman 1992). Instead, it offers general principles to guide conduct and the critical appraisal of conduct in situations that have ethical implications. Codes of ethics cannot solve our dilemmas—our professional judgment does that. This professional judgment draws on our reflective abilities and contextualized knowledge about values, ethics, principles, the professional code, and ethical decision-making frameworks.

The challenges of contemporary practice require codes of ethics to 'be seen as a "living" document, constantly under discussion and reconsideration' (Hugman 2003, p. 12). This position reinforces an emerging wider societal concern and heightened awareness about the ethical quality of decisions and policies.

Sensitivity to cultural and ethnic diversity is introduced as Value 1 in the CASW *Code of Ethics* (2005) which states, 'Social workers recognize and respect the diversity of Canadian society, taking into account the breadth of differences that exist among individuals, families, groups and communities. Social workers uphold the human rights of individuals and groups as expressed in the *Canadian Charter of Rights and Freedoms* (1982) and the United Nations *Universal Declaration of Human Rights* (1948)' (p. 4).

In the last twenty years, there has been an increasing awareness among social workers of the ways in which cultural and ethnic norms and history can affect clients' experiences, perceptions, and life circumstances. Pack-Brown and Williams (2003) exhort helping professionals to embrace ethical thinking and decision-making in a multicultural context and to guard against personal ethnocentrism, or seeing 'all people as people' and only looking for similarities, to determine the best practice for clients. For helping professionals to become truly culturally competent, they are advised to ask questions that encompass both differences and similarities: How comfortable am I personally and professionally with the idea of difference? How are similarities and differences helping and/or hindering my clients? What powers do similarities and differences bring to the helping relationship, process, and outcome?

Taking a critical stance in your practice means engaging with varying perspectives, facing conflict, and using critical reflection to arrive at a viable course of action. The professional code, along with ethical decision-making frameworks and guidelines, is a resource to aid decision-making.

## Activity 2.8  Clients' rights and social workers' responsibilities

Review the CASW *Code of Ethics*. Reflect on the following.

1. Within the context of the CASW *Code of Ethics*, what are clients' rights and the social workers' responsibilities?
2. What is the relationship between ethics and informed consent?

# Ethical issues and dilemmas

As a social worker, you have the absolute obligation to maintain ethical standards of practice. You have an *ethical issue* when you face the questions: What is the right thing to do in this situation? How can I avoid unethical behaviour in this case? You have an *ethical dilemma* when you must choose between two or more relevant, but contradictory, ethical directives or when every alternative results in an undesirable outcome for one or more individuals.

## Confidentiality and privacy

Ethical dilemmas related to confidentiality and privacy arise in practice. Common dilemmas faced by a practitioner involve disclosure of confidential information:

- to protect or benefit a client
- to protect a third party
- in response to a court order
- to parents or guardians concerning children who are minors

## Practice example 2.1

## Respecting privacy and maintaining confidentiality

As a social worker on a community-based psycho-geriatric assessment team, you have received a referral for a seventy-six-year-old retired judge. He lives on his own, and has been assessed by his physician as having the early stages of dementia, possibly Alzheimer's disease. He is not eating well, and his home is becoming untidy. He has left the stove on a couple of times, and

*continued*

has been seen, by neighbours, wandering around in his dressing gown at night watering their gardens. He has refused all services, and is adamant that he does not want any 'interference from his family'. His daughter calls you in some distress. She has just visited him after being phoned by a neighbour who told her that he should be 'in a home'. She was shocked by his appearance. He had refused to let her inside the house. She asks you what is wrong with him, and what services you are going to arrange for him.

Case example courtesy of Annette Riley.

### Questions for reflection

1. What perspectives emerge in this case?
2. What ethical theories or principles would you draw on to help guide you in your decision?
3. What possible outcomes are there, and on what ethical principles are they based?

## Self-determination and paternalism

Professional paternalism arises when social workers intervene in such a way as to direct the client's right to self-determination 'for their own good'. Rosemary Carter, a philosopher, offered a broad definition of paternalism as 'interference with a person's liberty of action justified by reasons referring exclusively to the welfare, good, happiness, needs, interests, or values of the person being coerced' (Carter 1977, cited in Wasserstrom 1975, p. 108). Paternalism can occur in three different forms (Reamer 1999):

- The social worker believes that it is justifiable to withhold information from clients for their own good—for example, certain diagnostic information, information about their mental health state, and prognosis.
- The social worker lies to the client for the client's own good, in contrast to merely withholding information—for example, telling a child, after parental separation, that their father wants to continue seeing them when, in fact, that does not appear to be the case.
- The social worker physically interferes with clients, against their wishes, for their own good—for example, forcing individuals to receive medical treatment or to reside in a shelter against their wishes.

## Practice example 2.2

## The challenge of self-determination

A general practitioner refers a sixty-four-year-old Italian woman to the community mental health service. The GP is concerned that the woman has not been attending follow-up appointments with

*continued*

him and that she may be mentally unwell as she has a history of mental illness. When you visit the woman, she appears dishevelled and frightened, and states that people have been shouting at her through the walls of her flat at all hours of the day and night. She also looks very thin but tells you at the door that she is fine and asks you to leave.

Case example courtesy of Sheila Nicolson.

## Questions for reflection

1. What would you do?
2. Is there a limit to self-determination in a case where the person appears to be neglecting themselves and possibly doing injury to themselves or others?
3. Can a case be made for acting paternalistically?

# Critical practice and ethical decision-making

Ethical decision-making in a given situation will involve the informed judgement of the individual social worker. Instances may arise when social workers' ethical obligations conflict with agency policies, or relevant laws or regulations. According to Reamer (1999, p. 76), 'no precise formula for resolving ethical dilemmas exists'. It is conceivable that differences about ethical principles and criteria, which ought to guide ethical decisions, might exist among thoughtful social workers in any given case.

Ethicists agree that it is important to do one thing, and that is to approach ethical decisions systematically, following a series of steps to ensure that all aspects of the ethical dilemma are addressed.

### Guidelines for ethical decision-making

Reamer (1999) offers one framework for ethical decision-making which follows a series of clearly formulated steps so that social workers can enhance the quality of the ethical decisions they make. A modified version of Reamer's (1999) guidelines for resolving ethical dilemmas follows:

- Identify the ethical issues, including the social work values and duties that conflict.
- Identify the individuals, groups, and organizations likely to be affected by the ethical decision.
- Identify all viable courses of action and the participants involved in each, along with the potential benefits and risks for each.
- Examine the reasons in favour of, and opposed to, each course of action, considering relevant:
  - Code of Ethics
  - social work theories and principles
  - ethical theories and approaches

  – personal values and cultural and socio-political ideologies, including those that conflict with one's own
  – consultation with colleagues, supervisors, and other experts
- make the decision and document the decision-making process.

# Practising critically

Self-reflective practitioners who are committed to critical practice must begin the ethical decision-making process by reflecting on and describing the main ethical tensions, presenting the 'for' and 'against' perspective of the issue, along with a justification for each perspective—and all within the framework of:

- systematically analyzing the ethical dimensions, both implicit and explicit, of ethical dilemmas in practice
- identifying and clarifying one's own personal value systems and ethical orientation, and the implications of that system on ethical choices.

Critical reflection on ethical theories and ethical principles adds insight to an ethical reasoning process. Knowing oneself ethically is important for critical practitioners. Most importantly, critical practitioners must at all times be mindful of the interplay between the individual and their particular social context.

Read the scenario in Practice example 2.3 and reflect carefully on the issues and questions before arriving at your decision.

## Practice example 2.3

### Applying ethical principles to practice

You are a social worker on a respiratory medicine unit. An elderly Korean woman, Mrs Kua, has been admitted with suspected tuberculosis, and is in isolation. All staff are required to wear masks and protective gowns. Her son and daughter-in-law are in constant attendance. Mrs Kua is in Canada on holiday from Korea, and has no medical insurance. She speaks no English. She is required to undergo compulsory treatment for tuberculosis if it is diagnosed. Her son asks to see you, and is very agitated. He does not want his mother to be told of the diagnosis, as she is a very proud woman, and will feel shame at contracting such a 'common' illness. The family has told her that she has a bad case of the 'flu', and that is why the staff is wearing masks. They have told her she will be discharged in a few days, and can return to Korea in the following week as planned. They are very eager for her to be discharged, as they say they cannot afford the hospital fees. The doctor is planning to inform Mrs Kua of the diagnosis, and the need for compulsory treatment, via a health care interpreter that afternoon. The family refuses for an interpreter to be involved,

*continued*

and insists on being present when the doctor sees her. That afternoon, as you are waiting for the doctor and the interpreter to arrive, the doctor rushes in, says the interpreter has cancelled, and that he will see Mrs Kua using the family as interpreters.

Case scenario courtesy of Annette Riley.

### Questions for reflection

Work through the scenario using Reamer's guidelines for ethical decision-making.

1. What ethical tensions do you identify in this scenario?
2. What conclusions do you arrive at by using the framework?
3. If you find you have a voice saying that something in particular 'should' happen, reflect critically on what this might be based on. From what ethical theories or principles might this 'should' emanate?
4. Consider all 'coulds', and the reasons you may consider or reject these.
5. Identify the knowledge that you would need to begin to formulate a social work response to the scenario.
6. Identify the skills that you may need to draw on to respond to the situation.

## Some final thoughts

In conclusion, let's return to the comments made by Tschudin and Marks-Maran (1993) at the beginning of this chapter. Incorporating the theories that inform ethical decision-making and the framework used to address conflicts and dilemmas can become part of routine critical practice. Indeed, the activities and practice examples you have worked through and reflected upon in this chapter demonstrate the 'everyday' nature of professional values and ethical practice.

## Questions for Review

1. Why is it important for any helping professions to be contextualized within Codes of Ethics and/or Standards of Practice?
2. What are the core values and principles of the Canadian Association of Social Workers *Code of Ethics*? In your opinion, are there any values or principles it should contain that are currently absent?
3. Is it possible for a Code of Ethics to reflect and respect the values and aspirations of the many different communities—cultural, ethnic, religious, political, economic, regional and local constituents—that it is designed to serve?
4. What are the basic steps in resolving ethical dilemmas? What sections of the *Code of Ethics* would you rely upon to guide you in your decision-making?

# References

Abramson, A. (1996). Reflections on knowing oneself ethically: Toward a working framework for social work practice. *Families in Society: The Journal of Contemporary Human Services*, April, 195–201.

Banks, S. (2001). *Ethics and Values in Social Work* (2nd edn). Basingstoke: Palgrave.

Barker, R. (1991). *The Social Work Dictionary*. Washington: NASW Press.

Beauchamp, T.L., & Childress, J.F. (1994). *Principles of Biomedical Ethics*. New York: Oxford University Press.

Biestek, F.P. (1957). *The Casework Relationship*. London: Allen & Unwin.

Bloom, M. (1975). *The Paradox of Helping: Introduction to the Philosophy of Scientific Helping*. New York: John Wiley & Sons.

Canadian Association of Social Workers (2005). *Code of Ethics*. Ottawa, Ontario: Canadian Association of Social Workers.

Clark, C.L. (2000). *Social Work Ethics: Politics, Principles and Practice*. London: Macmillan.

Dominelli, L. (2002). Values in social work: Contested entities with enduring qualities. In R. Adams, L. Dominelli, & M. Payne (eds), *Critical Practice in Social Work*. Hampshire: Palgrave.

Eby, M. (2000). The challenge of values and ethics in practice. In A. Brechin, H. Brown, & M.A. Eby (eds), *Critical Practice in Health and Social Care*. London: Sage.

Fowler, M., & Levine-Ariff, J. (1987). *Ethics at the Bedside*. Philadelphia: J.B. Lippincott.

Freedberg, S. (1989). Self-determination: Historical perspectives and effects on current practice. *Social Work*, 34, 33–8.

Gilligan, C. (1982). *In a Different Voice: Psychological Theory and Women's Development*. Cambridge, MA: Harvard University Press.

Hugman, R. (2003). Professional ethics in social work: Living with the legacy. *Australian Social Work*, 56(1), 5–15.

Johnstone, M.J. (1989). *Bioethics: A Nursing Perspective*. Sydney: Harcourt Brace Jovanovich.

Loewenberg, F.M., & Dolgoff, R. (1996). *Ethical Decisions for Social Work Practice*. Itasca, IL: Peacock.

Noddings, N. (1984). *Caring: A Feminine Approach to Ethics and Moral Education*. Berkeley: University of California Press.

O'Connor, I., Wilson, J., & Setterlund, D. (1995). *Social Work and Welfare Practice* (2nd edn). Melbourne: Longman.

O'Connor, I., Wilson, J., & Setterlund, D. (2003). *Social Work and Welfare Practice* (4th edn). Melbourne: Pearson Education.

Pack-Brown, S.P., & Williams, C.B. (2003). *Ethics in a Multicultural Context*. Thousand Oaks, CA: Sage.

Pellegrino, E., & Thomasma, D. (1993). *The Virtues in Medical Practice*. Oxford: Oxford University Press.

Perlman, H. (1976). Believing and doing: Values in social work education. *Social Casework*, 57(6), 381–90.

Porter, S. (1998). *Social Theory and Nursing Practice*. Basingstoke: Macmillan.

Reamer, F.G. (1999). *Social Work Values and Ethics*. New York: Columbia University Press.

Rhodes, M.L. (1991). *Ethical Dilemmas in Social Work Practice*. New York: Routledge, Chapman and Hall.

Shulman, L. (1992). *The Skills of Helping: Individuals, Families and Groups*. Itasca, IL: Peacock.

Timms, N. (1983). *Social Work Values: An Enquiry*. London: Routledge and Kegan Paul.

Tschudin, V., & Marks-Maran, D. (1993). *Ethics: A Primer for Nurses*. London: Bailliere Tindall.

Vigilante, J. (1974). Between values and science: Education for the professional during a moral crisis or is proof truth? *Journal of Education for Social Work*, 10, 107–15.

Vigilante, J. (1983). Professional values. In A. Rosenblatt & D. Waldfogel (eds), *Handbook of Clinical Social Work*. San Francisco: Jossey-Bass.

Wasserstrom, R. (ed.) (1975). *Today's Moral Problems*. New York: Macmillan.

# 3 Making the Most of Supervision

### Jude Irwin

In much of the growing research and literature on supervision in the human services, the primary focus is on the knowledge and skills of the supervisor, or the 'how' of being a supervisor (see, for example, Hawkins & Shohet 2000; McMahon & Patton 2002). There is, however, much less literature on the 'how' of being a supervisee. Although there is evidence to suggest that supervision is more effective when a supervisee is proactive in the supervision process and in the establishment of a partnership with a supervisor, there is little written that explores this in detail (Hawkins & Shohet 2000). This chapter aims to address this gap and, although it is written primarily for early career professionals and students, the suggested approach is relevant for all supervisees. While this chapter will focus on the knowledge and skills that are necessary to become proactive in the supervision process, the skills referred to in other chapters of this book (for example: chapter 1, 'Practicing Critical Reflection'; chapter 8, 'Effective Communication'; and chapter 12, 'Understanding and Managing Conflict') are also important in supervision.

It is frequently assumed that a good practitioner will be a good supervisor, but while practice and supervision may involve some overlapping knowledge and skills, supervision has its own theoretical base and specific knowledge, practice, and skills. Similarly there is a belief that supervisees will routinely be able to capitalize on supervision they receive. However, without knowledge of the theory and practice of supervision, supervisees may not be able to take full advantage of the supervision process. As supervisees, it is important to be proactive and take some responsibility for deciding what you want from supervision. According to the Oxford English Dictionary, being proactive refers to taking the initiative by acting, rather than reacting to events. By taking responsibility for your own learning, it is more likely that you will receive the type of supervision needed to meet your professional development/learning goals and develop into good practitioners.

I begin the chapter by stressing the benefits of being proactive in your role as a supervisee and exploring the roles and purpose of supervision. I then outline various learning styles and strategies, arguing that understanding your own learning style can help you to make the most of your supervision. This is followed by consideration of some of the critical issues to consider when preparing for the role of supervisee, such as the development and use of a learning contract that can guide and focus learning. In the final section, I identify some different methods and techniques that can be used in supervision.

# What is supervision?

Supervision is an established component of social work practice, and, in fact, a distinguishing characteristic of social work is the requirement for ongoing administrative and clinical supervision of credentialed and experienced practitioners. Supervision literally means 'overseeing'. If viewed in this narrow and involuntary manner, the primary focus is on accountability: 'checking up' to ensure practitioners are doing their jobs properly. While accountability *is* important, for supervision to be most effective in the helping professions, it needs to be understood more broadly than simply monitoring performance; it should be seen as an opportunity for the supervisee to explore, reflect, learn, and problem solve (Brown & Bourne 1996). Martin Davies defines supervision in the health, human, and community work services as 'a relationship-based activity which enables practitioners to reflect upon the connection between task and process within their work. It provides a supportive, administrative and developmental context within which responsiveness to clients and accountable decision making can be sustained.' (Davies 2000, p. 204). Inherent within these definitions are several identified purposes which range in a continuum from solely clinical consultation to administrative tasks.

Supervision can assist helping professionals to understand their practice better, to be aware of their reactions, to explore their interventions, and to examine alternative ways of working. This is done through reflection on, and exploration of, practice. For some, the primary purpose of supervision is to ensure that clients are provided with the best possible service, which reflects the belief that, ultimately, supervisors are accountable to the clients of the agency. Supervision creates space to explore and share some of the problems and difficulties that arise in day-to-day practice. Four principal interconnected functions or roles of supervision—educational, management, supportive, and mediation—have been identified in the literature, and they remain critical in the provision of good professional practice supervision (Kadushin 1976; Proctor 1988; Morrison 1993).

The *educational* function involves the development and fine-tuning of knowledge, skills, understandings, and abilities of practitioners and students. This includes exploring knowledge, skills, and values; learning new skills; and identifying professional development needs.

The *management* function focuses mainly on performance and ensures that supervisees work within the policies and practices of the organization. This includes time management, roles and responsibilities within the organizational context, and working in teams or with other agencies.

The *supportive* function focuses on the impact of practice on supervisees, ensuring they are not left alone to deal with some of the emotional effects that go with working in the health, human, and community services. An important aspect of this is the management and containment of anxiety and uncertainty. This function assists supervisees to take responsibility for their own work, to analyze what they do, and, as a consequence, to develop and improve their practice. This includes debriefing, exploration of the emotional responses, understanding blocks in their work, and assisting in dealing with job-related stress.

The *mediation* function assists with communication up and down the hierarchy in an organization. This involves ensuring that supervisees are informed about organizational changes, briefing management on resource deficits and key issues impacting on practice, and negotiating on behalf of supervisees when contentious or potentially problematic issues arise.

# Being proactive in supervision

According to the *Code of Ethics* (CASW 2005, p. 8), 'Social workers have a responsibility to maintain professional proficiency, to continually strive to increase their professional knowledge and skills, and to apply new knowledge in practice commensurate with their level of professional education, skill and competency, seeking consultation and supervision as appropriate.' Practitioners in the health, human, and community services can make the most of learning from supervision by preparing for and being active in the supervision process.

Being proactive is important for a number of reasons. Supervision and relational issues are inextricably intertwined, and can function as an important form of support for the practitioner. In this respect, supervision may be conceptualized in a similar manner to social work practice, in which the essence of change is equated with the relationship between the worker and client, rather than specific models/techniques of practice. As noted by Kadushin (1976) supervision must occur in the context of a positive relationship. This creates a space where you can focus on the challenges in your work. It is also an opportunity for ongoing learning and development where supervisees can learn how to use resources better, manage their workloads, increase knowledge and skills, and be open to challenge about ways of working. Supervision also enables a supervisor to take on some of the responsibility in difficult situations. It is therefore important to be clear about what is expected from supervision and to have some idea about how to achieve this. For supervision to be effective, it should involve mutual trust and an awareness of issues of authority and responsibility. It should also be provided on a regular and ongoing basis, and offer an opportunity to express feelings and go below the surface. An important part of a supervisor's role is to contain anxiety and to be cognizant of what a supervisee brings to the practice situation.

At the same time, it is important to note the ethical considerations for supervisors. A predominant theme in the literature is the absence of formal training for clinical supervisors that could be considered an ethical violation. Although the CASW (2005, p. 14) 'Standards for Practice' require that 'social workers who have the necessary knowledge and skill to supervise or consult do so only within their areas of knowledge and competence', there are no established professional development courses that prepare practitioners to assume a supervisory role.

# Learning styles and strategies

Having an understanding of learning styles and the most useful approaches to learning can contribute to optimizing your use of supervision (Shardlow & Doel 1996). Although, over time, you are likely to develop a balanced approach to learning, at particular stages in development you tend to learn more effectively from some activities than from others. Influences such as your age, gender, class, culture, ethnicity, and previous learning experiences are important in shaping learning. Learning styles change, and in supervision it is important to take risks and try out different and new learning activities.

In developing a model of experiential learning, Kolb (1984) argued that most people learn from experience and draw on four main learning strategies:

- experience
- reflection
- conceptualization
- experimentation.

These four elements of learning are related to four aspects of the human experience:

- being
- feeling
- thinking
- doing.

Learning involves converting *experience* into values, attitudes, behaviour, and skills, so, to learn, you must be aware of your experience (Jarvis 1995). In order to use supervision constructively you need to be able to share your experience with your supervisor.

## Activity 3.1  Self-supervision

Prior to engaging in a process of formal supervision, it is helpful to undertake a process of 'self-supervision'. This invites the supervisee to reflect on how he performed in an interview or client interaction. Self-supervision parallels the formal supervision process, with the added component of including one's reflection of feelings as each question is addressed. The supervisee reviews the first interaction with the client, how the interview was arranged, what questions were asked and with what intent, the nature and range of emotions expressed by the client, the assessment of the worker's response to the client's emotions, the degree of sensitivity demonstrated throughout the interaction, and a general sense of how the interview ended. Additionally, supervisees should reflect on what worked well throughout the interview, and what changes they would incorporate into the next interview. Processing these questions at an individual level provides a more informed perspective for the formal supervision session.

## Experience (observation) or being

Supervision at this stage will focus on recalling experiences and observations. The issues to consider include describing the key aspects of any activity undertaken (for example, a team meeting, home visit, assessment):

- What was the context?
- What did you observe?
- What did you do?
- What was the outcome?

This process can provide insight into a situation, which can then be further enhanced by engaging with the other aspects of Kolb's learning strategies.

## Reflecting or feeling

Reflecting on experience can lead to a greater understanding of the situation. It can involve exploring how previous professional and personal experience, skills, and knowledge can assist you in the current situation. Questions for consideration include:

- What feelings did the situation evoke for me?
- Were they familiar?
- What is influencing me in this situation?
- What values, attitudes, knowledge, and skills from similar situations are relevant here?
- Are there patterns or similarities between the current situation and my previous professional or personal experience?

## Conceptualization or thinking

Analyzing and thinking about a situation can introduce new considerations into a situation. This includes applying what is known about theory, research, and policy to the specific situation. You may also consider how your values and beliefs affect how you perceive the situation. Some questions to consider include:

- What approach am I taking in this situation, and why?
- How do my values in relation to gender, race, and class influence my approach?
- How am I understanding this situation?
- What assumptions am I making?
- What theory, research, or policy could help me to understand the situation?

## Experimentation or doing

Active experimentation is about drawing together observation, reflection, and analysis and, after discussion, deciding how you would approach the situation if it happened again. Experimenting could also involve anticipating or planning the next step of a practice activity such as the next contact with a client, a team meeting, or a meeting with a co-worker. Questions to consider include:

- How will I approach this situation next time?
- When you were in the situation, how did you experience yourself?

- How did you think that the other person (people) saw you?
- What are the different options and the gains and losses of these options?
- What outcome am I wanting and how can this be achieved?
- What is my action plan and my contingency plans if this does not work?
- What support do I want from my supervisor?

It is important to engage with all elements of what Kolb refers to as the learning cycle. Supervision can assist in this by helping you to become more aware of the details of your practice, to pay attention to and understand reactions, to analyze your practice, and to try out different ways of doing things.

Honey and Mumford (1986) used the work of Kolb to identify four groups of learners: activists, reflectors, theorists, and pragmatists. *Activists* thrive on new experiences and prefer new challenges. They focus on the issue and move quickly into activities, centering on themselves and taking little account of others. *Reflectors* are more contemplative, collecting and considering as much information as possible. They tend to be cautious and may avoid taking action. *Theorists* shape their observations into intricate and plausible theories. They are systematic in considering problems. *Pragmatists* are keen to experiment, problem solve, and apply new ideas and theories to the situation, and can have a tendency to move too quickly without considering all factors (Shardlow & Doel 1996). Kolb and other, more recent writers have developed various questionnaires and self-report measures, which will assist you to work out your dominant learning strategy (see, for example, Cleak & Wilson 2004, pp. 21–2).

Another influence on the choice of learning strategies is the learning stage of the practitioner. The developmental approach to learning reflects a stage model of supervision, and suggests that styles and learning strategies are modified as a practitioner gains experience and moves through different developmental stages. Based on the epigenetic principle, this model asserts that the practitioner must successfully migrate through one stage before progressing to the next. It should be noted that the stages outlined below are based on assumptions about professional development. We all learn in different ways and at different rates, so it is useful to regard these stages as signposts rather than fixed and universal dimensions of learning. Bertha Reynolds (1965) identified a number of stages that practitioners go through while learning: acute consciousness of self, 'sink or swim' adaptation, understanding the situation without necessarily having the power to control activities, and relative mastery. The salient factor of developmental models is their often exclusive focus on the beginning worker, to the exclusion of the developmental needs of the supervisor or, more importantly, the client.

At *the acute consciousness of self* stage, it is normal to experience a high level of anxiety and uncertainty about your role and your ability to fulfil it. This can be exacerbated by an absence of grounded experience on which to assess your performance and consequently, your dependence on your supervisor for this. This stage is temporary and it will pass as you gain more confidence. At this stage, supervision is supported by a structured environment, clear directions, small manageable tasks, and sufficient support. Also critical is feedback and encouragement to try out different responses to the situation and to reflect on your practice, carefully considering your actions and reasons for them.

At *the 'sink or swim' adaptation* stage, you have overcome your initial anxieties and are prepared to take risks. You have an idea of what is required without understanding the purposes behind your responses or being able to show the sensitivity required. At this stage, supervision should be less structured with a high level of both support and challenge to learn from your practice and to explore different ways of doing and thinking, which will enable you to act more purposively.

During the third stage, *understanding the situation without necessarily having the power to control your activities*, you will display an intellectual understanding of the issue without the ability to consistently put this into action. You will become much less self-conscious, demonstrate much more self-confidence, and have the capacity to analyze the problems and situations with which you have to deal. Supervision at this stage should continue to focus on support and advice but also on encouragement to translate the identified issues into appropriate actions.

The *relative mastery* stage epitomizes good professional practice when knowledge and skills become internalized. You will be able to undertake routine tasks competently and confidently and should be able to generalize your learning to other situations. You should also be able to evaluate your practice and change it if relevant.

## Practice example 3.1

## Stages of learning

Gian's situation illustrates some of these learning stages. Gian is a twenty-four-year-old social worker at a community health centre. This is her first job since graduating with her Bachelor of Social Work. She had previously worked part-time as a behavioural specialist in the disability area, had collaborated with practitioners at a community health centre, and had some knowledge of the tasks they undertook, so was confident that she could take on any tasks required. However, she was surprised about how anxious and self-conscious she was when she started her work at the community health centre.

Very early on, she was asked to make a phone call to the government department that dealt with financial aid, on behalf of a client. She became very self-conscious and froze, forgetting the questions she had prepared. Her supervisor, Margaret, was present in the room when she made the phone call, but to Gian's surprise Margaret did not seem overly concerned. Margaret stressed that this level of performance anxiety at the beginning of a new job was normal and, as Gian became more familiar with the agency and her role, this should diminish. Margaret encouraged Gian to prepare for and carefully consider each task prior to undertaking it. She also encouraged her to keep notes focusing on her role in a task, what she had done well, and what she would like to see changed. As Gian became more familiar with her role, this anxiety decreased, although it returned occasionally when she was confronted with a new task. As time progressed, she became aware that although the tasks Margaret was giving were becoming more complex, she

*continued*

was able to plan and perform them with greater confidence. She was also aware that Margaret was encouraging her to review and analyze how and why she approached tasks in a particular way and to consider a different approach and how this would play out in practice. Gian had never been extended in this way before and found this level of analysis assisted her to focus on the detail of her practice and be more aware of her approach.

# Contracting

For students in the helping professions it is now commonplace to develop a learning contract or plan with their supervisor. However, this was not always the situation with early career professionals, particularly when supervision was provided by their line supervisor. Some practitioners regard contracts or supervision agreements as too formal, but they are important for a number of reasons including:

- They signify that supervision is an important and valid aspect of practice.
- They make it more likely that there is a clear understanding between the supervisor and supervisee and that both are aware of their roles and responsibilities.
- They reduce the chances of misunderstandings yet also outline a process of review if there are differences of opinion.
- They specify feedback processes for evaluating practice (Morrison 2001).

Outlining what you desire from supervision and what you are prepared to give is an important step in the development of a learning/supervision agreement. Considering the following questions can assist you in preparing for an initial meeting and being ready to negotiate a supervision agreement or contract.

- What is your approach to practice? What are the values and attitudes that are important to you? How would you like this to be reflected in your professional practice?
- How do you learn best? In responding to this question, it may useful to think about both positive and negative learning experiences and to tease out what contributed to them being positive or negative.
- What do you expect of your supervisor in terms of time and availability, approach and methods of supervision, and level of expertise? Do you want someone who both challenges and supports you and moves beyond the analysis of a task? What are the implications of this?
- What do you bring to supervision? Given your educational and life experiences, in what areas do you have a sense of confidence or mastery? What are the areas you need to strengthen?
- What are your professional development or learning needs in terms of knowledge, skills, and values? How can you best achieve these in the organizational context?

Supervision is a relationship that does not happen by chance, whether organizationally imposed or not. Both supervisees and supervisors can be influential in how the relationship forms and develops. In many organizations, supervisors are allocated on the basis of administrative convenience (or, in the case of students, educational priorities). However, unless there is mutual respect and a similar approach to supervision and practice, there is a risk that the supervision will not be optimal. Negotiating a learning or supervision contract/plan can take a considerable amount of time, and it is important that both the supervisor and supervisee are active in the process. Developing a solid working alliance provides the context for a sound supervisory relationship that is built on trust and respect. The greater the role of supervisees at this early stage, the higher their commitments are likely to be. An interactive process where you and your supervisor both present some of your ideas, expectations, questions, and responses enables you to take responsibility and be proactive in supervision.

The areas to be negotiated in a contracting discussion would generally include:

- the learning or professional development goals and the tasks that can be undertaken to achieve these goals
- the roles, responsibilities, and expectations of the supervisor and the supervisee
- the approaches to both practice and supervision of both the supervisee and supervisor
- the methods to be used to achieve the learning/professional development goals
- the methods of assessment and the forms feedback will take
- how the work is to be evaluated
- the ongoing monitoring and reviewing of the contract
- the practicalities—for example, the dates, times, and duration of sessions; setting agendas; and agreements about renegotiating sessions

Questions flowing from these areas that you may wish to ask your supervisor in your initial meeting include:

- What is your approach/philosophy to practice and supervision?
- What are your expectations of my role and responsibilities?
- What do you consider as your area of expertise?
- What supervision methods do you use?
- How will my progress be evaluated?

In this initial meeting, differences in approaches and expectations may be evident. If so, it will be important to negotiate how these will be dealt with.

There are particular issues around the development and review of learning/professional development goals. It is important that, as a professional, you regularly self-assess your learning or professional development goals. These goals will be influenced by the organizational context in which you are working or undertaking placement. It is useful to develop goals that are both challenging and specific. The more specific the goals are, the greater the likelihood that relevant tasks can be identified to ensure their attainment. Broad goals may make this more difficult, although sometimes it may be important to begin with a broad goal and an understanding that this needs to be broken into more specific components at a later time, after some tasks related to the goals have been completed. For example, beginning students frequently identify very broad goals such as learning about casework or community work, or linking theory to practice. It can become easier to break these goals into more specific components after the student has more information about what is involved by undertaking some related tasks. As the supervisee becomes more experienced in the agency context, learning/professional development goals and associated supervision activities can be developed more specifically, which can contribute to them being more achievable.

# Issues of Diversity

A key theme within supervision literature is the recognition of the impact of the social group categories of gender, race, ethnicity, class, and sexual orientation on the supervisory milieu. Although there is an emphasis on examining the impact of social group categories on the relationships between social workers and clients, there is less awareness of how these factors influence the supervisor/supervisee relationship. As with traditional theories of human behaviour, counselling, or social work, the supervision literature is dominated by Western discourse. This suggests that it is important for supervisors to be aware that the dynamics that exist between groups can be isomorphic to the broader social, economic, and political realms. For example, Chapman and Sork (2001) provide a gendered analysis of the power differentials inherent in male supervisor/female supervisee relationships, and how these dynamics can (unconsciously) reproduce traditional male/female power differentials. Other authors (Nelson 2000; Vonk & Zucrow 1996) found that same-gender constellations provide marginally higher reports of satisfaction, but not to the degree that would indicate this to be the preferred arrangement.

Generally, ethnic minority supervisees are reluctant to discuss cultural issues in supervision (McRoy et al. 1986). This suggests that the power differentials that exist between supervisors and supervisees may be exacerbated when the individuals are from a different race, culture, gender, or other social group category. Page (2003) discusses the importance of majority member supervisors working to eliminate preconceived ideas, stereotypes, and prejudices about minority group supervisees, as these, too, can reproduce majority–minority group dynamics. For example, supervisors from the majority perspective may engage in practices that 'treat everyone the same' which can invalidate the unique needs of

## Practice example 3.2

## Community development supervision

Jini was able to refine her goals when she became more familiar with her role. She began her first job as a community development worker. At Jini's first supervision session her supervisor, Charlie,

*continued*

asked her about what she wanted to focus on in supervision. Jini said she wanted to learn more about the community she was working in and develop a greater knowledge about community development processes. Charlie suggested that these were very broad goals and suggested that Jini monitor what she did over the following month and try to break these goals down into more specific and achievable goals. Jini decided to keep an ongoing journal to help her with this. As she became more familiar with her role, she began to be clearer about her professional development goals. When she met with Charlie the following month she presented the following goals:

- to become familiar with particular issues facing this community through examining municipal, provincial, and federal documents about the area, as well as other relevant reports, and meeting with the residents, groups, and individuals that are connected to the community
- to learn more about the assets-based need approach and its applicability to community development by reading current literature and talking to community development workers and her supervisor
- to develop her group work skills and knowledge through reading, practice, and analysis in supervision
- to develop an understanding of professional values and ethics by identifying issues as they arise and discussing them in supervision
- to develop her skills in critical reflection by analyzing both the personal and structural implications of situations

minority group supervisees. Minority member supervisors/supervisees may also be subject to their supervisory practices being interpreted by reference to their culture. Clearly, supervisors need to aim for culturally competent supervisory practices that recognize and respect the dynamics of difference, appreciate the diverse world views that minority group supervisees bring to the process, recognize the differences that exist within groups, and engage in an ongoing process of reflexive awareness that is constituted in direct experience.

## Methods of supervision

The use of a broad range of supervision/learning techniques is critical in supervision. These can include:

- observation
- journals, diaries, and other forms of process recordings
- self-analysis using role recording (a written record of an interaction in which the focus is on the role of the learner) or tape recording
- discussion of readings

- simulation exercises including role plays
- teaching exercises including skills training

A number of factors need to be considered by both the supervisor and supervisee in deciding which methods are the most appropriate to achieve the supervisee's learning/ professional development goals. There needs to be a match between the supervision method and the approach that will be most effective or valuable for the particular task at hand. The following section outlines the processes involved in using observation and reflective journals or recordings.

## Observation

The two most frequently used observation methods are:

- a supervisee observes an experienced practitioner complete a skill
- the supervisor observes the supervisee completing a task either through direct observation, video- or audiotapes, and/or co-working

Learning from modelling or observing experienced practitioners enables supervisees to begin to understand the vast and complex array of knowledge, skills, and values that are part of everyday practice and to use this as a basis to develop their own approaches. Observations can take various forms, from sitting in on an interview or meeting, to the use of one-way mirrors, or video- and audiotapes. Observation should not be a passive process: the supervisee should be given particular tasks to complete or themes to scrutinize during the observed activity. Prior to the observation, the supervisee and supervisor will agree on how the material from the observation is presented—for example, discussion, or recording followed by discussion.

Direct observation of a supervisee creates an excellent opportunity for learning and professional development. Prior to any direct observation it is important to ensure that the supervisee is comfortable and able to trust the supervisor so as not to feel threatened; clearly specify the focus of the observation; and agree to debrief immediately after the activity. Other forms of observation include co-working with a supervisor; role-plays and other simulations; and audiovisual and audio recording to indirectly observe the supervisee.

## Reflective journals

Reflective journals can be used to both analyze practice and prepare for supervision sessions. There needs to be agreement about how these journals will be used. Are they to be available to the supervisor or are they only for the supervisee? Some supervisees choose to use their journals to prompt them during supervision sessions, without showing them to their supervisor. Journals can be organized in different ways but should focus on learning/professional development. They can assist in analyzing practice and advancing understanding by focusing on actions, feelings, values, and beliefs.

Reflective journals include recordings of interactions and events. They usually include a summary of what happened, the context in which it happened, and who was involved, as well as the supervisee's reactions and feelings. Other questions to consider addressing in a journal are:

- What was the stimulus for your action or response?
- How did you understand or read this stimulus?
- What did it mean to you?
- What did you hope to achieve from your action?
- What are the assumptions, dominant beliefs, or values that underpinned your actions?
- What are the competing views that can affect practice?
- What theories or reading are you drawing on and how has this influenced your approach?

Any notes developed from your analysis can be used in supervision sessions. The role of the supervisor in this situation would be to raise questions and pose challenges to extend your analysis.

This chapter has focused on the role that you as supervisees can take to be proactive in your supervision. Being clear about professional development/learning goals, being an active partner in the supervision process, and being open to challenges sets the scene for effective supervision. This promotes an environment where supervision is seen as part of everyday practice, which in turn enhances your professional development.

 ## Questions for Review

1. What are the four main functions of social work supervision?
2. What theoretical models apply to supervision in the helping professions?
3. What sections of the Canadian Association of Social Workers *Code of Ethics* apply to supervision? What are the benefits of including supervision in the *Code of Ethics*? What are some limitations?
4. How might membership in a particular social group category, for either the supervisee or the supervisor, impact the supervision process?

## References

Brown, A., & Bourne, I. (1996). *The Social Work Supervisor*. Buckingham: Open University Press.

Canadian Association of Social Workers (2005). *Code of Ethics*. Ottawa, Ontario: Canadian Association of Social Workers.

Chapman, V., & Sork, T. (2001). Confessing regulation or telling secrets? Opening up the conversation on graduate supervision. *Adult Education Quarterly*, 51, 94–108.

Cleak, H., & Wilson, J. (2004). *Making the Most of Field Placement*. Southbank, Victoria: Thomson.

Davies, M. (2000). *The Blackwell Encyclopaedia of Social Work*. Oxford: Blackwell.

Hawkins, P., & Shohet, A.R. (2000). *Supervision and the Helping Professions*. Buckingham, PA: Open University Press.

Honey, P., & Mumford, A. (1986). *The Manual of Learning Styles.* St Leonards: Allen & Unwin.

Jarvis, M. (1995). *Adult and Continuing Education.* London: Routledge.

Kadushin, A. (1976). *Supervision in Social Work.* New York: Columbia University Press.

Kolb, D. (1984). *Experiential Learning: Experience as the Source of Learning and Development.* Englewood Cliffs, NJ: Prentice Hall.

McMahon, M., & Patton, W. (2002). *Supervision in the Helping Professions: A Practical Approach.* Sydney: Prentice Hall.

McRoy, R.G., Freeman, E.G., Logan, S.L., & Blackmon, B. (1986). Cross-cultural field supervision: Implications for social work education. *Journal of Social Work Education*, 22, 50–6.

Morrison, T. (1993). *Supervision in Social Care.* London: Macmillan.

Morrison, T. (2001). *Staff Supervision in Social Care: Making a Real Difference for Staff and Service Users.* Brighton: Pavilion.

Nelson, S.E. (2000). A new paradigm for teaching counseling theory and practice. *Counselor Education & Supervision*, 39, 254–70.

Page, M. (2003). Race, culture, and the supervisory relationship: A review of the literature and a call to action. *Journal of Curriculum and Supervision*, 18, 161–75.

Proctor, B. (1988). Supervision: A co-operative exercise in accountability. In M. Maren & M. Payne (eds), *Enabling and Ensuring.* Leicester: National Youth Bureau and Council for Education and Training in Youth and Community Work.

Reynolds, B. (1965). *Teaching and Learning in the Practice of Social Work.* New York: Russell & Russell.

Shardlow, S., & Doel, M. (1996). *Practice Learning and Teaching.* London: Macmillan.

Vonk, E.M., & Zucrow, E. (1996). Female MSW students' satisfaction with practicum supervision: The effect of supervisor gender. *Journal of Social Work Education*, 32, 415–20.

# 4. The Practitioner's Use of Self in the Professional Relationship

### Agi O'Hara

Understanding the experience of the client is the foundation for effective work in the helping professions. Practitioner self-knowledge and self-awareness is the conduit through which client understanding develops. Self-knowledge can be defined as an understanding of ourselves in terms of our worldview, our values, beliefs, attitudes, the sources from which our lives gain meaning, and, hopefully, the reason for choosing to become a helping professional. Brearley (1995) warns of the potential for self-gratification and exploitation of clients if there has been insufficient exploration of the underlying motivations for our career choice. For example, one of the myths of the helping professions is that if an individual has experienced some degree of trauma, they will be in a better position to assist others. It is possible this may provide the helper with some insight into others' feelings, it is also important to remember that everyone will have different experiences. Although self-knowledge is available to all of us, we are not always conscious of all of its facets and need to be prompted to reflect on our beliefs and attitudes to ensure that the use of self in our professional role is in a disciplined and appropriate manner (O'Connor et al. 1995, p. 26). Self-awareness can be considered as the awareness of ourselves in the moment, quite often as a result of our interactions with others. It facilitates our level of involvement, appropriate to the situation, such that we are neither excessively distant nor overly involved (Collins et al. 1999). This is especially important when working with clients and should include developing an awareness of potential differences between our clients and ourselves.

Self-knowledge and self-awareness work well in tandem. Self-knowledge can enhance the benefits of self-awareness, by assisting the practitioner to develop an understanding of various perspectives and interpretations that may be relevant in their work with clients, particularly when issues of difference emerge.

## Activity 4.1  Critical self-reflection

1. What experiences from your life do you think invited you into a helping profession?
2. Was there a particular incident or memory that brought you into the helping professions?

*continued*

3. How do you think that your goal to help others developed throughout your own life?

4. What does your desire to help say about you as a person?

5. How might your desire to help facilitate your ability to help others?

6. How might the same desire impede your ability to help others?

7. How would you like others to view you as a helper?

8. How would you like to see yourself as a helper?

9. How is your self-view as a helper a part of your self-view outside your profession?

10. To what degree do you feel you have personal control in your work as a helper?

11. What do you like and dislike about being a helper?

12. What personal needs does being a helper fulfill?

13. How does your personality suit or not suit your being a helper?

14. What are the perceptions of helpers in your community?

## Practice example 4.1

### Clients giving gifts

As a psychologist, I am keenly aware of the guideline that gift-giving by clients should be discouraged. However, I sometimes experience discomfort when attempting to refuse a client's gift. On reflection, it is clear that my level of discomfort is dependent on various client characteristics and the nature of the working alliance developed between us. It is therefore insufficient to merely become aware of my discomfort. I also need to differentiate between the possible causes of the discomfort. Is it due to my assumption that the client is attempting to manipulate my responses or is becoming overly familiar with me (either of which may be personal triggers for me, as well as having professional consequences), or is it due to my concern that if I refuse to accept the gift, I will seem to be disrespecting the client's cultural custom of demonstrating his gratitude? Taking the time to consider my beliefs about the client, his possible motives, and our working relationship, will assist in formulating an appropriate response.

# Values

Working with people inevitably involves encountering value issues (Thompson 2002). The assumption that the only way to avoid biasing the work with clients is by isolating or hiding our values ignores the reality that, as people, we are neither value-neutral nor value-free. Despite this, it is possible to remain appropriately objective in our work with clients (Corey 2005). It is not necessary to maintain a rigid or unnatural separation between the practitioner's professional and personal selves (Shulman 1999). In fact, our authenticity as helpers is enhanced when the boundary between our personal and professional selves is fluid. There are other choices besides adopting extreme positions such as (a) total reluctance to express our values and beliefs, or (b) believing in the absolute correctness of our values and beliefs, and expecting them to be adopted by everyone (Corey 2005). What is required is balance and sensitivity.

Although practitioner self-disclosure regarding values and beliefs may assist clients in clarifying their own values and beliefs, great care needs to be taken to ensure that the client's perspective is not invalidated, overridden, or diminished. The client should not feel coerced, whether directly or indirectly (perhaps as a means of pleasing the practitioner) to alter their views to match those of the practitioner. An exception to this guideline is likely to arise when working with perpetrators of child abuse and domestic violence, or any behaviours that are legally prohibited. The role of the practitioner with regard to values in such situations is more complex and will necessarily involve discussion and modelling of pro-social behaviours (Trotter 1999).

As stated in chapter 2, 'Professional Values and Ethical Practice', possessing professional values and engaging in ethical practice are basic expectations of helping professionals. Although different professional groups may develop and prioritize their professional values differently—for example, 'social work is characterized by a commitment to social justice, while nurses may make health a higher priority' (Thompson 2002, p. 202)—the manner in which the fundamental expectations of professional practice are adhered to is, to a large extent, determined by the practitioner's personal values. It is therefore imperative that practitioners clarify their values and develop and maintain an awareness of the appropriate role of their values in their professional practice.

## Activity 4.2  Personal values

Develop a list of values that you consider to be the benchmark for the way you live your life and by which you are guided in relation to others (respect, honesty, and so on). It is helpful to identify specific examples of how these values are translated into your personal and professional lives, and to identify times when these values have been challenged.

The origin and development of professional values can readily be attributed to our professional training and can at any time be checked against the Codes of Ethics developed by the professional associations whose role it is to monitor and uphold the profession's standards of practice. However, the origin and development of our personal values and ethics is not so clear-cut. Where do our values come from? Do we just inherit or adopt those of our parents? Do we, as a means of rebellion, differentiation, or gaining of independence, reject and abandon parental-gained values? Or is the process a variation or combination of each of these extremes? Which other people and what other factors contribute to the development of our values? There are no simple answers to these questions. The process of values formation is complex and determined by many individual and cultural factors.

## Activity 4.3  Primary professional obligations

1. To what degree do you think you are able to keep your personal needs separate from your professional relationships with clients? Do you think that you will be able to meet your own needs through your work, yet not at the client's expense? How might you manage this?
2. What are some of your personal needs that you think will help you become a more effective communicator/helper?
3. What are some of your personal needs that you think will hinder you in establishing effective working relationships with people?

## Activity 4.4  Influences on moral development

The following exercise developed by White (1996) offers a creative means of considering the sources of influence on the development of moral values.

Consider the following question: *Should equal opportunities be given to people regardless of their race or gender?* Do you agree or disagree, or do you have difficulty in deciding? Briefly, provide a reason for your answer.

Rate the *amount of influence* each statement below has on your response using the following rating scale:

| 1 | 2 | 3 | 4 | 5 |
|---|---|---|---|---|
| no influence | little influence | moderate influence | strong influence | very strong influence |

1. My teachers' ideas on race and gender issues have _____ on my opinion.
2. The idea that all people are born equal and should be respected has _____ on my opinion.
3. My family's beliefs and expectations on race and gender issues have _____ on my opinion.
4. The idea that society will benefit from addressing race and gender issues has _____ on my opinion.
5. Satisfying my own interest on race and gender issues has _____ on my opinion.
6. Other considerations such as _____ have _____ on my opinion.

# Self-disclosure

Effective practitioner self-disclosure 'is grounded in authenticity and a sense of mutuality' (Corey 2005, p. 359) and can create additional trust between practitioner and client (Ivey & Bradford Ivey 2003). Practitioner self-disclosure, whether related to values and beliefs (see above) or to life experience, may assist clients in clarifying their own experiences. As previously stated, great care needs to be taken to ensure that the client's perspective or experience is not invalidated and that the client feels no coercion to change her perspective or actions, to be in line with those disclosed by the practitioner.

Although particular theoretical approaches may strongly encourage self-disclosure—for example, 'feminist therapists use therapeutic self-disclosure to equalize the client–therapist relationship, (and) to normalize women's collective experiences' (Corey 2005, p. 359)—we nevertheless need to regularly examine our motives for self-disclosure, recognizing the possibility that it may be related to our own needs rather than those of the client. In our desire to demonstrate our humanity, we may possibly end up burdening our clients (Corey 2005) with too many personal anecdotes of our own life struggles. A simple guide for determining whether self-disclosure of practitioner experiences and feelings is appropriate is to consider whether they directly relate to the immediate concerns of the client (Shulman 1999) and if they will genuinely assist the client in having a greater sense of their own experience. Generally, the role of the practitioner is 'to create a climate in which (clients) can examine their thoughts, feelings and actions and eventually arrive at solutions that are best for them . . . and congruent with their own values' (Corey 2005, p. 22). The focus at all times needs to remain on the client and not on the practitioner.

## Practice example 4.2

## Inappropriate self-disclosure

A client is worried about her weight and the possible effects of it on her health. She is particularly concerned about heart-related illness as her mother died after several heart attacks. During her appointment with a practitioner, the practitioner begins to talk about the factors contributing to his own heart attack several years ago. Although the client is at first pleased to know that the practitioner has personal experience of her issues of concern, after ten minutes of detailed discussion of the various medical procedures, the difficult recovery period, and its effects on the practitioner's lifestyle, she feels that her specific concerns are being overlooked. In a sense she has become a sounding board for the practitioner.

### Questions for reflection

Think of a situation in which you were discussing your issues or experiences and the listener spoke of a personal experience that was similar.

*continued*

1. How did you feel about the listener's self-disclosure?
2. Did it help or hinder you in the exploration of your experience? Why?

# Practitioners' emotions

The majority of practitioners would now accept that they do not appear as blank screens to their clients, and also recognize that they are not devoid of feelings in their interactions with clients (Goldstein 1984). Finding the appropriate balance between remaining open to being moved by clients' experiences and being sufficiently detached so as not to merge with or become overwhelmed by their experiences (Brearley 1995; Trevithick 2000) is probably one of the greatest challenges for beginning practitioners. What practitioners decide to do about their feelings and whether it will be appropriate for them to be expressed and/or discussed with the client, will depend on many factors. However, it is suggested that attempting to totally suppress their feelings may be counterproductive to working with clients, as it requires so much energy that it diminishes the practitioner's ability to focus on the client's emotions (Shulman 1999). Effective practice depends on synthesizing 'real feelings with professional function' (Shulman 1999, p. 162). This allows for appropriate spontaneity and enables the client to experience the practitioner as real, not overly controlled, and therefore someone to whom they are able to relate (Shulman 1999). Expression of practitioner feelings is discussed further in the sections on counter-transference and immediacy.

The nature of practitioner feelings generated when working with clients appears to be related to many factors, such as:

- practitioner characteristics (clinical training, therapeutic orientation, personality)
- treatment variables (client characteristics and issues—for example, the feelings elicited by clients who are depressed and/or suicidal will be different from those elicited by clients experiencing psychotic withdrawal [Najavits 2000])
- the atmosphere in the treatment/practice milieu

The effect of therapeutic orientation on practitioner feelings towards clients and, in turn, the effect of perceived practitioner feelings on outcomes for clients, has been demonstrated in studies cited by Najavits (2000).

## Practice points 4.1

- Twelve-step drug counsellors appear to have more positive emotions towards their clients than cognitive or supportive-expressive therapists or psychodynamic

*continued*

therapists, who are reported to experience more negative feelings (such as frustration, confusion, anger, disappointment) (Najavits et al.1995, cited in Najavits 2000)

■ Compliance of patients regarding their treatment for alcoholism was shown to be influenced by the perceived level of anger and anxiety in their doctor's voice at the initial interview, based on analysis of audiotapes (Milmoe et al. 1967, cited in Najavits 2000). Such findings may also be relevant to non-medical situations.

Unrecognized feelings towards the client, which is sometimes referred to as counter-transference (see below), have also been shown to impair interview performance in a medical setting (Smith 1984). Although some of the behaviours discussed were specific to medical contexts, others such as performance anxiety, fear of loss of control, and fear of harming the client, would be concerns for many novice helping professionals. Despite the fact that research results on the effect of practitioners' emotional reactions to clients or patients are diverse, and at times contradictory, it is nevertheless apparent that developing an awareness of feelings in relation to the client with whom we are working is beneficial. Feelings such as unrecognized or suppressed anger, hostility, sadness, and over-protectiveness will inevitably affect our working relationship with clients and potentially the outcome of the work they are doing.

# Counter-transference

'Counter-transference' is a term associated with psychoanalysis and traditionally refers to reactions of the practitioner to the client, based on the practitioner's 'unconscious conflicts or developmental arrests' (Goldstein 1984, p. 201), such that they unwittingly 'project onto clients their own unfinished family business' (Shulman 1999, p. 26). This results in practitioners responding to their clients as if they are the person with whom they still have 'unfinished business'. These responses are viewed as unrealistic as they are generally not connected to the here-and-now experience with the client, and the practitioner is urged to control, resolve, or work through their responses (Goldstein 1984) without burdening the client, or allowing the responses to interfere with their working relationship. Kendall-Tackett (2003) suggests that counter-transference is more likely when clients (especially abuse survivors) reveal aspects of their story that are paralleled in the history of the practitioner, and asserts that 'abuse histories are fairly common in both mental health and medical providers' (Kendall-Tackett 2003, p. 2).

There are, of course, many other aspects of the practitioner's history, besides abuse, that may parallel the experiences of the client, for example, unresolved parental issues, sibling rivalries, and failed relationships. Therefore, the issue of counter-transference is potentially relevant for the majority of practitioners. Goldstein (1984) suggests that counter-transference may also be considered as relating to the real, immediate, and conscious response of the practitioner to the client's behaviour as they work together. Irrespective of the label attributed to practitioners' emotional responses, whether in accordance with a traditional or a broader definition of counter-transference, practitioners need to understand themselves sufficiently well to be able to differentiate between the various sources of their emotional responses to clients. It is through this understanding that practitioners are able to determine whether to discuss their feelings with their clients, as a form of immediacy (see below) or perhaps work through the related issues in supervision.

## Activity 4.5  Emotions exercise

Think back to a recent encounter in which you adopted a helping response to someone that triggered some uncomfortable feelings within yourself. This could be a situation from your volunteer or field practice experience, or one in which you were discussing a sensitive issue with a friend or family member. For this activity, it is important to focus on your personal thoughts, emotional reactions, and subjective experiences during the session.

- What thoughts were going on in your mind during the session?
- What emotions were you feeling? Were there any going on 'below the surface'?
- What did you think the client was thinking about you?
- What did you want the client to feel/think about you?
- Does the client remind you of anyone?
- What did the client want from you?
- Were there any boundary violations?
- Who were you for the client at that moment?
- Who was the client for you at that moment?

# Use of immediacy

Immediacy is a communication skill by which the practitioner, in the helping relationship, offers the client self-disclosure related to the practioner's current experience with the client. It requires self-awareness, critical thinking, and judicious application (Cormier & Nurius 2003) as not all perceptions or feelings connected with the client's behaviour require reporting. Immediacy may concern feedback about the client's behaviour, in relation to not only what is being said but also to what remains unsaid (Evans et al. 2004), or a disclosure of the practitioner's thoughts or feelings about his or her own experience in the moment, as it relates to the helping relationship. Although its primary function is to address issues that may interfere with the helping relationship if not dealt with (Cormier & Nurius 2003), it also provides an opportunity for clients to develop an awareness of their behaviour and learn about others' responses to them, in a way that may not normally be possible. Practitioners sometimes find it difficult to provide feedback about a client's behaviour that may be embarrassing or confronting, but their ability to do so offers the client a unique opportunity for self-awareness and a potential for change.

Cormier & Nurius (2003, pp. 153–4) provide the following guidelines for formulating immediacy responses:

- become aware of feelings experienced and whether they relate to issues that need to be raised
- formulate an immediacy response that addresses the issue in the 'here and now', using the present tense and an opening phrase such as 'I'm aware . . . '
- describe the situation, rather than give an evaluation of it
- identify the specific effect of the situation or behaviour
- ask for feedback to check the client's response to what was said

## Practice example 4.3

# Use of immediacy

In working with a client named Anna, who has experienced a series of broken relationships, the practitioner becomes aware of the client's flattering and rather overly enthusiastic responses to everything the practitioner says. Anna appears to be extremely eager to please and begins to adopt quite child-like mannerisms in her responses. It would be helpful to provide Anna feedback regarding the changes in her behaviour and to explore its relevance to her experience with failed relationships.

Practitioner: 'Anna, this may seem like a strange question, but I wonder what your answer would be if I asked you how old you are feeling right now? I only ask because I've become aware of a change in the way you are speaking since we began exploring the strategies you could use in your interactions with your mother. You've become much quieter and seem to be speaking in a higher pitch than before. I'm beginning to feel more protective towards you and wonder if you are aware of the changes in the way you are responding to me.'

Anna's response could be followed by an exploration of her feelings and the context in which she experiences similar feelings.

## Questions for reflection

Consider the last few times when you became aware of negative feelings towards the person with whom you were interacting.

1. Are you clear about the reasons for the feelings you were experiencing?
2. If they were a direct result of the behaviour of the other person, did you discuss these feelings?
3. If not, what were your reasons for not doing so?
4. Do you generally have difficulty speaking about negative feelings?
5. Do you know why this might be the case?
6. How might this affect your work with clients?

# Self-care

The work of helping professionals is often demanding and gruelling due to the inevitable immersion into the 'inner worlds of distressed and distressing people' (Brady et al. 1995, cited in Norcross 2000, p. 710) frequently involving negotiations 'about the most diffi-cult aspects of human relationships' (Jordan 1990, cited in Brearley 1995, p. 59). Self-care requires the conscious recognition of the potential hazards of such work and the many serious consequences of practitioner self-neglect. Norcross (2000) warns of the conse-quences of over-personalizing the sources of stress and inappropriately attributing them to personal inadequacies rather than to the nature of the work being carried out. Although the potential for depression, emotional exhaustion, anxiety, substance abuse, disrupted rela-tionships, business and financial difficulties, excessive workloads, and other stress-related concerns (Kramen-Kahn & Downing Hansen 1998; Miller & McGowen 2000; Norcross 2000) is now recognized by many helping professionals, this has not necessarily resulted in their involvement in proactive behaviours to prevent such difficulties. Many of the strate-gies that practitioners devise with their clients to assist them in managing the stressors in their lives would be relevant to the practitioner, yet for many of them there appears to be a reluctance to practice what they preach to their clients. Some gender differences have been demonstrated in the use of coping strategies—for example, female psychotherapists were shown to use self-talk strategies, continuing education, and personal therapy more than male psychotherapists (Kramen-Kahn & Downing Hansen 1998). A study investigating counter-transference and boundary issues in clinicians found that female clinicians reported using more coping strategies than male clinicians (Little & Hamby 1996, cited in Kendall-Tackett 2003). Although it is encouraging that female practitioners will utilize a greater repertoire of coping strategies, this does not indicate that male practitioners would not also benefit from similar strategies, nor should this encourage complacency in either sex who work in the helping professions.

So why is it that so many of us seem to ignore what is so patently obvious? Perhaps the reluctance to focus on self-care can be blamed on an inadequate focus on such issues by the professional training bodies responsible for curriculum development in the various courses taken by helping professionals (Baruch 2004). It is in these professional develop-ment contexts that self-care issues and 'risk factors associated with . . . compassion fatigue, distress, and impairment' (Gilroy, Carroll, & Murra 2002, cited in Baruch 2004, p. 66) should be raised and emphasized. Significant focus on the inevitable hazards of being a profes-sional helper and exploration of strategies (beyond a cursory mention of supervision) for countering natural vulnerabilities, needs to be a compulsory component of all professional training courses (Baruch 2004).

Often mentioned in the literature on self-care is the need to create clear boundaries between one's professional and personal lives. This can be facilitated by engaging in activi-ties that re-energize the practitioner and that offer relief (Dlugos & Friedlander 2001) from the numerous sources of stress and pressure associated with being a 'helper'. The following experiences drain practitioners and leave them vulnerable to compassion fatigue, vicarious trauma and burnout:

- continually drawing on emotional resources from which to demonstrate our 'empathic attachment (and) active involvements' (Skovholt et al. 2001, p. 167)
- needing to choose the appropriate form of intervention from 'the plethora of . . . theoretical and clinical approaches' (Baruch 2004, p. 66) to which we are exposed
- frequent exposure to detailed accounts of our clients' trauma, particularly when working with adult survivors of abuse (Kendall-Tackett 2003)
- the experience of isolation for practitioners engaged in private practice

Practitioners who do not experience reciprocal relationships in their non-professional life, and who find themselves becoming too involved in the needs of others (at work, within the family, and among friends) and being only givers and not receivers of caretaking (Kendall-Tackett 2003) are not maintaining appropriate boundaries. As a result, they are at increased risk of developing burnout.

Burnout may be described as the decreased ability to attach with the next client because of the emotional depletion that comes from caring for others. Baruch (2004) reminds us that we do not always recognize the imminent dangers and that 'conscious burnout drains us; unconscious burnout is often taken out on the people we love' (Treadway 1998, cited in Baruch 2004, p. 66) or those with whom we are working (clients and colleagues). We therefore need to become aware of our state of health well before we are so exhausted that we are no longer able to connect with others and can only survive the end of the working week by seeking solace in silence and isolation from family and friends. Estrangement and withdrawal from others can be understood as both 'a response to the other symptoms of burnout and as a symptom itself' (Baird 1999, p. 123). Periodically-consulting inventories specifically designed for the purpose can quite dramatically alert practitioners to their state of burnout or vicarious trauma (Halpern 1995). According to Baird (1999), symptoms of burnout are both emotional and physiological, and can include:

- emotional distancing from clients and staff
- decreased empathy
- cynicism
- decreased self-esteem
- physical exhaustion
- sleep disturbances
- stomach pains and other stress-related physical complaints

In times of stress, it is quite common for helping professionals sometimes use belittling humour about their clients as a means of venting feelings among their peers. Almost 70 per cent of respondents in a 1999 study of Victorian social workers (Sullivan 1999) admitted to such venting. Despite its common occurrence, it is a source of conflict between personal needs for stress reduction and maintaining professional values of respect and the valuing of clients (Sullivan 1999). Such apparently light-hearted use of 'twisted' humour, though succeeding in its objective of stress release, is a source of cognitive dissonance for some practitioners. This was evidenced in the Sullivan (1999) study, in which 20 per cent of respondents expressed discomfort with their use of humour about their clients. Despite the assertion by Monteith (1993, cited in Sullivan 1999) that the discomfort experienced as a result of engaging in belittling humour lessens the likelihood of actually being discriminatory, Sullivan (1999) cogently asserts that such venting is 'one of the mechanisms by which "meta-discrimination" operates' (Sullivan 1999, p. 6) and should be avoided, particularly as other means of stress reduction and self-care are readily available.

## Questions for reflection

1. What do you value most about your work in the helping professions?
2. What are (or do you expect to be) the most stressful and the most rewarding aspects of this type of work?
3. How do you know when you are stressed?
4. How might your co-workers know when you are stressed?
5. What can others do for you when you are stressed?
6. What can you do for yourself?

Suggestions for self-care include:

- supervision (with professional mentors or peers)
- involving other professionals in the care of clients who have multiple needs and who would benefit from a team response
- seeking counselling if client issues are stirring up own issues
- maintaining a good social support network
- meditation and yoga
- exploration and engagement in religious practice
- physical exercise (for example, sports, walking, dancing)
- continuing education and professional development activities
- journaling
- hobbies or leisure activities (for example, painting, singing in a choir)

However, at times, even these activities appear to be 'too much to ask' as there may be effort and/or competency pressures associated with them. Simple leisure activities such as reading a 'light' or 'trashy' novel, and watching television or a movie, may not appear to be quite as worthy as the other strategies previously listed, but can nevertheless be a source of energy renewal for many. Joining a 'laughter' club is a more modern suggestion for re-connecting with the simple joys of life, which can be so easily forgotten when frequently exposed to life's hardships, tragedies, and the shadow sides of human nature. Such 'light' activities, however, should not be considered as long-term alternatives for specific strategies required for ethical practice, such as engaging in professional supervision. See chapter 3, 'Making the Most of Supervision', for a detailed discussion of supervision.

## Activity 4.6  Strategies for self-care

Create a list of strategies or activities that you are already using as a source of energy renewal from currently-experienced stresses. Are there others you would now consider since reading this section on self-care?

## Questions for Review

1. What interpretations of the concepts of transference and counter-transference can most usefully be adopted by helpers?
2. What might be some situations in which the use of self-disclosure would be helpful? In what situations might the use of self-disclosure be harmful?
3. How can the emotional aspects of the helping context that are particularly inhibiting or disruptive be addressed?
4. How might the cultural, ethnic, gender, racial, or other social group categories of either the client or the helper influence the helper's values and beliefs?

## References

Baird, B.N. (1999). *The Internship, Practicum, and Field Placement Handbook: A Guide for the Helping Professions* (2nd edn). Upper Saddle River, NJ: Prentice Hall.

Baruch, V. (2004). Self-care for therapists: prevention of compassion fatigue and burnout. *Psychotherapy in Australia*, 18(4), 64–8.

Brearley, J. (1995). *Counselling and Social Work*. Buckingham: Open University Press.

Collins, D., Jordan, C., & Coleman, H. (1999). *An Introduction to Family Social Work*. Itasca, IL: Peacock.

Corey, G. (2005). *Theory and Practice of Counselling and Psychotherapy* (7th edn). Belmont, CA: Thomson Brooks/Cole.

Cormier, S., & Nurius, P.S. (2003). *Interviewing and Change Strategies for Helpers*. Pacific Grove, CA: Thomson Brooks/Cole.

Dlugos, R.F., & Friedlander, M.L. (2001). Passionately committed psychotherapists: A qualitative study of their experiences. *Professional Psychology: Research and Practice*, 32(3), 298–304.

Evans, D.R., Hearn, M.T., Uhleman, M.R., & Ivey,

A.E. (2004). *Essential Interviewing: A Programmed Approach to Effective Communication* (6th edn). Toronto: Thomson Brooks/Cole.

Goldstein, E.G. (1984). *Ego Psychology and Social Work Practice*. London: Collier Macmillan.

Halpern, N. (1995). Who is helping the helper? Self-care for therapists working with traumatized and abused clients. Paper presented at the Australian Association of Trauma and Dissociation 4th Annual Conference, Melbourne.

Ivey, A.E., & Bradford Ivey, M. (2003). *Intentional Interviewing and Counseling: Facilitating Client Development in a Multicultural Society* (5th edn). Pacific Grove, CA: Thomson Brooks/Cole.

Kendall-Tackett, K. (2003). *Treating the Lifetime Health Effects of Childhood Victimization: A Guide for Mental Health, Medical and Social Service Professionals*. New York: Civic Research Institute.

Kramen-Kahn, B., & Downing Hansen, N. (1998). Rafting the rapids: Occupational hazards, rewards, and coping strategies of psychotherapists. *Professional Psychology: Research and Practice*, 29(2), 130–4.

Miller, M.N., & McGowen, K.R. (2000). The painful truth: Physicians are not invincible. *Southern Medical Journal*, 93(10), 966–73.

Najavits, L.M. (2000). Researching therapist emotions and countertransference. *Cognitive and Behavioral Practice*, 7, 322–8.

Norcross, J.C. (2000). Psychotherapist self-care: Practitioner-tested, research-informed strategies. *Professional Psychology: Research and Practice*, 31(6), 710–13.

O'Connor, I., Wilson, J., & Setterlund, D. (1995). *Social Work and Welfare Practice* (2nd edn). Melbourne: Longman.

Shulman, L. (1999). *The Skills of Helping Individuals, Families, Groups, and Communities* (4th edn). Itasca, IL: Peacock.

Skovholt, T.M., Grier, T.L., & Hanson, M.R. (2001). Career counseling for longevity: Self-care and burnout prevention strategies for counselor resilience. *Journal of Career Development*, 27(3), 167–76.

Smith, R. (1984). Teaching interviewing skills to medical students: The issue of 'countertransference'. *Journal of Medical Education*, 59(7), 582–8.

Sullivan, E. L. (1999). Discrimination and 'meta-discrimination': Issues for reflective practice. *Australian Social Work*, 52(3), 3–8.

Thompson, N. (2002). *People Skills* (2nd edn). Hampshire: Palgrave Macmillan.

Trevithick, P. (2000). *Social Work Skills: A Practice Handbook*. Buckingham, PA: Open University Press.

Trotter, C. (1999). *Working with Involuntary Clients*. Sydney: Allen & Unwin.

White, F. A. (1996). Sources of influence in moral thought: The new moral authority scale (MAS). *Journal of Moral Education*, 25(4), 421–39.

# 5

# Cultural Diversity in Practice: Working with Immigrants and Refugees

## Denise Lynch

## Activity 5.1  Early cultural experiences

(Adapted from Adams, Bell, & Griffin 1997)

Prior to reading this chapter, take a few minutes to reflect upon the following questions:

- What are your earliest memories of, or experiences with, people from another culture?
- What images, impressions, or feelings did you have as a child about people from another culture?
- What messages did the people around you (parents, teachers, friends) pass on to you about people from another culture?
- How did these messages affect how you thought about yourself?
- As an adult, what impressions, thoughts, feelings, or beliefs do you have about people from another culture? How have they changed or stayed the same over time?

## Processing

- What are some of the early messages and from whom or what did they come?
- What are some commonalities or themes that you notice in these messages?
- What cultures were included? What cultures were not included?
- What is it like to recall these early memories?

In its simplest form, 'diversity' means difference. It refers to people who are, or have been, landed immigrants in Canada. A landed immigrant is a person who has been granted the right to live in Canada permanently by immigration authorities. Some immigrants have resided in Canada for a number of years, while others have arrived recently. Diversity is an overarching Canadian value that signifies a positive response to change within the demographic and cultural landscape and an appreciation of differences between language and ethnic groups in the community. Yet, despite the unequivocal expression of commitment within federal legislation to diversity issues, the experiences of immigrants and refugees in Canada demonstrate that a parallel commitment by social service practice to the value of diversity has yet to be fully achieved. Understanding the experiences of immigrants and refugees requires an ecological analysis that incorporates how social, institutional, familial, and individual factors influence one's capacity for integration into a new country. From a critical perspective, it requires the service provider to be self-reflective by articulating their world view about cultural diversity, acknowledging bias, and evaluating the source of this information, as well as its validity.

Canada is considered a multicultural country, with extensive French and English histories; a long tradition of First Nations, Aboriginal, and Métis history; many different layers of immigrants, refugees, and skilled overseas workers; and a myriad of other international influences. Until the early 1970s, when greater public awareness and legislative changes solidified the acceptance and mainstreaming of diversity, our pluralistic society was steeped in racism as enshrined in overt federal government policy including immigration policies, as well as other, more subtle forms of discrimination against those perceived as 'different'.

How do practitioners ensure that the cultural diversity in our lives is incorporated into our philosophies, theories, policies, and practices? How do learning institutions engage with diversity and assist students to think, reflect, and develop appropriate practice strategies that will give the best assistance to the individual, group, or community with whom they are working? In summary, how does the practitioner move from an abstract understanding of diversity in Canada to being a 'practitioner of excellence', incorporating values and ideas that strategically develop the direction of their work in a culturally appropriate way? This chapter will address these questions and offer some strategies for practice in the helping professions and for community workers.

The knowledge base of the human services professional requires an understanding of the development of political, psychological, and sociological perspectives of immigration to Canada. They are the foundations that underpin expert practice in working with culturally diverse communities. These perspectives overlap and influence each other in many contexts and situations. Although we may work with individuals and families, it is imperative to have some clarity about this larger picture from historical and current perspectives. It gives us the opportunity to engage in work that can offer more than short-term solutions to often profound and lifelong issues.

# Social and political context

The Canadian Association of Social Workers (CASW) *Code of Ethics* (2005) states that the pursuit of social justice is one of the important mandates of our profession. In this respect, working with immigrants and refugees in the community needs to strongly reflect this ethic. Advocacy and respect for the individual, group, and community are also articulated in the *Code of Ethics* and practitioners, again, need to show they are cognizant of cultural diversity in their communities.

A macro-level analysis of the social and political context suggests that current immigration policy was not developed in pursuit of social justice goals. Prior to 1945, Canada's immigration policy reflected an 'open door' approach in terms of numbers, although 'preferred' immigrants were restricted to individuals/families from Western Europe, Britain, and the United States. The 'acceptable' category contained individuals from Eastern and Southern Europe, and members of visible minorities were prevented from entering Canada as they were considered less desirable. The intent of federal policy at this time was to promote the settlement of the West including the Prairies and beyond to Alberta and British Columbia, and thus farmers, farm labourers, and those 'who seemed likely to become successful agriculturalists' were encouraged to emigrate (Troper 2008). After the end of World War II, the economic needs of Canada changed, and immigration policy shifted to accommodate the large influx of Europeans, as well as the establishment of policies to support economic goals and ethnic quotas. In 1962, Canada abandoned its 'European [white] only' immigration policy to allow for visible minorities, and admission requirements shifted to individual and personal characteristics of the applicant, rather than nationality.

During the 1970s, the federal government undertook a formal review of immigration policies, and a Green Paper on Immigration Policy and a report to Parliament by a Special Joint Committee of the Senate and the House of Commons were prepared (Troper, 2008). This resulted in the proclamation of a new *Immigration Act* (1978) that established the fundamental objectives of Canada's immigration policy. These reflected a greater humanitarian component that prioritized allowing immigrants to sponsor family members (family reunification); the recognition of refugee status for particular groups, defined as those who 'by reason of a well-founded fear of persecution for reasons of race, religion, nationality, membership in a particular social group or political opinion' (Abella 2008) are outside their own countries and cannot, or fear to, return; in addition to the promotion of Canada's economic, social, demographic, and cultural enrichment.

Since the 1980s and 1990s, there has been a move to 'multiculturalism', reflecting an appreciation of the background of all Canadians, their sense of identity with their ethnic community, and pride in that identity and community. The *Canadian Multiculturalism Act* was proclaimed in 1988 with the stated goals being:

a) to recognize and promote the understanding that multiculturalism reflects the cultural and racial diversity of Canadian society and acknowledges the freedom of all members of Canadian society to preserve, enhance, and share their cultural heritage; b) to recognize and promote the understanding that multiculturalism is a fundamental characteristic of the Canadian heritage and identity and that it provides an invaluable resource in the shaping of Canada's future; and c) to promote the full and equitable participation of individuals and communities of all origins in the continuing evolution and shaping of all aspects of Canadian society and assist them in the elimination of any barrier to that participation (*Canadian Multiculturalism Act 1988*).

The diversity of our population since the settlement of the West has increased enormously. We now have national social policies that reflect the importance of multiculturalism and diversity in mainstream policies. Within the Canadian context, cultural diversity is not difficult to articulate within our many ethnic communities. It is also reflected in the key policy documents of the government such as the *Canadian Multiculturalism Act*, as indicated above.

In 2006, the proportion of the population who was born outside of Canada reached its highest level in 75 years, with the majority arriving from continental Asia, including the Middle East. Currently, immigrants to Canada may arrive under different classes representing different program objectives. The three classes are: Family Class immigrants who enter on the basis of family relationships; Independent Class immigrants (business class) selected on the basis of a point system that reflects occupational skills, experience, and likely adaptability to Canadian society; and Convention Refugee Class immigrants who are admitted on the basis of Canadian laws governing refugee admissions and likely adaptability to the Canadian environment (Citizenship and Immigration Canada 2008)

Although considered part of the immigrant population, there are significant points of divergence for those who enter Canada as refugees to escape persecution and danger in their home countries. (Abella 2008). In the past century and a half, Canada has accepted groups beginning with the United Empire Loyalists, and American blacks escaping slavery, to Quakers and Mennonites who refused to participate in the military, to Jews who were fleeing the genocide of Nazi Germany. The Doukabours, Hungarians, Czechs, and Vietnamese are among the many other ethnic groups who have found sanctuary in Canada. Currently, there are a significant number of African refugees who are settling in the larger urban centres of Toronto, Montreal, Calgary, and Vancouver.

From a social justice perspective, Lacroix (2006) suggests that it is important for social service professionals to begin with an examination of the various treaties and conventions that influence refugee policy, and that at times contribute to the ongoing marginalization of individuals and families. Legal identity is especially relevant for immigrant populations. People without formal legal identity linking them with the host country tend to be 'in limbo'. For refugees, this is particularly pertinent. They cannot begin to integrate into the community because they cannot formally access 'citizenship' rights, and it may be dangerous and emotionally devastating to return to their country of origin. This can also be understood more clearly within the discourse of inclusion and exclusion: those who can obtain citizenship or permanent residency are included, and those who are refugees are still mostly excluded. This is reflected in rights, benefits, and acceptance by the general public. Coates and Hayward (2005), in their review of barriers facing refugees in Canada, concluded that the system is 'highly inefficient' (p. 86) and likely impedes the integration of refugees into the community. For the individual, the authority of the law often makes the process a long and difficult journey.

## Institutional context

The conditions and obstacles for new arrivals are challenging, and remain so even after several years. For example, immigrants typically earn less than Canadian-born workers with the same amount of education and work experience (Statistics Canada 2008). The high rate of unemployment and underemployment of Canada's highly skilled immigrants has been widely documented (Picot, Hou, & Coulombe 2008; Smith & Jackson 2002). Although the political promotion of multiculturalism is critical to the success of immigrants and refugees, the reality for some people coming to Canada has often been very different and very difficult. There is generally positive support for multiculturalism; however, there remain beliefs that 'immigrants compete with Canadians for jobs' and threaten 'Canadian culture'. The degree of entrenchment of these attitudes is at odds with the emerging reality. Recent immigrants (between one and five years) who arrive in Canada with a university level education are more likely to be employed in positions that do not require university level education, including manual labour and the service industry. Of some concern is a similar trend for established immigrants (more than 10 years) with university level education, which suggests that employment and economic difficulties of recent immigrants do not necessarily dissipate the longer they stay in Canada (Statistics Canada 2003). The situation may be exacerbated for those who immigrate as refugees, as people who are forced to leave their homes in fear for their lives are less likely to have the skills and educational levels associated with success in the labour market. With government policy reflecting and directing mainstream community attitudes and the media supporting these attitudes, our ideal of multiculturalism and cultural diversity is often compromised (Jamrozik et al. 1995).

## Family and community context

Within an ecological framework, the mezzo level of analysis includes community and family-based factors. Each ethnic community has a great deal to offer the individual who is attempting to integrate into a new society. It can inform and assist individuals who wish to connect or reconnect with their culture and it can provide a sense of a 'belonging community'. The ethnic community can also be a valuable advocate in taking an individual's issues to broader arenas and facilitating connections to community resources. Since an individual is part of a community, practitioners can enhance their effectiveness by using the community to assist the individual. Each ethnic community will generally have identified support structures or informal networks to assist the individual. The practitioner needs to be cognizant of these community supports and their ability to assist their members.

The self-aware worker also needs to be mindful of the impact of immigration on the family system and how the family dynamics contribute to family adaptation. McGoldrick (2003) suggests that service providers begin from the position that cultural, class, religious, and political background will influences families' world view, and then collaboratively explore these world views with individuals and their families. People who leave their country of origin bring with them not only a factual history but also an emotional and perceptual history that is very important to the way that they make decisions about their lives and become integrated into the 'host' country. This history may involve feelings of grief and loss. It is very important to extract the relevant 'cultural' history in a respectful manner.

It is also important to be aware of the many factors that will influence families' capacity for integration. The developmental stage of the family life cycle, the degree of choice regarding the decision to immigrate, educational level, gender, age and generation, fluency in the language of the new country, and experiences with racism or discrimination will all influence the family's ability to adapt. There is extensive literature available that documents numerous difficulties and barriers to service utilization that impede the successful adaptation of immigrants to Canada. These include a significantly higher risk of homelessness (Danso & Grant 2000; Fiedler, Schuurman, & Hyndman 2006; Omidvar & Richmond 2003; Preston, Murdie, & Murnaghan 2007), barriers to accessing health services (Lai & Chau 2007), poverty (Kazemipur & Halli 2001), depression and mental health issues (Kuo, Chong, & Joseph 2008), and social isolation (Dunn & Dyck 2000).

Although all immigrants experience a wide range of difficulties related to adjustment and adaptation, individuals within the refugee class may experience additional issues including post-traumatic stress disorder, extended separation from family, limited access to employment and settlement services, a lengthy determination process, as well as the loss of country, identity, and status (Lacroix 2006; Thurston et al. 2006).

The immigration process may especially challenge parent–child relationships. Although immigrant or refugee status can be extremely stressful on all family members, children may be especially vulnerable to psychological distress (which impedes their adjustment to school), language barriers that reverse the parent/child roles; and exposure to far different influences than in their home country.

The two quotations below not only reflect the diversity between cultures but the different ways individuals have responded to the laws and policies within Canada. So while there is diversity between cultures, there is also great diversity in each immigrant's experience of Canada. This is dependent on when and how they arrived, and the structural and personal supports available both upon arrival and later in their settlement. The situation of the second generation has particular importance with respect to the long-term integration and success of immigrant families.

This is the greatest country on earth. You are free to speak your mind and your children have opportunities. They can be educated and they need not be fearful.

Raul, eighteen years of age, asylum seeker from Colombia.

I got my children out of hell in Palestine and now they are in limbo in Canada. They cannot concentrate at school or be all right, because they do not know that they will not be deported. They are fearful the whole time. This is terrible.

Mohammed, a father who has been waiting for the results of his application for refugee status for three years and three months. His ten-month-old baby, born in Canada, is considered a citizen, but not his father.

## Activity 5.2  Social service agencies and diversity

Within an ecological framework, the exo or legislative level examines the larger institutions of society that influence our personal systems and include social service agencies

*continued*

that have a strong, yet indirect, influence on our lives. Examples of these are services related to health, education, disability, employment, and income assistance.

Think of a particular social agency that you have had some experience with as a client, paid staff, or volunteer. How does the agency address the following issues:

- Does the agency provide outreach services to community members?
- What is the cultural background of workers compared to clients?
- Does the agency staff reflect the diversity of population?

# Individual context

How are immigrants perceived? Although the *Code of Ethics* (2005) clearly underscores the right—not the privilege—of self-determination, the experiences of immigrants with service providers suggest that the inherent goal is assimilation. According to Sakamoto (2007), new immigrants should be viewed as independent adults who may, initially, need information and guidance, but are able to decide for themselves what their goals of settlement are and select, as opposed to being directed to, the services needed to meet their goals. For people who leave their country of birth, the migration process means that their personal and national identities must be reframed. There is no choice. When they arrive in the host country, they no longer have the identity of their country of origin. Citizenship and a new identity do not immediately replace their former identity. Their sense of 'self' and sense of 'belonging' are blended into their new Canadian life. Young people, in particular, can find this very difficult, particularly when the construction of a new identity is very different to the ancestral identity of their parents or close relatives. The relevant concept here is 'belonging': often the pain and loss associated with 'not belonging' has long-standing negative health effects (Leavey et al. 2004, p. 776). The challenge for the practitioner is to holistically assess the meaning and relevance of identity for their clients in their current situation (Lum 1999).

A migrant's own language, and the adoption of English as an additional language, creates for the individual a sense of belonging to a group within their community. The individual's language of origin is often the factor that contributes to a 'sense of belonging'. Loss of language often means far greater losses: loss of esteem, loss of status, and loss of the ability to communicate one's most intimate and important stories about one's life. While language is only one aspect of culture, the ramifications of language and its link with culture need to be addressed and given due importance. Practitioners are often involved in verbal and written interactions with people who are speaking English as an additional language. Practitioners need to thoughtfully reflect on the client's difficulty in understanding conceptual matters when they are not spoken or written in their first language.

In this context, the role of human services practice is relevant and vital. We, as practitioners, have a role in assisting people to settle and integrate into this country, but we also have a role in assisting them to deal with the contradictions between national policy and the fact that many new arrivals are forced to live in communities that have a range of ways of including and excluding them. Thus, there are many levels on which practitioners can intervene that reflect professional values and beliefs. Our individual intervention can be matched with advocacy for individuals or groups within the community who are not able to access the full benefits of Canadian society. Barriers of language, religion, and gender often make it difficult for immigrants and refugees to be informed about services and their rights and responsibilities. Practitioners can only begin to work effectively with culturally diverse families, groups, or communities if they have a clear understanding of the many issues relevant to the process of migration.

# Meaning and understanding of 'cultural diversity'

Cultural diversity can have as many meanings and interpretations as is possible on any given day. A working definition is offered by Naylor:

> Cultural diversity is the acceptance and promotion of the variety of human cultures and their different value systems in a given society. Cultural diversity recognizes the importance of native languages, dress, traditions, and beliefs that govern self-identity (Naylor 1998, p. 1).

Another definition, by Mitchell, goes a step further:

> The concept of culture is an inclusive concept that recognizes and affirms difference in its many forms and dimensions. It refers not only to differences based on ethnicity or language, but also embraces differences of lifestyle, world view and social experience that characterize socially defined sub-populations such as young people, same-sex attracted and transgender people, people who use drugs, and people who are homeless. Culture can also capture the common experiences of exclusion and discrimination that are widely recognized as affecting sub-populations such as those listed above that have minority status in society (Mitchell 2000, p. 59).

Concepts and philosophies that impact on practice with culturally diverse communities can be extracted from a number of disciplines. There is no single theory that will direct the work of a practitioner, but the central theories and concepts that assist our understanding and direct our practice are:

- inclusion and exclusion (Vasta 2004)
- grief and loss (Ward & Styles 2003; Falicov 2003; Fazel & Stein 2002; Davies & Webb 2000; Fitzpatrick & Freed 2000; Papadopoulos 1999; Bowlby 1981)
- personal, institutional, and cultural oppression (Bishop 2002; George & Ramkissoon 1998)

Although these concepts seem dissimilar, they can contribute to the development of a holistic understanding of the migrant and refugee experience. For example, in respect to inclusion and exclusion, practitioners are more prepared and able to be effective in work with individuals, groups, and communities if they ask the following questions posed by Harris and Williams (2003, p. 205): 'How does "social inclusion" actually work? And what processes does the individual engage in, while becoming included or staying excluded?' It is also important to recognize that clients from marginalized cultures may have internalized society's prejudices about them, and those from dominant cultural groups may have internalized assumptions about their own superiority and right to be privileged within our society.

Additional questions that are central to an understanding of the difficulties of difference may be of assistance. These include:

- Who is included and why?
- Who is excluded and why?
- What are the costs and benefits of that exclusion?
- How can the excluded become included?

The second important set of concepts is linked with the grief and loss experienced by individuals who leave their homeland either through choice or involuntarily. The grief and loss often continues throughout the life of the person, and practitioners need to have an understanding and an integrated set of strategies to assist people and groups in this situation. No matter how positive the changes made to their lives, there is still grief and loss with respect to the life, and, often, 'way of life', that migrants or refugees have left behind. Immigrants and refugees experience multiple losses of friends, community, and family, ambiguous loss in terms of security, familiar situations, and physical, social, and cultural meanings. This grief is often linked with a loss of extended family, and the familiarity of being in one's own country. These feelings are exacerbated if there is no clear sense of belonging to the 'new country'. The concept of 'cultural bereavement' is relevant here (Rechtman 2000; Shapiro 1995; Eisenbruch 1991). This is particularly important for people who have been forced to leave their homeland and therefore have not made a conscious choice to come to Canada. 'Cultural bereavement includes the refugees' picture—what the trauma meant to them; their cultural recipes for signalling their distress; and their cultural strategies for overcoming it' (Eisenbruch 1991, p. 673). Thus, cultural bereavement encapsulates both the experience of being in a place where the refugees are not 'included', and grieving for the loss associated with this position.

A practitioner must consider the meaning given by the individual to important life 'experiences', and how they can assist individuals or groups in dealing with their loss in a meaningful way. This means practitioners may have to critique, and perhaps discard, the 'Canadian' ideas of survival and 'good life', recognize that not everyone who arrives in Canada is unequivocally accepting of the move, and be able to accept that people 'heal' in many different ways. Practitioners need to have excellent assessment skills as no person or situation is the same. The literature supports the notion of the individual's collective experience and the individual's particular experience, being characterized and determined, in part, by their 'culture' (Eisenbruch 1991).

The psycho-social impacts of oppression on individuals and families may include alienation from self, group, and culture, and coping mechanisms may include distancing from members of one's own group as well as from members of the majority group. It is important for practitioners to recognize how people on the margin have frequently been silenced, and to, therefore, focus on drawing people and their stories out. Self-awareness is critical, and we must refrain from interpreting people's experiences through our own lens to ensure that the client experiences a sense of personal power within the helping relationship. Traditional theories of 'helping' have been based on the centre and extended to the margin, without any awareness of the level of 'fit'. We need to recognize that understanding the immigrant and refugee experience is a challenge to our privilege, that how we experience the society in which we live is different from those who are new to the country. As professionals, we need to adopt a critical perspective and understand the dynamics of the experience for both those in the margin and for those in the centre, and avoid developing interventions based on stereotypes rather than a cultural assessment.

Recently there has been a use of models of 'cultural competency', which define a set of techniques to assist workers in diverse communities (Sue & Sue 2003; Brach & Fraseri-rector 2000). For example, no one can ever fully understand another's culture, but curiosity, humility, and awareness of one's own cultural values and history can contribute to sensitive and culturally competent practice. These techniques have greater relevance when they complement the understanding of cultural diversity outlined earlier in this chapter (Husband 2000, p. 231).

Combining theories to explain and analyze culturally diverse communities can assist the practitioner. The challenge is to carefully explore the core principles outlined above and develop positive strategies. These core principles can be summarized as an understanding of:

1. Canada's political and social history of immigrants and refugees,
2. the current socio-political context,
3. inclusion and exclusion, and its many applications to immigrants and refugees,
4. the grief and loss experienced by immigrant groups—in particular, cultural bereavement,
5. the dynamics of oppression and empowerment,
6. the positive contribution that difference has made to the Canadian community.

# Practice

Social service practice is never disconnected from the policy framework. The intent of integration forms the core of Canada's immigration policy. Of particular note within this legislation is the expectation that the social service sector will collectively promote the adaptation of newcomers to Canadian society. The following discussion gives strategies for the practitioner who is working with culturally diverse communities. It builds on the above discussions and on the skills and knowledge developed in professional education. It has relevance for practitioners in policy development, non-government agency work, mandated social service agencies, individual counselling and therapy, and legal advocacy. At the same time, practitioners need to be mindful of the different considerations for counselling, therapy, group work, and community interaction. It is important to consider and respect the meaning and status of therapeutic counselling and support in the country of origin, which can often vary considerably from Western values and beliefs.

## Individual history

Cultural competence is more a process of learning and critiquing our own practice rather than a clearly defined goal. From a critical perspective, it is important to begin by exploring and acknowledging our own individual cultural history and immigration experience.

## Activity 5.3  Your own cultural heritage

Using your family of origin, beginning with your grandparents (or earlier if you have access to that information), develop a cultural timeline that traces your family's migration to Canada. Try to identify specific organizing principles (positive or negative) that are particular to your culture of origin. These are fundamental constructs that shape the perceptions, beliefs, and behaviours of members of a group. For example, in First Nations families, colonization and the residential school system are two organizing principles that have influenced families in significantly negative ways. For children whose parents were Holocaust survivors, the experiences of their parents during the war had an enormous impact upon their family. It is important to note that for some practitioners the answer to one or more of these questions may be unknown. For example, some adults may have been adopted as children. Others may not know their heritage, particularly if they have been in the same country for one or two generations (for example, those from settled Anglo-Celtic families).

Use the following questions to guide your narrative.

- What nationality were your grandparents and great-grandparents? If non–First Nations, why did they come to Canada?
- What has been your own experience of Canada?
- Has your family's experience been fair and egalitarian?
- What has been your group's experience with oppression?
- What positive and negative 'cultural baggage' do you have? This may include cultural, language, racial, or other issues.
- What are some of your group's ideas about family? About gender roles?
- Are there issues that divide members of your group?
- What bias do other groups have about your group? What bias does your group have about other groups?

*continued*

- How does your group view outsiders in general, and members of the helping professions?

1. Spend some time on this exercise. It often raises many issues about nationality, forced migration, poverty, and the intergenerational impact on the individual.
2. Consider the different cultures represented in the grandparents' group. It might be useful to compare notes with someone you know well, or do this activity together to highlight the different cultures represented in people's backgrounds. It is also an excellent group activity.

Once a level of personal cultural awareness has been established, the next step is to explore how these cultural characteristics influence the manner in which the service provider will build relationships with clients, assess situations, resolve dilemmas, and develop intervention plans. Culturally competent practice also requires the worker to acquire cultural knowledge about groups in question and develop skill in discovering each person's unique cultural outlook. Knowledge may be accessed in various ways, and nurturing cross-cultural awareness requires one to locate oneself within a cultural milieu that encourages interaction in an environment that is controlled by the other culture.

By eliciting stories and explanations within a cultural framework, the service provider can learn from clients through the telling of their own familial and cultural stories. However, at the same time, it is important to develop sensitivity to cultural differences without over-emphasizing them. It is equally important for the practitioner to be aware that although people may be connected to the same culture and share many of the same beliefs, rituals and practices, there is divergence within cultures as well. Differences within groups may include patterns of migration, generational status, degree of assimilation and acculturation, degree of fluency in one's traditional language, degree of fluency in English, and the level and location of education.

## Intervention considerations

Intervention methods that are congruent with culturally competent practice begin with a paradigm shift: moving from a deficit-based model in which the personal pathology of the individual is emphasized (rather than the social conditions that created the problem), to a strengths-based model that acknowledges client strengths in the context of cultural diversity. Practitioners need to understand how the client copes with the oppressive structures they encounter, and discover those areas in which the client feels personally and politically powerless. Through these processes, the practitioner can facilitate the client moving from a position of alienation to one of change and empowerment.

In summary, when assessing the experience of immigrant and refugee families, there are several key issues that service workers need to address:

- timely access to the labour market
- recognition of human and cultural capital of newcomers
- access to skills training and education programs
- culturally sensitive access to social services
- strong community-based and neighbourhood-based social networks
- inclusive public spaces for leisure and activities that allow the expression of difference
- access to high-quality services and affordable housing
- recognition of cultural differences in planning and policy-making
- anti-discrimination measures in employment and housing

## Practice example 5.1

## Alice: understanding her point of view

Consider the following case study. Alice, who is nineteen years old, lives with her Vietnamese parents and brother. The parents came to Canada as refugees via the internment camps in Hong Kong. Alice is studying sciences at university, which she dislikes. She is very unhappy at home and is constantly fighting with her parents. They do not like her boyfriend, her friends, her attitude to her education, and the manner in which she addresses them. She wishes to leave home and wants to know about income assistance programs that will help her support herself.

### Questions for reflection

1. What skills would assist the interviewer in gaining information from the client?
2. What particular skills or knowledge would be required to gain a good understanding of the relevance of the cultural issues?
3. How would the individual's narrative contribute to the assessment?
4. What is the role of the ethnic community in assisting the family members?

## Activity 5.4  What is identity?

Draw a circle and write your name in the middle.

Then draw eight 'spokes' out from the middle circle.

On each spoke, write something that is important to your identity. For example, it can be a word, like 'Asian' or 'gay' or a phrase like 'parents divorced when I was 5' or 'Huge Leafs Fan' or 'love being with friends and family'.

Be prepared to share most or all of the qualities you write down with the rest of the group.

The following guide may be used for reflection or sharing:

*continued*

- Reflect upon/share the thing you are most proud of or happy about right now.
- Reflect upon/share the thing that is most controversial for you, or that you are struggling with right now.
- Reflect upon/share the thing that you put down that surprised you.
- Reflect upon/share two or three others things you want the group to know about you.

1. What did you think of the exercise?
2. Were you surprised by any of the words that you chose for yourself?
3. Are there words that your friends or family might use that you did not use? Why is it that others see us differently than we see ourselves?
4. Is race/ethnicity a major factor in identity circles for yourself or members of this group? Why or why not? How about gender? Why or why not? How about sexual orientation? Age? Family upbringing? What else did you notice as important common factors?
5. What are some of the other ways we differ from each other? What ways are we similar? What can we learn from our differences and similarities?
6. Why is learning about ourselves and/or each other in this way important in terms of our work as social service practitioners?

## Role of interpreters and translators

For the majority of immigrants to Canada, English is not their first language. Practitioners need to thoughtfully reflect on clients' difficulty in understanding conceptual matters when they are not spoken or written in their first language.

Most practitioners will need to work with interpreters. They are now frequently used and can be important where language is a barrier to communication (Maidment & Egan 2004, p. 169). It is also important, though, to consider that interpreters do not exist in isolation. They bring with them their own values, organizational context, and history. The following scenario and questions may assist with understanding the positive contributions and limitations of interpreters.

## Practice example 5.2

## Working with interpreters

A practitioner who works for the provincial child welfare service is called to assess a situation where there has been an allegation of sexual assault against a twelve-year-old Peruvian girl,

*continued*

Nelida. Nelida is part of a family that migrated to Canada two years ago. Her parents do not speak English and she has two younger sisters, aged ten and eight years. The three girls speak English quite well. The family migrated to Canada from a farming village in Peru and the parents speak Spanish and Quechua, the indigenous language of Peru.

The family lives in a relatively poor part of a large urban city in the province of Ontario. They rent a small apartment. They are practising Catholics and their religion is very important to them. The father, José, is currently out of work and the mother, Cecilia, has a cleaning job. They have landed immigrant status.

The school has reported concerns to the child welfare service, as the girl disclosed to a friend at school that she was being inappropriately touched by a neighbour, who cared for them while the parents were away from the home.

The practitioner contacted the immigrant support services and arranged for a Spanish-speaking interpreter to be present for an interview with the girl's parents. A female interpreter was requested.

When the interpreter arrived at the home, her credentials were explained. She was originally from Spain, had a degree in languages, and had been working as an interpreter in Canada for one year. She was dressed formally, with a lot of expensive jewellery, and spoke with a great deal of authority to the parents about her role.

When she began to interpret the practitioner's concerns about Nelida to Nelida's parents, her tone and way of speaking were formal and authoritative. She allowed for very few questions and was somewhat disdainful of the parents' concerns and their inability to understand the situation. The parents seemed overwhelmed by her and she seemed frustrated with them.

Finally the practitioner had to stop the interview as Nelida was becoming distressed and the parents were noticeably intimidated by the interpreter.

## Questions for reflection

1. What is your analysis of the interpreter in the above scenario?
2. What is the responsibility of the practitioner in this situation?
3. What lessons are learned from this scenario in relation to the criteria that defines and determines 'excellent interpreters'?
4. How can social workers assist interpreters in preparation?

## Integration into Canadian life

An important consideration for practice is clarifying the goal of new immigrants with regards to their settlement. Canada's immigration policies suggest that immigrants are selected not only on the basis of potential for economic success but also on their ability to successfully integrate into Canadian society. Working with people from diverse communities involves sensitivity to history, language, and their process of integration into Canadian life. Although the federal and provincial governments lay out the framework, it is the social service sector that promotes social integration, assists in the settlement of immigrants, and helps them find housing, work, and schools for their children. Practice may be located in communities where individuals and groups require assistance as they work towards settlement. Certain groups, and their vulnerabilities as well as their strengths, are well documented in the literature. Children and young people who are refugees are a particularly vulnerable group who require specialist services to assist their settlement (Lynch 2004).

The important lesson for practitioners is that the 'meaning' of this settlement lies with the immigrant or refugee rather than with the practitioner. Our challenge is to assist the person, group, or community in planning for their future so that they can have a place in the Canadian landscape, where they will have dignity and esteem, and no longer feel categorized as 'other'.

## Potential areas of conflict

There are a number of conflict areas in which practitioners need to have skills of mediation, negotiation, and advocacy (see chapter 11, 'Advocacy in Practice', and chapter 12, 'Understanding and Managing Conflict'). As stated throughout this chapter, from a national perspective through to an individual one, the path towards contentment and integration has many difficulties. It is important to separate individual responsibilities from the structural barriers that immigrants and refugees experience on their path to settlement in this country.

Professionals are also in a difficult position. They are often caught between being an agent of mainstream institutions and, in attempting to assist people and advocate for communities, being kept out of these institutions (Goldberg 2000).

Canadian practitioners have a great deal to contribute to the research process. We need to be far more active in this area and bring international research findings to our work which may assist the immigrant or refugee. This not only needs to be encouraged in our educational institutions, but the voices of culturally diverse populations in Canada need to be part of the discourse.

Working with culturally diverse populations is a complex, constantly evolving area in which there are no easy analyses or simple solutions. Social work professionals have an important part to play in realizing social justice principles and strengthening community awareness about human rights and citizenship. There is much support in the community for the models of 'multiculturalism' that acknowledge and respond to the difficulties faced by immigrants and refugees. By developing and maintaining positive systemic and structural supports for multiculturalism, the benefits to the country that flow from our diverse populations are inestimable.

## Questions for Review

1. Compare and contrast the different immigration periods in Canada. For example, what are the national origins of the current immigrants? How are these different

from previous generations? Are people mostly immigrating as single individuals or are they arriving as families? What are some motivations for wishing to leave their countries of origin?

2. What are the key areas in which immigrants intersect with the social service system?
3. What are the essential elements of culturally competent social work practice?
4. What are some barriers to culturally competent social work practice?
5. What are the important policy considerations when working with individuals, families, and groups who have emigrated from another country?

# References

Abella, I. (2008). Refugees. *The Canadian Encyclopedia*, Online edition. http://www.thecanadianencyclopedia.com/index.cfm?PgNm=TCE&Params=A1ARTA0006738

Adams, M., Bell, L.A., & Griffin, P. (1997). *Teachings for diversity and social justice: A sourcebook*. New York, NY: Routledge.

Bishop, A. (2002). *On becoming an ally: Breaking the cycle of oppression in people*. Toronto: ON: Zed Books.

Bowlby, J. (1981). *Attachment and Loss: Loss, Sadness and Depression*. Harmondsworth: Penguin.

Brach, C., & Fraserirector, I. (2000). Can cultural competency reduce racial and ethnic health disparities? A review and conceptual model. *Medical Care Research and Review*, 57(1), 181–217.

Canadian Association of Social Workers (2005). *Code of Ethics*. Ottawa, Ontario: Canadian Association of Social Workers.

*Canadian Multiculturalism Act* (1988). Government of Canada, Ottawa, Ontario: Department of Justice.

Coates, T., & Hayward, C. (2005). The costs of legal limbo for refugees: A preliminary study. *Refuge*, 22, 77–87.

Danso, R., & Grant, M. (2000). Access to housing as an adaptive strategy for immigrant groups: Africans in Calgary, *Canadian Ethnic Studies*, 32, 19–43.

Davies, M., & Webb, E. (2000). Promoting the psychological well-being of refugee children. *Clinical Child Psychology and Psychiatry*, 5(4), 541–54.

Dunn, J., & Dyck, I. (2000). Social determinants of health in Canada's immigrant population: Results from the National Population Health Survey. *Social Science and Medicine*, 51, 1573–93.

Eisenbruch, M. (1991). From post-traumatic stress disorder to cultural bereavement: Diagnosis of South East Asian refugees. *Social Science Medical*, 33(6), 673–80.

Falicov, C. (2003). Immigrant family processes. In F. Walsh (Ed.), *Normal Family Processes* (3rd edn). New York: The Guilford Press.

Fazel, M., & Stein, A. (2002). The mental health of refugee children. *Archives of Disease in Childhood*, 87, 366–70.

Fiedler, R., Schuurman, N., & Hyndman, J. (2006). Hidden homelessness: An indicator-based approach for examining the geographies of recent immigrants at-risk of homelessness in Greater Vancouver. *Cities*, 23, 205–16.

Fitzpatrick, T., & Freed, A. (2000). Older Russian immigrants to the USA, their utilization of health services. *International Social Work*, 43(3), 305–23.

George, U., & Ramkissoon, S. (1998). Race, gender, and class: Interlocking oppressions in the lives of South Asian women in Canada. *Affilia*, 13, 102–19.

Goldberg, M. (2000). Conflicting principles in multicultural social work. *Families in Society: The Journal of Contemporary Human Services*, 81(1), 12–21.

Harris, P., & Williams, V. (2003). Social inclusion, national identity and the moral imagination. *The Drawing Board: An Australian Review of Public Affairs*, 3(3), 205–22.

Husband, C. (2000). Recognising diversity and developing skills: The proper role of transcultural communication. *European Journal of Social Work*, 3(3), 225–34.

Jamrozik, A., Boland, C., & Urquhart, R. (1995). *Social Change and Cultural Transformation in Australia*. Cambridge: Cambridge University Press.

Kazemipur, A., & Halli, S. (2001). Immigrants and 'New Poverty:' The case of Canada. *International Migration Review*, 35, 1128–56.

Kuo, B.C., Chong, V., & Joseph, J. (2008). Depression and its psychosocial correlates among older Asian immigrants in North America: A critical review of two decades research. *Journal of Aging and Health*, 20, 615–52.

Lacroix, M. (2006). Social work with asylum seekers in Canada: The case for social justice. *International Social Work*, 29, 19–28.

Lai, D., & Chau, S. (2007). Predictors of health service barriers for older Chinese immigrants in Canada. *Health and Social Work*, 32, 57–65.

Leavey, G., Sembhi, S., & Livingston, G. (2004). Older Irish migrants living in London: Identity, loss and return. *Journal of Ethnic and Migration Studies*, 30(4), 763–79.

Lum, D. (1999). *Culturally Competent Practice: A Framework for Growth and Action*. Pacific Grove, CA: Brooks/Cole.

Lynch, D. (2004). The protection, care and adjustment of refugee children in Australia. Paper presented at the 15th International Conference on Child Abuse and Neglect, Brisbane.

Maidment, J., & Egan, R. (2004). *Practice Skills in Social Work and Welfare*. Crows Nest, NSW: Allen & Unwin.

McGoldrick, M. (2003). Culture: A challenge to concepts of normality. In F. Walsh (Ed.), *Normal Family Processes* (3rd edn). New York: The Guilford Press.

Mitchell, P. (2000). *Valuing Young Lives: Evaluation of the National Youth Suicide Prevention Strategy*. Melbourne: Australian Institute of Family Studies.

Naylor, L. (1998). *American Culture: Myth and Reality of a Culture of Diversity*. Westport, CN: Bergin and Garver.

Omidvar, R., & Richmond, T. (2003). Immigrant settlement and social inclusion in Canada. Laidlaw Foundation's Working Paper Series, Perspectives on Social Inclusion. Toronto, Ontario: Laidlaw Foundation.

Papadopoulos, R. (1999). Working with Bosnian medical evacuees and their families: Therapeutic dilemmas. *Clinical Child Psychology and Psychiatry*, 4(1), 107–20.

Papillon, M. (2002). *Immigration, Diversity and Social Inclusion in Canada's Cities*, http://www.cprn.org, accessed 15 December 2004.

Picot, G., Hou, F., & Coulombe, S. (2008). Poverty dynamics among recent immigrants to Canada. *International Migration Review*, 42, 393–424.

Preston, V., Murdie, R., & Murnaghan, A.M. (2007). The housing situation and needs of recent immigrants in the Toronto Census metropolitan area. CERIS Working Paper No. 56. The Ontario Metropolis Centre, Toronto, Ontario: CERIS.

Rechtman, R. (2000). Stories of trauma and idioms of distress: From cultural narratives to clinical assessment. *Transcultural Psychiatry*, 37(3), 403–15.

Sakamoto, I. (2007). A critical examination of immigrant acculturation: Toward an anti-oppressive social work model with immigrant adults in a pluralistic society. *British Journal of Social Work*, 37, 515–35.

Smith, E., & Jackson, A. (2002). Does a rising tide lift all boats? The labour market experiences and incomes of recent immigrants 1995–98. Canadian Council on Social Development, Ottawa, Ontario; Canadian Council on Social Development.

Statistics Canada (2003). Longitudinal survey of immigrants to Canada: Process, progress and prospects. Statistics Canada, Social and Aboriginal Policy Division. Catalogue no. 89-615-XIE. Ottawa, Ontario: Statistics Canada.

Sue, D.W., & Sue, D. (2003). *Counseling the Culturally Diverse: Theory and Practice*. New York: John Wiley.

Thurston, W. (2006). Immigrant women, family violence, and pathways out of homelessness. Report prepared for the National Secretariat on Homelessness. Calgary, Alberta: National Secretariat on Homelessness.

Troper, H. (2008). Immigration. *The Canadian Encyclopedia*, Online edition. http://www.thecanadianencyclopedia.com/index.cfm?PgNm=TCE&Params=A1ARTA0003960

Vasta, E. (2004). Community, the state and the deserving citizen: Pacific Islanders in Australia. *Journal of Ethnic and Migration Studies*, 30(1), 195–214.

Ward, C., & Styles, I. (2003). Lost and found, reinvention of the self following migration. *Journal of Applied Psychoanalytic Studies*, 5(3), 349–67.

Williams, F. (1996). Postmodernism, feminism and the question of difference. In N. Parton (ed.), *Social Theory, Social Change and Social Work*. London: Routledge.

This chapter will explore the area of working with Indigenous people, where positive outcomes are always possible but not always achieved. Whether practitioner, client, Indigenous, or non-Indigenous, an informed knowledge base regarding the history of Aboriginal and non-Aboriginal relationships is critical in addressing issues of social justice for Indigenous people, particularly within the social service context. It is hoped that this chapter can assist in providing some key practical skills that will enable professionals to undertake more culturally competent interactions with Indigenous social workers, clients, organizations, and communities. Taking into account practice and field specifics, particularly those of health and social welfare, the information contained in this chapter should be generic enough to be useful in a broad range of settings. The chapter will discuss the major concepts being utilized across a range of areas where improvement in cultural interaction is crucial in producing beneficial outcomes for all involved.

Given the importance of recognizing that the present and future have an inescapable historical context, the chapter will also briefly touch on the journey that has brought Indigenous and non-Indigenous groups to this meeting place. To work together effectively, it is important for both Indigenous and non-Indigenous participants to understand and respect the past and the present, on which the future will be based.

## Historically speaking: listening, hearing, and understanding

Indigenous people in Canada, also known as First Nations, Inuit, and Métis, are people who belong to recognized Indigenous groups as defined by the Canadian *Constitution Act, 1982*. As a starting point, it is important to address the language used to describe members of this group. Although 'Aboriginal' has typically been used, writers are currently referring to members of this group as 'Indigenous', with a view toward recognizing, valuing, and respecting the diversity of the many First Nations, Inuit, Aboriginal and Métis groups in Canada, and the fact that they were the first inhabitants of the country, long before European contact.

It has been well documented in numerous sources (Bennet & Blackstock 2002; Bourgeault 1991; Dominelli 2000; Fournier & Crey 1997) that the relationship between Indigenous and non-Indigenous people in Canada has been fraught with oppression, systemic discrimination, and racism, as evidenced by institutionalized social, political, and economic power differentials. Moreover, we appear to be slow at learning from the lessons of history, which have been constructed and written from the point of view of the 'colonizers', not the 'colonized', and from this frame of reference, our knowledge is inevitably distorted.

It is not possible to understand any of the contemporary social issues affecting Indigenous peoples without an examination of the history of colonization from Indigenous perspectives. Colonization is a pervasive structural and psychological relationship that is reflected in the dominant institutions, policies, and histories of the occupying powers. From the Aboriginal perspective, it refers to loss of lands, resources, and self-direction and to the severe disturbance of cultural ways and values (Larocque 2006). One of the key mechanisms for colonization was the residential school system through which Aboriginal children were removed from their families and communities and sent to be educated within dominant, often religious-based, institutions. The intent of federal policy at the time was to undermine, if not eradicate, the existence of Aboriginal communities and families, and contemporary Aboriginal families are continuing to bear the burden of the residual trauma associated with this period (Funk-Unrau & Snyder 2007).

Given this significantly incomplete historical context, a legacy of colonization is a complex trail of hurdles both big and small, over which positive race relations need to jump, in order to produce positive outcomes for all. This cannot occur unless the foundations of this positive future are nurtured with sensitivity, awareness, and, above all, accurate and inclusive knowledge.

For example, consider the following excerpt from the *Educational Policy Statement* of the Canadian Association of Schools of Social Work:

> All social work students shall be prepared with a transferable analysis of the multiple and intersecting bases of oppression. Diversity refers to ethnic or linguistic origin, culture, race, colour, national origin, religion, age, disabilities, gender, sexual orientation, socio-economic status, and political orientation (CASSW 2008).

To foster positive relationships between Indigenous and non-Indigenous people, a shift in the way the two come together will determine whether we find ourselves physically, emotionally, and spiritually fit to clear the hurdles, or whether we fail in our attempts. As human services practitioners, it is fair to say that at some stage of your professional practice you will come into contact with Indigenous people. Why? Because although Indigenous persons make up only 3.8 per cent of the total Canadian population, according to the 2006 census figures (Statistics Canada 2008), First Nations and Indigenous persons measure the highest on every possible key indicator of social and economic disadvantage. The cumulative impact of colonization and the residential school system on Indigenous people has resulted in disproportionately higher rates of incarceration within the criminal justice system (Bracken, Deane, & Morrisette 2009; La Prairie 2002), overrepresentation within the child welfare system (Trocmé, Knocke, & Blackstock 2004), poor academic performance and employment outcomes (Barnes, Josefowitz, & Cole 2006), elevated risk for violence victimization (Brownridge 2008), poor maternal health (Moffitt 2004), and poor health outcomes including higher rates of chronic and contagious diseases and shorter life expectancy (Health Canada 2007). Institutionalized racism and socio-economic disadvantage appear to feed off each other in a never-ending cycle of dispossession, poverty, and despair for many Indigenous groups in this country, regardless of demographics. Beyond statistics, this issue represents one of the worst significant human rights and social justice challenges facing all citizens in Canada.

## Activity 6.1  Deconstructing the power of stereotypes

Make a list of the stereotypical ways in which Indigenous people have been described and portrayed in Canadian society.

1. Where do you think these stereotypes come from?
2. Do you believe they are a true representation of Indigenous people? Why or why not?
3. How do they influence interactions between Indigenous and non-Indigenous peoples?

'Culturally appropriate' is one term that is frequently used when discussing services provided for Indigenous people and communities, and its application is very broad. Basically, it implies that the service that is given to Indigenous groups will, in fact, meet and address their needs using skills, knowledge, and methods that are relevant and understandable in an Indigenous cultural context. In terms of process and protocols, it must reflect the traditions and values of the local community.

It is argued that understanding sociological concepts and applying them to definitions of Indigenous health and social service issues will encourage a more critical perspective. Therefore, an understanding of the socially-situated knowledge arising from colonial and post-colonial contexts will enhance the way practitioners relate to Indigenous peoples in a variety of settings. This critical approach will emphasize the importance of evaluating our own cultures, and the knowledge base, perceptions, and expectations that underlie them (Anderson 1999; McGibbon 2000).

The provision of adequate service to Indigenous peoples means that human services practitioners must acquire the knowledge and skills to provide services in a culturally appropriate manner. For example, culturally appropriate practice by service providers includes knowledge of the particular issues that Aboriginal women may experience, traditional teachings and practices, and Aboriginal spirituality; an inviting physical environment; and Aboriginal staff (Bucharski, Reutter, & Ogilvie 2006). Culturally appropriate ways of practice also promote more positive social outcomes. The Health Canada report (2007)

'Continuing Care in First Nations and Inuit Communities: Evidence from the Research', for example, outlines the outcomes of culturally appropriate behaviours that are applicable across a range of professions. The intent of culturally appropriate interactions are to engage in effective communication, contribute to clients' confidence in accessing service, affirm clients' sense of control with respect to their health and well-being, and promote the social and emotional health of Indigenous patients.

## Activity 6.2  Culturally appropriate practice

Think back to a time when you had an encounter or an interaction with an Indigenous person and what the result of that meeting was.

- Were you confident in your knowledge and skills in practising in a culturally appropriate way?
- Did the encounter go well for you? For the other person?
- If not, what hindered the encounter?

## Practice points 6.1

- Culturally appropriate practice invites service providers to be self-reflective and recognize biases within themselves as well as within their profession, and integrate this knowledge and reflection into their practice (Zellerer 2003). Those from dominant cultural groups may have internalized assumptions about the right to be privileged within our society.

- It is critical that practioners move beyond intellectual understanding and 'book knowledge' about others' socio-cultural realities and listen to the lived experience of those whose cultural context is different: individual and collective narratives are important. They need to fully explore the individual history, culture, community, and contemporary realities of specific clients, and listen to and observe the unique elements of individual situations.

- It is important for professionals to acknowledge the strength and resilience of Indigenous peoples. Even though great efforts were taken to assimilate them into the dominant culture, Indigenous traditions and values remain strong.

- Practitioners would be advised to consider the possibility of heterogeneity within a given cultural group and not uncritically use a 'one-size-fits-all' approach—for example, avoidance of eye contact might mean different things to different people within the same cultural grouping.

*continued*

- It is important for practitioners, who strive to be culturally appropriate in their practice, to question the dominant culture's often-accepted wisdom of the meaning of certain words and behaviours and what they think they 'know' before drawing conclusions regarding the meaning of those words and behaviours.
- Culturally appropriate practice builds on the fundamental helping skills that begin with a respectful, nonjudgmental, and open-minded attitude, and the abilities of listening and tolerance of silence.

## Crossing cultures or cultures crossed? Cross-cultural interaction

Much has been written about the relevance and importance of cross-cultural communication and interaction. Nonetheless, within the context of Indigenous health and education, this appears to have had limited success in terms of more positive outcomes. Whether this is a positive experience for both parties will depend, to some extent, on what each cultural group brings to this interaction.

McKenzie and Morrisette (2003) suggest a number of guidelines for respectful social work practice that may be conceptualized as the foundation for a framework of practice with Indigenous Canadians:

- an understanding of the world view of Aboriginal people and how this differs from the dominant Euro-Canadian world view
- recognition of the effects of the colonization process
- recognition of the importance of Aboriginal identity or consciousness
- appreciation of the value of cultural knowledge and traditions in promoting healing and empowerment
- an understanding of the diversity in Aboriginal self-expression

There needs to be recognition that individual and personal obstacles may influence the way that cross-cultural interaction is carried out. It should be understood that this might also be derived from within the context of larger, more generic and societal obstacles, which Eckermann et al. (1992, p. 125) define as 'structural' obstacles, particularly in relation to the health and social welfare institutions. These include:

- systems that have become highly institutionalized, where service is frequently administered in isolation from issues related to personal, family, and community care,
- a history of colonialism, and individual, scientific, and institutional racism, which has created a legacy of negative legislation, minority anxiety, and dependence, as well as a climate in which many Indigenous/non-Indigenous interactions are based on mutual stereotypes,

- professional structures and demands, which sometimes overshadow and override clients' as well as caregivers' personal needs,
- a philosophy and concept of health and well-being based on a biomedical model that focuses on curative, rather than holistic, health.

## Practice example 6.1

## Challenging rules and regulations

Ensuring access to social services through their location within communities is an important aspect of practice. Furthermore, it is important, however, to ensure that sufficient attention is given to addressing the psychological barriers that may prevent Indigenous people from accessing services. If we consider that it is imperative to have policies, rules, and regulations in regard to running a large health institution such as a hospital, it's also interesting to think about how, and by whom, these policies, rules, and regulations are developed.

In many instances, Indigenous people do not live within a standard 'nuclear' family, but have more complex extended families. Health professionals must accept that different healing processes exist for different people. For example, some (not all) Indigenous people like to have many family members with them in the hospital, which can create tension for staff and other patients. This tension often arises from restrictions around visiting times and certain entrenched behaviours. So a rule about visiting hours from 2 p.m. to 8 p.m. with two visitors at a time could become an impossible task for many Indigenous families. The question should become: Is it possible to have an optimal healing environment if we change how we think about visiting hours? In more remote areas, family members may have had to travel hundreds of kilometres to get to the nearest hospital to visit a family member only to be told that they will have to come back the next day. Limited transport options cause another layer of burden. Within one community there may not be sufficient vehicles to transport everyone who wishes to visit the patient. Also consider whether the community is, in fact, connected by roads to the larger centres or can only be accessed via air transport. For example, in many Northern communities in Manitoba and Ontario, ground transportation can only be utilized during the winter months, when the lake is sufficiently frozen to support the weight of a vehicle. Although it is understood that the rules are justified in relation to the welfare of the patient, this justification is rationalized from within a dominant cultural knowledge base. In many instances, the health and well-being of an Indigenous patient may be enhanced by the nurturing of kinship interaction between the patient and his or her family.

## Cultural competence

*Cultural competence* refers to the relationship between the helper and the client, and focuses on the capacity of the professional to integrate culture into the clinical context, with the view towards ensuring more meaningful outcomes. Cultural competence is defined as a congruent set of behaviours, policies, and attitudes that come together in a system or agency, or among professionals, which enables those professionals to work effectively within culturally appropriate cross-cultural situations (Isaacs & Benjamin 1991; Cross, Bazron, & Isaacs 1989). Benchmarks of culturally competent practice include:

- ethics and values that explicitly identify how professional values may facilitate or hinder the self-determination of Indigenous people
- self-awareness that addresses the multiple identities that we all experience
- cross-cultural knowledge about the history, values, language, family systems, and practices of Indigenous groups (for example, the value placed on sharing circles and the medicine wheel)
- cross-cultural skills, including mobilizing resources and advocacy that reflect professional understandings of how to incorporate culture into the helping process, and social action directed towards social justice by assisting people to increase their access to power, at both a psychological and political level

Understanding what is meant by 'culturally competent' is integral to acting on this imperative and making it work (Osher & Osher 1995). Cultural competence extends far beyond notions of cultural awareness and cultural sensitivity and finds legitimacy in the positive experience of clients and improved service outcomes. Cultural competence must be integrated into the delivery of social services in order to reduce the institutionalized racism that maintains current Indigenous health standards (Sambono 2004). For example, many Northern communities do not have regular access to physicians, and must rely upon the limited resources of the nursing stations that are often inadequately staffed. At the same time, Indigenous Canadians struggle with significantly higher rates of diabetes, and other chronic health conditions. Services that are culturally competent to engage in these health care issues have, within them, individuals who are culturally competent and who advocate and proactively assist in the attainment of self-determination for Indigenous peoples and communities by supporting the concept and processes of Indigenous control. In this way, both client and practitioner engage in a relationship—a partnership—that is built on rapport and values the contribution that each brings to this encounter. This engagement reinforces a cultural exchange that is equal, adaptable, and flexible, and builds a foundation for future interactions by allowing for mutual respect to be developed. Such engagement encourages positive interactions within the context of work with Indigenous individuals, groups, and communities, and leads to improved services.

# Cultural safety: safety in numbers?

The concept of *cultural safety* brings into focus the experience of the recipient of service, rather than the perspective of the service provider. While cultural competence focuses on the capacity of the worker to improve client outcomes by integrating culture into the clinical context, cultural safety centres on the experiences of the person. The concept of cultural safety was developed by a Maori nurse to describe how the dominant health care culture in Australia and New Zealand disregarded the health and illness belief systems of the Maori, and, instead, privileged those of the dominant 'Euro-white' culture (Ramsden 2000). The concept of cultural safety draws attention to the impact of colonizing processes on Indigenous persons, and shifts the service paradigm to respect the inclusion of Indigenous knowledge, as opposed to the imposition of Western ideas within local contexts. Colonization has not only affected the health and well-being of Indigenous persons, it has also perpetuated inequalities in the present social service system. In contrast to cultural awareness, cultural competence, or cultural sensitivity, cultural safety 'enables safe service to be defined by those who receive the service'. (Ramsden 2000, p. 6). Cultural safety has implications in terms of policy, research, and practice as it explicitly incorporates Indigenous knowledge in terms of assessment, planning, and intervention into health and social services. Indigenous knowledge can be defined as 'a body of knowledge built up by a group of people through generations of living in close contact with nature' (Johnson & Rattan 1992, p. 30). When practising from a position of cultural safety, indigenous knowledge is accorded the same degree of respect and consideration, if not to a greater degree, than that which the service provider brings to the interaction.

Cultural safety may also be understood as a position of personal reflection upon one's own cultural identity and how this impacts upon one's practice. As a perspective, cultural safety aims to enhance the delivery of services by identifying the client's needs and empowering the client to take full advantage of the service offered. Unsafe cultural practice is any action that diminishes, demeans, or disempowers the cultural identity and well-being of an individual. The social, geographic, economic, and political distance between Indigenous and non-Indigenous Canadians is frequently manifested in client–professional relationships. Indigenous Canadians have often been confronted with a very negative 'looking glass' from others who have considerable power over them. For example, Harding (2006) has documented the historical representation of Aboriginal people within the mainstream media, and concluded that issues are framed, much as they were in colonial times, in ways that protect dominant interests and signify Aboriginal people as a threat. Consequently, in relation to social services, there is an overwhelming insecurity felt by Indigenous persons with regard to their self-perception, traditions, and background. People who feel unsafe and who are unable to express degrees of felt risk may subsequently refuse service, perhaps contributing to increased risk. Cultural safety in practice gives Indigenous people the power to comment on the service provided, leading to the reinforcement of positive experiences. It also enables them to be involved in changes to any service experienced as negative.

Within the idea of cultural safety there is recognition that inequalities within health, social welfare, and educational systems are isomorphic to the inequalities experienced by Indigenous groups throughout history that are entrenched within the social, political, and economic institutions of Canada. Cultural safety in practice accepts the legitimacy of difference and diversity in human behaviour and social structure. It does not analyze cultural diversity as a way of finding validity for this difference, but values it in its own right. It recognizes that the attitudes, beliefs, policies, and practices of service providers and other professionals in various fields can act as barriers to service access. At its core, cultural safety in practice is concerned with quality improvement in service delivery and consumer rights of all cultural groups (Sambono 2004).

## Activity 6.3  Working towards cultural safety

(adapted from People's Experiences of Colonization 2008)

You are a social worker in a post-surgical unit of a large urban hospital. One of your clients is an older male of Euro-Canadian ancestry. Each time you engage with your client, he makes a disparaging remark about the patient in the adjacent bed, who is of Indigenous ancestry. Your client complains about the number of visitors his roommate has at all hours of the day and evening and the fact that he and his family speak another language when they visit together. Your client is quite outspoken about his concerns and speaks loudly, possibly within hearing range of his roommate. Some of his comments are offensive to you, and you are worried they will be offensive to the other client and his family.

What cultural safety issues are at play in this scenario? Which issues affect which people? How did you feel after reading the scenario? Has anything like this happened in your practice? Does this scenario alter your views on how people are treated in the social service system? How you approach your practice? Reflect on the possibilities.

## Practice example 6.2

## Hypothetical responses to training opportunities

I haven't got time for training sessions. I've worked in many reserve communities and we've never had any training. You just learn as you go. There are usually other more important health issues—life and death issues—which take priority within the community. They'll let you know if you are not doing it right.

*Midwife–Remote area nurse.*

Basically all communities are the same, and health problems are pretty much the same. I don't like to distinguish between one community or another. We should be treating everyone the same, with no discrimination—that's what it says in the Hippocratic oath.

*Midwife–Remote area nurse.*

Sometimes I'm so tired, being so isolated with no one to help. They make policies, but they mean nothing out here. We just do the best we can, but we can't solve all the issues. I won't be here

*continued*

for long anyway so it's no use striking up good friendships with them. What they really need is better health outcomes, not friends.

*Midwife–Remote area nurse.*

There are many people here in the community who have helped me do what I came to do. Their knowledge and skills are extremely useful, and they want to assist. The elders held a sharing circle, which really gave me a deeper insight into the way they do things. It's very different to ours. . . . I can go to them for anything. There is some real progress being made out here.

*Midwife–Remote area nurse.*

### Question for reflection

1. Consider the above responses. If you were about to give birth, which midwife would you prefer to be looking after you? Give reasons why.

Cultural safety training for practitioners is becoming increasingly necessary, particularly in remote Indigenous communities. In this training, practitioners are given the opportunity to learn about Indigenous cultures, issues, knowledge, and perspectives from the community themselves. However, many of these cultural safety training or cross-cultural sessions are generically based; rather, it is essential to utilize the *local* knowledge, to learn from the people with expertise within the community itself. This avoids the 'blanket approach' to fixing a particular social problem since what is appropriate for one community may not be appropriate for another. Research undertaken in the Northwest Territories found that frustrations were rife within communities where it was evident the service providers lacked social and cultural knowledge. To address this, strategies included regular sharing of information and community-based engagement by the service providers (Graham, Brownlee, Shier, & Doucette 2008; Waldram, Herring, & Young 2006).

# Researching the researcher? Indigenous research practice

'Ethical considerations, like all conceptual and behavioural phenomena, are constructed and enacted within specific cultural contexts' (Smith 1999, p. 25). A rapid process of change is occurring in relation to the guidelines and practices of Indigenous research. Previous to this, it is argued, research was prescribed for the most part by non-Indigenous researchers, and this is now being heavily debated at the community level, policy level, and within the vast array of academic disciplines. Concerns have centred around the lack of consultation with Indigenous participants, the inability of researchers to share the aims and methods of research as well as results of their study, the disregard for Indigenous cultural heritage, and intellectual property issues. A continuous and 'constructive' dialogue with Indigenous people and researchers regarding the nature and practice of ethical research is highly desirable and central to the issues that arise when conducting research of Indigenous affairs.

Key organizations such as the Canadian Institutes for Health Research have developed specific guidelines for health research involving Indigenous people (CIHR 2007), which health researchers, for example, need to follow to assist them in making informed and considered decisions while undertaking research. These guidelines are premised on a need for researchers to understand and respect Indigenous world views, particularly when engaging in the sphere of traditional and sacred knowledge, and the corresponding responsibility that possession of such knowledge entails. Researchers need to understand the broader senses of accountability in order to understand the responsibility they have when entering into a research relationship with Indigenous people (p. 3).

Meaningful engagement and reciprocity between the researcher and Indigenous people must occur at every stage of the research process. The guidelines state three main areas for consideration when working with Indigenous individuals and communities. They are: 1) ensuring open consultation, negotiation, and mutual understanding of the research questions, research process and consent processes, 2) ensuring the respect and involvement of community members as well as the recognition of the diversity within communities and, 3) ensuring that the benefits and outcomes of the research benefit the communities by addressing the identified needs. For example, community members are entitled to due credit and to participate in the dissemination of results. Publications from the project should recognize the contribution of the community and its members as key participants.

## Activity 6.4  Working towards ethical practice

Does your organization or workplace encourage ethical practice in regards to working with Indigenous persons? Take some time to investigate the policies and/or strategies (if any) that ensure that your practice is culturally appropriate and ethically sound. Talk about this openly with other colleagues in an effort to engage in constructive and critical discussion.

1. What strategies would you consider necessary to achieve best practice for your organization in respect to working with Indigenous persons?

2. In your practice, is there support for an organizational holistic approach to the subject, as opposed to individuals working in isolation?

3. Do policies or strategies exist? If so, are they hidden somewhere on a shelf? If not, what could be done to develop and establish procedures to support your work in this area?

4. If policies or strategies are in place, are they reviewed regularly? How is this process maintained, both within the organization and out in the field?

What would it be like to be fit to undertake your work with Indigenous people without fear, without prejudice, and with common goals? To try to understand and operate within the dominant society, Indigenous persons have had to develop and maintain processes for effective cross-cultural communication on a daily basis. In an increasingly multicultural society it is more than appropriate, relevant, and timely that other citizens attempt to do the same.

## Questions for Review

1. What are the key guiding principles to consider when working with Indigenous people?
2. What are the culturally relevant principles of practice that helpers must be mindful of when working with Indigenous people?
3. What is meant by the term 'cultural safety'?

## References

Anderson, I. (1999). Aboriginal well-being. In C. Grbich (ed.), *Health in Australia, Sociological Concepts and Issues*. Sydney: Prentice Hall.

Barnes, R., Josefowitz, N., & Cole, E. (2006). Residential schools: Impact on Aboriginal students' academic and cognitive development. *Canadian Journal of School Psychology*, 21, 18–32.

Bennet, M., & Blackstock, C. (2002). A literature review and annotated bibliography focusing on aspects of aboriginal child welfare in Canada. Winnipeg, MB: First Nations Research Site of the Centre of Excellence for Child Welfare.

Bourgeault, R. (1991). Race, class and gender: Colonial domination of Indian women. In O. McKague (ed.), *Racism in Canada* (129–50). Saskatoon, SK: Fifth House.

Bracken, D., Deane, L., & Morrisette, L. (2009). Desistance and social marginalization: The case of Canadian Aboriginal offenders. *Theoretical Criminology*, 13, 61–78.

Brownridge, D. (2008). Understanding the elevated risk of partner violence against Aboriginal women: A comparison of two nationally representative surveys of Canada. *Journal of Family Violence*, 23, 353–67.

Bucharski, D., Reutter, L., & Ogilvie, L. (2006). 'You need to know where we're coming from': Canadian Aboriginal women's perspectives on culturally appropriate HIV counseling and testing. *Health Care for Women International*, 27, 723–37.

Canadian Association of Schools of Social Workers (2008). *Educational Policy Statement*. Ottawa, Ontario: Canadian Association of Schools of Social Workers.

Canadian Institutes of Health Research (2007). *cihr guidelines for health research involving Indigenous people*. Ottawa, Ontario: Canadian Institutes for Health Research.

Cross, T., Bazron, K., & Isaacs, M. (1989). *Towards a Culturally Competent System of Care, Volume I*. Washington, DC: Georgetown University Child Development Center, CASSP Technical Assistance Center.

Dominelli, L. (2000). Tackling racism in everyday realities. A task for social workers. In S. Hessle & S. Strega (Eds.) *Valuing the field: Child welfare in an international context*, 141–56). Burlington, VT: Ashgate Publishing.

Eckermann, A., Dowd, T., Martin, M., Nixon, L., Gray, R., & Chong, E. (1992). *Binan Goonj, Bridging Cultures in Indigenous Health*. Armidale: University of New England Press.

Fournier, S., & Crey, E. (1997). *Stolen from our embrace: The abduction of First Nations children and the restoration of Indigenous communities*. Vancouver, BC: Douglas & McIntyre.

Funk-Unrau, N. & Snyder, A. (2007). Indian residential school survivors and state-designed ADR: A strategy for co-optation? *Conflict Resolution Quarterly*, 24, 285–304.

Graham, J., Brownlee, K., Shier, M., & Doucette, E. (2008). Localization of social work knowledge through practitioner adaptations in Northern Ontario and the Northwest Territories, Canada. *Arctic*, 61, 399–406.

Harding, R. (2006). Historical representations of aboriginal people in the Canadian news media. *Discourse & Society*, 17, 205–35.

Health Canada (2007). Continuing Care in First Nations and Inuit Communities: Evidence from the Research. H34-182/2007. Ottawa, Ontario: Ministry of Health.

Isaacs, M., & Benjamin, M. (1991). *Towards a Culturally Competent System of Care, Volume 2, Programs Which Utilize Culturally Competent Principles.* Washington, DC: Georgetown University Child Development Center, CASSP Technical Assistance Center.

Johnson, M., & Rattan, R. (1992). Traditional environmental knowledge of the Dene: A pilot project. *Lore: Capturing traditional environmental knowledge.* Yellowknife, NWT: International Development Research Centre (Canada).

La Prairie, C. (2002). Aboriginal over-representation in the criminal justice system: A tale of nine cities. *Canadian Journal of Criminology*, 4, 181–208.

Larocque, E. (2006). The colonization of a Native woman scholar. In M.E. Kelm & L. Townsend (Eds) *In the days of our grandmothers: A reader in Aboriginal women's history in Canada*, 397–406. Toronto, ON: University of Toronto Press.

McGibbon, E. (2000). The 'situated knowledge' of helpers. In C.E. James (ed.), *Experiencing difference*, 185–99. Halifax, NS: Fernwood Publishing.

McKenzie, B., & Morrisette, V. (2003). Social work practice with Canadians of Aboriginal background: Guidelines for respectful social work.

*Envision: The Manitoba Journal of Child Welfare*, 2, 13–39.

Moffitt, P. (2004). Colonialization: A health determinant for pregnant Dogrib women. *Journal of Transcultural Nursing*, 15, 323–30.

Osher, D.M., & Osher, T.W. (1995). Comprehensive and collaborative systems that work: A national agenda. In C.M. Nelson, R. Rutherford, & B.I. Wolford (Eds), *Developing Comprehensive Systems that Work for Troubled Youth*. Richmond, KY: National Coalition for Juvenile Justice Services.

Peoples' Experience of Colonization (2008). http://web2.uvcs.uvic.ca/courses/csafety/mod1/resource.htm, accessed 12 January 2009.

Ramsden, I. (2000). Cultural safety/Kawa whakaruruhau ten years on: A personal overview. *Nursing Praxis in New Zealand*, 15(1), 4–12.

Sambono, A. (2004). Indigenous Australian history and health (lecture notes). Sydney: Koori Centre, University of Sydney.

Smith, B. (1999). Community consultation: It's essential. In R. Craven (ed.), *Teaching Indigenous Studies*. Sydney: Allen & Unwin.

Smye, V., & Browne, A. (2002). Cultural safety and the analysis of health policy affecting Indigenous people. *Nurse Researcher*, 9(3), 42–56.

Statistics Canada (2008). Aboriginal identity population by age groups, median age and sex, percentage distribution for Canada. Release number 5, 15 January 2008.

Trocmé, N., Knoke, D., & Blackstock, C. (2004). Pathways to the over-representation of Aboriginal children in Canada's child welfare system. *Social Service Review*, 78, 577–600.

Waldram, J., Herring, A., & Young, K. (2006). *Aboriginal health in Canada: Historical, cultural, and epidemiological perspective.* Toronto, ON: University of Toronto Press.

Zellerer, E. (2003). Culturally competent programs: The first family violence program for aboriginal men in prison. *The Prison Journal*, 83, 171–90.

# 7 Risk Assessment: Working Within a Legal Framework

## Fran Waugh

Practitioners are often required to undertake risk assessments of service users. In fact, risk assessment and risk management are at the centre of professional practice (Gilmour et al. 2003, p. 406; Goddard et al. 1999, p. 254; Alaszewski, et al. 1998, p. 89). Professional practice often involves working with highly vulnerable groups and their families, such as children or young people who have been abused or neglected; children with multiple disabilities; families where there are issues of domestic violence; children, young people, and adults where there are mental health concerns; older people, whose mental capacity is deteriorating; and service users facing end-of-life issues. Practice with such groups can be extremely difficult, very stressful, and, at times, dangerous to workers, and is frequently criticized (Stanley & Goddard 2002, p. 254). As noted in chapter 2, 'Professional Values and Ethical Practice', ethical, moral, and emotional issues abound in highly complex practice situations (Goddard et al. 1999, p. 254). Risk assessment combined with professional judgment form an important element of the comprehensive multidisciplinary and multi-dimensional assessment undertaken when practitioners are required to make sense of, and intervene in, the complex and uncertain situations of the service users' lives.

There are no straightforward, prescriptive, easy answers to these complex situations despite governments' wishes to address such social problems in efficient and effective ways. This is why practitioners, with their professional knowledge and skills, and analytical and critical reflective abilities, are called on to intervene and display the compassionate face of social justice to vulnerable groups whose human rights are frequently being neglected or violated in society.

The practitioners' assessments of the level of risk, together with their professional judgment, inform their decisions about what actions are required to address the identified risks and needs. These decisions may have major consequences for service users. For example, an older person with dementia may be assessed as being unsafe or incompetent to remain living at home alone and be forced to move to a residential aged care facility, or a child may be assessed as being no longer safe to remain in her/his parents' care.

Working knowledge about relevant legislation, such as child protection, mental health, and disability or aged care, is important for practitioners as legislation provides the framework for their intervention and shapes their responsibilities in their interactions with service users (Swain 2002, p. 2). Legislation together with the agency's purpose, policies, and procedures; the theoretical perspectives informing practice; and the practitioners' experience, knowledge, and skills, intersect at various levels and provide the multidimensional context of the risk assessment with service users (Hall & Dixon 2001, p. 1; Kennedy & Richards 2004, p. 28; Waugh 2000, p. 63).

The purpose of this chapter is to outline:

- the purpose of risk assessments,
- the approach and ideal features of risk assessments,
- social work theories underpinning risk assessments,
- what is meant by 'risk' and what is meant by 'harm',
- risk from whose perspective and risk to whom,
- child protection as a case example and applying the principles in other fields of practice,
- the skills required in undertaking risk assessments.

## The purpose of a risk assessment

Without being overly simplistic, the general purpose of risk assessments (in any field of social work) is to address any identified safety concerns—namely, factors that pose immediate danger to the service users—and to determine possible harm if the care or circumstances continue in the current manner. In situations where there have been specific incidents that have caused harm, the practitioner is required to assess the risk, that is, the likelihood that this will happen again or the likelihood that the situation might deteriorate and how serious the resultant harm would be.

## Selecting an approach to risk assessment

Risk assessment models began to be developed to standardize workers' responses in different areas of practice (D'Cruz 2004, p. 28; Hall & Dixon 2001, p. 3). There are three distinct models referred to in the literature on risk assessment. All three models are claimed to be evidence-based, that is, they are grounded in research (Baird et al. 1999, p. 723).

Firstly, there are actuarial models in which selected items are included in assessments and the significance of such items assigned numeric values, which are then totalled to provide an overall numeric level of risk. These actuarial models are developed following an audit of files in a particular location—such as child protection, senior care, mental health, and criminal offenders—to identify specific risks for that population. For example, the Correctional Service of Canada found that detention decisions based on actuarial or structured risk assessment measures were more accurate than the detention decisions being made in the absence of risk assessment measures (Nugent & Zamble 2001). Thus the particular checklist is validated for a specific population. However, such models frequently fail to take into account the heightened risk as a result of the interaction of the particular risk items in the unique situation of each service user. A common critique of such models is that they are mechanistic and prescriptive, as workers merely tick the box and add up the scores to determine the overall level of risk. For a thorough evaluation of actuarial risk assessment models, see Baumann, Law, Sheets, Reid, and Graham (2005).

Second, there are consensus models in which items are generated through sources such as theory, research, and practice wisdom. As with the actuarial models there is minimal value placed on the importance of the professional judgment and skills of the worker in making sense of the complex situations.

This leads to the third type, professional judgment models, which are based on individual or collective practitioner judgment, sometimes supported by a decision-making framework, and informed by professional knowledge, values, and skills (Hall & Dixon 2001, p. 3). In child protection, the professional judgment model is based on key knowledge from research on child development, attachment theories, parenting practices, the resilience and vulnerability of children and young people, and safety planning. For example, according to the Centre of Excellence in Child Welfare, risk assessment instruments measure specific risk factors such as the nature and severity of previous maltreatment, characteristics of the family environment (for example, domestic violence), caregiver characteristics (for example, substance abuse), and child characteristics (for example, age, problem behaviour) (Knocke & Trocme 2004). It is this third model that this chapter focuses on as being core in social work practice where risk assessment of service users is required regardless of the context of practice.

# Ideal features of risk assessments

Ideal features of risk assessments in child protection are ones that:

- assist with the identification of risk of maltreatment in the first place (interestingly, there is no clear agreement between practitioners, policy-makers, and researchers about what one should consider when assessing risk) (Hall & Dixon 2001, p. 3);
- assist with assessment of immediate concerns and safety (Berg & Kelly 2000, p. 15);
- enable interpretation of the seriousness or significance of concerns (Hall & Dixon 2001, p. 5);
- provide for uniform case overview and holistic assessment clearly related to risk issues (Dalgleish 2004, p. 1);
- enable and make transparent the process for analysis of information and decision-making and planning, that is, the rationale for action (Dalgleish 2004, p. 1);
- provide for specialist assessment requirements in relation to different service user groups, different problem types, phases of protective involvement, and significant decision-making points (Corby 1996, pp. 16–17);
- improve the consistency of the service response as it provides an authorized, standard framework as the basis for rationale for intervention within protective services and in respect to evidence presented to court (Department of Human Services 1998, p. 1);
- help protective services attain a high-quality response by providing clear guidance regarding expectations based upon legislation, policy regulations and guidelines, research, theory, and practice wisdom (Baumann & Fluke 2004);
- are understandable to families (Turnell & Edwards 1999, p. 27);

- are culturally sensitive (Hall & Dixon 2001, p. 2);
- provide a basis for shared understanding and assessment practices between protective services and other child, family, and youth services engaged in risk assessment and case management roles (Turnell & Edwards 1999, p. 166);
- are embedded within a culture of supervision, professional development, and ongoing training (Hall & Dixon 2001, p. 8);
- promote a practice style that builds on family strengths and is sensitive and respectful (Turnell & Edwards 1999, p. 27).

The majority of these ideal features pertain equally to other fields of practice, such as domestic violence, mental health, senior care, disability services, alcohol and other drugs, and end-of-life care, where practitioners are required to undertake risk assessments as part of their duties. You could choose a field of practice other then child protection and consider the extent to which these ideal features are relevant.

## Theories underpinning risk assessment

Risk assessments are about gathering information, sorting, judging, and planning. The systems theory and the strengths perspective underpin risk assessments and strongly influence what type of information is required, how it is assessed, and what is required in the judging and planning stages of risk assessment.

In systems theory, the term 'system' refers to both informal and formal systems. Systems theory emphasizes the role and interaction of these systems in contributing to well-being or, in this case, 'risk'. It provides a framework for understanding and responding to service users in their social context. It involves understanding service users at the micro level, such as individual and family systems, through to the macro level, such as impact of income level, housing, health, education, and availability of community resources and services. As Fernandez notes, 'practitioners are provided with a multi-interactional view of problems and needs in order to intervene to change the interaction between people and environments' (Fernandez 1996, p. 60). In addition, information is required on the protective factors or the strengths in a situation. The strengths approach focuses on the capacities and potentialities of service users rather than their problems—it is future orientated. According to Saleebey, the strengths perspective formula is simple: 'Mobilize clients' strengths (talent, knowledge, capacities) in the service of achieving their goals and visions and the clients will have a better quality of life on their terms' (Saleebey 1997, p. 4). The focus on strengths is not with the view to minimize issues, but aims to obtain a balanced perspective in a climate where defensive practice often guides decision-making (Hall & Dixon 2001, p. 3).

## What is meant by 'risk' and 'harm'

When undertaking risk assessments of service users, it will be helpful to clearly map out some of the key areas you are required to address by teasing out the following questions:

- How is risk defined?
- Who has the power to define risk in a situation?
- Who is posing the risk (the service user or others)?
- To whom does the risk pertain (the service user or others)?
- When is the risk threshold reached?
- What action is required to address the identified risk?
- What resources are required to minimize the risk?
- How do practitioners evaluate whether the intervention has lessened the risk to an acceptable societal level?

## Activity 7.1  Reflections on risk

How do you define risk? Describe a situation in which you considered yourself or someone else to be at risk.

1. What factors made you assess there was a risk?
2. Who had the power to define risk in that situation?
3. Who or what posed the risk?
4. Whom did the risk involve?
5. What did you do?
6. When did you think it was necessary for someone to take action to address the risk?
7. What action did you think was required to address the identified risk?
8. Were there any particular resources needed to minimize the risk?
9. Do you think the risk was resolved in a satisfactory manner?

There is a tendency to use the words 'risk', 'danger', and 'uncertainty' interchangeably in practice. Risk is a highly complex concept and the meanings attributed to it by non-professionals and professionals, including practitioners from various settings, may be different (Goddard et al. 1999, p. 251). Initial definitions of risks 'linked [it] with the concepts of harm or danger or as a chance to gain benefits in a situation where harm is also possible' (Gilmour et al. 2003, p. 405). This definition can be operationalized in practice in a variety of ways from a narrow focus to a broader focus. In narrow definitions, the emphasis is placed on equating risk to harm, and the negative outcomes of events; whereas in the broader definition, the focus is on balancing negative consequences against positive outcomes (Alaszewski 1998, p. 10). Therefore, it is important for practitioners to be aware of the theoretical position(s) from which they are coming and to critically reflect on how their own values and personal experiences influence how they define 'harm'.

It is equally important for practitioners to be aware of how the parameters of risk are shaped by their agency and the legislation that is underpinning their practice. For example, in Canada, child protection is a provincial responsibility, and all provinces and territories have child welfare legislation that mandates the reporting of all suspected child neglect/abuse situations to the provincial child welfare authorities. Reportable situations include those wherein reasonable and available information indicates a child or young person is at risk of imminent harm, or current concerns exist for the safety, welfare, or well-being of the child or young person because of the presence of one or more of the following circumstances:

a)  The child's or young person's basic physical, emotional, or psychological needs are not being met or are at risk of not being met.
b)  The parents or other caregivers have not arranged for the child or young person to receive necessary medical care.
c)  The child or young person has been, or is at risk of being, physically or sexually mistreated.
d)  The child or young person is living in a household where there have been incidents of domestic violence and, as a consequence, the child or young person is at risk of serious physical or psychological harm.
e)  A parent or other caregiver has behaved in such a way towards the child or young person that the child or young person has suffered, or is at risk of suffering, serious psychological harm.

How then would you define 'harm'? What other underlying values and beliefs would influence your decision in determining whether or not a situation you were assessing was harmful? What are the elements that you would look for in the following situations outlined in Activity 7.2 in assessing the level of harm?

## Activity 7.2  Reflecting on harm

What do you consider to be the level of harm to a child in the following situations? Assign a number between 1 and 5 where 1 = no harm, 2 = minimal harm, 3 = considerable harm, 4 = serious harm, and 5 = extreme harm.

a)  Mary is a twenty-year-old mother of three children, all under four years. She lives with her partner of 11 months who is the father of the youngest child. Both she and her partner have an alcohol problem. Mary has recently been charged for shoplifting and is on probation. Her eldest child seems very withdrawn to you and his mother does not want him to continue at preschool.

b)  Betty is a thirty-year-old single mother of Joanne, who is fourteen months old, and Michael, who is three years old. Both children are the result of Betty being sexually assaulted. Betty has been involved with many other services and is known to have significant mental health issues. The children's physical development appears delayed.

c)  Nathan, who is fourteen years old, lives with his parents and two sisters aged ten and twelve years. A teacher at school is concerned that Nathan's concentration in

*continued*

class has declined and that he is aggressive in his interactions with other students. This change in behaviour has occurred over the past month. When the teacher approached Nathan about his concerns, Nathan told him that his father was continually fighting with his mother and that it was getting worse.

d) Bill, aged twelve years, and Margaret, aged fourteen years, attend private schools. Their parents run a family business and employ a housekeeper to ensure the physical needs of their children are addressed. Margaret appeared to be highly distressed at school, and disclosed to one of her friends that she feels enormous pressure from her parents to excel in her studies.

What factors do you take into account in your initial assessment with the family to determine each level of harm, namely:

a) no harm,

b) minimal harm,

c) considerable harm,

d) serious harm, or

e) extreme harm?

It is important to be clear about your interpretation of these terms as your assessment of the level of harm may determine the level of intervention that will be used in the lives of the children, young people, and their families.

## Other factors underlying risk assessments

In addition to understanding what definitions of risk and harm are shaping their practice, practitioners need to be aware of their value positions in regards to various issues and what influence they may have on their risk assessments. See Activity 7.3.

## Activity 7.3  Values, beliefs, and assumptions

Consider the following questions and reflect on the underlying values, beliefs, and assumptions that inform your answer.

1. What is 'good enough' care for the group in question, whether it be people with mental health issues, children, or older people who are living alone?

2. What is the range of outcomes that a society considers to be in the normal range of 'good enough'?

*continued*

3. How can intervention with service users ensure that maximum autonomy and independence is respected when it is clear that practitioners are sometimes exercising statutory authority and have a duty of care to interact with service users who clearly protest such intrusion?

4. How do practitioners grapple with the tension of being an agent of social control and their desire to be the compassionate face of social justice?

5. Whose rights are paramount when practitioners frequently intervene in the lives of service users and their families? How do practitioners balance the interests of the various players and society?

6. How can practitioners ensure anti-oppressive and anti-discriminatory practice as they undertake risk assessments?

7. How can practitioners engage with involuntary and sometimes hostile service users as they undertake the task of completing a risk assessment?

8. How can practitioners ensure their own safety in situations of extreme stress and threat?

## Risk from whose perspective and risk to whom

While practitioners might have a clear understanding of their definition of risk, it is important that assessment takes account how risk is perceived by the other key players—for instance, other workers and service users and their families. For example, in research on community-based senior care by Gilmour, Gibson, and Campbell (2003, pp. 405–6), the construction and definition of risk by health and social service agencies were different from those held by people with dementia and their caregivers. Whereas professionals emphasized the physical aspects of safety, people with dementia and their families gave the maintenance of self-identity and interpersonal relationships more importance. Therefore, it is important to share different perspectives of risk, as this would lead to professional practice that includes the understanding of who the key players are. Practitioners are also required to make an assessment of whom the risk pertains to, namely:

- Is it solely risk to the service user or others as well?
- Is the risk caused by the service users themselves or by others or by a combination of both?
- Is there possible risk posed to the professionals who are undertaking the risk assessment?

## Child protection as a case study

As mentioned previously, the four stages of risk assessment are gathering information; analysis; making a professional judgment; and management of the identified risks, needs, and concerns. Each of these will be considered in turn using child protection as a case study.

# Gathering information

Although, currently, there is no single risk assessment tool that is widely accepted or utilized across provinces/territories, the majority of child welfare authorities employ some form of a child protection risk assessment framework. Two commonly used instruments are the Washington Risk Assessment Matrix and the California Family Assessment Factor Analysis (Baird & Wagner 2000). These are based on the principles of systems theory and strengths perspective. As well, a research team from the Faculty of Social Work at the University of Toronto developed the Risk Assessment Model for Child Protection in Ontario that defines how cases are investigated and determines follow-up steps for cases where a risk of harm exists (Ontario Association of Children's Aid Societies [OACAS] 2000). Although the specific questions vary in each of these approaches, information is required under the five essential categories: the child or young person; parents; opportunity for harm; harm; and networks. Table 7.1 lists the type of information that is required under each of these categories.

**Table 7.1**  Child protection risk assessment framework

| | CATEGORIES | | | | |
|---|---|---|---|---|---|
| | **Child or young person** | **Parents** | **Opportunity for harm** | **Harm** | **Networks** |
| *Information required* | Age | Attitudes to harm and to child | Access of person responsible for harm | Incident/ harm-causing behaviour | Formal and informal |
| | Development Functioning | Relationship with child | Exposure to harm | Severity | Alternative care givers |
| | Behaviour | Functioning | Environment | History and pattern | Significant others |
| | Their presentation | Parenting capacity | | | Cultural context |

From the framework in Table 7.1, it is apparent that practitioners have clear guidelines as to what information they need to obtain in their risk assessments. They are then required to make sense of this information, however limited it may be.

# Analysis: making sense of the information

Analysis is a difficult stage in risk assessment as practitioners are required to consider the information they obtained and make a risk assessment in terms of the following four areas:

- severity: type and degree of harm
- vulnerability: age, development, and functioning
- likelihood: pattern, beliefs, complicating factors such as domestic violence, mental health issues, drug and alcohol issues, neighbourhood issues
- safety: strength and protection

## Making a professional judgment

Practitioners are required to make a professional judgment based on their analysis. Using the evidence obtained in the analysis stage, a judgment is required about the existing harm and its consequences and the probability of future harm, that is, how likely or unlikely it is to occur in the future. In essence, a statement about immediate safety and possible consequences of interventions is required. While some practitioners feel uncomfortable with their responsibility for making professional judgments, it is a key stage in risk assessment and requires a clarity and openness about how the professional judgment is reached (Healy 1998, p. 909). Professional judgments need to be accessible, transparent, and accountable to the service users (Hall & Dixon 2001, p. 5). As Campbell (1997) states:

> Active participation by family members requires professionals to demonstrate their willingness to inform and listen respectfully: to give full and frank information on their evidence of risk to the child, their interpretations of that evidence, and the resources and services they have to offer the family; and to hear what the family has to say about the evidence, their own views and interpretations and what resources they have at their disposal and feel they need (p. 8).

## Management

Once the risks and strengths are identified, an action plan is developed which addresses two key questions:

- What action, including services and resources, is required to reduce the identified risks and needs?
- What action, including services and resources, is required to increase the safety?

The action plan outlines the responsibilities of the key players and the time frame in which the action is to take place. In other words, the action plan outlines the intervention decision.

These four stages and the associated issues are also relevant to other fields of practice in which practitioners are required to undertake risk assessments. While the information will differ depending on the field of practice and the relevant research evidence, the analysis, professional judgment, and decisions about ongoing management follow a similar process. For example, practitioners who work with older people with dementia who live alone are required to make a decision about their intervention choices based on their risk assessment of the situation. Gilmour, Gibson, and Campbell (2003, p. 406) suggest that such workers have three intervention choices, namely:

- leave the person in charge and accept the risk
- persuade the person to accept help/lessen risk
- take control by mandated means

# Skills required in undertaking risk assessments

Risk assessments are dependent on the following skills:

1. *Interviewing and communication skills* entail, in particular, the ability of the practitioner to elicit salient information about the service user's situation. As risk assessments are conducted across the life span for different purposes, it is critical that practitioners develop sound engagement, rapport building, respectful listening, and clear verbal communication skills with their specific service user group. Practitioners may be performing a statutory role so it is important that they are up front about their role, responsibilities, and the authority/power they have in the situation. In addition, practitioners need to have knowledge about service users' rights and responsibilities.

   In eliciting any information, Kennedy and Richards note that it is important that practitioners keep an open mind at all times about the 'facts' in a situation and keep questioning their accuracy (2004, p. 38). Following on from this is the need for practitioners to identify additional information or 'facts' that are required for an informed decision to be made (Kennedy & Richards 2004, p. 38). Consider the scenario in Practice example 7.1.

## Practice example 7.1

### Reflections on a 'good enough' case

Mrs Z is a ninety-five-year-old client living in a house within the inner core of a large urban centre. She has a post-surgical cancerous wound under her breast and moderate to severe dementia. She has no family other than a nephew who lives approximately 100 kilometres away. He commutes to the city one day a week and makes a point of visiting his aunt, occasionally shopping or bringing a meal. He has little or no understanding of her condition. He has enduring power of attorney and manages her finances.

The referral to the psycho-geriatric assessment team came from the client's family doctor via the public health nurses. The doctor had attempted to refer the client for home care service prior to her surgery, but the client would refuse help and not allow access to workers. Public health nurses from the Regional Health Authority come daily to dress the wound. She accepts this.

*continued*

Upon inspection, the home was found to be in total disarray. Both bedrooms were littered and looked as though intruders had been through all the drawers and cupboards. The kitchen was cluttered, full of leftover food with flies and ants gathering everywhere. The fridge had a life form of its own and the freezer contained a solid layer of ice, with the kettle frozen in among it all. The bath had bowls of dentures in it, none of which fit the client, the shower was unused and filled with things, and the toilet was unclean. The client, however, says she showers daily. Nurses have tried to persuade her to shower, but she has refused. Her clothing is usually worn for a few weeks at a time until, strongly encouraged by the nurses, she will change, and then that outfit will remain on for weeks. An additional problem was an elderly cat, which had scratched and bitten the client on numerous occasions, and whose diet and health the client had difficulty managing.

This case study describes a condition known in the field of public health as 'senior squalor syndrome'. This condition can occur when seniors stop taking care of themselves and their surroundings. A senior's home becomes cluttered and there is a consequent, real risk to the senior owner-occupant of falling. Health effects can also include dehydration, malnutrition, and hypothermia.

Case study provided by Mercy Community Care, Catholic Health
Care Services, Waitara, Australia.

## Questions for reflection

1. What additional information would you require to undertake a risk assessment of Mrs Z?
2. Outline the skills you would be drawing on in undertaking the risk assessment.

2. *Assessment skills* consist of the ability of practitioners to establish the meaning of the information for the service user and their family in their cultural, developmental, and community context. It requires that practitioners listen to all the parties involved and ensure that their rights are respected. See chapter 10, 'Conducting Assessment: Some General Guidelines'.

3. *Analytical skills* encompass the ability of practitioners to process, weigh, and organize interrelated factors that influence a situation to form an overall judgment of risk.

    Risk assessments are not merely a tick-the-box checklist of specified items. They require that workers apply their analytical skills to the given situation. How would you make sense of the information you have collected in Activity 7.3?

4. *Professional judgment* includes the ability of practitioners to balance the twin goals of protecting whoever is the focus of the intervention while maintaining connections with the service users' social networks including families, significant others, and communities. It entails weighing competing forces within and between the different identified

risks and determining which ones are most compelling, to whom, and why. According to Kennedy and Richards (2004, p. 38), in professional judgments, workers need to consider:

- urgency
- levels of risk to public, agency, self, service user, and others
- cost of legal and other actions
- resources available
- timelines of any proposed action plan

## Activity 7.4  Practitioners' use of discretion

In making a professional judgment, Kennedy and Richards assert that practitioners need to be aware of information about legal mandates, duties, powers, and protections, and the less obvious legal dimensions of the agency and worker role. In addition, it is important that practitioners seek advice on matters or questions outside of their professional expertise (Kennedy & Richards 2004, p. 38). In other words, practitioners must be clear about their roles, responsibilities, and authority within the relevant legislative and policy framework for their particular practice area. They also need to consider that, as a result of their responsibilities and professional judgment, there are at times limits to service user confidentiality and their level of self-determination.

1. Can you think of situations when you are working with children, young people, and their families; people with mental health concerns; or older adults where this may be the case?
2. Discuss what level of discretion you as a practitioner are likely to have in these situations.
3. What does this mean in terms of your interaction with the service user and their families and other key professionals?

# Conclusion

While this chapter has focused on the issues that practitioners need to address and the skills and knowledge they need to continually develop in undertaking risk assessments, it is important to remember that practitioners are often part of a team. Practitioners' contributions in terms of completing a risk assessment are only a piece of a jigsaw puzzle that helps convey some aspect of the service users' lives. Other professionals are required to contribute their parts of the jigsaw puzzle and, together, multidisciplinary teams can provide a richer, more complete understanding of the complexities and uncertainties that commonly characterize vulnerable service users' lives.

It should also be noted that practitioners who are charged with the responsibility of undertaking risk assessments in their day-to-day practice have a responsibility to themselves to participate in ongoing supervision; briefing and de-briefing meetings; peer support activities; and professional development. Such activities are key strategies to ensure self-care of practitioners, who are frequently faced with challenging and stressful situations. Organizations employing such practitioners have a responsibility to support such activities, as it is only when such a commitment exists within organizations that practitioners have the ongoing opportunity to critically reflect on the process of undertaking risk assessments based on relevant research theories, knowledge, legislation, and practice wisdom. It is only then that practitioners can claim that they are undertaking evidence-based risk assessments that can contribute to making a difference to the lives of vulnerable service users.

## Questions for Review

1. After reading this chapter, how would you define 'risk'? Assess risk? Intervene in situations in which some level of risk is present?
2. What tools would you consider useful in assessing risk? Why did you choose one particular tool over another? How would social work practice differ based on the implementation of different risk assessment measures?
3. To what extent do you think organizational mandate and culture would impact on risk assessment measures, processes, and outcomes? For example, do you think seniors should be 'protected' to the same degree that children are?
4. Within a risk assessment framework, what are some implications for social policy? How might risk assessment impact upon policies that relate to social workers' decision-making, training, intervention methods, and client relationships?

## References

Alaszewski, A. (1998). Risk in modern society. In A. Alaszewski, L. Harrison, & J. Manthorpe (eds), *Risk, Health and Welfare*, 3–23. Buckingham, PA: Open University Press.

Alaszewski, A., Alaszewski, H., & Harrison, L. (1998). Professionals, accountability and risk. In A. Alaszewski, L. Harrison & J. Manthorpe (eds), *Risk, Health and Welfare*, 89–103. Buckingham, PA: Open University Press.

Baird, C., Wagner, D., Healy, T., & Johnson, K. (1999). Risk assessment in child protective services: Consensus and actuarial model reliability. *Child Welfare*, 78(6), 723–48.

Baird, C., & Wagner, D. (2000). The relative validity of actuarial- and consensus-based Risk

Assessment Systems. *Children and Youth Services Review*, (11/12), 839–71.

Baumann, D., & Fluke, J. (2004). *Steps to a Decision Making Ecology for Child Protective Services: A Multi-National Research Perspective*. Paper presented at the 15th International Congress on Child Abuse and Neglect, Brisbane.

Baumann, D.J., Law, J.R., Sheets, J., Reid, G., & Graham, J.C. (2005). Evaluating the effectiveness of actuarial risk assessment models. *Children and Youth Services Review*, 27, 465–90.

Berg, I., & Kelly, S. (2000). *Building Solutions in Child Protective Services*. New York: Bytheway.

Campbell, L. (1997). Family involvement in decision-making in child protection and care: Four types of case conferences. *Child and Family Social Work*, 2, 1–11.

Corby, B. (1996). Risk assessment in child protection work. In H. Kemshall & J. Pritchard (eds), *Good Practice in Risk Assessment and Risk Management*, 13–30. London: Jessica Kingsley.

Dalgleish, L. (2004). *Steps to a Decision Making Ecology for Child Protective Services: A Multi-National Research Perspective*. Paper presented at the 15th International Congress on Child Abuse and Neglect, Brisbane.

D'Cruz, H. (2004). *Constructing Meanings and Identities in Child Protection Practice*. Melbourne: Tertiary Press.

Department of Human Services (1998). *The Victorian Risk Assessment Framework, Version One*. Melbourne: DHS.

Fernandez, E. (1996). *Significant Harm*. Aldershot: Ashgate.

Gilmour, H., Gibson, F., & Campbell, J. (2003). Living alone with dementia. A case study approach to understanding risk. *Dementia*, 2(3), 403–20.

Goddard, C., Saunders, B., Stanley, J., & Tucci, J. (1999). Structured risk assessment procedures: Instruments of abuse? *Child Abuse and Review*, 8, 251–63.

Hall, K., & Dixon, J. (2001). *The RARM: A strengths based and collaborative approach to risk assessment*. Paper presented at the 8th Australasian Conference on Child Abuse and Neglect, Melbourne.

Healy, K. (1998). Participation and child protection: The importance of context. *British Journal of Social Work*, 28, 897–914.

Kennedy, R., & Richards, J. (2004). *Integrating Human Service Law and Practice*. Melbourne: Oxford University Press.

Nugent, P., & Zamble, E. (2001). Affecting detention referrals through proper selection. *Forum on Corrections Research*, 13.

Saleebey, D. (1997). Introduction: Power in the people. In D. Saleebey (ed.), *The Strengths Perspective in Social Work Practice*. New York: Longman.

Stanley, J., & Goddard, C. (2002). *In the Firing Line: Violence and Power in Child Protection Work*. New York: John Wiley & Sons.

Swain, P. (2002). Why social work and law? In P. Swain (ed.), *In the Shadow of the Law: The Legal Context of Social Work Practice*, 1–6. Annandale, NSW: Federation Press.

Turnell, A., & Edwards, S. (1999). *Signs of Safety: A Solution and Safety Oriented Approach to Child Protection Casework*. New York: Bytheway.

Waugh, F. (2000). Initial assessment: A key stage in social work intervention. *Australian Social Work*, 53(1), 57–63.

# 8

# Effective Communication
## Zita Weber

Communicating effectively as a practitioner, in both spoken and written forms, is fundamental to all good practice. Communicating effectively results in communicating purposefully. Practitioners in their activities across contexts will be required to speak *to* or *in* a group and to write, for instance, conference papers, reports, and submissions. The skills involved in speaking to or in a group and writing are learned through practise, critical reflection, and critically-directed practice.

Since few of us are 'natural' orators or writers, most of us have to learn how to overcome the nervousness we feel about making a speech or giving a public address or the apprehension that grips us when we must commit our professional thoughts to paper in report format and other, more informal writing tasks. By practising, critically reflecting on your performance, and then receiving feedback and accepting critical direction, you can hone these skills and overcome the embarrassing false starts that we have all experienced.

This chapter is divided into three parts: first, the spoken word as it is practised when speaking *to* a group; second, the spoken word as it is practised when speaking *in* a group; third, the written word as we strive to write for effect.

## The spoken word: speaking to a group

Whether you have to give a speech at a public meeting, sit as a speaker on a panel discussion, deliver a conference paper, or conduct a seminar or workshop, you will be speaking to a group. Learning to speak effectively to groups of people is important if you are to be an effective practitioner. Understanding your speaking background might help you to better plan for your future in speaking to groups. Activity 8.1 is a reflection exercise that allows you to look backwards and forwards.

### Activity 8.1 Reflections on biography and power

#### Biography and speaking out

1. Who got to speak in your family of origin?
2. How did position, order, or gender in the family affect this?
3. What was 'allowed' to be spoken about?

*continued*

4. What was disallowed?

5. What effect do you think this has had on your ability to speak up and speak to others today?

6. Was there one occasion you can think of when you broke your silence and spoke out?

7. What happened when you did this?

8. How does your biography affect your level of confidence regarding speaking to others?

9. When do you find yourself speaking up?

10. What stops you?

11. What changes would you like to make?

## Power

1. Who in the public sphere is given a voice, and whose voice is never heard? Why do you think this may be?

2. Analyze power relationships with respect to 'air space', referring to politicians, radio presenters, and television journalists as examples.

When called on to speak to a group, many people complain that they 'freeze up', are too nervous or afraid of embarrassing themselves to act. It's interesting to note that few people experience nervousness or fear embarrassment when speaking to two or three friends, particularly when the topic is familiar and the surroundings are comfortable. Now imagine shifting this scenario to a more formal setting where there are six people, three of them unknown to you. What we might find is that in this more formal setting, some nervous symptoms may arise—for instance, our hands trembling, our mouth going dry, and our pulse rate increasing.

Many of our nervous mannerisms fall under the heading of non-verbal communication. It is incorrect to think that non-verbal communication relates only to the positions and movements of our body, that is, body language. Non-verbal communication also incorporates such non-physical things as:

- the sound of your voice—what is its 'music' like?
- the speed of speech
- the use of emphasis and pauses—do listeners have time to reflect?
- the spatial relationship you create with listeners—do you prefer to be close to listeners or do you prefer to have a barrier—either spatial or physical—between you and them?

You know how it is to watch a speaker who is not coping: how edgy you become, how you feel for them, how off-putting it is. So you owe it to yourself and your audience to be as relaxed as possible. Personal uneasiness will be mirrored in your verbal and non-verbal communication. It is hard to rephrase your body's non-verbal communication language, but with practice, you can alter the more extreme expressions that would work against you.

To help you to better understand the way your body behaves when you are nervous, reflect on what you know about yourself from past situations when you have been asked to speak to a group by completing Activity 8.2.

## Activity 8.2  Nervous mannerisms inventory

Many people find it hard to look at the audience and, instead, focus on the floor or the ceiling. Others adopt a wooden posture with a hand placed in their pockets or, worse still, jingle the keys in their pockets. Some people twist their wrist-watches, play with their hair, or fiddle with their notes continually. All of these mannerisms indicate nervousness and are related to a set of factors including eye contact with the audience, gestures, facial expressions, stance, and body tension.

Think back to a time when you were asked to speak to a group and list all your known nervous mannerisms.

Windschuttle and Elliott (2002) suggest that the best way to prevent nerves overwhelming you is to do a thorough job of preparation. If you have made notes about the major points you want to cover, practised, or rehearsed what you intend to say, perhaps even written out your speech beforehand and, most importantly, gained a clear idea of your audience and its needs, then you will feel more settled. As Windschuttle and Elliott (2002, p. 357) put it, 'Well prepared notes backed up by visual material are essential aids for the beginner.' Some simple relaxation techniques before you give your speech also might be helpful. Generally speaking, the most effective relaxation techniques are simple and involve becoming aware of tense muscles and relaxing each one individually, combined with deep breathing.

This brings us to the two critical elements in the area of speaking to a group: preparation and delivery.

## Preparation

Essentially, the sequence of activities you follow is similar to that used when writing an essay or preparing a report.

Preparation can be divided into the following sections:

1. interpreting the topic
2. interpreting your audience
3. interpreting special requirements
4. gathering material/researching
5. organizing your talk
6. structuring of the speech

Of course, these preparatory tasks will vary in terms of the time and commitment you give them, depending on the nature of the talk. You may well be familiar with your audience and therefore need not spend much time thinking about their needs, or you might have your material partly prepared from giving a similar talk previously, and need to hone points rather than do your research from scratch.

## Interpreting the topic

First, define as accurately as possible just what it is you are expected to do. Develop a working definition to help you classify what should, and what should not, be included in your talk. By stating the topic clearly, you can move onto designing and eventually delivering your speech.

## Activity 8.3  Two ten-minute talks

Study the following two topics that could be used for a ten-minute talk and reflect on the questions that follow.

A Outline the short-term employment prospects for early school leavers without a high school diploma.
B Discuss the long-term lifestyle prospects for young people who have suffered serious injuries in car accidents.

1. How would you define:
   a) short-term?
   b) long-term?
   c) employment?
   d) serious injuries?
2. What, at a minimum, would you need to say to get your message across about these topics in ten minutes?

## Interpreting your audience

It is essential to know something about your audience and to have some background information. For instance:

- Who is your audience? Are you going to speak to experts or to people with little knowledge about the topic, or both?
- How many people are expected?
- For what purpose are they gathering? What are their expectations?

Windschuttle and Elliott (2002) suggest that you strike a balance between what you want to speak about and what you believe your audience wants to hear.

## Interpreting special requirements

Vallence (1987) points out that you need to know a number of basic things that relate to the particular context of your talk. For instance:

- For how long will you be expected to speak?
- Will you be introduced or will you do this yourself?
- Are there any names you need to commit to memory?
- Is there a protocol to be observed?
- Will members of the audience be invited to ask questions?
- Will you be seated or standing?
- Is all equipment available and compatible?

From personal experience, I would urge everyone to take the time to interpret the particulars of the context in which they are going to speak. It might sound silly, but you can easily overlook such simple things as asking about protocol (and possibly being embarrassed on the day) or, indeed, whether your audiovisual equipment will work at the venue! We have all sat through worrying minutes as a presenter struggles with technology that is unknown to them, and we have become more and more anxious with them, hoping that the next strategy will work.

Flood and Lawrence (1987) in *The Community Action Book* highlight that different contexts will demand different interpretations regarding audiences and special requirements. Talking at a conference is different from giving an informal talk to members of your team in your agency. If you are on a panel discussion, for instance, you need to remember that you probably were chosen because you represent a different opinion from the other people on the panel. There are usually three to five panelists and a chairperson, who introduces the topic and ensures that all speakers have an opportunity to state their case. You can expect questions directed to you on the panel after everyone has spoken or, occasionally, after each presentation. Questions may be directed to a particular panelist or may be open to comment from any member of the panel.

## Gathering material/researching

Researching can be a challenging yet enjoyable stage. Your research should include written sources, Internet searches, newspapers, magazines, and radio and television programs; in fact, include any source from which you can draw material legitimately. Perhaps the most overlooked yet important source is personal experience. People sometimes discount personal experience when gathering material, believing it may not be an authoritative enough source. Yet, as Windschuttle and Elliott (2002, p. 364) argue, 'Well-prepared speeches based on personal experiences can be among the most convincing and moving of all forms of communication.'

Whatever sources you decide to use in your research, remember it is important to be selective. A small number of well-made points are better than many poorly made ones. Selectivity keeps you focused. If you are not selective, you run the risk of giving a talk that lacks specific information, repeats what might already be known, and may prevent you from including any new ideas and insights that your audience would appreciate.

## Organizing your talk

You have done the research and it is now time to organize and plan your speech. You might think this stage is tedious and unnecessary, but by specifically organizing and planning, you can gain confidence. In effect, organizing and planning brings direction and form to your research material. In planning your talk, remember the golden rule of starting engagingly and finishing conclusively and pertinently. Of course, there should be no meandering in the middle!

To achieve this, consider beginning in such a way that your audience will immediately be captivated and interested for you to continue. It follows then that, having emphasized your major points, you should attempt to leave your audience on a high note with them wishing for more. Organizing your talk helps you to visualize your material. If your material is clear and well organized, your speech will flow more readily.

### Structuring of the speech

It is a truism as well as a little hackneyed to say that the simplest structure is the best: tell them, tell them, tell them. The beginning or introduction is where you tell your audience what it is you are going to tell them. The middle or body of the speech is where you tell them what you promised to tell them. The end or conclusion of the speech is where you tell them what you have told them.

## Activity 8.4  Developing a plan and structuring your ten-minute speech

Look at your responses to Activity 8.3 and write out how you would now plan and organize your speech about short-term employment prospects for school leavers and long-term lifestyle consequences for young people who have suffered serious injury. How does this differ from your earlier plan?

## Delivery

Speaking to a group is a performance, which is why many people feel anxious at the prospect of doing so. However, if you have prepared well you will find that you are 75 per cent of the way there!

## Activity 8.5  Feedback to a speaker

Reflect on a talk you attended recently. What did you think of how the speaker handled the delivery of his/her speech? What feedback would you give him/her if you had the chance? Remember, it is always more helpful to give specific feedback, rather than vague, general comments. (See chapter 13, 'Introduction to Working with Groups', for guidelines on providing constructive feedback.)

Good delivery of your speeches is a practised skill and you might like to critically reflect on your performance after you give your next talk. Go even further and ask for feedback and accept critical direction from your peers who attended your talk. It may seem like a scary proposition, but receiving feedback and critical direction from others helps you understand what effect you had on your audience. This, in turn, allows you to further reflect on how you might do things differently next time to improve on your delivery.

In the beginning, when planning speeches, it is wise to have an honest 'critical friend' watching your rehearsal. If this can not be arranged, then standing before a mirror and speaking aloud will give you some idea of how you might look and sound to your audience. After you have had some practice, and experience, with speaking to a group, you should continue to consider the benefits gained from rehearsal. This point cannot be emphasized enough. Rehearsals give you confidence and allow you to work through any part of your talk that does not fit or sound right, or that needs some modification.

## Starting your speech

Give plenty of thought to how you intend to start your talk. If you are confident in this, you will feel more confident about the whole talk unfolding as you envisage. Beware of using humour. Some people can use humour to start their talk but before you decide to do this, ask yourself whether you tell jokes well and whether you know how your audience will react to the humour. There is nothing more unsettling than 'putting your foot in it' from the start!

## Developing your speech

Keep in mind that 'proportion' is an important organizational consideration. Anecdotes, tangents, and digressions may be entertaining, and they may be tempting because they feel 'comfortable' to you; however, they may distort the proportion in your talk. Each part of your talk should be given the amount of time that corresponds with its comparative importance. Generally speaking, it is the 'middle' part of your talk that has the most relevance for the audience.

## Concluding your speech

We have all heard poor conclusions to talks. They may have started well, but then we were disappointed with the end. Just as the beginning of the speech is your first chance to impress your audience, the conclusion is your last chance. Your conclusion should be as well planned and rehearsed as your introduction. Good speeches easily can be ruined by long, ineffectual, or boring conclusions.

Books on public speaking often spend many pages guiding the would-be public speaker through instructions and checklists related to such factors as body language and the use of voice, clothing, and audiovisual aids (McCarthy & Hatcher 2002; Windschuttle & Elliott 2002; Le Clair & Fortune 1986). For helping professionals, the essential points can be summarized as follows:

- Your body conveys a diverse range of messages. Practise standing or sitting naturally, moving your body, and gesturing as needed, and being conscious of exaggerations in movement, gestures, and posture.

- Your voice quality also will signal meanings to your audience. Practise speaking clearly and pronouncing your words, varying the pitch, and projecting your voice so that it can easily be heard in the back row.
- Your clothing conveys messages to your audience. With this in mind, choose your clothing carefully and appropriately to convey the message you wish to send.

## Radio interviews and television appearances

Getting your message out is important and if you are asked to speak on a topic in a radio interview or appear on television, you should take the opportunity to do so. Flood and Lawrence, in *The Community Action Book* (1987), point out some golden rules:

- use short, direct points
- be selective and choose two or three vital points and make sure you get them across
- avoid long sentences
- speak clearly
- avoid jargon and clichés
- try to aim for the greatest audience comprehension

Always do your homework and make good use of the time available to you. Suggest questions to the interviewer and know the key points you want to make.

In the radio studio, look at the interviewer, not at the microphone, and try not to shuffle your papers! For television, acquaint yourself beforehand with where you will be sitting and try to sit as naturally as possible. Remember, television is a visual medium, so make sure you are as comfortable in what you are wearing as well as with what you are saying. Be as much yourself as possible, use plain language, listen to the questions, and give simple, direct answers.

Juliet Jordan (1991), an actress and voice trainer, coaches people, particularly women, for public speaking. She has pointed out five behaviours speakers should try to avoid:

- nasality—speaking through the nose can sound whiny and lifeless
- speaking too loudly or too softly
- speaking too fast, which makes listeners hold their breath, or too slowly, which makes them impatient
- sounding monotonous, which she calls a 'well-known trance induction technique'
- mumbling, about which she has said: 'You don't want to be heard because if you were, you would be responsible for what came out of your mouth' (Jordan 1991, p. 10).

## Your audience

Many speakers confess that they are afraid of the audience. Kaplan (1997, p. 42) asks: 'Does the audience loom up like some hydra-headed monster, teeth bared?' To prevent this he advises that you should 'identify with your listeners; know as much about them as you can. And remember why you're there; to tell them something in which they're going to be interested.' (Kaplan 1997, p. 42)

## Activity 8.6  Tricks of the trade

Think back to the last really impressive speaker you saw or heard and analyze their speech performance. What makes them effective? Draw up a list.

Maintaining eye contact with your audience is important and will connect you to them more readily. Do not look over their heads or down to their feet. Try not to focus on one person. Meet their eyes and keep your gaze moving across the audience.

# The spoken word: speaking in a group

In this section, you will be guided through the process of how to speak effectively in a group. We spend much of our lives in groups, listening and speaking. In the workplace, knowing how to speak effectively in various group settings is an essential part of practice. Speaking in a group implies that you are part of the group and that you have a membership role. Consequently, you have both proprietary thoughts about the group and responsibilities towards it.

You will experience both informal and formal groups in the workplace. Groups form for countless reasons and most of the time they are informal, that is, they have no overt rules. What you need to understand is that no amount of formality, nor sheer weight of attendant rules, will negate the basic necessity of your having the confidence and ability to speak your point of view. Communicating effectively, as the last section highlighted, presupposes your confidence in your identity and the integrity of your point of view.

Practitioners attend many different sorts of meetings, for example, staff meetings, team meetings, committee meetings, public meetings, and information forums. While these meetings have different purposes, what they all have in common is that they are meetings with objectives. That objective is best served through a group—that is, where a grouping of concerned participants has been consciously decided upon as the method most likely to meet the objective.

## Activity 8.7  Communication Issues

In the next week, take note of any instances of 'miscommunication' or 'misunderstanding' you experience or observe, particularly in group settings. Arguments are often the result of miscommunication, so especially note these. Try to figure out what caused the miscommunication. If nothing happens this week, try to remember a miscommunication or misunderstanding from the recent past. Then, take some time to think about the issue in terms of how you perceive 1) what caused the miscommunication, 2) what could have been done to prevent it, and 3) how this miscommunication relates to the rules of effective communication.

## Meetings, meetings, meetings . . .

We have all heard the old joke about meetings: Are you lonely? Hate having to make decisions? Rather talk about it than do it? Then why not hold a meeting? In meetings you can learn to write volumes of meaningless notes, feel important, sleep in peace, and impress (or bore) your colleagues. A punchline is added, 'Meetings: The Practical Alternative to Work'.

The reality is that meetings are an important part of working life.

## Activity 8.8  Purposes for a meeting

List as many purposes as you can for meeting in a group—for example, to share information and to elicit ideas.

According to Windschuttle and Elliott (2002), the most frequent complaint about working in organizations is that there are too many meetings and that they take up too much time. Despite this, however, meetings 'have become part of our organizational culture for some sound reasons. Decision-making is, on balance, more effective in groups than individually.' (Windschuttle & Elliott 2002, p. 406) For groups to work effectively, there have to be some common, agreed upon elements and participants need to know their responsibilities.

First, as participants, you should clearly understand the objectives of the group meeting. Second, you should practise effective discussion behaviour and keep self-centred interests in check. Avoid the temptation to commandeer time. You have to accept that the discussion will not always be to your liking and that by adopting blocking tactics you are not playing 'fair'. Always be prepared to welcome differences of opinion, and you might find such challenges occasionally help shift your point of view. Third, arrive at the meeting with a positive attitude to your participation, to the group, and to the objectives. By attending with a closed mind, convinced your view is the only right one, your effective contribution will be negligible. Fourth, cooperate in the processes of the group meeting, speak effectively in the group, and speak up if you believe the time is not being used effectively. Finally, be punctual as commitment can often be measured by the lateness of a participant.

It is inevitable that from time to time there will be tension and conflict in groups. Sometimes disagreements can be strong. The reconciliation of differences and the building of points of agreement can be facilitated by the chair of the meeting or any of its members. Windschuttle and Elliott (2002) believe that this role is a political one that confers leadership status on the person or persons who assume that role. It is important to consider building into the group a mechanism for the release of tension. If there is disagreement and conflict, then people can be tense and this may impair their ability to contribute. Using humour or taking a coffee break are simple ways of releasing tension. According to Flood and Lawrence (1987), ten-minute breaks after fifty minutes can be beneficial. Their reasoning is based on research that shows that a person's ability to take in information drops off after fifty minutes.

See chapter 12, 'Understanding and Managing Conflict', and chapter 13, 'Introduction to Working with Groups', for further discussion on small group interaction.

## The Importance of Culture

Context refers to the amount of (largely unconscious) understanding a person can be expected to bring to a particular communication setting. High context cultures tend to be highly developed, with expectations around refined ways of behaving, and because of this, communication tends to be indirect, as there is less need for direct words. People carry within them clear ideas of how most interactions will unfold, of how they and the other person will behave in a particular situation. Because people know and understand each other quite well, they have evolved a more indirect style of communication. There is less need to be explicit and rely on words to convey meanings, especially the *literal* meaning, and there is more focus on nonverbal communication. In high context settings, people often convey meaning by manipulating the context—*not* doing or *not* saying something that is always done or said in that situation. The overriding goal of the communication exchange is maintaining harmony and saving face.

Direct or low context cultures tend towards greater heterogeneity, and there is much greater diversity between and amongst the members. There is a greater reliance on direct communication, and the giving or receiving of information is the overall goal of communication. As low context cultures are usually more heterogeneous than high context cultures, less is known about each member of the team. In these situations, one cannot depend merely on manipulating context or communicating nonverbally to make themselves understood. They must rely more on words, and on those words being interpreted *literally*.

In the context of a group discussion, cultural differences can lead to misunderstanding, miscommunication, and different interpretations of non-verbal interactions. For example, in high context cultures, it is necessary to have established a personal relationship prior to 'getting down to business'. This may be accomplished through sharing a meal together or spending some time interacting on a social/personal basis. Group discussions in Western cultures tend to focus on business discussions first, prior to social interaction. This style would be interpreted as being extremely rude in many non-Western cultures.

## Starting a group discussion

One of the most difficult tasks in meetings is to initiate group discussion, particularly when participants do not know each other well.

The following are some techniques for starting a group discussion:

### Names

Begin with an exchange of names and reason for attendance at the group. This enables people to feel more comfortable and able to address everyone else by name right from the start.

## Role or interest

Use role or interest in combination with exchange of names—for example, people can be asked to briefly share with the group their name, their role, and their special interest. Also, sometimes people are invited to participate in groups because they have a specific role or special interest—for example, a case conference. These can indicate or reflect their objectives or 'agendas'.

## Whip-around

This, again, is an exchange of names and ideas. All participants are asked to take turns and make a brief statement of their position, attitude, and proposal.

# Meeting procedure

As a rule, there should be a record kept of every meeting. This necessitates taking minutes on the major points and decisions. Minutes are important documents for the organization and should be filed and kept as a record.

Meetings may be informal or formal; however, all meetings should have some ground rules so that everyone in the group understands their speaking rights and what procedure is being used.

## Formal meetings

Formal meeting procedure uses the rules of debate and is controlled by a chairperson, has a minute taker, and is conducted in a way that is calculated to allow all participants the opportunity to speak. Flood and Lawrence (1987) point out that the chairperson's chief responsibility is to the participants and not vice versa.

## Activity 8.9  Reflections on meetings

What experience do you have of meetings? What observations would you be comfortable sharing with others?

### Roles in a formal meeting

*Chairperson*

All discussion takes place through the chairperson, whose responsibility it is to:

- open the meeting and explain what it is about
- introduce speakers, guests, or new members
- have an agenda ready to propose at the meeting
- direct the meeting by steering questions to those people who can answer them and

drawing out people, ensuring that shy and nervous people get to speak along with the articulate and confident

- control the length of contributions
- keep the meeting moving along and work towards forward movement when the meeting is 'stuck'
- keep only one issue before the chair at a time
- summarize the discussion at the end of each item and at the end of the whole meeting
- accept motions and control debate according to the rules

*Secretary or minute-taker*

The minute-taker is elected and writes brief notes of the agenda items discussed, records the motions passed, and their movers and seconders. The minutes provide a description of the meeting, a list of those present, and a list of apologies. The minutes are a record of the business of the meeting as well as a record of the action decided by the meeting, naming those delegated to perform the action, along with any relevant dates. It is the responsibility of the minute-taker to write up the notes as the minutes of the meeting as soon as possible after the meeting.

**Meetings glossary**

It is helpful to understand the terms used in meetings. A resource list follows.

**addendum**: adds words to a motion, but does not otherwise change it.

**agenda**: a list of items to be discussed at the meeting. If an agenda has been circulated, then the chairperson raises items as they are listed. Items may be re-arranged, for instance, to discuss one item earlier in the proceedings to ensure full participation and time to do so. A typical sequence might be:

1. Opening
2. Apologies/Regrets from absent members
3. Welcoming visitors
4. Confirmation of minutes of previous meeting
5. Business arising from minutes
6. Head of Department's report
7. Report from working party on agency changes re: intake
8. Special business
9. General business
10. Date and place of next meeting
11. Closure

The agenda establishes order to the meeting, informs participants so they can be prepared, and ensures that no important item will be missed.

**amendment**: a change or addition to a motion. So, if the mover of the motion agrees to incorporate an amendment to the motion then no debate of the amendment is required.

However, if the mover of the motion does not agree, then the amendment must be debated first, and if accepted, it becomes part of the motion. If there is a seconder, the chairperson accepts the amendment and then the motion is debated and voted on. After the mover speaks in its support, the chairperson calls for further speakers to speak against and in favour of the motion. The mover then has a right of reply, following which the chairperson puts the motion to the vote.

**committee**: a small group of people selected to perform a task that cannot be done efficiently by a large group, the organization, or by one person. It may plan a single activity or a long-term program, act as an advisory body, study a particular problem, promote or publicize a particular event, or evaluate a particular activity.

**motion**: the expression of an idea for acceptance or rejection by the meeting.

**original motion**: the first motion on the particular subject. When an amendment is lost, or voted down, the meeting reconsiders the original motion.

**point of clarification**: a point that may be raised if the motion is unclear to someone in the meeting and before further discussion takes place.

**point of order**: a point that may be raised by anyone in the meeting if they think a speaker is out of order—for example, straying off the topic, breaking the rules of debate, or going on for too long. The chairperson then makes a ruling on whether the speaker is out of order.

**quorum**: the number of members who must be present to constitute a valid meeting.

**resolution**: a decision reached by the meeting and the name given to a motion that has been passed.

Most meetings are not so formal as to incorporate all of the previous elements; however, in formal meetings such terminology and protocol are in use.

Returning to the theme at the beginning of this section, it is important to re-emphasize the point that no number of rules and no amount of formality and structure can negate the necessity of having the confidence to speak clearly about your point of view in a meeting. That is the main challenge.

Being positive about meeting and speaking with others in a group can be a rewarding, pleasurable, and creative experience. Communicating and cooperating with others and reaching decisions is constructive. Beware of the cynic who quips, 'a camel is a horse designed by a committee', as it can disguise an autocratic tendency.

Every grouping of people is different. Meetings can be well run and the group of people motivated to work towards goals in the spirit of goodwill and full participation. On the other hand, meetings can be poorly run and inefficient in their functioning. Knowing a little about group dynamics and what Windschuttle and Elliott (2002) call 'humanizing meetings' is important if you are to reflect on the purpose and functioning of the group.

## Group dynamics

Group dynamics concerns how people act as a group and as individuals towards each other. As each group is different, there are no hard and fast rules. However, there are some matters and issues that help or hinder communication in groups.

Generally speaking, if people are content and believe they are gaining something from the group, they are more likely to contribute and be active group members. Interactions in groups will depend on the individuals who make up the groups. Nevertheless, as Reed et al. (1985) suggest, there are some things that need fostering in groups. First, offering support to each other is important as it creates trust and commitment, and enables people to facilitate each others' interactions and ideas. Support leads to respect for each other and a respectful hearing of each others' ideas. Second, fostering group identity leads to unity and everyone's energies being turned outwards towards a single goal. A divided group has its energies turned inwards. Third, a group that works well is one in which people encourage one another's participation, are flexible, and encourage compromise between extreme positions in the group. Fourth, a group is supported by the verbalizing of accepted group standards in conflict situations and by working towards relieving tension with breaks and humour.

The sorts of things that hinder group interaction include distrust, negativity, internal subversion, subgroups, exclusion of unfavoured members, self-centredness, and refusals to experiment, to try new things, and to make an effort, both as individuals and as a group. In chapter 13, 'Introduction to Working with Groups', you can find more about group dynamics.

Windschuttle and Elliott (2002) suggest that physical setting has important effects on the relationships between people in the group. Be mindful of how the group forms physically— for instance, the more people want their relationships to be equal at a meeting, the more they will be inclined to sit on the same level and face each other. Similarly, lighting, heating, and decor can play a part in ensuring people's comfort and their ability to stay alert and participating. Even factors such as providing simple refreshments can be appreciated by people and demonstrate that group members are valued and their needs considered important.

## And finally . . .

Groups may gather for a variety of reasons and take many forms. Critical practitioners should inform themselves about the purpose for the group, understand the structure of the group, and appreciate that tensions will arise from time to time. Being prepared to be part of a group, having a positive attitude, and harbouring goodwill towards others in the group will ensure a level of comfort, making speaking up in a group an easier task.

# Effective writing

Sometimes social work students say they are amazed by the amount of writing that is required of them in the organizations where they were placed for practicum. It is true that the practice of helping professionals requires writing in a wide range of different formats. It follows then that effective writing skills are crucial for practitioners. Being able to organize thoughts in clear sentences using proper standard English is essential in recording work of all kinds. Practitioners may find themselves writing many different types of documents—for example, letters, reports, policy statements, memoranda, planning documents, newsletters, pamphlets and brochures, press releases, articles and papers, and posters and flyers.

## Some general guidelines

All effective writing shares the following qualities (Flood & Lawrence 1987; Windschuttle & Elliott 2002):

- is simple and direct
- uses short sentences and the active voice
- keeps paragraphs short and confined to one point
- avoids abstract words
- avoids jargon

In short, effective writing means writing clearly. Making yourself understood is the goal of writing, but it takes time and patience to write effectively. As Flood and Lawrence advise (1987), be prepared to do a few drafts before putting your signature to your written piece. They also suggest that when you have got it as good as you can, show other people what you have written (if confidentiality is not an issue) and ask for their comments and feedback. For instance, if you have been charged with the responsibility of writing a flyer for a community event, it would be good practice to get some input once you have written a draft you are prepared to share with colleagues.

Getting started can be daunting. Again, Flood and Lawrence (1987, p. 73) advise that a good technique is to 'just write out what you want to say and don't worry about grammar, spelling, punctuation, and whether anyone is going to understand it or read it'. Once you have your thoughts down on paper, you can work on making it letter perfect.

Working to perfect your written piece is absolutely essential if you pride yourself on being a credible professional. 'Close enough' is not good enough when it comes to your written work. There are many books available that can give you simple, yet comprehensive, advice regarding writing, grammar, and style. If you are in doubt, it is useful to consult such a book to help guide your efforts. A good way of developing your writing is to practise writing short pieces that need to be clear and contain a message. Activity 8.10 will assist in this development.

## Activity 8.10  Letter to the editor

Write a letter on a topic of relevance to social welfare for hypothetical submission to your city or regional newspaper. To prepare for this activity, you need to read the papers and acquaint yourself with a topic that has a social justice, social policy, and social issue component.

Flood and Lawrence (1987, p. 76) posit that a golden rule when writing letters is 'clarity with courtesy'. Remember that a letter is a permanent record of your contact with the other party and, therefore, needs to be planned carefully and written clearly. Flood and Lawrence (1987, p. 76) suggest that 'a letter should be as short as clarity, sufficient information and courtesy allow. Clarity implies using simple, natural English and arranging the points in a logical order, preferably with a new paragraph for each point. Courtesy helps make a letter acceptable to the reader—you need to compromise between being too wordy and being too abrupt, though the length will depend on the purpose of your letter.'

Your letter should be tidy in appearance and well written. It is a good idea to read other letters that can give you ideas for improving the letter that you write. Although it might seem obvious, pay attention to the obvious! Remember to include:

- your address and the date
- your telephone number or e-mail address (if appropriate)
- a reference number (if appropriate)
- recipient's address
- a subject heading (if appropriate)—for example, 'Re: Permission to hold community meeting'
- endings—for example, 'Yours sincerely' or 'Regards', and your signature with your printed name and title beneath

Generally speaking, recording is important in human services practice. According to O'Connor et al. (2003, p. 186), 'Good records are an essential practice skill, and recording, like other skills, takes practice if it is to be done effectively and efficiently. Poor recording can lead to unintended but serious consequences.' If records are incomplete or inaccurate and where there is no attempt to separate fact from opinion, then dire consequences might follow in practice. The source of your information should always be made clear (Prince 1996), and you must accept the understanding that the records are not your private property, but in law, belong to your employer, with clients having the right to gain access to many records (Bateman 2000).

Why and what to record are important questions to be explored.

## Purposes for recording

One essential purpose for recording client case details is that it helps you organize your thoughts on what is happening, why it might be happening, and what might be done to address the situation. Pare and Allen (1995, pp. 166–7) have summarized the early work done in 1925 by Mary Richmond, who gave nine reasons for recording. Records:

1. help workers to be more effective by providing the full complications of a case;
2. allow someone else to continue working with clients when workers get sick, go on holiday, or move to new points of service;
3. can be used as a starting point when people return for service years after the case has been closed;

4. help in the supervision of staff;

5. help to train new workers;

6. offer data for the study and improvement of services;

7. can be grouped around presenting problems to provide help in deciding on appropriate services;

8. contain the full and detailed descriptions that allow for problem solving in difficult cases;

9. provide public evidence of the activities of social work.

The question that beginning practitioners often ask is, 'How much recording should I do?' There is no convenient, universal answer to this important question. You should be guided by the knowledge that each piece of writing and recording should be specific to its purpose. As Doel and Shardlow (1998, p. 108) point out, 'The student learns that being clear about the purpose of making a written record helps to decide what needs to go in it.'

However, having some minimum guidelines is helpful in practice. The CASW *Guidelines for Ethical Practice* (2005, p. 9), Section 1.7, Maintenance and Handling of Client Records, advise as follows:

Social workers maintain one written record of professional interventions and opinions, with due care to the obligations and standards of their employer and relevant regulatory body. Social workers document information impartially and accurately and with an appreciation that the record may be revealed to clients or disclosed during court proceedings. Social workers are encouraged to take care to:

- report only essential and relevant details,
- refrain from using emotive or derogatory language,
- acknowledge the basis of professional opinions,
- protect clients' privacy and that of others involved.

Doel and Shardlow (1998, p. 109) point out that social workers have become increasingly aware of the power of language and suggest that asking 'questions about the use of language in social work practice helps them to think not only about how and what to record, but also to be critical of the use of labels for people.' The aim is to be clear and accurate and to avoid jargon and labels.

Confidentiality and clients' right to privacy are paramount considerations when writing and lodging your report. It is good practice to know who can gain access to the information contained in the report, as this will affect what you include, and how the report will be physically safeguarded (whether paper or electronic). A clear understanding of your agency's policy in relation to matters of confidentiality, privacy, and storage of records is fundamental to your practice. This allows you to be accountable to your clients and to be able to explain the situation clearly to them. Doel and Shardlow (1998) propose the idea of 'open or shared records', suggesting that a good way of checking the fairness of your information is to share it with your clients.

Practitioners across contexts will find themselves writing reports of one kind or another. As O'Connor et al. (2003, p. 187) state, 'Reports are written for many reasons and this will have an impact on the structure and style of report writing.' The practitioner may write interview, assessment, and planning reports, journal entries, and submissions. Some of these reports may be paper or electronic, you may be the sole author, and, on occasion, you might be co-writing with another or many others. Increasingly, in some agencies, there are templates that guide the practitioner as to what specific information is needed and what must be collected and recorded. One type of report is that written for assessment purposes after an interview has taken place.

## Interview report

After an individual, couple, family, or group interview, you first need to analyze, integrate, and organize the information you have obtained. Then you are in a position to present the information; the traditional medium for doing so is the report. A report deserves great care and consideration in its writing. It is an important document that may influence crucial future decisions and have effects on the lives of the people who are the subject of the report.

Sattler (1998) points out that a good report does not only present facts, but rather it brings together known and prior information that is obtained during the interview. Consequently, each report is individual and unique and respectful of the subject of the report. Nevertheless, two qualities that all good reports share are that they are well organized and written in such a way as to be easily readable.

To assist in formulating and constructing your report, you need to consider who your audience is: a colleague, another helping professional, a teacher, a magistrate or judge? Always keep in mind the need to explicate important points you have made. You can do this by providing examples to illustrate and emphasize selected statements you have made. When making your recommendations, be mindful of their ability to be translated into action. It is useless making recommendations that are either not realizable or unable to be effectively implemented. Before you sign off on a report, study it carefully for signs of how your values have affected your judgment and writing. A professional report is one where the reader is able to readily identify how you have arrived at your recommendations and be satisfied in the knowledge that the information gathered, rather than your value system, guided the process.

A sample interview report appears in Practice example 8.1. This report relates to Practice example 10.2. Read the report and reflect on the Practice points that follow.

## Practice example 8.1

### Assessment report

Community Mental Health Service

**Presenting situation**

Jane is a thirty-two-year-old divorced woman who has been escorted by police to the emergency department following an expression of suicidal ideation. Jane is reported to have had an

*continued*

argument with her boyfriend of six months who resides with her. Jane has a fifteen-year-old daughter who was staying with a friend at the time of the argument. Neighbours were allegedly concerned about the escalating conflict and contacted the police. Police report both Jane and her boyfriend to have been intoxicated by alcohol at the time.

### Personal history

Jane became pregnant and had one daughter at age sixteen years. She reports no contact with the biological father of her child. Jane reports a history of traumatic relationships including a marriage of five years. Jane reports ongoing verbal and physical abuse by her ex-husband requiring a two-day hospital admission twelve months ago, which instigated her separation from him and subsequent divorce.

### Family history and early development

Jane describes being estranged from her family of origin. She states she was always the 'black sheep' of the family and her parents did not accept her teenage pregnancy.

### Social circumstances

Jane resides in a two-bedroom unit with her daughter and current boyfriend. She works as a checkout clerk at the local supermarket. Jane reports ongoing financial stressors. Her relationship with her daughter is described as positive, and there is no evidence to indicate a referral to the child welfare authorities is required at this stage.

### Mental health

Jane reports feeling anxious and describes herself as a 'worrier'. She is agitated in behaviour during the assessment and her mood appears low with limited responses. She reports no formal

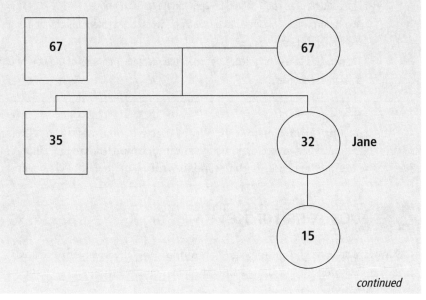

*continued*

treatment but states she uses cigarettes and marijuana to manage this. Jane reports past alcohol abuse and is reported by police to have been intoxicated prior to attending the emergency department.

**Suicide risk assessment**
Risk indicators: Jane reports anxiety features and possible depressive symptoms in the context of alcohol and substance use as well as relationship and financial stressors.

**Protective factors**
Jane identifies her relationship with her daughter and her job as significant positive influences in her life that keep her going.

**Recommendations**
Jane requires intervention to address her mental health and psycho-social needs. Referrals for a full psychiatric assessment and provision of practical supports in the short-term to alleviate immediate financial and accommodation pressures may minimize her suicide risk.

Sheila Nicolson BSW
Social Worker

## Practice points 8.1

- The content of a report should be appropriate for its purposes.
- In a report, clear links need to be made between assessment information and recommended interventions.
- There needs to be congruence between the recommendations of a report and the available resources.

This chapter has focused on the centrality of effective communication skills for the practitioner in the human services sector. Effective communication leads to practitioners being more effective in arguing their cases, verbally and in writing, on behalf of clients and themselves.

## Questions for Review

1. How are speaking, listening, and communicating effectively interrelated?
2. What are some important considerations when preparing a speech for a group of colleagues?

3. What factors influence speakers' ability to communicate effectively?
4. How do speakers use the media to successfully get across their message?
5. What are the key steps in effective letter-writing?

# References

Bateman, N. (2000). *Advocacy Skills for Health and Social Care Professionals*. London: Jessica Kingsley.

Canadian Association of Social Workers (2005). *Guidelines for ethical practice*. Ottawa, ON: Canadian Association of Social Workers.

Doel, M., & Shardlow, S. (1998). *The New Social Work Practice*. Aldershot: Ashgate.

Flood, M., & Lawrence, A. (1987). *The Community Action Book* (2nd edn). Sydney: Maxwell.

Jordan, J. (1991). Catching slips from lips. *Sydney Morning Herald*, 18 April, 10.

Kaplan, B.J. (1997). *A Nurse's Guide to Public Speaking*. New York: Springer.

Le Clair, M., & Fortune, P. (1986). *A Lazy Man's Guide to Public Speaking*. Sydney: Fortune.

McCarthy, P., & Hatcher, C. (2002). *Speaking Persuasively*. Sydney: Allen & Unwin.

O'Connor, I., Wilson, J., & Setterlund, D. (2003). *Social Work and Welfare Practice* (4th edn). Melbourne: Pearson Education.

Pare, A., & Allen, H.S. (1995). Social work writing: Learning by doing. In G. Rogers (ed.), *Social Work Education: Views and Visions*. Dubuque, IA: Kendall/Hunt.

Prince, K. (1996). *Boring records? Communication, Speech and Writing in Social Work*. London: Jessica Kingsley.

Reed, H., Cameron, D., & Spinks, D. (1985). *Stepping Stones: A Management Training Manual for Community Groups*. Hurstville: Community Management Training Scheme.

Sattler, J.M. (1998). *Clinical and Forensic Interviewing of Children and Families: Guidelines for the Mental Health, Education, Pediatric, and Child Maltreatment Fields*. San Diego, CA: Jerome M. Sattler.

Vallence, K. (1987). Speaking in a group. In K. Vallence & T. McWilliam (eds), *Communication That Works*. Melbourne: Thomas Nelson.

Windschuttle, K., & Elliott, E. (2002). *Writing, Researching, Communicating: Communication Skills for the Information Age*. Sydney: Irwin/McGraw-Hill.

# 9

# The Microskills of Interviewing

### Agi O'Hara

Communication between helping professionals and their clients generally occurs within the context of an interview. Interviews can be considered as purposeful conversations (Thompson 2002; Trevithick 2000; Collins et al. 1999; Seden 1999) and, therefore, require the interviewer to employ strategies and skills to achieve the intended objective(s) of the interview. This chapter will cover a range of interviewing skills that assist in appropriately structuring an interview and gathering the information required to fit the purpose of the helping professional in a variety of settings. Chapter 10, 'Conducting Assessment: Some General Guidelines', is the ideal companion to this chapter as it offers the rationale or purpose for interviewing in a great many contexts.

When thinking about interviewing, we need to do so in a way that is, at all times, cognizant of the individual before us, and the various sources of difference between the client and ourselves. These differences may be associated with 'class, race, gender, age, disability, sexual orientation, religion, culture, health, geography, expectations and outlook on life' (Trevithick 2000, p. 2), so our approach to working with clients requires an awareness of how this diversity may affect the client's interactions with us. The wide variety of practice situations also may require adaptations in our interviewing skills. For example, as pointed out by Rowland and McDonald (2009), a variety of interviewing skills and techniques are needed to ensure that the human worth and dignity of those with communication barriers is maintained and human rights in health care are being met.

This requires an appreciation of the fact 'that healer and patient, practitioner and client, are part of the same equation in that the cultural values of both parties are an integral part of understanding the interaction and relationship to best advantage' (Gabb 2000, p. 6). Each of the skills to be discussed, therefore, will be considered as arising from a foundation of professional competencies based on awareness of diversity and ethical and multicultural practice (Ivey & Bradford Ivey 2003). These necessary competencies can be acquired through appropriate professional training that avoids overly rigid representations of cultures that may result in perpetuating 'cultural stereotypes and treatment of persons from a common culture as the same' (Hartel & Trumble 1995). Reading relevant texts and articles (Ivey & Bradford Ivey 2003; Ivey et al. 2000; Vicary & Andrews 2000; Nguyen & Bowles 1998) and consulting specific guidelines that have been developed by professional or cultural associations is also recommended. For example, Mckenzie and Morrissette (2003) outline that an integral component of social work practice with Aboriginal persons requires knowledge of the particular nature of oppression experienced by Aboriginal persons as well as an understanding of the world view of Aboriginal persons and how this differs from the dominant Euro-Canadian world view. The guidelines, though specifically written for working with Aboriginal Canadians, are also relevant to working with various other cultures. They further highlight the importance of sensitivity regarding:

- forms of greeting and leave taking,
- culturally appropriate use of questioning,
- respectful intergenerational communication,
- use of personal names,
- non-verbal communication,
- public displays that are likely to result in feelings of embarrassment.

There is much to consider before we begin to examine the microskills of interviewing. Connected with the above indicators of respectful practice is the notion of 'intentionality'. The term implies a clear understanding of the professional role being undertaken and the ability to choose strategies and responses that are appropriate to the needs of each client. It necessitates a critical evaluation of the practice strategies employed, a flexibility in the choices made, and the recognition that merely relying on one's 'natural personal style' (Ivey & Bradford Ivey 2003, p. 15) is insufficient in the majority of cases. Intentionality involves professional discipline such that we consciously examine our own competencies, the effectiveness of our interviewing style, and the consequences of previous interactions with clients, and that we formulate our own theory of interviewing practice (Ivey & Bradford Ivey 2003). Shulman's (1999) review of social work practice skills remains an excellent introduction to those skills considered most useful in the helping professions.

Furthermore, an effective interview depends not only on the interpersonal skills of the interviewer but also the extent to which the interviewer has prepared for the interview. Generally this would involve consideration of:

- the context of the interview,
- the role and purpose of the interview,
- the structure of the interview.

## Interview context

The context in which an interview takes place not only influences the level of engagement, mood, and responsiveness of the client but also the potential outcome of the interview. As Lishman (1994, p. 141) points out, there are a range of possible contexts:

- an office of a non-profit social service
- a home or other residential setting
- a prison
- a school
- a hospital (whether general or psychiatric)

- a government agency or organization (for example, a Child and Family Services office, Employment and Income Assistance settings, Juvenile Probations)
- a daycare centre
- a community centre
- an informal, transitory, or detached setting (for example, conversations in cafés and on car rides)

Of course, regardless of the context, the initial task for the interviewer is to connect with the client by making them feel as comfortable as possible and building a relationship with them. The physical environment can assist or detract in this regard. Conducting the interview in unpleasant (for example, dark, squalid, cramped) surroundings generally makes it more difficult to engage the client in the interview process.

## Activity 9.1  The purpose of interviews

Consider the various settings in which helping professionals might conduct interviews (see the list above) and identify the different purposes for which interviews might be conducted in these contexts.

# Role and purpose of the interview

The purpose of the interview will be determined by the needs of the various people involved. This includes the needs of the professional practitioner who will be conducting the interview, the person(s) being interviewed, and others involved with this person(s), the agency or organization for which the interview is being conducted, and other professionals who may also be involved (Trevithick 2000).

Not infrequently there will be an expectation that a report will be written as a formal or informal record of the interview undertaken. In such situations, preparation for the interview should involve consideration of the content and structure (for example, headings) of the report to be written, as they will generally influence the questions to be posed. For a discussion of report writing see chapter 8, 'Effective Communication'.

# Structure of the interview

It is possible to identify various stages within each interview. Some writers consider interviews in a general way, such as moving through beginning, middle, and end stages. Ivey and Bradford Ivey (2003, p. 23), on the other hand, delineate the following five stages in their microskills hierarchy:

- initiating rapport and structuring
- gathering data

- mutual goal setting
- working: exploring alternatives and confronting incongruity
- terminating and generalization to daily life

As previously mentioned, in the beginning we need to help the client feel at ease and to develop 'confidence in our personal and professional integrity' (Trevithick 2000, p. 76). Clearly defining our role and the purpose of the interview assists in this regard. The middle stage could be considered the working stage of the interview, during which the focus is on exploring the relevant issues and using appropriate skills and techniques. The end, as implied, is the time to appropriately conclude the interview. A detailed discussion of these stages will follow.

## Activity 9.2  Planning for an interview

Prepare a general checklist of items you would find helpful to remember when planning an interview with a client (for example, booking and preparing the interview room, catering to special mobility needs of the client).

## Beginning stage of the interview

### Welcoming skills

Clients' anxieties, fears, or concerns can be reduced if they feel welcomed when entering the facility in which the interview will be conducted. The response of the receptionist (if one is present) and the decor of the reception area (Lishman 1994) may provide initial cues about the interview to follow. When the interviewer meets the client, simple social interchanges that are commonly a part of greeting conversations (for example, comments or questions related to transport, parking, and the weather) and shaking hands (when appropriate) also assist in making the client feel welcome. Determining the length of such informal conversations can be tricky, but Trevithick (2000) suggests we are generally guided by our intuition in this regard.

### Establishing a relationship

The ease with which clients develop trust and connection with the interviewer is largely determined by the rapport between them. Trevithick (2000) differentiates between a superficial, instant 'clicking' between people and a deeper, 'genuine and meaningful point of contact' (Trevithick 2000, p. 76) that develops into a trusting working relationship, often referred to as a *working alliance*. The benefits of establishing a relationship often go beyond merely assisting in conducting the work of the interview. It can result in the client developing 'a heightened sense of self-worth (and) a growing desire for more rather than less connection with others' (Jordan, cited in Trevithick 2000, p. 78). Kadushin (1990, pp. 39–57) identifies the following behaviours as assisting in building rapport and trust between interviewer and client:

- engaging with interest and warmth
- offering acceptance and empathic understanding
- demonstrating a respect for the client's individuality
- being genuine and authentic

It is important to keep in mind that, despite the interviewer's best intentions, particular circumstances of the interview, such as whether the client attends voluntarily or is mandated to attend, the perceived power differential between interviewer and client, and the anticipated consequences of the interview, will significantly influence the client's willingness to engage in the interview process and the nature of the relationship developed.

## Activity 9.3  Reluctant clients

Create a list of contexts in which the practitioner may be working with clients who are likely to be reluctantly involved in the interview process.

## Middle stage of the interview

### Microskills of effective interviewing

Communication between practitioner and client involves not only words but non-verbal features such as 'facial expressions, gestures, posture and tone of voice' (Satir, cited in Collins et al. 1999, p. 108). Although the interview process is quite complex, it is possible to break it down into its constituent parts and identify the microskills involved (Evans et al. 2004). Interviewing microskills have been analyzed and organized in various ways (Cormier & Nurius 2003; Trevithick 2000; Ivey & Bradford Ivey 2003; Egan 2002), but a common differentiation is that between listening and influencing responses (Cormier & Nurius 2003).

The following section provides a practical discussion of many of the microskills involved in effective interviewing, but it is important to remember that discussing skills individually is artificial (Egan 2002) and cannot depict the manner in which practitioners naturally combine these skills in a myriad of ways. The suggestions made are only general guidelines that may need to be modified depending on the individual and cultural needs of the person being interviewed. Also, though many of the skills to be discussed are relevant to both adult and child clients, it is recognized that a child's ability to engage in verbal communication is generally age dependant, and when working with children under twelve years of age, verbal communication is often augmented with various forms of play (Webb 2003). To successfully interview children, the practitioner requires specialized understanding of developmental psychology, particularly cognitive development related to language ability—that is, the speaking and understanding of varying complexities in sentence structure (Wilson & Powell 2001).

As it will not be possible to adequately cover the many specific skills required for interviewing children in this chapter, the focus will be limited to adult clients. Consulting the

Wilson & Powell (2001) text is recommended for practitioners wishing to enhance their work with children.

## Attending

Attending behaviour involves both a physical orientation and a style of responding to client communication (Evans et al. 2004). It is important that a practitioner's verbal communication reinforces, rather than confuses or contradicts, non-verbal messages conveyed to clients by physical posture, gestures, facial expressions, and tone of voice. In essence, the intended message needs to be that we are interested in what the client is telling us and that we are able and willing to offer our undivided attention to our client. Egan's (2002) guidelines for appropriate physical attending, which are incorporated into his 'SOLER' model, offer a simple reminder of non-verbal messages that may be conveyed or interpreted from our physical posture. The acronym 'SOLER' represents the following:

S   *Face clients **squarely**, indicating availability and interest in working with the client.*
    Although this seems to imply that the knees of the client and interviewer need to be directly facing each other, the point is more that the client and interviewer need to be generally facing each other, rather than side by side, or back to back. This is particularly important for clients who are visually impaired and who rely on voice direction as one of the cues regarding the interviewer's attention. The arrangement of chairs in the interview room should be given considerable attention. There should be sufficient distance between chairs to avoid physical contact, so that personal boundaries are not violated. Slight angling of chairs is a common set-up, particularly if the space is restricted. The cultural group to which the client belongs or the number of people who attend the interview are also considerations. For example, the Aboriginal sharing circle is a respectful way to demonstrate equality amongst group members. Sitting side by side is less confronting than sitting face to face and should perhaps be considered with any client who is feeling threatened or unable to engage in the interview due to excessive discomfort. However, such unexpected changes in seating arrangements should be checked out with the client first, allowing them to determine their preference in this regard. This can be very helpful when working with child and adult clients who are distressed.

O   *Adopt an **open** posture, indicating an openness to the client, and a non-defensive attitude to what is being spoken about.*
    Beginning practitioners sometimes mistake this guideline as meaning that it is inappropriate for them to cross their legs, and therefore attempt to sit in ways that are unnatural and uncomfortable. This becomes counterproductive to guideline R below, relating to appearing relaxed.

L   ***Lean** towards the client, responding naturally to the ebb and flow of the conversation with the client.*
    Moving towards and away from the person with whom we are conversing is a natural and mostly unconscious behaviour that is part of everyday interactions. Practitioners

need to be aware of not 'leaning too far forward . . . or doing so too soon' (Egan 2002, p. 69) as this may be too threatening for the client. Excessive leaning away from the client is also inappropriate, as it gives the impression of disinterest.

E    *Maintain appropriate* **eye contact***, showing interest in the client and the client's concerns, while demonstrating cultural sensitivity.*

A great deal has been written about various cultural groups and their customs regarding direct eye contact and the implied disrespect when such customs are ignored. However, the benefit of such guidelines depends on an awareness of the cultural background of our clients, which is not always apparent. Similarly, individual differences within cultures and differences due to situational factors also need to be considered. Many people find it disconcerting to be in the situations in which they are being interviewed. Even if not adhering to particular cultural imperatives and not generally being concerned about maintaining direct eye contact, the interview situation may limit the extent to which they are able to do so. It is therefore advisable to allow our clients to lead us in their preferred manner of maintaining eye contact without negatively evaluating them as reluctant to engage in the interview, or being evasive or timid. Being sensitive to our client's needs regarding eye contact demonstrates respect and will assist in making them feel more at ease.

R    *Remain relatively* **relaxed***, indicating confidence, thereby helping the client to also feel more relaxed.*

There is nothing more distracting to a client than an interviewer who fidgets incessantly whether by tapping their fingers, clicking a pen, or playing with their hair. Each of these types of behaviours implies nervousness and is therefore counterproductive to creating an impression of professionalism.

## Activity 9.4  Contravening the SOLER model

In your next conversation with a friend, consider the five components of the SOLER model and attempt to contravene each of the guidelines and observe the consequences. For example, do the following one at a time:

1. Turn your back while your friend is talking.
2. Cross your arms and legs, allowing your body to become hunched over.
3. Lean in very close or move well away.
4. Refuse to make eye contact or, alternatively, continue staring despite your friend's attempts to disengage from your stare.
5. Keep fiddling with your hair, tapping your foot, or clicking a pen.

    Is your friend able to continue the conversation with you? Which of the guidelines did you find the most difficult to maintain inappropriately?

A note of caution regarding attending behaviour: inexperienced practitioners in their earnestness sometimes adopt postures that appear to be overly intense and inappropriate for the content of the discussion taking place. If, from the very beginning, the interviewer is already leaning forward, face set in a serious, intense manner, and the client is merely talking about difficulties in finding a parking spot, it will be difficult for the interviewer to indicate a greater degree of attending when the real and often difficult issues begin to be discussed.

The actress Carrie Fisher, when interviewed on the Parkinson television show, offered an insightful anecdote regarding attending behaviour that is worth recounting. She remarked that when telling friends and practitioners about being recently diagnosed with bipolar disorder, she found it extremely irritating that many of the people to whom she was speaking developed what she referred to as 'heavy hair'. This affliction was indicated by their almost automatic shift in posture such that their head tilted to one side. I had not previously considered this aspect of physical attending, but since hearing the anecdote I have become aware of just how often my head is tilted to the side when intently listening. Although not everyone may find the 'heavy hair' posture irritating, it is perhaps helpful to occasionally check our posture and consider whether aspects of it that may be a source of distraction, if not irritation, to our clients.

## Activity 9.5 Indicators of inadequate listening

Sometimes the best way to understand the rationale behind specific guidelines regarding new skills or techniques being learned is to experience interactions in which the guidelines have been ignored or contravened. Personally experiencing the effects of inappropriate behaviour greatly assists in remembering what not to do.

Think about recent conversations with friends or colleagues and consider features of these conversations that would be inappropriate in a professional context and indicative of inadequate attending (for example, interrupting, side-tracking the conversation).

## Empathy

Empathy has been described as seeing the world through another person's eyes or experiences. The ability to demonstrate genuine empathy is not only a communication skill but one of the core qualities, alongside warmth and genuineness, necessary for establishing a working alliance with clients. Collins et al. (1999) caution against forced expressions of empathy. When experiencing difficulty in understanding a client's perspective, their preference is to ask clients to provide more information to clarify their situation, rather than attempting to offer inaccurate or false empathy. As empathy is generally conveyed by the accurate reflection of feelings, practitioners need to be aware that there are cultural and individual differences in the extent to which clients directly focus on feelings. Practitioners therefore need to find alternative means of conveying empathy (Collins et al. 1999) such as focusing on behaviours and experiences (Egan 2002). A variety of response styles have been devised (Collins et al. 1999) to assist practitioners who find it difficult to express empathy to their clients:

- 'you feel _____ [emotion] because _____ [restatement of client's experiences and/or behaviours]'
- 'it sounds like _____'
- 'you seem to feel _____'
- 'I get the impression that _____'

However, an overreliance on these suggestions can be problematic if the use of such responses comes across as rehearsed and formulaic. It is preferable merely to keep the essence of such phrases in mind and to respond more naturally.

## Activity 9.6  Difficulty in conveying empathy

Consider contexts in which you may be asked to work with clients who have issues for which you would find it difficult to genuinely convey empathy. Empathy blockers include interactions in which the practioners' expressions of domination, manipulation, disempowerment, denial, cut-offs, empty responses, or sympathy override the interview. As interviewers, it is important for us to reflect upon what it is about these clients or issues that spark these reactions in ourselves.

## Activity 9.7  Empathy blockers

Think of a time when you wanted to tell someone something and that person's response made you shut down your communication. What did not work?

Reflect upon your triggers—some phrases that might really irritate you, or at least cause you to shut down. What are they?

Working with a partner, take a few moments to discuss which blockers you find the most difficult.

- What responses do they invite in yourself?

Working with a partner, have one person share a problem (not too deep) and the other person respond with an empathy blocker of choice. After several minutes, reverse roles.

- How did it feel to receive the empathy blocker?
- How did it feel to use the empathy blocker?
- Are some more familiar than others?
- Are some more difficult to deliver than others?
- Are some more difficult to receive than others?
- What is your reaction to this exercise?

## Observation skills

Observation skills are required for keeping track of both the client's and our own responses and interactions in the interview. They assist us in our awareness of the diversity between our clients and ourselves, and facilitate the formulation of appropriate responses. By being aware of both verbal and non-verbal responses, we are better able to gauge how the interview is proceeding, whether we have managed to help the client trust us, and if the client is feeling safe enough to open up about their experiences or issues of concern. Countless books and articles have been written about non-verbal behaviour, and, although some general guidelines may be helpful, it is imperative that we remain tentative in our interpretations and do not assume that our interpretation of the client's experience is necessarily correct. When in doubt, it is always best to ask for clarification from the client. Good observation skills can greatly enhance the rapport between practitioner and client, and include more than simply observing physical aspects. Observing the client's use of language, mirroring it, or referring to it can make the client feel better understood.

### Practice example 9.1

## Use of metaphors

If your client Barry has mentioned that he is a rowing enthusiast and occasionally uses metaphors such as 'it has to be a team effort' or 'you have to put your oar in the water', then questions or responses that expand on the metaphor can be very effective. Barry has explored the possibility of becoming a stay-at-home dad while his wife goes to work, but his friends have been giving him a hard time about this. Responding empathically, by saying 'going against the current must take such effort' is likely to make him feel better understood than if the response had been a more general one. As well, metaphors may also be used to reframe a situation for a client. For example, if one is interviewing a single mother who has expressed that she does not have control over her 10-year-old son, the interviewer may ask whether it feels like the son is 'driving the car' and question what the mother may need to do in order to 'get back in the driver's seat'.

### Appropriate and effective use of questions

Asking questions is an essential and expected component of interviewing. They determine the direction of the interview and assist the client in focusing on particular aspects of their experience. New practitioners generally ask too many questions when feeling unsure about how to proceed, in an effort to ensure that they have collected all the required information, or as a means of filling uncomfortable silences, assuming that as long as they are gathering information they are being effective. It is important to ensure that questions are not merely a 'random search for information that is of little value' (Egan 2002, p. 121) and that appropriate forms of questions are chosen from the variety available, according to the needs of the situation.

Practice example 9.2 will be used to illustrate various forms of questions and other microskills to follow in the text.

## Practice example 9.2

### John, a reluctant client

You are a counsellor in a child and family health team at the local community health centre. John has come to see you about marital difficulties. His wife, Helen, had made the appointment and from the outset it is obvious that he does not want to be there. His opening sentences clearly indicate his reluctance:

> Let me be quite frank, I'm only here because my wife has threatened to leave me if I don't speak to someone. Despite telling her otherwise, she thinks I have a problem. So it appears that I have no choice but to talk to you.

It may be tempting to launch into a series of questions that may elicit information regarding the 'problem', but that would be ill-advised before acknowledging John's reluctance to seek help and to be interviewed. A fairly informal empathic response will assist in beginning to build rapport with John, for example:

*Practitioner:*   It must be tough being forced to come here when you don't think you have a problem.

After validating his feelings about being forced to attend, I would explain to John that it is important that he recognize that he is able to exercise considerable choice. Just as he chose to keep the appointment, he could choose to use our time together for his benefit in whatever way he wishes to, or he could choose to merely be physically present to satisfy his wife's request that he attend.

The following is a discussion of various question formats. It is not intended as an illustration of a specific sequence of questions in an interview with John.

### Open questions
Open questions are said to facilitate conversations, as they require more than a single word response. Responses to the following opening words provide different types of information:

- *What*—will generally result in 'factual' information being provided ('What is the issue that your wife wants you to talk about?').
- *How*—will generally result in 'feeling' or 'process' information being provided ('How do you feel about being forced to come and see someone?').

- *Why*—will generally result in 'reasons' or 'explanations' being provided ('Why do you think your wife wanted you to talk to someone?'). Too many 'why' questions may be experienced as accusatory; therefore 'what' is preferable ('What's happening, as you see it?').
- *Could*—will generally result in a 'general picture' being provided ('Could you tell me a little bit about your relationship with your wife?').

## Closed questions

Closed questions elicit specific information in a brief format. Questions facilitating quick, often single word responses are appropriate at times, when particular information is sought that does not require elaboration. Closed questions generally begin with the following: 'do', 'did', 'is', 'are', 'does', or 'have', for example:

*Practitioner:*  Do you smoke marijuana each day?

Closed questions may also be effective in challenging the client to consider the consequences of their actions or plans, for example:

*Practitioner:*  Is that what you really want to happen?

However, closed questions should not be used excessively as they limit the respondent's ability to provide information about their experiences. They often lead the practitioner to continue asking a series of questions that may make the client feel as if they are being interrogated. Despite the above examples of sentence constructions, it should be noted that it is not necessarily the opening word that determines the type of question, whether it is open or closed, or the brevity of the response to it. For example:

*Practitioner:*  How often do you smoke marijuana?

may still get a single word response, for example:

*John:*  Daily.

whereas:

*Practitioner:*  Could you tell me about when and how often you smoke marijuana?

is likely to lead to a more detailed response.

## Circular questions

Circular questions elicit information about connections between the client and other people, 'highlighting how individuals relate to one another or to a particular problem' (Trevithick 2000, p. 90). They are particularly helpful when working in a family context, assisting family members to understand that the problem is connected to each of them and is not only a problem for just one of them (Collins et al. 1999). Circular questions also help individuals to realize the effect of their behaviour on other family members, for example:

> *Practitioner:*  How does it make you feel when you hear Helen making excuses to your daughter about you missing her concert?

Collins et al. (1999) offer a detailed discussion of other question types frequently used when working with families.

Excessive questioning, whether open or closed, can be experienced as threatening by the client, and can inhibit the interview process. Leading questions, in which suggestions are offered, limit the extent to which clients can express their thoughts and feelings, and should be avoided. They force the client to respond to the alternative(s) offered instead of exploring their own versions of issues or experiences, and may misrepresent the client's experience, for example:

> *Practitioner:*  Do you smoke marijuana to avoid dealing with your feelings?
> *John:*  No!

could be replaced by:

> *Practitioner:*  What do you see as the advantage in smoking marijuana?
> *John:*  I get so uptight and anxious going to all of these interviews, it just helps to make me feel more relaxed.

Similarly, overly complex questions in which multiple questions are embedded—particularly when each is closed and could be responded to by a mixture of affirmative and negative responses—are unhelpful, for example:

> *Practitioner:*  Although I try to make everyone feel welcome, many clients find the first interview somewhat threatening. Have you found it to be so? Would you like to make another appointment?

### Paraphrasing

Paraphrasing should never be mistaken for 'parrot-phrasing'. The intention is not to repeat exactly what the client has said but to capture the highlights and essence of what has been said, thereby demonstrating genuine active listening and understanding.

## Activity 9.8  Paraphrasing a client's comment

John has made the following statements:

*continued*

How many more interviews will I need to go to? It's always the same. They say I'm overqualified and there are thousands of others like me looking for work in it. But she doesn't get it . . . she won't get off my back, just keeps nagging and telling me I'm lazy and useless.

Provide a response that paraphrases what John has said.

## Reflection of feelings

Appropriate and accurate reflection of feelings is a key factor in effective interviewing, but skills to do so are perhaps the least likely to come naturally, and the most difficult to learn for many practitioners. The advantages in specifically training practitioners in this regard are highlighted by the results of studies in medical contexts in which the effectiveness of training in patient-centred interviewing was evaluated. The primary advantage between groups of medical residents who received specific training in patient-centred interviewing (which included reflection of feelings) and residents who did not, was their ability to reflect patients' emotions (Oh et al. 2001).

Cormier and Nurius (2003, p. 97) identify specific steps involved in reflecting clients' feelings, including:

- listening for the presence of feeling words in the client's messages (positive, negative, ambivalent),
- watching the non-verbal behaviour such as body posture, facial expression, and voice quality as indicators of client emotion,
- constructing an appropriate statement to reflect client feeling (for example, 'It appears that / it sounds like / it looks like you are angry now'),
- accurately representing the feelings expressed and not going beyond the intensity of the emotion expressed by the client (for example, angry or outraged would be inappropriate if the client had spoken of feeling irritated).

## Activity 9.9  Reflection of feelings

Consider John's statements in Activity 9.8. Identify the feelings that he seems to be expressing and devise a response that accurately reflects these feelings.

## Prompting, offering encouragers, and probing

Many clients experience difficulty in speaking about and exploring their issues of concern. Finding ways to encourage the client is a crucial skill for practitioners. Prompts can be both verbal and non-verbal and can signal to the client that you are attending and keen to hear more from them. These may be a simple nod or gesture, a slight forward lean towards the client, or a response such as 'I see', 'yes', or 'uh-huh'. However, too many of these minimal responses may be counterproductive if they appear to indicate that you are on automatic pilot and not attending (Egan 2002).

Probing questions, statements, or interjections (Egan, cited in Trevithick 2000) can be used to explore and clarify the client's perspective or to assist in focusing the client on particular aspects of the story or issue being discussed, or perhaps being avoided. Trevithick (2000) reminds the practitioner to be cautious in their use of probes so as not to increase the client's defensiveness.

### Summarizing

When clients have spoken for a while, referred to several issues, or expressed various feelings or thoughts, it is helpful for the practitioner to summarize key points or themes that have emerged (Cormier & Nurius 2003) and identify significant highlights that have been shared. Accurate summarizing promotes confidence in practitioners by demonstrating their attentiveness, and facilitates the working alliance between client and practitioner. It assists the client to become aware of issues that may be common to several situations, and to focus on the issues whose further exploration would benefit the client. It may also be used to 'moderate the pace' (of the interview) or interrupt a client who is speaking in a rambling or unfocused manner, helping to bring 'direction to the interview' (Cormier & Nurius 2003, p. 101). Despite its many benefits, summarizing skills do not necessarily need to be used in all interviews and should be used discerningly (Shulman 1999).

### Activity 9.10  Summarizing a client's comment

John has spoken for some time and finishes with the following comment:

A lot of people think smoking marijuana is preferable to drinking alcohol—at least you don't have a hangover. There's no point in taking the moral high ground, going on about the fact that it's illegal. Helen's a bit of a hypocrite. She can wipe herself out and feel too sick to play with Jodie the next morning but that doesn't seem to be a problem. But if I've been smoking and don't want to surf the Internet for jobs she goes off her head.

Provide a summarizing response to this comment.

### Use of silence

Silence in interviews causes concern and discomfort for many practitioners as well as their clients (Trevithick 2000). It is at times difficult for practitioners to interpret its cause (and meaning for the client) and they fear that they may have been inappropriate in their response. Shulman (1999, p. 153) suggests an appropriate strategy in many cases is to offer encouragement to the client to discuss their feelings and thoughts by saying, 'You've grown quiet in the last few moments. What are you thinking about?' However, frequently, the best strategy is to allow the client to remain silent (for a reasonable length of time), giving them the opportunity to collect their thoughts, or really experience feelings that may be new or previously resisted. In the view of Shulman (1999, p. 152), the client may be silent because they are:

- dealing with emotions that have surfaced,
- reflecting on the implications of the conversation preceding the silence,
- experiencing uncertainty about exploring difficult issues.

Whatever the reason, resisting the temptation to quickly fill the silence demonstrates respect and sensitivity, and the client will feel supported by the worker (Thompson 2002). Sometimes clients remain silent as a way 'of letting the practitioner know their previous response was inaccurate or misrepresented their perspective or experience' (Shulman 1999, p. 152). The client's body language will generally provide clues if this is the case. If the client is silent and not making eye contact, perhaps looking down or having their head and eyes slightly tilted up, we can generally infer that they are processing thoughts, feelings, or responses and should be given space to do so. However, if they are silent and looking directly at you, irrespective of the manner in which their face is composed (relaxed, irritated, surly, and so on), they are letting you know the ball is in your court and are waiting for a question or response.

## Activity 9.11  Dealing with silence

Consider social situations you have been in recently where you or others present had difficulty making conversation.

1. How did everyone react to the silences?
2. What feelings did you experience?
3. How would this experience relate to working with clients who are having difficulty speaking?

## Self-disclosure

The appropriateness of self-disclosure is determined not only by its content but also to whom it is given and in what context. Speaking in detail about one's romantic or sexual experiences may be perfectly fine with a group of friends in a private location but will more than likely be inappropriate with one's service manager in the office or one's client. Determining what aspects of personal experience to disclose to clients is difficult for many practitioners. I have always been helped by pausing to consider my motives before self-disclosing. Clarifying the benefit for the client—for example, modelling that it is safe in this environment to speak about particular issues, or demonstrating an understanding of the client's issues by speaking of shared experiences (not uncommon in drug- and alcohol-related work) is generally appropriate. Responding to a client's curiosity about my personal situation, however, is rarely appropriate. Although clients are often curious about the practitioner's personal life, they may feel threatened by the practitioner's self-disclosure if it refers to having experienced similar difficulties and perhaps implies that they should also be able to deal with things, in the way the practitioner had. Self-disclosure therefore needs to be selective, timely, and infrequent. Egan (2002, p. 208) suggests mentioning it in the opening stages of the professional relationship, perhaps saying 'From time to time, I might share with you some of my own life experiences if I think they might help.'

See chapter 4, 'The Practitioner's Use of Self in the Professional Relationship', for further discussion of self-disclosure.

## Activity 9.12  Discomfort with self-disclosure

Consider a situation in which you felt uncomfortable when someone disclosed personal information.

1. What was the reason for your discomfort: what was being said, the people present, or the location in which the disclosure took place?
2. What was your response?
3. In reviewing this experience, what have you learnt about self-disclosure that would be applicable to working with clients?

## Ending the interview

Appropriately bringing an interview to a close involves creating opportunity for reflecting on the interview, considering both the content covered and the processes engaged in. Where relevant, it may also involve the setting of tasks for homework and the consideration of goals for the next interview. It is the time when the client (if present on a voluntary basis) considers if she is benefiting from the time with the practitioner and agrees, or not, to make another appointment. If the interview is the final one and therefore the termination of the professional relationship, it should involve a review of the work done overall, changes achieved over time, and drawing together the learning that has taken place. A discussion of feelings about the termination of the relationship and strategies for managing without the professional support should also be facilitated. The ending process should never be trivial-ized as clients may have quite strong feelings about the end of the professional relationship, particularly if the client has experienced major losses (Dillon 2003) or is dealing with issues of abandonment. An abrupt or insensitive ending may undo the work that has been done and increase the likelihood that further professional assistance will be required.

## Questions for Review

1. What are the purposes of conducting interviews?

2. What is your working definition of empathy? How does the expression of empathy facilitate the interview process?
3. What are some empathy blockers? Why do you think these would impede the interview process?
4. What does the SOLER model stand for?
5. What are reflecting behaviours?

## Activity Answers

### Activity 9.2

Trevithick (2000, p. 188) includes the following items as a memory aid: book the interview room, if necessary; refer to records; send for information, leaflets, and so on that may be needed; make or plan phone calls to liaise with other agencies if necessary; inform others in the workplace (for example, receptionist) if you do not wish to be disturbed while conducting the interview; prepare the interview room; consider any special client needs; consider what notes or records you need to take with you to the interview.

### Activity 9.5

The following list of inappropriate behaviours draws on the work of Egan (2002), Evans et al. (2004), and Townshend (cited in Seden 1999, p. 28): daydreaming, mind reading, interrupting, rehearsing, poor listening, contradicting, advice giving, appearing bored, joking to side-step difficult emotions, filtered listening, and evaluative listening.

## References

Collins, D., Jordan, C., & Coleman, H. (1999). *An Introduction to Family Social Work*. Itasca, IL: Peacock.

Cormier, S., & Nurius, P.S. (2003). *Interviewing and Change Strategies for Helpers*. Pacific Grove, CA: Thomson Brooks/Cole.

Dillon, C. (2003). *Learning from Mistakes in Clinical Practice*. Pacific Grove, CA: Brooks/Cole Thomson Learning.

Egan, G. (2002). *The Skilled Helper* (7th edn). Pacific Grove, CA: Brooks/Cole.

Evans, D.R., Hearn, M.T., Uhleman, M.R., & Ivey, A.E. (2004). *Essential Interviewing: A Programmed Approach to Effective Communication* (6th edn). Toronto: Thomson Brooks/Cole.

Gabb, D. (2000). Development of transcultural mental health education by the Victorian Transcultural Psychiatry Unit. *Synergy*, Summer, 5–30.

Hartel, C.E.J., & Trumble, R.B. (1995). IDADA: The individual difference approach to cultural-awareness. Paper presented at the Inaugural Industrial and Organisational Psychology Conference, Sydney.

Ivey, A.E., & Bradford Ivey, M. (2003). *Intentional Interviewing and Counseling: Facilitating Client Development in a Multicultural Society* (5th edn). Pacific Grove, CA: Thomson Brooks/Cole.

Ivey, A.E., Rathman, D., & Colbert, R.D. (2000). Culturally-relevant microcounselling: Australian Aborigines and the Eurocentric tradition.

*Australian Journal of Counselling Psychology*, 2(1), 14–21.

Kadushin, A. (1990). *The Social Work Interview* (3rd edn). New York: Columbia University Press.

Lishman, J. (1994). *Communication in Social Work*. Basingstoke: Macmillan/BASW.

McKenzie, B., & Morrissette, V. (2003). Social work practice with Canadians of Aboriginal background: Guidelines for respectful social work. In A. Al-Krenawi and J.R. Graham (eds.) *Multicultural social work in Canada: Working with diverse ethno-racial communities*, 251–82. Don Mills, ON: Oxford University Press.

Nguyen, T., & Bowles, R. (1998). Counselling Vietnamese refugee survivors of trauma: Points of entry for developing trust and rapport. *Australian Social Work*, 51(2), 41–7.

Oh, J., Segal, R., Gordon, J., Boal, J., & Jotkowitz, A. (2001). Retention and use of patient-centred interviewing skills after intensive training. *Academic Medicine*, 76(6), 647–50.

Rowland, A., & McDonald, L. (2009). Evaluation of social work communication skills to allow people with aphasia to be part of the decision making process in healthcare. *Social Work Education*, 28, 128–44.

Seden, J. (1999). *Counselling Skills in Social Work Practice*. Philadelphia, PA: Open University Press.

Shulman, L. (1999). *The Skills of Helping Individuals, Families, Groups, and Communities* (4th edn). Itasca, IL: Peacock.

Thompson, N. (2002). *People Skills* (2nd edn). Hampshire: Palgrave Macmillan.

Trevithick, P. (2000). *Social Work Skills: A Practice Handbook*. Buckingham, PA: Open University Press.

Vicary, D., & Andrews, H. (2000). Developing a culturally appropriate psychotherapeutic approach with Indigenous Australians. *Australian Psychologist*, 35(3), 181–5.

Webb, N.B. (2003). *Social Work Practice with Children*. New York: Guilford Press.

Wilson, C., & Powell, M. (2001). *A Guide to Interviewing Children: Essential Skills for Counsellors, Police, Lawyers and Social Workers*. Sydney: Allen & Unwin.

# 10

# Conducting Assessment: Some General Guidelines

## Zita Weber

Many words have been devoted to the subject of assessment over the years. Assessment is said to be the cornerstone of professional activity across different contexts. Whatever the practice context, assessment of the situation by the practitioner is the foundation of decision-making and planning for future action. Assessment may be an end in itself or it may be the first part of a process that aims to achieve specified outcomes. This chapter covers assessment in direct practice as the starting point from which further understanding regarding the diverse activities that are subsumed under the assessment banner may be gained. Chapter 7, 'Risk Assessment: Working Within a Legal Framework', and chapter 16, 'Asset-based Community Development: Recognizing and Building on Community Strengths', also address assessment issues.

Much of what has previously been written on assessment may be seen as prescriptive in nature, in the form of directives, guidelines, and specific 'know-how', yet paradoxically, lacking the ability to capture the interaction between people meeting for the purpose of assessment and, indeed, the interaction between people within their contexts. There is now an understanding that the qualitative human attributes of identity, autonomy, and competence within the framework of a lived experience and the interplay of personal and structural factors work to create complexities in defining 'assessment' (Milner & O'Bryne 2002; Ellis 1993; Cowger 1992).

Nevertheless, it is important to acknowledge that without the foundation stones of the now seemingly simplistic perspectives on assessment, we would not have had the luxury to progressively build more complex and sophisticated perspectives on the process of assessment. As Fook (2002) points out, the context of the historical period is crucial in our understanding of a particular perspective, and influences how we might assess any practice.

## Through a historical lens

By adopting an historical lens, it would be unreasonable to label Mary Richmond's important contribution to social work assessment, or what she called 'social diagnosis', as naïve. 'Social diagnosis', a term derived from the medical industry, was used by Mary Richmond (1917) and other early social workers (Hollis 1972; Friedlander 1958) to describe assessment. Within the context of the times, Mary Richmond's early work was revolutionary and provided a starting point for the development of the process of assessment in practice. Over the years, subtle and dramatic shifts in emphasis have occurred (Seden 1999), primarily from a focus on the individual only, to the wider social context and the interplay between the person and his environment. More recently, there has been a challenge to the once strongly held practice of 'one of us will talk, the other will listen' (Konrad 1987), favouring instead one in which the professional enters into a dialogue with the client and together they co-construct a more helpful account of the narrative presented as problematic (Milner & O'Byrne 2002). According to Fook (2002, p. 120), such an approach also creates a relationship in which 'the worker needs to "own" (that is, locate him- or herself reflexively in relation to) the narrative which is created jointly between worker and service user'. Parton and O'Byrne (2000) go further by suggesting that assessment presupposes reflexivity and action, and that professionals need to become aware of the socially-constructed nature of social work itself.

For the critical practitioner, it is important to maintain a sense of balance and a respect for historical developments, while also questioning and challenging previous and current ways of 'doing assessment'. Earlier preoccupations with individual assessment, borrowing heavily from the medical models of psychiatry and psychology, have been replaced by approaches that balance internal and external elements, give more emphasis to strengths rather than deficits, and acknowledge the client as the 'expert' of him- or herself (Cowger 1992; Sullivan 1992). Current assessment practice covers individuals, families, groups, and communities (the last in chapter 16, 'Asset-based Community Development: Recognizing and Building on Community Strengths') along dimensions such as assets, needs, resources, and risk (in chapter 7, 'Risk Assessment: Working Within a Legal Framework'), and is conducted by practitioners working alone, jointly, in group or a team, or across disciplines (Trevithick 2000).

Critical practice emphasizes collaboration with clients, open-mindedness, and uncertainty, which allow for dialogue to take place. By adopting this position, the practitioner accepts that assessment is not the 'truth', but rather, as Milner and O'Byrne (2002) posit, a process whereby worker and client build an understanding of the problematic scenario and thereby help identify difficulties and mobilize people's strengths. Nevertheless, practitioners, while not searching for 'the truth', need to be clear about what it is they are doing. Everitt et al. (1992, p. 33) point out, 'It needs to be stated that clarity is not the same as certainty. Certainty in theory leads to dogma and blinkered practices. Clarity opens it up for scrutiny.'

## Conceptualizing assessment

If you pick up and read any book that covers assessment, you will find there is general agreement that assessment involves the formulation of professional judgments, opinions, and interpretations regarding a particular situation. Underpinning everything you might read about assessment is the assumption that the process calls for an understanding of theories and values that inform that professional opinion.

By reflecting on our own narratives of 'being assessed', we place ourselves in a strengthened position to understand how others might perceive the process. Did we experience the person assessing us as being open-minded, flexible, and willing to hear our story? Or was our experience one in which we felt that the other person was sitting in judgment of us, having already made up her mind and operating from a set of stereotypes and prejudices? Did the assessment meet our needs? Was it a positive experience in terms of the outcome?

## Activity 10.1  Being assessed

Most of us have had some experience of being 'assessed' for something at some time. Based on your personal experience:

1. In twenty-five words or less complete the sentence beginning with 'Assessment is . . . .'.

2. Reflect on your own experiences of assessment, in whatever context you believe you have been 'assessed'. What was the context? What thoughts and feelings were raised in the situation for you? What was the outcome?

It would be erroneous to view the assessment process as a necessarily discrete, finite one: no assessment should be set in stone. The practitioner should be mindful of possible new developments and be prepared to incorporate these into the fabric of the original assessment, and generally approach assessment as an ongoing process.

# Assessment in the contemporary context

Assessment has always been a challenging task. It is generally agreed that assessment is the first phase of a process that involves the formulation of professional judgments, opinions, and interpretations regarding a particular situation (O'Connor et al. 2003; Fook 2002; Milner & O'Bryne 2002; Compton & Galaway 1994; Hepworth & Larsen 1993). For the critical practitioner working in the contemporary context, procedural manuals, extensive intake forms, and a series of checklists are often imposed to assist in conducting assessments (Milner & O'Bryne 2002; Seden 1999). However, as Seden (1999) points out, the situations in which people find themselves are invariably more complicated than manuals might imply. Milner and O'Bryne (2002) alert us to the dangers of shaping information to fit favoured theories, concentrating on risks rather than needs, and guarding against assessment taking on the status of 'truth'. In an era replete with guidelines and templates, the critical practitioner needs to remain flexible and take a holistic approach to the task of assessment.

Such a flexible approach to assessment turns on the acceptance that assessment presupposes an understanding of the knowledge, values, and broader theoretical position that might inform that professional opinion. This is echoed in the stance of Everitt et al. (1992, p. 4), who stress the value of the spirit of enquiry, and the need to make assumptions explicit, to think through theoretical perspectives, and to engage with and listen to people's worlds while remaining conscious 'of the pervasiveness of ideology in the way we see the world'.

For critical practitioners, reflection on and awareness of their set of ideas about the world, or their world view, is an essential part of practice. When working with people from diverse backgrounds, what are our ideas about human nature, culture, human activity, and relational orientation of different groups of people? What are their ideas? For instance, when assessing clients from a cultural background in which beliefs regarding spiritualism and magic are strong, the critical practitioner would need to understand how such beliefs affect the client's life and the perceptions of what might be helpful.

When I was working in the US, I became aware that many Hispanic people believe that mental problems may be the result of witchcraft (hex) or bad spirits. Martinez (1986) found that many clients also believe that mental health problems may be resolved with the assistance of traditional helpers (espiritistas or curanderos) in conjunction with the expertise of mental health professionals. In such a case, the practitioner's ability to explore, understand, and accept the client's magical or spiritual explanatory model of life and mental health problems is crucial. In assessing the situation, the practitioner needs to work outside an exclusively Western world view and incorporate other ways of seeing. In the words of Martinez (1986, p. 80), practitioners must be 'prepared to function within both systems' in order to justly assess the narrative account presented by a client who has beliefs different from their own.

Research by Ibrahim and Kahn (1987), Pedersen (2000) and Sue and Sue (2003) has linked earlier findings by Kluckhorn and Strodtbeck (1961) on categories for viewing culture in promoting cultural competence and sensitivity for practitioners when assessing people from diverse backgrounds. Kluckhohn and Strodtbeck (1961) summarized five primary areas for viewing culture:

1. how people view human nature (bad, good, or bad and good)
2. the relation of people to nature (in control of, subjugated to, or having respect for and living in harmony with)
3. the temporal or time orientation of the cultural group (past, present, future, or a combination of these perspectives)
4. what people believe about human activity (doing, being, or being-in-becoming)
5. the relational orientation of people to other people (lineal, collateral, or individualistic)

## Activity 10.2  Your world view and how it affects your assessment

Reflect on Kluckhohn and Strodtbeck's five primary areas for viewing culture and nominate your preferred view in each category. How might your particular way of viewing the world affect your assessment activity?

# Towards a framework for assessment

Over the years, many frameworks for assessment have been proposed, including the systems ideas of Pincus and Minahan (1973), who suggested that in any assessment there was a change agent system, a client system, a target system, and an action system. Vickery (1976) asked: What are the problems in this situation? Who are the clients? What are the goals? Who has to be changed or influenced? What are the tasks and roles of the social worker? Forder (1976) took the systems thinking further, and posited that each system and each person needs to be analyzed in terms of (1) information, values, and knowledge; (2) resources, including skills and coping; (3) goals; (4) power; (5) communication within and between them; (6) external systems that interact with them; (7) the stage of development (life cycle); and (8) morale. These earlier frameworks gave rise to a person–environment or ecosystemic approach to assessment. An ecosystemic approach involves understanding the 'interrelated, complex reality in people's lives' (Meyer 1983, p. 30). This approach is said to open up many possibilities for intervention on the micro, mezzo, exo, and macro levels for both practitioners working in direct practice and those committed to social planning and policy making.

Systems frameworks have had an enduring influence on practice, possibly due to the assumption that systems thinking focuses on interactions between individuals and systems, and thereby does not pathologize individuals, and the recognition that such thinking values the social context, including the contribution of formal and informal social systems. Another model that is useful for assessment is the application of a solution-focused approach. Rather than focusing upon past events, this model frames the conversation toward a description of how the situation will be different when the 'problem' is solved. Assessment within this model directs the worker towards an understanding of how the client will perceive her situation after engaging in a counselling or helping process.

- What would it take for the client to feel as if she were making progress towards her goals?
- What would it look like if the client were moving towards her goals?
- What is a beginning step the client can take towards getting where she wants?
- Are there times when the client has been happier, freer, and more successful at juggling life's challenges than she is now—how did she do this?

In the 1990s, anti-oppressive or radical social work theorists put forward the importance of considering in our assessment the issues related to race, gender, disability, and social and sexual orientation (Thompson 1997). The core themes of this approach articulate that:

1. the origins of the problems faced by clients lie in social structures,
2. social workers should understand the multiple forms of oppression faced by service users,
3. the personal is the political (that is, how one experiences problems in one's life is a reflection of how that particular social category is understood in the environment),
4. the role of the social worker is a political one.

Fook (1993, p. 7) states, 'A radical perspective in social work first and foremost assumes an analysis which constantly links the causes of personal and social problems to problems in the socio-economic structure, rather than the inadequacies inherent in individual people or in socially disadvantaged minority groups.' She suggests that there is an interplay between personal and structural elements and that the practitioner should understand social control and social-labelling processes.

An anti-oppressive or radical framework encourages practitioners to understand the structural context of their assessment practice, and is empowering in that it works towards enabling people to gain more control of their lives through addressing potential obstacles such as barriers to participation and lack of confidence or skills. Such a framework emphasizes working in partnership, which involves valuing the client, reflecting on your own biography (and the shaping of identities within society), conducting open and clear communication, and encouraging shared decision-making. The appeal of this framework for assessment practice is that it makes social structures visible and seeks to enlist the client as a collaborator in change, rather than the subject of change. Friere's concept of 'praxis' is also relevant here as it focuses on working with clients to raise their personal consciousness with respect to issues of class and power, and how these may impact upon their personal situations.

The 1990s also gave rise to another view: the strengths perspective. However, as far back as 1958, Friedlander (p. 221) suggested, 'Ordinarily, the social worker would not focus on the pathology or the weaknesses in the situation but rather would attempt to identify the strengths or positive factors that can be brought to bear in helping the client or community in the problem-solving or developmental process.' Perlman's (1957) casework model also emphasized client motivation and capacity. Maluccio (1979, p. 401), based on his research findings, argued for a shift from 'problems or pathology to strengths, resources, and potentialities in human beings and their environments'. However, as Cowger (1992) points out, there was, for many years, an incongruity between this theoretical perspective and daily practice. Even more fundamentally, Saleebey (1996, p. 297) suggests that a strengths-based practice 'based on ideas of resilience, rebound, possibility and transformation is difficult because, oddly enough, it is not natural to the world of helping and service.'

The danger of using a deficit model of practice is that it may lead to self-fulfilling prophecies, related to clients' self-doubts and the practitioner ascribing blame, and possibly to the practitioner assessing that the client should receive services longer than is necessary. Hepworth and Larsen (1993, p. 194) maintain that social workers appear to focus on weaknesses 'despite the time-honored social work platitude that social workers work with strengths, not weaknesses'. The strengths perspective asks that practitioners reorient their focus from a deficit model to an assets model. Strom-Gottfried (1999, p. 66) summarizes this reorientation by stating, 'Because much of our work with clients is focused on the particular difficulties they are having, it is easy to dwell on their shortcomings and problems and overlook the "assets" at play in their lives.' Such strengths can include personal strengths, abilities, and accomplishments, and material resources and social support networks. Questions that might be asked include: How has the client coped before? What have been the consequences of previous coping? What is the client's perspective of his capacity? What does the client see as constraining and perpetuating his situation? What resources might mitigate the problem? Can the client develop an inventory of the resources available to him as well as those he perceives as not being available? What is the client's working knowledge of his strengths in relation to the impinging stress from the client's environment?

The strengths perspective makes explicit that strengths are fundamental to the value stance of the helping professions. According to Cowger (1992, p. 141), 'It provides for a leveling of the power social workers have over clients and in so doing presents increased potential for the facilitation of a partnership in the working relationship. Focusing on strengths in assessment has the potential for liberating clients from stigmatizing diagnostic classifications that reinforce "sickness" in family and community environments.' Some practice principles that emerge from the strengths perspective include:

1. collaboration with clients by respecting their views and challenging a deficit or pathological orientation,
2. focusing on assets by doing an assets audit and aiming to understand what skills and capacities clients have to achieve their goals,
3. challenging pathologizing language and a deficits orientation—for instance, the person is living with schizophrenia, and is not a 'schizophrenic',
4. focusing on empowerment and finding practical ways that clients might achieve their goals,
5. promoting resilience by affirming and supporting clients' goals and achievements,
6. identifying strengths that can be used as resources.

# Reflecting on two theoretical frameworks: anti-oppressive and strengths

If we assume that what you see depends on where you look and our assessment reflects our perspective as assessor, then critical practitioners are challenged to critically reflect on their perspectives—and the possible alternatives—and be broad in their approach rather than being 'shaped by what we think we can do' (Siporin 1975, p. 244) in practice or, indeed, 'shaping' information to fit a favourite theoretical perspective.

Developing precision and clarity in our professional role as assessors works towards enhancing our understanding of the concepts and theories we use and alerts us to the need to be continually sensitive to the 'disconfirming' information (Sheppard 1995) that confronts us and refuses to be categorized tidily into our favoured theoretical framework.

Practice example 10.1 allows you to reflect on two theoretical approaches: anti-oppressive and strengths, and to understand the ways in which theory might affect your assessment.

## Practice example 10.1

## Putting theory into action in assessment

You are working in a non-profit family support agency and the child protection worker has referred a family to you for assessment and family work. The family comprises a twenty-three-year-old

*continued*

mother, Julie, a twenty-seven-year-old father, Brendan, and an eight-month-old baby, Cherie. Both parents have an unstable family history and neither has frequent contact with their family-of-origin members. They have been together for two years and their relationship has been turbulent, with one report of domestic violence. They met in a drug rehabilitation program. Julie, who has a history of self-harming behaviour, was a sex trade worker from the age of sixteen until she discovered she was pregnant. Brendan has had many jobs, usually unskilled, temporary labour jobs, but has not remained in a job for more than a few months. They are currently receiving income assistance and Brendan is attending a basic computer skills training course. Julie is on a regime of Serepax administered by the drug and alcohol clinic where she collects her methadone daily. She used Serepax during her pregnancy. Brendan drinks heavily and uses marijuana 'to relax'. Julie has one 'good friend', a woman who is older than her and for whom she worked in an escort service about five years ago. This woman is supportive and sometimes babysits Cherie. In addition, Julie occasionally speaks with her younger sister but has no desire to re-establish contact with any other family members. Brendan has some friends he drinks with at the bar and he sees his father about once a year. Brendan has two other children, a boy aged six and a girl aged four, from a previous relationship. The children live with their mother and Brendan sees them a few times a year for birthdays and Christmas. He could exercise his right to see them more frequently, but at this stage, has no desire to increase his contact with them. They live in a public housing complex.

## Questions for reflection

1. From an anti-oppressive perspective, what are the most significant elements in this case?
2. From a strengths perspective, what are the most significant elements in this case?
3. What needs or vulnerabilities have you or others identified?
4. What strengths or assets have you or others identified?
5. How would you apply an anti-oppressive perspective in this case?
6. How would you apply a strengths perspective in this case?
7. What are the benefits of applying an anti-oppressive perspective in this case?
8. What are the benefits of applying a strengths perspective in this case?
9. What are the limitations of an anti-oppressive perspective in this case?
10. What are the limitations of a strengths perspective in this case?
11. How is your assessment the same or different when applying the two theoretical perspectives?

Working within any framework will still necessitate moving through various stages to achieve an assessment outcome. The literature, both early and contemporary, provides various stage models as well as frameworks for questioning during the assessment activity. For instance, Hepworth and Larsen (1993, pp. 228–9) have devised a comprehensive set of questions to be answered in assessment. Their questions include: What are the indications or manifestations of the problem(s)? What persons and systems are implicated in the problem(s)? How do the participants and/or systems interact to produce and maintain the problem(s)? What meanings do clients ascribe to the problem(s)? What is the frequency of the problematic behaviours? What unmet needs and/or wants are involved in the problem(s)? What are the skills and strengths of the clients? What external resources are needed by clients? These are just eight of their eighteen questions.

## Activity 10.3  Questions for eliciting information

Devise a set of questions that you would use when conducting an assessment of a situation in which a sixteen-year-old girl, who is a good student, has recently begun missing school. What sort of questions would enable you to discover information about this girl and her current behaviour?

One stage model of assessment that uses a research orientation and refers to information as data has been proposed by Milner and O'Bryne (2002). They suggest that there are five stages of assessment: (1) preparation, (2) data collection, (3) weighing the data, (4) analyzing the data, and (5) utilizing the analysis. An adapted version of the stage model of Milner and O'Bryne (2002, p. 61) appears below.

# Stages of assessment

## 1. Preparation

- Make a list of all key informants—for example, people, agencies, documents.
- Prepare a plan for collecting data from all key informants—adapt agency checklists for this purpose. Ensure that appropriate consents to release/receive information are completed.
- Make a list of questions to which answers are needed.
- Make a note of early hypotheses or tentative explanations.

## 2. Data collection

- Check verbal data for authenticity by repeating and summarizing. Provide all key informants with copies of summaries for further checking.
- Check all written data for factual accuracy and highlight any unsubstantiated opinion clearly.

- Consider widening your data sources if there are gaps or concerns about accuracy of information.
- All data at this stage is worthy of consideration but note any obvious inconsistencies or incongruities.

## 3. Weighing the data

- Consider the situation and how well the client is functioning in the circumstances.
- Identify and list any recurrent themes or patterns that emerge.
- Rank themes in order of priority.
- Identify any gaps in the data.
- List any people to be consulted, including those who will help with reflexivity.

## 4. Analyzing the data

- Identify theoretical perspectives, using them to gain depth of analysis and being mindful of their implications in practice.
- Develop more than one hypothesis or tentative explanation, particularly around what the intervention strategies might be.
- Test the explanations for possible theoretical bias and for language that might have created a certain 'fit' with a particular theoretical orientation.
- Check out explanations with key informants.
- Consult with others for 'reflexive' purposes and to guard against selective use of information.
- Develop possible further explanations and ways in which they might be tested.

## 5. Utilizing the analysis

- Determine what help is needed by the client.
- List all outcomes expected to be achieved and the consequences that might be avoided.
- Prepare recommendations for an intervention plan.
- Prepare a draft report that reflects the sources of information, analysis, and professional judgment.
- Obtain feedback on the report and revise it if necessary.

In any assessment, critical practitioners must be mindful of the framework they have adopted to guide them in their questioning and through the various stages of the assessment process. They also must be mindful of agency requirements regarding the use of set questions and ordering of information, confident enough to challenge the utility of these, and flexible enough to include other relevant information, pursue appropriate questioning, and complement the information required on intake documents. Assessment is more than a technical exercise; from the outset, the practitioner's self-awareness regarding this important activity must be heightened. At all times, the practitioner should strive to adopt a flexible position in which they potentially can accept, reject, or challenge information received and be prepared to be self-confronting in their task. By adopting such a position, the critical practitioner minimizes the danger of closed-mindedness and reinforces the words of Goldberg (1974, p. 150): 'Definition of a problem is a potent force in determining action to alleviate it, for the way in which a problem is formulated places constraints on the range of alternatives from which a solution can be drawn.' Positively reframing Goldberg's comment would lead us to say that self-awareness regarding our values and knowledge of theoretical perspectives, from the outset, heightens our understanding of what clients bring to us and allow us more opportunities to 'define' problems in more than one way.

# Key elements in assessment activity

Maximizing the number of sources from which information is derived and checking the degree of congruency between those sources is a key element in assessment. For instance, it is not only good practice to conduct an interview, but also to consult with practitioners previously involved, as well as to read all available records and reports when doing an assessment. It is important to know who the referring source is and the reason for the referral for assessment. It might also be useful to know how the presenting problematic situation previously has been handled and any other agencies involved.

At the very minimum, assessment involves:

- using professional and political skills to facilitate the process of assessment,
- gathering information from as many sources as possible,
- defining the problematic situation,
- making links between the individual's world and the larger structural forces,
- an exchange of ideas between you and the client, working in partnership,
- taking a short-term and long-term perspective,
- thinking through all available options,
- helping to mobilize the mutually-accepted option,
- developing answers to specific questions.

Often practitioners must act on the basis of incomplete information as they do not always have the luxury of postponing the assessment and the recommendations until a later time. Understanding and accepting that you can only work with what you have, yet knowing that should further information come to light, you need to incorporate it, makes for a flexible approach to practice. Yet, the reality is that assessment is usually a one-off event with little opportunity for re-evaluation. As such, it is vital that practitioners take the time to do a thorough assessment.

When conducting assessments, it is important to keep in mind the notion that it involves applying generalized knowledge to a particular situation and the necessity to arrive at a clear statement based on accountability of values and the offering of a professional opinion.

# Reflections on theory

Assessments are influenced by the theoretical perspective of the person doing the assessment; practitioners using a feminist perspective would conduct assessments differently from those informed by psychodynamic theory. The danger for practitioners of adhering to their world view (including theoretical orientation) to the exclusion of that of clients and the narratives they unfold is illustrated in Ellis's (1993) study of assessment. She observed assessors and disabled clients during assessments and found that some social workers made assessments based on their theoretical positions rather than on the clients' needs. These practitioners were assessing not in relation to how the clients perceived their situation, but rather were imposing their own theoretical explanations and practice techniques. For example, some practitioners perceived physical impairment in terms of loss and bereavement with people who had become disabled being thought of as going through a grieving process. Sight loss, in one case, had radically changed the life of an older woman, who previously had pursued an active life. She now lacked the self-confidence to go out. Depressed by her situation and afraid her sight would further deteriorate, she lost weight and consequently her clothes no longer fitted, which compounded her isolation as she felt embarrassed and did not want friends to see her. The social worker, using a hierarchy of losses paradigm, theorized that the traumatic loss of a parent was the most fundamental one and that the loss of sight had become the focus for other losses but was the least significant loss. A colleague, a rehabilitation worker, not using the same theory, decided that mobility training would be helpful in developing the woman's confidence, and believed that the main issue related to lack of social contact. It seems the social worker believed the woman was 'emotionally housebound' and to be more capable than she claimed, doubting the usefulness of mobility training. In the end what this client found most helpful was someone taking her out occasionally—for instance, assisting her to go shopping. This difference in what is considered most needed or helpful prompted Hanvey and Philpot (1994, p. 6) to comment when referring to the client in this case that, 'She, too, had not read the right books on social work theory!'

Similarly, Sheldon (1995) found that social workers were guided in their assessments by interviewing techniques, which then served to 'shape' the assessment information to fit a favoured theoretical model. In another study, Scott (1998) found that social workers' reasoning was not supported by exploration or the development of hypotheses, but rather the tendency to seek confirming information rather than disconfirming information in the assessment process. The danger, then, is the temptation for practitioners to become fixed in their assumptions and ideas and to try to make the facts fit them, rather than the other way around. Critical practitioners must learn when and how to alter initial assumptions as an essential part of practice.

Assessment should be a joint activity between the practitioner and the client. The end product, the assessment plan, should be mutually agreed upon. Only if assessment is open and shared can the client feel that she shares in the ownership of the process and that the practitioner is not harbouring a secret assessment agenda.

In Practice example 10.2, you can bring together your understanding of the assessment process and reflect upon questions that might challenge that process and practice points that guide your activity.

## Practice example 10.2

### Jane's story

You are a social worker based in the emergency department of a hospital in a major capital city. It is your responsibility to assess people who present with possible mental health issues and to facilitate follow-up when they are discharged from the hospital.

Jane is referred for an assessment after she is escorted by the police to the emergency department following an argument with her current boyfriend. Both Jane and her boyfriend were intoxicated at the time of the argument and neighbours contacted the police. Jane expressed suicidal ideation in the presence of the police.

Jane is a thirty-two-year-old woman who works as a check-out clerk in one of the local supermarkets. She is estranged from her family of origin. Jane's parents and one brother live in a rural area, approximately 200 kilometres away. She describes herself as always having been the 'black sheep' of the family. At the age of sixteen years, Jane became pregnant and had a daughter. Neither Jane nor her daughter has contact with the biological father. Jane's daughter is now fifteen years of age and Jane reports an overall good relationship with her. Jane states that her daughter and her job are the two positive aspects of her life. Jane's daughter was not at home at the time of the argument with her boyfriend. Jane reports a history of traumatic relationships, including a common-law marriage of five years in which she was a survivor of verbal abuse and physical assault on a regular basis. Assault by her ex-partner resulting in Jane requiring a two-day hospital admission instigated her separation from him twelve months ago.

Jane currently resides in a two-bedroom unit with her daughter and boyfriend of six months. Jane states that she often feels 'worried', especially about finances, so she smokes cigarettes and marijuana to 'calm down'. Jane reports past alcohol abuse but denies this currently.

At the time of assessment, Jane presents as slightly agitated and restricted in responses to questions. She is minimizing the circumstances that prompted her presentation to the hospital.

### Questions for reflection

1. What are the issues for Jane from both a personal and political perspective?
2. What may be some of the strengths and difficulties affecting Jane?
3. Identify possible supports that are available to Jane.
4. What would be important considerations in developing a plan with Jane following an assessment?
5. What theoretical perspective are you using?

## Practice points 10.1

- The personal history of Jane, including estrangement from her family of origin and her negative experiences in relationships, may influence her ability to engage in an open and trusting relationship where she is required to self-disclose. The assessment process may require an emphasis on engagement and building a therapeutic alliance in order to gather information from Jane and be able to determine her suicide risk status.

- Political influences affecting Jane may include her identity as a female and single mother, experiences of domestic violence, potential diagnosis of a mental disorder or illness, and contact with the police. These influences may have a significant impact on her self-perception and subsequently on how she is able to access and negotiate resources. Exploring strengths and resiliencies as well as the issues that have precipitated contact with you as a social worker may help to empower Jane and assist her in problem solving.

- Identification of supports and development of a discharge plan require generation of possible options with Jane. A brokerage approach would indicate an adequate assessment as Jane appears to have a range of issues. Some may be addressed by you directly and others by referral to existing service providers elsewhere.

Courtesy of Sheila Nicolson, Acting Deputy Director, Ryde Community Mental Health Service.

An assessment report based on this case scenario can be found in Practice example 8.1.

##  Questions for Review

1. How do you think your own experiences of 'being assessed' will influence your work with clients?
2. How does theory guide the assessment process?
3. What types of questioning formats should be avoided when conducting an assessment?
4. What types of interview questions facilitate the exploration of client situations?

## References

Compton, B.R., & Galaway, B. (1994). *Social Work Processes*. Pacific Grove, CA: Brooks/Cole.

Cowger, C.D. (1992). Assessment of Client Strengths. In D. Saleebey (ed.), *The Strengths Perspective in*

*Social Work Practice*. New York: Longman.

Ellis, K. (1993). *Squaring the Circle: User and Carer Participation in Need Assessment*. York: Joseph Rowntree Foundation.

Everitt, A., Hardiker, P., & Littlewood, J. (1992). *Applied Research for Better Practice*. London: Palgrave Macmillan.

Fook, J. (1993). *Radical Casework*. Sydney: Allen and Unwin.

Fook, J. (2002). *Social Work: Critical Theory and Practice*. London: Sage.

Forder, A. (1976). Social Work and System Theory. *British Journal of Social Work,* 6(1), 23–42.

Friedlander, W.A. (1958). *Concepts and Methods of Social Work*. Englewood Cliffs, NJ: Prentice-Hall.

Goldberg, G. (1974). Structural approach to practice: a new model. *Social Work,* 150–5.

Hanvey, C., & Philpot, T. (1994). *Practising Social Work*. London: Routledge.

Hepworth, D.H., & Larsen, J.A. (1993). *Direct Social Work Practice*. Pacific Grove, CA.: Brooks/Cole.

Hollis, F. (1972). *Casework: a psychosocial therapy* (2nd edn). New York: Random House.

Ibrahim, F.A., & Kahn, H. (1987). Assessment of worldviews. *Psychological Reports,* 60, 163–76.

Kluckhohn, F., & Strodtbeck, F. (1961). *Variations in value orientations*. Evanston, IL: Row Peterson and Co.

Konrad, G. (1987). *The Caseworker*. Harmondsworth: Penguin.

Maluccio, A. (1979). The influence of the agency environment on clinical practice. *Journal of Sociology and Social Welfare,* 6, 734–55.

Martinez, C. (1986). Hispanic psychiatric issues. In C. Wilkinson (ed.), *Ethnic psychiatry*. New York: Plenum.

Meyer, C.H. (1983). The search for coherence. In C.H. Meyer (ed.), *Clinical social work in the eco-systems perspective*. New York: Columbia University Press.

Milner, J., & O'Byrne, P. (2002). *Assessment in Social Work* (2nd edn). Basingstoke: Palgrave Macmillan.

O'Connor, I., Wilson, J., & Setterlund, D. (2003). *Social Work and Welfare Practice* (4th edn). Sydney: Pearson.

Parton, N., & O'Bryne, P. (2000). *Constructive Social Work*. Basingstoke: Palgrave Macmillan.

Pedersen, P.B. (2000). *A handbook for developing multicultural awareness* (3rd edn). Alexandria, VA: American Counseling Association.

Perlman, H. (1957). *Social casework: A problem-solving process*. Chicago: University of Chicago Press.

Pincus, A., & Minahan, A. (1973). *Social Work Practice: Model and Method*. Itasca, IL: Peacock.

Richmond, M. (1917). *Social Diagnosis*. New York: Russell Sage Foundation.

Saleebey, D. (1996). The strengths perspective in social work practice: Extensions and cautions. *Social Work,* 41, 296–305.

Scott, D. (1998). A Qualitative Study of Social Work Assessment in Cases of Alleged Child Abuse. *British Journal of Social Work,* 28, 73–88.

Seden, J. (1999). *Counselling Skills in Social Work Practice*. Philadelphia, PA: Open University Press.

Sheldon, B. (1995). *Cognitive-Behavioural Therapy, Research, Practice and Philosophy*. London and New York: Routledge.

Sheppard, M. (1995). *Care Management and the New Social Work: A Critical Analysis*. London: Whiting and Birch.

Siporin, M. (1975). *Introduction to social work practice*. New York: Macmillan.

Strom-Gottfried, K. (1999). Social Work Practice. Thousand Oaks, CA: Pine Forge Press.

Sue, D.W., & Sue, D. (2003). *Counseling the Culturally Diverse*. New York: John Wiley and Sons.

Sullivan, W.P. (1992). Reconsidering the Environment as a Helping Resource. In D. Saleebey (ed.), *The Strengths Perspective in Social Work Practice*. New York: Longman.

Thompson, N. (1997). *Anti-Discriminatory Practice* (2nd edn). Basingstoke: Palgrave Macmillan.

Trevithick, P. (2000). *Social Work Skills: A Practice Handbook*. Buckingham, PA: Open University Press.

Vickery, A. (1976). A Unitary Approach to Social Work with the Mentally Disordered. In M.R. Olsen (ed.), *Differential Approaches in Social Work with the Mentally Disordered*. Birmingham: British Association of Social Workers.

# 11

# Advocacy in Practice
## Zita Weber

Advocacy has a long tradition in the helping professions. This obligation is reflected, for instance, in the social work profession's *Code of Ethics* (CASW 2005, p. 5), which clearly articulates in the associated principles of Value 2, 'Pursuit of Social Justice', the ethical responsibility for social workers to serve as advocates for clients:

- Social workers uphold the right of people to have access to resources to meet basic human needs.
- Social workers advocate for fair and equitable access to public services and benefits.
- Social workers advocate for equal treatment and protection under the law and challenge injustices, especially injustices that affect the vulnerable and disadvantaged.

Jane Addams, a social worker and social reformer during the turn of the twentieth century, was an early advocate in her work in the settlement houses of Chicago. The motto attributed to her, 'There's power in me', foreshadowed the empowerment movement that was to take firm hold in the 1980s. Clement Attlee, in his book *The Social Worker* (1920), highlighted the advocacy role of social work in addressing social injustice. Over the years, many writers have addressed the necessity of the social worker acting as an advocate. Common themes in these writings include those of empowerment and the protection of people who are vulnerable, poor, and disempowered, and the use of advocacy to further their empowerment and protection. Davies (1994, p. 90) states, 'Strategies of change in social work might sometimes need to be directed, not at the client, but at dysfunctional elements in the client's environment.' In elucidating on this, Davies describes two forms of advocacy in social work: personal (often called 'case') and structural (often called 'class') advocacy. The personal focuses on the individual need, and the structural on the needs of a group or community. Davies (1994, p. 90) continues by stating, 'In either case, the assumption is that the social worker has skills and qualities or access to resources that are likely to tip the balance in favour of those whose interests would otherwise be overlooked or overridden.' Continuing in this vein, Payne (1997, p. 266) writes, 'Advocacy seeks to represent the interest of powerless clients to powerful individuals and social structures.' In Jordan's view (1987, p. 145), advocacy assumes a set of skills and, when conducted by social workers, ought to include clients and empower them, rather than social workers acting in an 'expert, lawyer-like' manner.

Advocacy is an activity that most practitioners engage in frequently and is part of everyday practice for many and, for some, such as social workers, is believed to be an integral responsibility to their clients. Advocacy requires the worker to know the different kinds of action to take and the consequences of each action, obtain resources through the use of pressure, ensure that the client is not punished once a request has been met, and model skills that will enable the client to self-advocate in the future. In essence, advocacy involves an effort to enhance the responsiveness of socio-legal arrangements to people's needs within the context of their lives. Rights to services, adequate income, decent housing, humane treatment by social and welfare organizations, and to participate in society on equal terms are at the core of advocacy.

Again, it has long been held that advocacy subsumes two separate, yet related, facets: case advocacy and class advocacy. First, the advocate in case advocacy corresponds closely to the definition of an advocate in the *Concise Oxford Dictionary* as 'one who pleads for another' (1985, p. 15). Second, advocacy can involve acting to effect changes in policy, law, or practice that affect all people in a specific group or class. In this regard, class advocacy is much broader in scope and may be considered as a form of social action. Holmes pointed out the possible interrelatedness of the two types of advocacy. Consider, for instance, the case where a social worker might serve as a case advocate for a client who has been denied a particular service or benefit. If that case advocacy action results in setting a precedent and leads to a change in policy affecting all others in the same position, then 'class advocacy may be viewed as an extension of case advocacy' (Holmes 1981, pp. 33–4).

# Integrating case advocacy and class advocacy

In many provinces, individuals who are in receipt of income assistance are constrained in their entitlement to keep any income that comes as a result of paid employment. Typically, any income that came from paid employment was 'clawed back' by income assistance. Clearly, this resulted in a disincentive to work, as well as punished people for being honest in reporting outside income. As direct service workers, social workers advocated for changes in the income assistance legislation to allow individuals who were employed on a part-time basis to retain a larger portion of their income, without losing benefits such as expenses for medications or dental care.

## Practice example 11.1

### Case advocacy to class advocacy

Recognizing that the majority of individuals on income assistance have the desire to work but were penalized for doing so, social workers who were employed as financial workers advocated for policy changes within the existing legislation. Case studies drawn from individual advocacy

*continued*

efforts were incorporated into a written submission resulting in the introduction of legislation for individuals on income assistance to supplement their benefits through paid employment. This provision was extended and additional employment allowances were introduced for other categories of individuals on assistance including people with disabilities or mental health issues.

Another example of class advocacy involves the proliferation of 'payday loan' lenders in Canada. According to the Public Interest Advocacy Centre, the payday lending rate in Ontario is 'astronomically high' (2008). This is particularly problematic as borrowers who use this system are frequently low- or middle-income earners and have been refused credit through other institutions. For some families, the use of payday lenders can quickly lead them into poverty as the interest rates on the loans are exceedingly high. In an effort to reduce the financial strain for consumers, several advocacy groups including the National Anti-poverty Organization and the Canadian Association of Retired Persons have been successful in advocating for legislation that caps interest rates in British Columbia, Manitoba, Nova Scotia, and Saskatchewan. These provinces also entered into indemnity agreements with major banks that allow non-bank customers to cash cheques—regardless of the issuer—for no fees with the required identification.

Courtesy of Deborah Hart.

# Critical practice and advocacy

For practitioners practising from a critical/structural perspective, there are challenges inherent in advocacy. Critical practitioners must never lose sight of the fact that they are being instructed by the clients for whom they are advocating. Clients must not be used as a means to achieve ends for practitioners' own personal or professional purposes. Critical practitioners must guard against imposing their perspectives onto the client, or controlling the goals, tasks, and processes. Critical practitioners have a responsibility to explain in clear and realistic terms what the advocacy action hopes to attain and what is achievable, as well as the potential negative outcomes. In terms of advocating on behalf of others, practitioners must strive to convey in clear and well-argued terms the perspective of the client(s) to the decision-maker. Critical practitioners will question the position they take, reflect on viable alternative positions, and be familiar with the possible outcomes and consequences of adopting different approaches and making different demands.

The CASW *Code of Ethics* (2005, p. 9) recognizes that advocacy involves action 'with and on behalf of clients', which is reinforced by Fook (2002), who points out that there are tensions inherent in the idea of the advocate as a practitioner who 'acts for' other persons. Fook believes that the idea of advocacy needs to be reworked to reflect the complexity of everyday lives and everyday practice, and to avoid the inevitable binary assumptions of a simplistic perspective on advocacy. First, Fook contends that the critical practitioner must recognize both the 'outcome and process aspects of advocacy' (2002, p. 150). It is important to ensure that the process of working towards the outcomes (rights and entitlements being secured for people) is as empowering an experience as possible. Second, she emphasizes the importance of identifying 'multiple points of contradiction, alliance, complexity and resistance' (Fook 2002, p. 150). Essentially, not all decision-makers will necessarily oppose the interests of the client, and not all clients will be blameless in their presentation; the best strategy calls for forming alliances with potential adversaries rather than setting them up as impossible opposition from the very beginning. Such advocacy presupposes using what Fook (2002, p. 151) calls the 'language of alliance'—for example, 'How can we help you?', 'How can you help us?', and 'What can we do about this?' In essence, the role of the advocate is to make it easy for the resource provider to say 'yes'. If this perspective is adopted then advocates are less likely to take the moral high ground and more likely to organize their actions so that it allows for the challenge of working with others in ways that let everyone feel they can act morally. Finally, Fook offers the advocacy–empowerment link in suggesting that critical practitioners do not 'other' the client but offer empowering ways of working with clients who might feel powerless and unheard in their lives. In a similar vein, Ife (1997, p. 181) cautions critical practitioners against adopting the absolute role of advocate, thereby 'making it the social workers' voices that are heard, rather than those of the people they claim to represent . . . . From the critical theory perspective, the authentic voices of the marginalized must be heard, and the role for social workers is to make sure that this becomes possible, by helping the marginalized people to develop the skills and vocabulary needed to address the structures of power and domination.'

## Advocacy, negotiation, and mediation

Advocacy may occur in the course of negotiation but can and should be distinguished from it. It is a prerequisite for negotiation where the other party is not willing to enter a negotiation process. An example of this distinction is where, during the course of negotiation, social workers are explicit about what it is they want to achieve and the reasons for doing so. Such advocacy may take only a short time in the otherwise protracted negotiation process. Compton and Galaway (1994, p. 434) point out the distinction that whereas in mediation the effort is to secure resolution to a dispute through give and take on both sides, in advocacy 'the effort is to win for the client'.

## What are the indications for advocacy?

Advocacy may be employed in many instances, some of which are listed below (Hepworth & Larsen 1993, p. 504):

- when a person is denied services to which they believe they are entitled—for example, housing, income assistance, or disability-related services
- when services are delivered by service providers in a dehumanizing manner—for example, during treatment of victims of sexual assault
- when a person is discriminated against on the basis of ethnicity, religion, sexual orientation, or other factors

- when gaps in services cause hardship
- when a person is unable to act effectively on their own behalf—for example, vulnerable people in institutions such as nursing homes and prisons and people with chronic mental or developmental disabilities
- when a person is denied civil or legal rights—for example, unlawful detainment of a juvenile, illegal eviction of a tenant, illegitimately being cut off from employment insurance
- when organizational procedures or facilities adversely affect a person
- when a number of people have common needs for which resources are not available—for example, homeless youths
- when a person has need for immediate services and is in a crisis situation—for example, immigrants or refugees who are seriously ill or have dire financial needs

### Activity 11.1  Appropriate use of advocacy

Reflect on your own experiences. Has someone advocated on your behalf? Have you advocated on behalf of another? For what purpose? With what result?

Think of two situations where advocacy can be used.

## Advocacy in practice: a rights perspective and the empowerment approach

### A rights perspective

Bateman (2000, p. 40) points out that the word 'rights' is frequently linked to advocacy, and believes that rights are 'the fulcrum upon which advocacy balances'. An important part of advocacy practice lies in welfare rights (Bateman 2000; Payne 1997), which is concerned with ensuring that clients who benefit from welfare services receive their entitlement to other welfare provisions. As Payne (1997, p. 270) suggests, 'Ensuring that clients receive all their entitlements to other services is an important part of many other formulations of social work.'

Jordan (1987, p. 135) states that advocacy is 'the unambiguous championship of the oppressed'. Donnison (1991) extends this view by arguing that advocacy is concerned with securing people's rights, and that it is powerless people whose interests are ignored by those in power, precisely because the powerful have possession of things they would rather not surrender. In this context, the goal of advocacy is to win.

Bateman (2000) notes that the concept of 'citizenship' is centrally placed in the activity of advocacy. He suggests that there are three basic elements to the idea of citizenship: political, social, and civil. As a citizen, rights in any of these areas, theoretically, can be realized. Hence, as a first step, Bateman (2000, p. 40) posits that where rights are unclear or the opportunity to enforce them is limited, 'the question of citizenship is addressed to push back the limitations for those affected'. In terms of the political dimension of citizenship, the right to participate in the exercise of power and, at a minimum, the right to vote, are seen as essential. The social dimension of citizenship centres around the right to enjoy a minimum standard of welfare and security—for example, the right to adequate education, health care, and social security. Any obscuring or denial of rights in this respect means effectively denying the chance of people to be full citizens of the society in which they live. Civil rights encompass the liberty of people, their right to free speech, thought, and faith; the right to own property and to act on their own behalf in securing valid contracts; and the right to justice. Marshall (1975) put forward the view that exercising civil rights presupposes the access to appropriate institutions for people in order to remedy any breaches of their rights to citizenship.

According to Bateman, the client's rights to a service means that they have the right to accept or decline a standard of service and that they are then entitled to exercise their formal rights. However, he argues that these formal rights are not enough. If clients and advocates are to be effective in their participation in obtaining services then they need knowledge in the form of information and 'clear legally enforceable rights to services' (Bateman 2000, p. 41).

## Practice example 11.2

## Vicki's case

Vicki, who is fifty years old and suffers from severe anxiety, is living in a women's shelter. She reports a childhood history of sexual abuse. She has been married for twenty years and has recently left her marital home. She describes ongoing marital discord and reports physical and emotional abuse by her husband over a long period of time. Throughout her marriage she has been a housewife and her husband has maintained full control of the household finances.

Advocacy in this context may be both written and verbal. The role of the practitioner may involve advising the client of her entitlement to income assistance, public housing accommodation, and possibly legal aid support. Liaison and negotiation with the relevant government departments may be required as well as the completion and submission of applications, support letters, and reports. Written consent of the client for the service provider to release information must be sought prior to consultation with other service providers.

Courtesy of Sheila Nicolson.

It follows then, that clients and advocates must work in partnership and that practitioners must work to minimize any professional barriers to client participation. Many clients might feel disinclined to advocate on their own behalf, believing they have little formal status or power in presenting their case and pressing their rights. This is evident in many contexts, particularly in relation to housing and social security issues.

## Practice example 11.3

### Reluctance to exercise formal rights

Following the death of her husband six months ago, Frances left her full-time job and moved with her six-year-old son, Luka, into a two-bedroom unit in a low income housing complex. Frances had found it very difficult to locate affordable accommodation within walking distance of Luka's school. Luka suffers from asthma and requires frequent medication.

Heavy downpours of rain cause water to leak into Luka's bedroom through the window frames and the carpet is often saturated. Frances believes the continuously damp carpet is exacerbating Luka's asthma. She advised the caretaker about the leak on three occasions but nothing has been done to rectify the problem.

Frances attended the local drop-in centre on days that they distribute food hampers. The centre coordinator advised Frances about her entitlement to exercise legal tenancy rights to urgent repairs. However, Frances did not wish to take further action because the original lease was about to expire and she did not want to risk losing this relatively cheap property. Frances decided to move Luka into the dry bedroom with her rather than do anything that might place her tenancy at risk.

Courtesy of Deborah Hart.

## An empowerment approach

A different form of advocacy, and one that stems from Jane Addams' oft-repeated quote about power residing in the individual, is that of rights and their enforcement acting to empower the client. Participation and empowerment involve providing clients with access to information, including them in decision-making processes, and listening to their stated needs and views of services and service delivery. An empowerment approach to advocacy practice, which became popular in the 1980s, is linked to the notion of consumerism, which promotes opportunities for consumers to criticize services that do not meet their needs and to seek changes in these services through campaigning and group activity (Beresford & Croft 1993).

Also at that time was a movement to assist people with mental illness and learning disabilities living in institutions and those leaving institutions through the deinstitutionalization process, to increase their capacity to manage their lives and achieve their civil rights. Empowerment for and self-advocacy of people with disabilities was encouraged by practitioners working in these areas. The concept of 'normalization' (Wolfensberger 1972) or 'social role valorization' (Wolfensberger 1984) is linked to an empowerment approach. People were being encouraged to speak for themselves and to form self-help organizations and groups, through which they could gain support from one another, work together to represent their needs, and ensure their rights to assist in their recovery from difficulties in their lives. An example of this is parents of children with disabilities. It was through parent-to-parent connections that the disability support system began to change to reflect parents' needs and not simply those of the child as determined by the professionals. Rose and Black (1985) believe that an advocacy/empowerment approach restores a sense of human dignity and personal responsibility to people living with a mental illness when they return to live in the community. Dane (1985) discusses the use of professional and lay advocacy aimed at enhancing the education of disabled children. These authors stress that the sense of empowerment that clients gain through organized advocacy and self-help may be more significant than the changes themselves.

Other authors write in recognition that assisting self-help groups to develop has been an important area of practice (Jack 1995; Wilson 1995; Thursz et al. 1995). Practitioners have supported groups of clients sharing concerns and encouraged them to come together for support. From these groups new responses to services and ideas regarding more appropriate services can arise. Notions of social and political rights drawn from citizenship are important elements for people taking power in groups. The philosophy of personal responsibility and self-direction through empowerment is grounded in knowledge about recognizing and building on strengths and competence. A strengths perspective focuses on people's ability to define their interaction within their particular social context (Saleebey 1996). Rose and Black (1985) base their approach on the work of Freire (1997) (liberation from struggle requires revolutionary change) and believe empowerment means encouraging people to become subjects rather than objects in their lives and actively involving them in the process of advocacy. Friere further highlights the importance of 'praxis', the process in which the social worker ensures that the personal dimensions of a client's problem (the way a client thinks, feels, and acts) are understood in relation to the dominant ideology and the material conditions in which the client lives.

In further developing an empowerment paradigm, Rose and Black (1990) propose three principles of advocacy and empowerment practice:

1. *Contextualization* involves enabling clients to express, elaborate, and reflect on their own feelings and understanding of life: their 'social being' rather than the practitioner's understanding, assumptions, or policies. This leads to the development of a 'dialogical' relationship based on clients' views of their reality.
2. *Empowerment* is a process that centres on assisting clients to make their own decisions and assume responsibility for their lives. Practitioners support clients by identifying the possible range of responses that might meet clients' needs.

   Reflection on the case of Vicki in Practice example 11.2 raises significant practice issues associated with advocacy and empowerment. Contextualization means that a client with a history of abuse, as well as current social stressors, is seen positively as a person with knowledge and expertise about her current situation which can be utilized to enable her to identify her needs. Empowerment practices may include consultation with the client regarding problem-solving strategies and possible solutions, such as accessing social security benefits and applying for public housing. The environment of the women's shelter may assist in the process of collectivity in addressing and reducing negative experiences such as isolation, which can affect an individual's self-image and sense of worthiness. Support groups are often effective therapeutic vehicles in assisting clients who have experienced domestic violence to reconnect and establish new relationships and support networks. This may be an option generated through discussions with the client (courtesy of Sheila Nicolson).

3. *Collectivity* emphasizes the importance of connecting clients to relationships and minimizing feelings of isolation and alienation. It is believed that stronger feelings of self-worth evolve from an experience of socialization. Moreau (1990) highlights the need to collectivize rather than personalize experience for people as it acknowledges that the problems of individuals have social and structural causes.

## Practice example 11.4

### Empowering young parents to take action

A 'parenting young' support group was established by a family support worker within a community women's health centre in an area with a high concentration of young families. The program developed out of individual casework with women aged between fifteen and twenty-two who were young parents. Women who attended the centre for counselling and support expressed a sense of feeling isolated and stigmatized because of their relative youth and their life choices. Given the similarity of their experiences, the family support worker decided to invite young women to participate in a peer network to address these challenges. The worker initially acted as a group facilitator but later withdrew from active membership of the group and did not attend unless invited by the young women for a specific purpose.

Over time, the group evolved into a self-advocacy network, the Parenting Young Network, to address negative perceptions of young parents held in the local community. The network sought funding for support activities and devised a newsletter, which they distributed to other young families in the area.

At one point, the Parenting Young Network learned that local landlords were refusing to rent properties to young single parents because of fears they would renege on rental payments or damage property. The network decided to advocate for change by inviting office managers from several rental property agencies to a 'positive parenting' forum. This event provided an opportunity for the network to establish ongoing relationships with local landlords/rental agents and to portray a positive image of young parents. The family support worker used her local media contacts to showcase the event and to promote community understanding of the strengths of local parents who happened to be young.

Courtesy of Deborah Hart.

# Ethical principles for advocacy

Bateman (2000) identifies six principles for effective advocacy:

■ Principle 1: Act in the client's best interests.

- Principle 2: Act in accordance with the client's wishes and instructions.
- Principle 3: Keep the client properly informed.
- Principle 4: Carry out instructions with diligence and competence.
- Principle 5: Act impartially and offer frank independent advice.
- Principle 6: Maintain rules of confidentiality.

Bateman (2000) suggests that these six principles form a fundamental approach to advocacy and a Code of Ethics for advocates.

## Practice example 11.5

## Soheila and Ali

You are a counsellor in a child and family health team at the local community health centre. Soheila and her twelve-year-old son, Ali, are driven to the centre by a man who lives in the same block of units after he found them sitting in a bus shelter with their suitcases at 6 a.m. this morning. Soheila is a widow who was born in Afghanistan. Until this morning, she was living with her two widowed sisters and their six children in a three-bedroom unit in the local area. The whole extended family spent three years in refugee camps in Pakistan before being accepted into Canada as refugees.

Soheila explains that Ali has suffered from a 'damaged brain' since his birth in the refugee camp. He is attending a special purpose school for children with moderate to profound disabilities in an affluent suburb about 15 kilometres from home. He is picked up by minibus every morning and driven to and from school.

Soheila tells you that she was ordered by her older sister to pack her belongings and to leave the unit because Ali attacked one of the younger children in the middle of the night. He had become increasingly aggressive towards the other children and adults in the crowded unit.

Soheila receives income support payments from the provincial welfare system. She cannot take Ali to a shelter because of his special needs and his behavioural problems. She is on the waiting list for public housing but she has been advised that it will be at least another year before she can be housed in the area of her choice. She is worried that no private landlord will lease a property to her because she has no references and fears she may be discriminated against because of Ali's behavioural problems. As well, the amount that she receives from the provincial welfare system for shelter is completely inadequate to meet the rates in the private rental market. Soheila would like your assistance to advocate for urgent public housing assistance in the area of her choice. She did not seek assistance from her own community because she does not want people to know about her personal situation. She asks you not to contact her sisters or anyone else in the Afghani refugee community to discuss her situation. She is fearful and distressed as a result of her life experiences.

*continued*

## Questions for reflection

1. What factors will you explore when assessing Soheila's and Ali's 'best interests'?
2. What challenges might you face in acting as an advocate for Soheila and Ali?
3. What else will you need to know in order to be an effective advocate in this case?
4. How will you maintain the principles of confidentiality?

## Practice points 11.1

- Soheila and Ali are currently experiencing a crisis in their lives that may exacerbate pre-existing distress caused by traumatic refugee experiences. Soheila is likely to feel overwhelmed by her current situation. She requires patient support and clear information about realistic options in order to actively participate in decisions about her future.

- Like all refugees, Soheila has been forced to demonstrate courage and strength in order to rebuild her life in a new country. These strengths should be acknowledged, respected, and harnessed throughout the decision-making and advocacy process.

- Strategic and effective advocacy relies on a good understanding of rules and entitlements. It will be necessary to obtain as much information as possible about guidelines on applying for priority housing in order to represent Soheila adequately. This is only possible when social workers have invested time and energy into developing strong advice and referral networks among local service providers. Seek Soheila's permission to discuss her situation with service providers and keep her informed about any progress.

- Encourage, support, and resource Soheila's active participation in the advocacy process wherever possible in order to further develop her knowledge, skills, and existing strengths. Advocacy can result in feelings of enhanced confidence and agency if it is used effectively.

Courtesy of Deborah Hart.

## Practice example 11.6

## Kate

Kate, who is forty-five years old, has been diagnosed with a developmental disability. Five years ago she moved into supported accommodation; prior to that, she had resided with her parents.

*continued*

However, her parents were concerned about their own aging and wanted to ensure Kate had adequate supports in place for the future in case they were unable to care for her. As part of Kate's transition from her home environment to supported accommodation, she regularly resided at her parent's home at weekends. This routine had been maintained for five years, was satisfactory to all parties, and Kate appeared happy in the supported accommodation. However, Kate's father died six months ago and her mother has moved into a nursing home. Since this time, Kate's behaviour has changed. She is frequently tearful and has become increasingly agitated. She often shouts at fellow residents. Recently the families of fellow residents have approached you, as a social worker, wanting to talk about Kate and stating they want her to leave. When you raise this with Kate, she cries and shouts loudly that she wants to stay.

## Questions for reflection

1. What are some of the ethical principles implied in this scenario and why?
2. What are some of the issues that may require advocacy by a social worker?
3. What interventions would you adopt in the process of advocating for Kate?

## Practice points 11.2

- Kate's developmental disability may affect her ability to advocate on her own behalf.
- Possible reasons for the change in Kate's behaviour will need to be explored in order to act in her best interest and in accordance with her wishes and instructions. Grief and loss issues associated with the death of her father and relocation of her mother from the family home may be contributing factors.
- Discussion of Kate's circumstances with the families of fellow residents is a breach of her confidentiality.
- Keeping Kate properly informed implies a responsibility to ensure she is in a position to, and is able to, make informed decisions for herself.

Courtesy of Sheila Nicolson.

# Some approaches to advocacy

As with every practice situation, the practitioner must decide on an approach that best suits what needs to be done. For what are you advocating? Who are the decision-makers? How do the decision-makers make their decisions? How do the decision-makers perceive their relationship to the advocacy practice: are they neutral, positive, or hostile? By determining the answers to these questions and, in particular, whether the advocacy situation is within an alliance, a neutral context, or an adversarial context, practitioners are better placed to decide what is to be advocated, and what level of advocacy is most appropriate: individual, administrative, or policy or legislative level. Sosin and Caulum (1983) developed a typology that identifies three levels to which advocacy can be directed.

First, the *individual level* involves addressing specific individual or group issues in a factual manner and not seeking to actively challenge agency rules or processes. In this context, the advocate puts forth new information or highlights errors that may have been made previously by the decision-maker.

## Practice example 11.7

## Frank and guardianship

Frank, a fifty-five-year-old man with Down's syndrome, has been living in the community for ten years, having been moved into a public housing apartment with another man with whom he had shared a supported accommodation facility. This occurred in the context of de-institutionalization. Services were put in place to assist Frank and his roommate to adjust to and participate in community living. This was going well until Frank had a major heart attack and was diagnosed with early-onset dementia after several episodes of being unable to get home from the sheltered workshop at which he had been working for ten years. Frank was allocated an advocate in the form of a substitute decision-maker under the *Vulnerable Persons Act*.

Twelve months ago, Frank was placed under the guardianship of the Public Trustee after his advocate expressed concern over the management of his financial affairs as he had no living relative or interested person to manage his financial affairs or make decisions for him in relation to his health care or accommodation. Frank's dementia has been getting worse, requiring additional assistance from a local community non-profit agency to escort him to the bank, help him to complete and sign forms, and escort him to and from work to ensure that he catches the bus and gets off at the appropriate location.

The substitute decision-maker was in the process of attempting to cease the order as few decisions had to be made on Frank's behalf during the twelve months. A hearing before the panel reviewed this matter. The advocate advised that Frank had been tested by the memory clinic and there was marked cognitive deterioration, that there had been a number of incidents where the police had contacted the advocate as Frank had been found lost and without money, and that there were some significant decisions to be made in relation to a large inheritance. In addition, it was becoming clearer that decisions associated with Frank's accommodation would need to be made with a view to his moving to a facility with twenty-four-hour assistance. On several occasions

*continued*

he has been stopped from leaving shops while holding goods he had not paid for. The advocate expressed concern for Frank and recommended that decision-making processes needed review.

The Public Trustee, upon reviewing the new information presented by the advocate, ruled that an additional guardianship order be made for a period of another two years with a review at the end of that time.

Courtesy of Andrea Taylor.

Second, the *administrative level* is targeted when the advocate is accepting of the basic rules of the agency or organization, but the advocacy effort is directed towards changing the way that the agency or organization applies those rules. For instance, in the case of victims of domestic violence, the advocate might accept that police need to uncover facts and evidence that are private and painful to share. In these cases, the advocate would argue for a more empathic and sensitive approach in gaining such evidence.

## Practice example 11.8

## Advocacy at the administrative level

Betty is a seventy-five-year-old woman living in community housing with a moderate intellectual disability. She resides with another person with an intellectual disability. Both had been in supported accommodation until fourteen years ago when they were moved to their current accommodation. Betty has recently been diagnosed with dementia. The agency that has supplied services to her for these fourteen years is a rehabilitation service, but now that Betty has dementia her situation has been deemed as not within the scope of this agency (it is considered that she cannot be rehabilitated), and she will need to be supported by another agency.

This change produces a number of major repercussions. Betty's support has been reduced from twelve hours per week to four despite her additional and more complex needs. She is separated from the people whom she has known for so long and who have acted as a de facto family (she only has one living relative, an elderly sister in a nursing home). Betty has been in receipt of provincial disability support for the past twenty years. The social worker who was assigned case management responsibilities became aware of Betty's plight when the home care worker noticed that Betty was always in the same clothes whenever she arrived at the home and the clothes were in a deteriorating state of hygiene.

The social worker, after much networking, has established that the maximum service provision Betty can have from the new service is six hours per week, which is clearly insufficient. The social worker advocates that Betty's hours be increased to this maximum and attempts to source addition-

*continued*

al support from other like services. She is unable to obtain any additional support. The social worker writes to the Minister about these issues. Some time after these letters were sent, funding was received by the relevant agency to increase Betty's hours of assistance to fifteen hours per week.

Courtesy of Andrea Taylor.

Third, the *policy* or *legislative level* is identified as the level to which the advocacy effort should be aimed when the practitioner seeks to change the rules that affect the individual client or group. For instance, a practitioner might advocate a change in the rules of eligibility for services.

## Practice example 11.9

### Advocacy at the legislative level

A social worker working in a managerial role in a mental health service was requested by senior management to complete a submission reflecting the challenges that the current *Intoxicated Persons Detention Act* presented to community mental health crisis teams. The social worker presented the submission to the senior management committee of the Regional Health Authority. This submission detailed the impact that persons who come within the scope of this Act have on services, families, and their own lives, and it made some practical suggestions for change.

The *Intoxicated Persons Detention Act,* in a practical sense, assists with the involuntary hospitalization of persons who are intoxicated frequently and, as a result, end up in more seriously dangerous situations. The downsizing of the number of psychiatric institutions has resulted in a loss of programs and appropriate facilities to rehabilitate and educate persons who fall within the scope of this Act. The Act is rarely utilized because when a person is deemed to be intoxicated in a public place by a peace officer, they are now housed within mental health in-patient units. There are no appropriate programs: rather than acting as rehabilitation units, they are containment units and are inappropriate.

Persons who are regularly intoxicated often present to emergency departments (either under their own steam or in the company of others—for example, police) stating that they are suicidal. The community mental health service team is called to assess them and make a plan for their management in the short-term. Once these individuals sober up, they want nothing to do with any service. These individuals often have families, who go through this ordeal nightly.

The social worker was called in before the Regional Health Authority to provide more information in relation to the practical utilization of the Act and how it could be improved for services, families, and the individuals themselves.

Courtesy of Andrea Taylor.

## Practice example 11.10

# Three levels of advocacy

Matthew is sixteen. He has been attending a local youth centre to participate in social activities and an independent living skills program for the past six weeks. He had been living in a group home, under the care of the provincial child welfare authorities. Matthew was in receipt of an independent living allowance that was conditional upon good behaviour and attendance in the living skills program.

Matthew suddenly stopped turning up to the centre. One of his friends advised the youth worker at the centre that Matthew had left the group home because he assaulted his mother's new partner. Matthew has been 'couch-surfing' for the past three weeks, as well as sleeping in a friend's garage. The agency has stopped Matthew's independent living payments because he did not attend a traineeship interview lined up for him by the Youth Employment Services agency. This is the third time Matthew has incurred a penalty for breaching the agency's guidelines so he will not receive any payments for eight weeks. The youth worker sends a message to Matthew to invite him back to the centre for assistance with restoring his youth allowance and addressing his family problems.

Effective advocacy begins with knowledge about the most appropriate level at which to address a well-planned argument.

## Advocacy at the individual level

The youth worker calls a social worker at the local child welfare office and advises that Matthew was unable to attend the job interview because he was homeless at the time. This results in Matthew's independent living allowance being restored immediately, which resolves Matthew's specific concerns but does not touch on systemic issues.

## Advocacy at the administrative level

The youth worker is aware of many similar situations where young people in the local community have had their income support payments stopped because they failed to meet administrative requirements in the midst of a personal crisis. The youth worker decides to raise a concern about the way this policy is administered by the local child welfare office at the next youth interagency network meeting. A representative from the Youth in Care Network arranges a meeting with the local child welfare team manager to advocate for procedural reforms that take account of the circumstances of young people in a crisis situation.

## Advocacy at the policy or legislative level

The Youth in Care Network goes on to make a written submission to a federal inquiry into the government's activity test policy. This high profile advocacy campaign results in a change in

*continued*

government policy whereby young, unsupported people must be seen by a social worker before any action is taken to impose activity test penalties.

Courtesy of Deborah Hart.

# Skills of advocacy

As Bateman (2000, p. 83) points out, advocacy 'often starts with an interview, and interviewing will be the main method of obtaining instructions and for keeping clients informed'. He maintains that the skill of interviewing is the interface between the client and the organization. Consequently, poor interviewing will lead to an incomplete picture being formed and a poor basis on which to proceed. Therefore, in the context of advocacy, Bateman (2000) urges practitioners to use a range of skills (covered in chapters 4, 5, 6, 8, and 9 of this book):

- listening
- questioning
- understanding non-verbal aspects
- recording
- cultural sensitivity
- feedback
- assertiveness
- negotiation
- legal research

Other skills that may be useful include presenting written and oral submissions, providing expert evidence, lobbying, and providing different forms of public education. In Bateman's view, the practitioner also needs the following skills: assertiveness, negotiation, and legal research. It is useful to adopt Bateman's (2000, p. 138) definition of legal research skills: '"Legal research" is a generic term for the skills involved in assembling a coherent and logical argument in support of the client's case, making the best use of the law or rules governing the situation. Your argument may not just consist of references to the relevant law, but may also include policy and practice statements which are not being fully complied with or which support your argument.'

## Practice example 11.11

## Challenging a subpoena

A subpoena was received by a community agency requesting a copy of the clinical file of Celia (a previous consumer). Celia, who is seventy-four years old and lives alone, had come to the

*continued*

attention of the psycho-geriatric mental health service for the first time after being referred by a neighbour for shouting into her large garbage bin. This behaviour had been noted by the neighbour over a number of years but recently was becoming more frequent and louder, often disturbing the neighbour late at night. Celia had been seen by the community mental health service and, while she was unable to adequately explain the shouting into the garbage bin, had demonstrated no other behaviour that was of concern. Celia was polite and engaging with the mental health service but declined any further intervention and agreed to keep the noise down so as not to disturb her neighbour.

Closer review of the subpoena identified that it had been lodged by a private solicitor acting for another neighbour of Celia in another matter. Celia was contacted by the community agency and advised of the subpoena and its parameters. Celia requested that her neighbours not be provided with a copy of the health service record. Acting on this request, and a review of relevant privacy legislation, a manager of the community agency presented to court and filed a copy of Celia's file in an envelope marked for the magistrate's eyes only, complying with both the subpoena and Celia's instructions.

Discussions ensued in the court. The magistrate reviewed the file and supplied the manager of the community agency with the legislation relevant to evidence law. The magistrate then broke for coffee and tea while the manager read the provincial *Personal Health Information Act*. The manager presented her case, advising that there was no information relevant to the hearing that would justify the release of private health information to the neighbour. The magistrate agreed with the summation of that piece of law and thus denied the neighbour's access to Celia's file. Celia was advised of the outcome.

Courtesy of Andrea Taylor.

## Advocacy skills: helping Matthew tell his story

The following text (courtesy of Deborah Hart) continues to outline the use of advocacy skills in helping Matthew, introduced in Practice example 11.10, tell his story.

It is not uncommon for young people in Matthew's situation to avoid taking action to resolve a crisis or to mask anxiety about addressing a difficult problem with apparent indifference. It is very unlikely that Matthew will know how to exercise his legislated rights in this situation. Matthew may need assistance from the youth worker to negotiate his way through a complex and intimidating income support system. Effective advocacy will require attention to the following types of skills.

- *Patient communication skills*: Sixteen-year-olds in Matthew's situation are not always articulate and confident communicators. An effective advocate will use patient communication and interviewing skills to assist Matthew to tell his 'story'. Relevant details will be recorded and Matthew will be consulted about what information can be disclosed to the child welfare authorities.

- *Negotiation skills*: First, you need to negotiate with Matthew about what needs to be done to address his problems regarding income support. Second, you need to decide who has the organizational power within the agency to resolve Matthew's problem. Negotiation requires a forward plan: what outcome are you looking for and what can you contribute to the resolution of this problem? Perhaps it will help to devise a plan with Matthew for meeting agency requirements once his current crisis is resolved.
- *Legal research skills:* Effective advocacy goes beyond arguing that something is unfair, particularly when you are trying to change a decision based on the application of rules, policy, or law. In Matthew's case, it is important to relate advocacy efforts to the agency's guidelines about the exercise of discretion in situations of personal crisis. It is not always possible to know all the rules, particularly when dealing with complex policy. Effective advocacy involves research and consultation about the decision you want to challenge.
- *Assertiveness:* Once you know the legal or procedural basis of the decision and you have conducted research on exceptions to the rules, you are in a position to mount an assertive argument to support Matthew through this process. Advocates are less likely to revert to frustration and anger if they are confident in their argument.

Well-prepared advocates also know when and where to take further action if the initial advocacy effort fails.

# Appropriate advocacy strategies

With the foregoing skills in the practitioner's repertoire and an awareness of the level to which the advocacy effort is to be directed, the practitioner needs to consider appropriate advocacy strategies. According to O'Connor et al. (2003, p. 194), 'Underpinning all advocacy strategies must be an educative strategy, which seeks to raise the level of understanding in the (specific and general) community about the issue of concern.' Sosin and Caulum (1983) have devised a typology of three strategic approaches to advocacy:

1. *Normative strategies* rest on an assumption of common values and moral arguments. Where there is shared understanding of the needs and issues involved and a recognition of the legitimacy of the advocacy effort, this is the most appropriate strategy to employ.
2. *Utilitarian strategies* are dependent on bargaining and negotiation and are appropriate to use when decision-makers are neither particularly favourable nor antagonistic to the advocacy practice.
3. *Coercive strategies* are used in an adversarial context and presuppose conflict and complaint. Coercive strategies are appropriately employed to force the attention of the decision-makers where there is no willingness to change the existing policies/regulations nor an atmosphere that suggests any inclination towards a shared understanding of the needs involved.

Of course the practitioner's decision to use one strategy over another will depend on careful reflection on the obvious needs involved, the rights that require redressing, and the facts of each particular situation in context.

# Self-determination and advocacy

Earlier in this chapter, the practitioner was urged to observe ethical principles in the practice of advocacy. Practitioners must be mindful of strictly observing the client's right to self-determination. Self-determination is covered at length in chapter 2, 'Professional Values and Ethical Practice'. Suffice to say that if clients do not wish to assert their rights, practitioners are ethically bound to respect their wishes. If clients do want to pursue action, it is important to ensure that the client's interests, as the client defines them, are addressed and not an agenda belonging to the practitioner. As Hepworth and Larsen (1993) suggest, the ethic of self-determination dictates that practitioners should go only as far as the client wishes to, and no further, in their advocacy. This point must be appreciated by practitioners because clients may be anxious about the potential risks of generating antagonism or ill will with others, which may prove disadvantageous in the future. Some clients may be fearful of the consequences should they press fully for their rights and witness an unfavourable outcome. Even if such fears are seemingly irrational, the client may be convinced of the dangers and risks in any advocacy effort.

## Practice example 11.12

### The importance of self-determination

Clarissa is a very tall twenty-nine-year-old transsexual residing in a large public housing complex that is regularly attended by the police and other emergency services due to the behaviours frequently occurring there.

Clarissa was found wandering naked and dazed, with obvious trauma, along a major street by a passerby, who called the police. Clarissa was taken to the nearest hospital emergency department to be medically reviewed. The sexual assault social workers were called in. Clarissa refused to disclose to the social workers what had happened to her, claiming not to remember and refusing any physical testing for sexual assault.

Later, Clarissa disclosed to her case worker that she had been sexually assaulted by a resident of the block of units. This individual was known to supply drugs, utilize threatening tactics to get residents to hand over money, and was rumoured to have been involved in some serious assaults. Clarissa was scared of this particular male, his behaviours, and his friends. She felt that as a transsexual she was that much more vulnerable, desperately attempting to get society to accept her, and the last thing she wanted was pity associated with being raped. Clarissa advised

*continued*

that this was not the first time that it had happened but due to her sexuality, and probable reper-cussions, she was not prepared to provide a statement to police about what occurred and would deny the incident if pressed by the police.

Clarissa did agree to apply for an urgent transfer to other public housing with the assistance of her case worker.

## Practice points 11.3

■  If the police had been notified of the sexual assault, Clarissa could have been placed in danger (real or otherwise). Thus the advocate's role is to trust this information and work around it.

Courtesy of Andrea Taylor.

From a critical practice viewpoint, it must be acknowledged that discussing possible adverse consequences must be balanced with not being unduly discouraging and assisting the client to weigh pros and cons. Ultimately the final decision is up to the client. Critical practice recognizes that implementing advocacy actions can involve strains, tensions, and difficulties. Furthermore, it must be acknowledged that a positive outcome can never be assured.

Advocacy should only be undertaken when the practitioner has considered the situation closely and is certain that the client's predicament justifies assertive action. This means not only being familiar with, but also being certain about the accounts given by clients regarding denial, discrimination, or shabby treatment. The complaints must be based in fact: the advocate's case is weakened by any distortions or omissions.

Practice example 11.13 allows for an overview of skills in relation to advocacy.

## Practice example 11.13

## Challenges in advocacy—the case of Robert

You are a social worker in a community mental health rehabilitation team. You visit a local room-ing house and meet Robert, who asks to see you in a private room. Robert is clearly distressed and asks for your assistance to advocate on his behalf with his probation officer.

*continued*

Robert is fifty-five years old. He was released from prison three months ago after serving a fifteen-year sentence for manslaughter. Robert advises you that he has lived in institutions of one sort or another since he was twelve years old. He has a record as a violent offender and he was released from prison on the condition that he remain in the local area in supported accommodation and attend sessions with a psychiatrist once every two weeks. He receives a disability pension because he cannot work due to a brain injury he sustained in a fight when he was an adolescent. He also suffers from anxiety and depression.

Robert discloses that he is very close to committing another violent offence because of a build-up of tension caused by living in shared accommodation with men of all ages, many of them mentally ill and alcohol dependent. He is finding it very difficult to live 'on the outside' after so many years behind prison walls. He wants to escape the city to live in a rural town so he is not bothered by anyone. His probation officer refuses to negotiate and insists that he remain where he is for at least twelve months. Robert tells you he cannot talk to his psychiatrist and he gains no benefit from their meetings.

Robert tells you he is about to 'explode' and he is worried that he will hurt someone else if he does not get away from his current situation. He does not want you to tell the probation officer about his fears of re-offending because he is worried he will be sent straight back to prison. He feels confident he can stay out of trouble if he lives alone. He wants a chance to live peacefully in his old age in a place where nobody knows about his past life.

## Questions for reflection

1. What challenges would you face in advocating to achieve Robert's 'best interests'?
2. Identify competing tensions and interests in this situation.
3. What are the risks of adhering to Robert's request not to disclose his fears of re-offending to his parole officer?
4. What skills would you employ to achieve a positive outcome for Robert?
5. What additional knowledge would you need to inform your advocacy efforts?
6. What would you hope to achieve in performing the role of advocate for Robert?

Courtesy of Deborah Hart.

# Questions for Review

1. What are the indications for advocacy?
2. What is the difference between a rights perspective and an empowerment approach?
3. What are the key ethical principles one must abide by when acting as an advocate?
4. Why is self-determination an important factor in advocacy?

# References

Attlee, C. (1920). *The Social Worker*. London: G. Bell and Sons.

Bateman, N. (2000). *Advocacy Skills for Health and Social Care Professionals*. London: Jessica Kingsley.

Beresford, P., & Croft, S. (1993). *Citizen Involvement: A Practical Guide for Change*. London: Macmillan.

Canadian Association of Social Work (2005). *Code of ethics*. Ottawa, ON: Canadian Association of Social Work.

Compton, B.R., & Galaway, B. (1994). *Social Work Processes*. Pacific Grove, CA: Brooks/Cole.

Dane, E. (1985). *Professional and Lay Advocacy in the Education of Handicapped Children*. New York: Routledge and Kegan Paul.

Davies, M. (1994). *The Essential Social Worker*. Aldershot: Arena.

Donnison, D. (1991). *A Radical Agenda: After the New Right and the Old Left*. London: Rivers Oram Press.

Fook, J. (2002). *Social Work: Critical Theory and Practice*. London: Sage.

Freire, P. (1997). *Pedagogy of the Oppressed*. New York: Continuum.

Hepworth, D.H., & Larsen, J.A. (1993). *Direct Social Work Practice*. Pacific Grove, CA: Brooks/Cole.

Holmes, K. (1981). Services for victims of rape: A dualistic practice model. *Social Casework*, 62, 30–9.

Ife, J. (1997). *Rethinking Social Work: Towards Critical Practice*. South Melbourne: Longman.

Jack, R. (1995). *Empowerment in Community Care*. London: Chapman and Hall.

Jordan, B. (1987). Counselling, advocacy and negotiation. *British Journal of Social Work*, 17, 135–46.

Marshall, T.H. (1975). *Social Policy*. London: Hutchinson Educational.

Moreau, M.J. (1990). Empowerment through advocacy and consciousness-raising: Implications of a structural approach to social work. *Journal of Sociology and Social Welfare*, 17(2), 53–68.

O'Connor, I., Wilson, J., & Setterlund, D. (2003). *Social Work and Welfare Practice* (4th edn). Melbourne: Pearson Education.

Payne, M. (1997). *Modern Social Work Theory*. Basingstoke: Macmillan.

PIAC (2008). Comments of the Public Interest Advocacy Centre (PIAC) and the National Anti-Poverty Organization (NAPO) to the maximum total cost of borrowing advisory board.

Rose, S.M., & Black, B. (1985). *Advocacy and Empowerment: Mental Health Care in the Community*. New York: Routledge and Kegan Paul.

Rose, S.M., & Black, B. (1990). Advocacy/empowerment: An approach to clinical practice for social work. *Journal of Sociology and Social Welfare*, 17(2), 41–52.

Saleebey, D. (1996). The strengths perspective in social work practice. *Social Work*, 41, 296–305.

Sosin, M., & Caulum, S. (1983). Advocacy: A conceptualization for social work practice. *Social Work*, 28(12–17).

Thursz, D., Nusberg, C., & Prather, J. (1995). *Empowering Older People: An International Approach*. London: Cassell.

Wilson, J. (1995). *How to Work with Self-help Groups: Guidelines for Professionals*. Aldershot: Arena.

Wolfensberger, W. (1972). *The Principle of Normalisation in Human Services*. Toronto: National Institute on Mental Retardation.

Wolfensberger, W. (1984). A reconceptualization of normalization as social role valorization. *Mental Retardation*, 32, 22–5.

# 12 Understanding and Managing Conflict

## Agi O'Hara

*People . . . are trying to either shun conflict or crush it. Neither strategy is working. Avoidance and force only raise the level of conflict . . . They have become parts of the problem rather than the solution.*

DeCecco and Richards 1974,
cited in Johnson & Johnson 1997, p. 351.

Conflict is a natural part of everyday living. It develops in both personal and professional contexts when there is a clash of interests related to needs, values, opinions, or activities. As practitioners, we need to understand our own beliefs about the nature of conflict and to develop an awareness of the range of strategies we employ in managing conflict, before we can consider the skills required to assist our clients in managing or resolving their conflicts. We need to understand that conflict is ubiquitous and avoiding it, undesirable. Understanding conflict also allows the worker to shift from the paradigm of order and stability to that of conflict and change, thereby opening up multiple targets for intervention. Social workers will inevitably encounter conflict whether it is occurs in direct practice situations including high-conflict divorce, family violence, sexual assault, or child/elder abuse, or indirect practice such as unfair labour or housing legislation, employee terminations, or income redistribution policies.

## Activity 12.1 Connotations of 'conflict'

Take ten seconds to write down any words or phrases that come to mind as you read the word 'conflict'. Look at the words you have written and put them into three columns, depending on the positive, negative, or neutral connotations associated with the words listed.

1. In what order did these responses emerge? Did any single group (positive, negative, or neutral) emerge first?
2. Can you think of an explanation to account for these different reactions to the word 'conflict'?

A possible explanation for your response to Activity 12.1 is that often our initial or gut reactions are purely emotional and stem from earlier negative experiences with conflict, most likely during childhood, when we were vulnerable and, to some extent, at the mercy of others more powerful than ourselves. The positive reactions are generally more cognitive. These have been learned later in life once we have developed inner resources with which to empower ourselves. The benefit of understanding the presence of both emotional and cognitive responses to conflict will be developed later, in the discussion of skills for managing conflict.

Beliefs about conflict could be viewed on a continuum (let us call this the 'conflict–behaviours continuum') where avoidance of conflict is at one end and confliction—engaging in behaviour that deliberately promotes or encourages conflict (de Bono 1985)—at the other. Viewing conflict as something to avoid is a recipe for further conflict, whether in the short-term or long-term, as avoidance of conflict creates 'defensiveness, hostility and a general lack of trust' (Schneider Corey & Corey 1997, p. 183) between the people concerned.

One of the key factors that assists us in our understanding of conflict is the recognition that there is no single experience of conflict, that in fact there are various forms of disagreement and levels of conflict. If we recognize this, then we may prevent an escalation of what, originally, may be a quite manageable situation into one that involves a crisis. Hollier et al. (1993) identify the following steps or developments in interactions when conflict is involved. Conflict often begins with a sense of *discomfort* when we know something is not quite right, but it is still vague because nothing has been said to clarify what might be wrong. What generally follows is some type of *incident*, which may lead to an uncomfortable exchange that leaves you feeling temporarily upset or irritated. Without appropriate discussion and airing of the issues, this will most likely lead to *misunderstandings* such that motives and facts are misperceived and tension develops, and the relationship is strained and becomes a cause of worry and concern. Continuing to avoid dealing with the issues will result in a situation of *crisis* in which 'behaviour is affected[,] normal functioning becomes difficult [and] extreme [responses] contemplated' such as ending a relationship, resigning, or even perhaps some form of violence (Hollier et al. 1993, p. HIII.2).

Johnson and Johnson (1997) distinguish between controversy and other forms of conflict as they consider controversy arises 'when one person's ideas, information, conclusions, theories and opinions are incompatible with those of another person' (Johnson & Johnson 1997, p. 290). According to the authors, such disagreements are a natural part of all relationships, both personal and professional. A hint of controversy (and indeed the previously described discomforts and incidents in the early levels of conflict) need not produce the same feelings of anxiety and apprehension as a full-blown conflict, in which emotions have escalated. This is quite possible if we recognize our response patterns to controversy and seek to expand our repertoire of strategies, if required. Johnson and Johnson devised an inventory, 'Understanding my controversy behaviour' (1997, pp. 287–9), which assists in creating awareness of the strategies we already use by analyzing responses to statements such as: 'When I get involved in an argument with others, I become more and more certain that I am correct, and argue more and more strongly for my own point of view.'

Graded responses to thirty statements in the inventory (regarding frequency of behaviour) are analyzed according to the extent that they reflect the following perspectives:

- problem-solving
- confirmation
- perspective-taking
- win/lose
- rejection
- avoidance

The scores are tallied and range from 0 to 25 for each perspective. The first three perspectives are seen as constructive strategies and the last three as destructive strategies. The scores provide a profile of strategies used and those that appear not to be utilized. Understanding the appropriateness and the advantages or disadvantages of each of these perspectives assists in developing alternative and more appropriate and productive strategies for responding to controversy.

## Activity 12.2  Handling conflict

1. Think of a conflict that was handled in a destructive manner. What were some of the outcomes in that situation?
2. Now, think of a conflict that was handled in a constructive manner. What were some of the outcomes in that situaiton?

# Conflict strategies

As indicated above, different people use different strategies when encountering conflict. These strategies are often learned in childhood and they seem to emerge almost automatically (Johnson & Johnson 1997). As practitioners, we are able to see that objectively when our clients experience difficulties with regard to conflict in their lives, it is quite often due to the fact that they respond from habit, not stopping to consider whether what they are about to do is beneficial or appropriate to the particular conflict with which they are involved. Through introspection and the help of the practitioner, clients can become aware of their conflict strategies and, if deciding they are inappropriate, can change them 'by learning new and more effective ways of managing conflicts' (Johnson & Johnson 1997, p. 339).

Many people consider conflict merely in terms of winners and losers, thereby buying into a 'win/lose' paradigm, which views conflict in rather narrow and unnecessarily dualistic terms. Such a view ignores the potential for a resolution of the differing needs of the people concerned, such that each gains a type of 'win' because a fair compromise between their conflicting needs has been developed. By returning to our 'conflict–behaviours continuum', we can see that in the middle of the continuum would be people who recognize that conflict is a natural part of all relationships, that it can be considered 'as a problem to be solved' (Johnson & Johnson 1997, p. 359), that it requires management, and that it is possible to create a 'win/win' outcome so that benefits will accrue for all parties concerned.

It is helpful to offer a note of caution at this point. Although we may perceive our professional role as a facilitator for our clients' conflict management or resolution, it would be foolish to assume that everyone would prefer to eliminate the conflict in their lives. Clients may have numerous reasons for resisting processes of conflict resolution. They may genuinely believe they are right and fear that only by hanging on to their anger will justice be done or an apology offered. If they assume that only a 'win/lose' outcome is possible, the potential for loss may be seen as unacceptable due to the consequent 'loss of face'. They may also experience considerable gains or pay-offs for maintaining conflict, such as not having to admit they may be in the wrong and being able to continue to blame the other person.

Consideration of both the importance of the client's personal goals and the relationship between the parties concerned, facilitates an understanding of the client's willingness or reluctance to engage in conflict resolution. Johnson and Johnson's (1997) reference to the dual concern model of conflict assists in this regard. The two concerns are:

- Achieving personal goals—clients are in conflict because they have a goal that conflicts with another person's goal. Their goal may be highly important to them, of little importance, or somewhere in between.
- Keeping a good relationship with the other person—clients may need to be able to interact effectively with the other person in the future. The relationship may be very important to them, of little importance, or somewhere in between.

## Activity 12.3  Possible conflict strategies

Consider a situation of conflict, perhaps in a retail situation in which you are a customer wishing to return an item and the salesperson is resisting your request for a refund.

1. Devise, in writing, a forceful response to the saleperson's resistance that does not consider his perspective and that demonstrates your rights and your determination that nothing will stand in the way of getting what you want. Plan your argument as if you do not care about the other person's needs and the relationship is of no importance to you.
2. Having written your response, read it aloud, listening to the emotion in your words and reflecting on the likely feelings of a salesperson if he was to be on the receiving end of your response.

*continued*

3. Now reconsider your approach. Devise a response that is delivered in a respectful manner, while still focusing on achieving your goal. This time, the shop is one that you regularly frequent, and the salesperson is someone that you have got to know quite well.

4. Also read this response aloud, anticipating the likely response.

5. Consider the differences in the strategies and outcomes.

6. From this exercise, what learning could you pass on to clients who may be experiencing difficulties in managing conflict?

One of the most common means of analyzing conflict strategies (Johnson & Johnson 1997; Hollier et al. 1993; Bundey 1983) is to regard them as one of the following:

- taking flight from conflict—for example, sulking, crying, avoiding, pretending the incident did not happen, giving in
- engaging in a fight during conflict—for example, screaming, physical violence, emotional manipulation, refusing to listen
- attempting to manage or fix the conflict—for example, discussing the issue, taking time-outs, explaining one's own perspective and needs, listening to others

There are advantages and disadvantages in each of these responses (see below for a further discussion of Bundey's (1983) analysis) depending on the context and content of the conflict, as well as the nature of the relationship between the people involved. Fight and flight strategies stem from a 'win/lose' perception of conflict outcome, whereas 'manage/fix' strategies stem from perceptions that 'win/win' is possible.

## Activity 12.4  Responses to conflict

1. Think about the last personal conflict you were in.
   a) Where were you?
   b) Who was the conflict with?
   c) What was it about?
   d) What was your response—FIGHT, FLIGHT, MANAGE, or a combination of these?
   e) What do you see as the advantages and disadvantages of your response?

2. Now think about the last work situation in which you were involved in a conflict. Again, provide an answer to the above questions.

3. Now analyze your two sets of answers. Can you see any parallels? Do you appear to have favoured responses to conflict, irrespective of the context?

## Fight strategies

It seems to be a fact of life that not everyone avoids conflict. There are many who enjoy the energy or stimulation that comes from provoking others and promoting the disturbance that conflict produces, without apparently considering the needs of those involved. It is tempting to hypothesize that these people are always on the winning side of conflicts, whether by fair or foul means, and therefore seem to have little to lose. Similarly, the strategy of conflict avoidance could be assumed to be more likely if the person has frequently experienced the invalidation, humiliation, and demoralization of being the loser. We need to be wary of making either of these assumptions as they are likely to be an overly simplistic understanding of human behaviour. It needs to be remembered that we are influenced not only by our own experiences but also by those we have observed, particularly people close to us, such as family members.

### Advantages

The advantages of fight strategies (Bundey 1983) are:

- They challenge all of one's resources to win the battle.
- They may be exciting.
- They may obtain rewards in the audience's eyes if they result in overpowering the opponent.
- Their destructiveness may fill inner needs.

### Disadvantages

The disadvantages of fight strategies (Bundey 1983) are:

- Contenders lose sight of the ultimate consequences (generally more fighting) because of the enormity of the short-term goal (winning).
- The cost of battle (emotionally and financially) may far exceed the payoffs.
- The diminished self-esteem of the victor may be greater than the glory of victory. People do not usually value the destructiveness in themselves or in others.
- Battling markedly impairs the likelihood of future co-operation in the relationship.
- Fighting compounds the issues so that the extent and frequency of negative feelings and behaviours is likely to increase.

## Practice example 12.1

## Rationale for conflict strategies

Barry, who comes from a family in which conflict was frequent and distressing and where the outcomes for winners and losers were readily observed (an environment in which Barry had also

*continued*

frequently been a 'loser' as a child), decides to never be in a losing situation again. He therefore develops conflict strategies to ensure, at all costs, that his position is on the winning side, finding satisfaction in creating conflict as a means of maintaining a positive self-esteem.

## Questions for reflection

Consider someone you know who frequently seems to create conflict, or at least seems to derive great satisfaction from being in conflicts.

1. What would be this person's perception of the outcomes? Would she see herself as a winner?
2. What do you know about her that would help you to understand her behaviour?

# Flight strategies

To view the avoidance of conflict or 'taking flight' as an inferior or powerless position is to misunderstand the possible motives involved and the potential outcome for the parties concerned. Reluctance to be involved may be wise when we are fearful of being hurt or inflicting further hurt on another party.

### Advantages
The advantages of flight strategies (Bundey 1983) are:

- They avoid immediate conflict.
- They create an illusion of peace and stability.

### Disadvantages
The disadvantages of flight strategies (Bundey 1983) are:

- They can create resentment and anxiety.
- If frequently used, they may create an unstable relationship as resentment builds.
- They do not provide experience and tools to deal with the conflict when it finally surfaces.
- Conflict is likely to become exaggerated through suppression and may be too explosive to manage when it finally bursts through.

# Managing or fixing strategies

Attempting to fix or manage conflict will inevitably involve negotiation between the parties concerned. As with the strategies of fight and flight, depending on people's motivations and perspectives, there are both advantages and disadvantages associated with managing or fixing strategies.

## Advantages

The advantages of managing or fixing strategies (Bundey 1983) are:

- Both parties may end up as friends.
- The process is likely to breed future co-operation.
- The process is usually less costly (emotionally and financially) to both sides.
- The real issues underlying the conflict are likely to surface and be resolved.

## Disadvantages

The disadvantages of managing or fixing strategies (Bundey 1983) are:

- They require some discipline and self-restraint.
- They may be seen as 'weak' in the eyes of a blood-thirsty audience.
- They are not as exciting as fighting, for many.

It is also important to recognize that conflicts become increasingly difficult to resolve when there is intense mutual distrust or fear and no positive basis for the relationship between the parties involved. Significant imbalance in the financial or personal power of the two individuals, the expectation of a loss of face, and a determination by one or both of the parties to maintain their position also significantly reduces the likelihood of resolution (Bundey 1983).

In such situations, it is unlikely that the persons involved will be able to resolve the conflict without the assistance of a neutral third party. Helping professionals can be this neutral, objective person, who creates a safe and structured process to assist clients in resolving conflict (Bundey 1983) through a process of mediation. Mediation will be discussed later in the chapter.

Johnson and Johnson (1997) expand on the fight/flight/fix analysis of conflict strategies, drawing on the dual concern model of conflict. They refer to five types of conflict responses:

- withdrawing
- forcing
- smoothing
- compromising
- problem-solving

Johnson and Johnson developed an inventory of responses to conflict, 'How you act in conflicts' (1997, pp. 338–43), which seeks responses to thirty-five proverbs that 'reflect traditional wisdom for resolving conflict' (1997, p. 338). Responses are analyzed according to their five criteria and a conflict profile developed. Although the inventory seems a little unusual in its use of proverbs, the results are surprisingly beneficial in clarifying the strategies currently being used. The description of the five profiles is a useful educative tool for exploring other options, thereby offering the potential to expand the repertoire of strategies currently used.

# Negotiation

Negotiation is a process by which persons willingly try to solve shared and opposing interests (Johnson & Johnson 1997). Most interpersonal disputes are handled by negotiation. When finding ourselves in a conflict situation in which there appears to be a possibility for resolution, depending on past experiences with conflict, we generally tend to try negotiation, that is, working things out for ourselves, perhaps getting advice from friends or family. There are a great many situations in which negotiations take place, for example:

- buying a car
- arranging a salary package
- determining different roles and responsibilities at work
- arranging a fair division of household chores
- making divorce settlements and custody arrangements
- agreeing with a child (or a parent) on a study schedule or curfew times

The type and complexity of the strategies employed will depend on the people involved—the relationship between them, their expectations and needs, their level of trust and willingness to be honest and open in the negotiation, and the information required for the negotiation to take place (Johnson & Johnson 1997).

If only negotiations were always as simple as that in Practice example 12.2. Unfortunately, they are frequently more complex and emotionally taxing, requiring considerable skill to achieve success. Johnson and Johnson (1997), reporting on the statistics related to conflict in the workplace, state that on average 9.2 per cent of management time is involved with dealing with conflicts between employees who have not been able to negotiate their own solutions.

## Practice example 12.2

## Simple negotiations

Negotiation can be a very brief and simple interchange:

'I need a computer to finish this project. Can I use the one you're working on?'

'Well, I'm really enjoying playing this game on the computer.'

'How about I lend you my Playstation, while I use your computer? You always seem to enjoy playing with it.'

'Sure, that would be fun.'

## Activity 12.5  Negotiation outcomes

Consider your recent experiences with conflict. Briefly summarize two or three examples of both positive and negative experiences of your attempts at negotiating the conflict situations. Can you identify the differences in these situations that may account for the positive or negative outcome?

The negative consequences of failed negotiations can be financial, emotional, and psychological. Within a work context, they are likely to lead to a reduction in productivity (Johnson & Johnson 1997) and, if the conflict remains unresolved, may also result in experiences of stress and depression. In my work with clients referred through an employment assistance program, the majority of issues of concern are related to conflict with managers and, to a lesser extent, with co-workers. In the former situation, negotiations are generally more difficult due to the imbalance in power and the concern that an honest airing of issues may be counterproductive.

To explore the process of successful negotiation let us turn our focus to organizations and situations in which practitioners may find themselves. Successful professional practice depends on understanding the complex relationships and dynamics within our organizations or agencies. 'Frequently there is a lack of understanding of the roles of various professions who comprise the staff of an agency' (Brearley 1995, p. 113) and there are a myriad of opportunities for differences in beliefs and attitudes, goals and work practices to emerge, resulting in tensions that require negotiation (and, at times, mediation). Successful negotiation is much more likely when time and effort have been invested in preparing for the process of negotiation.

## Preparing for negotiation

Negotiation is successful when it results in agreements to which people feel committed. This is generally not possible unless people's needs have been adequately considered. These needs may be tangible, covering such aspects as the need for money, time, goods, resources, or territory. They may also relate to procedural requirements—for example, to the way things are to be done or how they may relate to psychological or relationship needs (Hollier et al. 1993). Mapping conflict (see below) is a means by which the needs of the parties involved may be explored. Preparation also involves taking the time to understand the negotiation process itself and the various strategies involved (Nierenberg 1981), as well as carefully considering the timing and context in which the negotiation will take place. The location or venue should, if possible, be neutral, comfortable, free of interruptions or distractions, and afford sufficient privacy (Tillett 1991). The timing needs to suit all parties and provide enough time for preparation. Preparation by each party should not only involve the clarification of needs and hoped for outcomes if the negotiation succeeds, but also the anticipated outcomes if the negotiations fail (Stitt 1998; Hollier et al. 1993). It is helpful to develop what is often referred to as the 'best alternative to a negotiated agreement' (BATNA) if the negotiation does not resolve the dispute (Stitt 1998) and also the 'worst alternative to a negotiated agreement' (WATNA), because 'having a bottom line makes it easier to resist pressure and temptations of the moment' (Fisher & Ury 1999, p. 102).

Another important aspect of preparation is to try to anticipate the emotions that may be experienced by all concerned and how to respond to the emotions of the others in the conflict (Hollier et al. 1993). Suggestions for managing emotions can be as simple as planning a self-calming statement that can be repeated, and remembering to breathe, taking slow, deep breaths before responding (Drew 2004). As emotions are experienced in both mind and body (Hollier et al. 1993), we need to become aware of how and in which part of our bodies we store our unexpressed emotions. We should also devise and 'practice ways of handling difficult emotions in others [such as engaging in]:

- active listening
- giving support and reassurance
- selecting out what is valid from emotional dumping
- re-directing statements that create or inflame conflict towards positive possibilities' (Hollier et al. 1993, p. 6.10).

## Activity 12.6  Physical responses to conflict

Think about the last conflict you were in when you felt unable to express your needs or emotions. Can you remember if you felt tension in any part of your body? It will be helpful if, the next time this happens, you consciously try to relax that particular body part, while taking slow, deep breaths.

Despite planning and preparing for negotiation, there are no guarantees that expectations of what will happen in the negotiation will match the reality encountered. Perhaps planning what we might say to begin the negotiation is the one thing on which we can truly depend. Hollier et al. (1993) extol the benefits of planning a thirty-second opening statement that engages the other person's interest, states your objectives, and invites a response from the other person, which may indicate their ideas on what the next step of negotiation might be (Hollier et al. 1993).

# Mapping conflict

Understanding people's needs in conflict is a key to successful resolution. Although it will not be possible to discuss it at length, it is beneficial for the practitioner to become aware of a process devised by Hollier et al. (1993, p. 8.2) for mapping conflict by 'graphically representing a problem, showing everyone's perspectives [and providing] sufficient distance to see issues . . . that may otherwise go unnoticed'. The map assists in the analysis of the needs and concerns of all the key stakeholders in a conflict situation. It is a constructive and efficient process, and if the mapping process is handled with sensitivity and skill, it not only facilitates the emergence of appropriate solutions but also results in all people involved feeling validated and understood. Mapping can be used for simple and complex situations, indeed, whenever 'we need greater clarity about a problem . . . [i]t can be used individually, with a partner, or with a small or large group' (Hollier et al. 1993, p. 8.8), and therefore it is readily incorporated into the negotiation–preparation process.

Mapping the conflict involves:

1. Defining the issue—ensuring that a person is not defined as the problem. Label the issue in terms that everyone can agree upon. On a large sheet of paper, position the issue in a circle in the middle.
2. Identifying who is involved as either individuals or groups. Draw segments from the circle with which to identify each person or group.
3. Listing the major needs and concerns of each party involved in their segment.
4. Reflecting on the map—working as a group, identify what the common points are that connect people. What are the similarities? What are the differences? How does this influence everyone's perspective on the original issue?

The dynamics in Practice example 12.3 draw on Practice example 15.3. The conflict between the various employees is not uncommon in many organizations, including those employing helping professionals.

## Practice example 12.3

### Conflict in a work team

Sylvia, the manager of a youth centre in an inner-city area, employs six workers from a number of different professional backgrounds to conduct a broad range of programs for homeless youth. She has become aware of escalating conflict between team members but is reluctant to address underlying tensions in case it jeopardizes the smooth running of the centre. It seems there has been a long-standing history of division between team members, who adopt very different positions on implementing government policy. Some members of the team believe there is no use challenging government policy, while others wish to resist all changes unless they are consistent with social justice values. Some team members are beginning to openly attack colleagues, whom they label as 'troublemakers'. In response, others are accused of being uncritical government functionaries who are out of touch with the needs of service users.

Over the past month, there has been a sudden increase in unexplained staff absences and Sylvia is coming under increasing pressure from her management committee to implement staff disciplinary action. Team members are feeling stressed and despondent, and two of them are

*continued*

thinking about leaving the centre, despite their passion for working with homeless youth in this community.

Using the above scenario, construct a map of this situation.

Case scenario courtesy of Deborah Hart.

## Questions for reflection

Imagine you are the manager of the youth centre and are planning to have individual meetings with each of the workers at the centre.

1. Develop a thirty-second opener that you could use to begin the meetings with those who have been labelled the 'troublemakers'.
2. What do you anticipate the reactions of the workers might be?
3. What feelings might be expressed?
4. What strategies might you use to manage these feelings?

# Mediation

'Mediation is an extension of the negotiation process and is a collection of strategies to promote more efficient and effective negotiations' (Johnson & Johnson 1997, p. 397). In mediation, a neutral third party assists those in conflict to 'identify the disputed issues, develop options, consider alternatives and endeavour to reach an agreement' (Martin 2000). The role of the mediator is to advise on the process to be used but not the actual content or outcome of the dispute (Martin 2000). There are many models of mediation or alternative dispute resolution, ranging from quite simple (Bundey 1983) to others of greater complexity (Stitt 1998; Moore 1996; Hollier et al. 1993). 'Mediation is practised in various degrees of intensity and structure, informally [and formally,] in most professions dealing with people' (Martin 2000, p. 34).

Although many of the skills required for successful mediation are the same as those acquired by practitioners associated with the helping professions, and 'there are parallels between mediation' and interviews conducted by helping professionals (Martin 2000, p. 36), it is recognized that specific training is required to be a professional mediator (Martin 2000). Therefore, the process of mediation that is to be briefly discussed here is one that involves only four steps and was developed by Bundey (1983) for working with groups. It is a simple process that does not require specific training and is equally applicable to working with couples, families, and, indeed, most situations in which the practitioner might be required to facilitate the resolution of conflict. The role of the practitioner in this model of mediation may require anything from a subtle facilitation of the negotiations between the parties involved in conflict, to a tightly structured facilitation of the mediation process. The success of the mediation process depends on the motives of those involved in the mediation and the extent to which the parties in conflict develop trust during the process. This obviously becomes more difficult when prolonged conflict has emotionally scarred the individuals involved (Bundey 1983).

### Step 1—Setting the stage
In this opening stage, the rules for the process and a climate of trust and safety are established so that participants can genuinely commit to the mediation process (Bundey 1983). The role of the mediator is to 'take charge' of the process, and ensure that both parties recognize that they will each have equal time to present their views without interruption.

### Step 2—Defining the issues
This can be a very difficult and risky stage as what is perceived to be the problem may not in fact be the real problem. Therefore, the parties involved need to feel safe enough to open up and disclose their real concerns (Bundey 1983). The role of the mediator is to assist each party in focusing and defining their needs, using concrete examples.

### Step 3—Processing the issues
This stage is a continuation of defining the issues, focusing on the communication process between the parties. The mediator's role is to ensure they are listening and understanding each other's perspective and to manage the emotional climate, deal with any competition or intimidation, and facilitate empathy between the parties (Bundey 1983).

### Step 4—Resolving the issues
By this stage creative alternatives are encouraged and begin to emerge, as each person feels respected due to the mutual respect and trust that has been part of the mediation process (Bundey 1983). What are the identified areas of agreement between the two parties? The role of the mediator is to ensure that each party acknowledges the common ground that exists, ensure that each party demonstrates a degree of flexibility, develop a variety of options, and ensure that there are some measurable criteria for change.

Successful mediation not only achieves the resolution of the current conflict situation but also creates a learning opportunity for the parties concerned, promoting their trust and confidence in conflict resolution, so that future conflicts may not require the involvement of a neutral third party (Bundey 1983).

It is probably true for many people that conflict is likely to be associated with negative experiences and outcomes. Therefore, the most beneficial strategy when working with clients is to help them to recognize and focus on conflict's positive potential (Johnson & Johnson 1997; Tillett 1991) for encouraging change, creativity, self-awareness, and better decision-making (Johnson & Johnson 1997; Bundey 1983).

## Question for reflection
1. In what everyday situations do you find yourself assuming the mediating role?

## Activity 12.7  Mirroring

Working with a partner, practise the skills of active listening and 'I' statements. Each partner should think about a situation that has recently caused him some difficulty.

Partner A begins by making an 'I' statement expressing how he feels about the situation. Partner B actively listens to the statement, and reflects back what he hears. Try to reflect back both the content and feeling of the statement. Partner A either agrees by indicating 'Yes, that is what I said' or 'No, that is not what I said'. The process repeats until some movement is made towards a shared understanding of the issue.

Reflection: Did either person become defensive? Was the reflected statement free of judgment? Did both partners feel heard?

## Activity 12.8  Conflict learning outcomes

1. Has your understanding of conflict management changed in any way since reading this chapter?
2. In what way might this affect the strategies you use when you next experience conflict, or the way you work with clients who are involved in situations of conflict?

## Questions for Review

1. What are three basic responses to conflict? What are the advantages and disadvantages of each?
2. What are the basic steps in mediation? In what conflict situation is mediation an appropriate response?
3. What are the advantages of mediation?

## References

Brearley, J. (1995). *Counselling and Social Work.* Buckingham, PA: Open University Press.

Bundey, C. (1983). Group Leader Training Course. Sydney: Unpublished workshop handouts.

de Bono, E. (1985). *Conflicts: A Better Way to Resolve Them.* London: Harrap.

Drew, N. (2004). *A Leader's Guide to The Kid's Guide to Working Out Conflicts: How to Keep Cool, Stay Safe, and Get Along.* Minneapolis: Free Spirit Publishing.

Fisher, R., & Ury, W. (1999). *Getting to Yes: Negotiating an Agreement Without Giving In.* London: Random House.

Hollier, F., Murray, K., & Cornelius, H. (1993). *Conflict Resolution Trainers' Manual: 12 Skills.* Sydney: The Conflict Resolution Network.

Johnson, D.W., & Johnson, F.P. (1997). *Joining Together: Group Theory and Group Skills* (6th edn). Boston: Allyn & Bacon.

Martin, J. (2000). Social workers as mediators. *Australian Social Work*, 53(4), 33–9.

Moore, C.W. (1996). *The Mediation Process: Practical Strategies for Resolving Conflict*. San Francisco: Jossey-Bass.

Nierenberg, G.I. (1981). *The Art of Negotiating*. New York: Simon & Schuster.

Schneider Corey, M., & Corey, G. (1997). *Groups: Process and Practice*. Pacific Grove, CA: Brooks/Cole.

Stitt, A.J. (1998). *Alternative Dispute Resolution for Organizations*. Toronto: John Wiley & Sons.

Tillett, G. (1991). *Resolving Conflict: A Practical Approach*. Sydney: Sydney University Press.

# 13 Introduction to Working with Groups

### Agi O'Hara

*A team without clearly defined goals is like an orchestra being called together without knowing what piece of music they are going to play. Each individual musician may be a splendid performer but without a common goal to bring them together the result will be noise.*

Williams, cited in Healy 1992, p. 2.

Group membership is a natural and frequently occurring human experience. From birth, we are involved in a range of groups, both formal and informal, beginning with family and continuing, for many, through 'school, church, political, friendship, interest, leisure and work groups' (Benson 2001, p. 3). So what is a 'group'? There are perhaps as many definitions as writers on group work, so perhaps a simple definition of a group offers a general but meaningful description: a number of people drawn together for 'a natural and purposeful experience involving . . . mutual interaction, over a period of time' (Benson 2001, p. 5). For Benson (2001, p. 6) this is 'not just any arbitrary massing of people'. He excludes from his definition of a group, for example, people lining up for a bus or shopping in a supermarket. Generally, this may well be an accurate differentiation in the majority of cases; however, it does ignore the potential for a relationship to develop among such people randomly massed together. People at a bus stop, for example, may quickly become a group if there is a motor vehicle accident in their proximity and they begin to process reactions and offer support to each other. In such circumstances, social relationships have formed and the previously mentioned 'arbitrary massing of people' have become a group, albeit of short duration.

## Types of groups

There are a variety of groups and group purposes. Within the social service sector, groups can take the form of consciousness-raising groups in which members promote dialogue, critical thinking, and action: intervention-/treatment-oriented groups—for example, survivors of childhood sexual assault or adults struggling with obsessive-compulsive behaviours; cognitive–behavioural groups to address anxiety or substance abuse; social action groups that bring members together to advocate for a particular cause—for example, highlighting the discrepancies between federal and provincial funding for reserve-based and non-reserve child welfare services, environmental groups; network and support groups—for example, groups for parents of children with disabilities; and skill development groups that focus on the attainment of particular skills—for example, The International Toastmaster's Clubs, or learning how to apply principles of Applied Behavioural Analysis when working with children with autism, at http://www.aaswg.org/.

Group membership facilitates social relationships that enable individuals to develop personally as well as to contribute to the attainment of a particular group's goal. Social workers have long recognized the benefits of group membership in assisting members to develop greater skills associated with psycho-social functioning (Northen 1988) as well as achieving institutional and community change through citizen action (Hartford 1972). During the 1960s there was a re-burgeoning of interest in small groups, particularly in social work practice, as social science research provided valuable understanding of group processes and dynamics (Hartford 1972). Since that time, understanding of group phenomena has continued to grow, as have the purposes and contexts within which groups now occur. Social workers are often involved in running groups for members of the general community who are in some way at risk or disenfranchised. Greif and Ephross (1997) offer a summary of the types of group membership with which social workers (and other helping professionals) might work:

- people with illness or disabilities—for example, cancer, HIV/AIDS, head injuries,
- mental illness
- support groups—for example, widows/widowers
- non-custodial parents
- children of divorce/separation
- elderly people
- victims and perpetrators of violence—for example, domestic violence
- substance abusers—for example, adolescent alcohol/drug abusers
- people on a methadone program
- gay and lesbian groups
- schools and workplace groups—for example, unemployed people

The nature of groups, whether educational, therapeutic, support, community, or political, generally determines the goals and membership of the group, as well as the contexts in which they meet. Group membership may be described as heterogeneous or homogenous, group members may be fully invested or marginal, or they may be transient members.

Despite the variety of purposes for group formation, many processes and dynamics are common to all groups. It is these frequently found group phenomena that will be dealt with in this chapter. Adapting principles developed in the context of interviewing (highlighted in chapter 9, 'The Microskills of Interviewing'), it is important to recognize that group members bring with them many dimensions of diversity to the groups they join. Competency based on awareness of diversity, and ethical and multicultural practice is therefore a necessary prerequisite and the foundation (Ivey & Bradford Ivey 2003) for respectful and equitable work with groups. Refer also to chapters 2, 5, and 6 for detailed discussions of ethics and diversity issues. It is also recommended that professionals consult their appropriate professional associations for specific ethical guidelines. In Canada, the Canadian Group Psychotherapy Association brings together group therapy practitioners from a variety of disciplines with the goals of providing education and training for mental health professionals in group psychotherapy, and encouraging research and social action by promoting the use of group psychotherapy in both community and hospital settings. Further information can be located at http://www.cgpa.ca. As well, The Association for the Advancement of Social Work with Groups is an international organization that has developed Standards for Social Work Practice with Groups, available at http://www.aaswg.org/.

## Activity 13.1  Group experiences

Write a list of the various groups of which you have been a part, together with three or four words that best describe your experiences in the groups. It will be beneficial to think about these groups and your relations with the leader and other group members as you consider the material to follow.

# Group leader tasks

Taking on the role of group leader involves engaging in a variety of tasks and using a range of skills, many of which are crucial in the very first group meeting. It is perhaps the first meeting more than any other that determines the overall quality of the group experience to follow. People join groups with a myriad of questions or concerns they seek to have answered before being able to commit to the group. Common concerns, often influenced by previous group experiences, include:

- who the other members will be;
- if they will fit in, or feel accepted by the others in the group;
- if they will be able to meet others' expectations;
- if the group will provide what is being sought;
- if the leader will be someone who can be trusted.

Issues related to identity and intimacy also frequently arise (Birnbaum 1986). How they will be perceived and if they will be able to offer sufficient self-disclosure and engage in the level of closeness expected by others is a source of anxiety for many group members. Feelings at the beginning of groups can be likened to those commonly experienced on the first day of school (Napier & Gershenfeld 1993). Although experienced through an adult lens, the experience for many evokes child-like insecurities. It is therefore the leader's role to create a safe, supportive, welcoming group environment so that feelings of discomfort based on fear, insecurity, embarrassment, doubt, and hesitation are diminished, allowing curiosity, hope, and excitement to prevail.

Culture acts as a primary source for explaining human development and functioning. Within group interactions, there is a need to account for cultural differences in relation to group dynamic issues such as self-disclosure, affiliation, individual versus group goals, personal boundaries, and degree of familiarity. For example, group building and attention to group identity are particularly important to Aboriginal people, who value, in ascending order, the needs and well-being of the individual, the family, and the community (Dickson 2000). Therefore, singling out individuals within groups, even with the intent to provide additional support, may not be appropriate for some Aboriginal group participants. As well, within heterogeneous cultural groups, leaders need to be mindful of what constitutes culturally-appropriate expressions of validation, nurturing, warmth, caring, acceptance, sincerity, and openness.

# Group rules

Facilitating a discussion of expectations around how group members will treat each other, quite early in the first session, is an effective means of increasing feelings of safety and trust. The products of such discussions are sometimes referred to as group contracts, group guidelines, or group rules. These guidelines are frequently recorded on paper but may also be provided as a handout for group members to keep. Exploring group members' concerns about group membership at this time also provides an indication of what could be included in the guidelines.

Formulating group rules is both a preventative and curative strategy. It encourages appropriate behaviour among the group and therefore minimizes the likelihood of problems arising in the group (Dick 1991). However, if difficulties do arise between group members, the guidelines can also be referred to and thus facilitate a more disciplined exploration of issues than would be possible if interaction guidelines had never been developed. The content of group rules varies depending on the nature of the group but the following are common to many groups:

- to respect each other
- to put aside prejudices and assumptions and value the diversity that often exists in groups
- to be non-judgmental of each other, despite potential differences of opinion
- to provide constructive feedback (see below for guidelines)
- to listen to each other without interrupting
- to maintain confidentiality regarding identifiable information discussed in the group
- to take responsibility for own learning/participation
- to permit group members *not* to participate in structured exercises (see below)

Although group rules are developed early in the life of the group, the possibility of adding items needs to be emphasized. As the group develops, new experiences sometimes raise issues that can benefit from inclusion in the group contract.

## Practice example 13.1

## Working with adolescents

Working with a group of adolescents who are attending a voluntary support group for people recovering from excessive drug use, the group leader introduces an exercise in which group

*continued*

members are asked to talk about their initiation into drug use. The majority of group members take a few minutes to self-disclose. Angela appears very agitated and when it's her turn begins to cry, saying she's unable to talk about her experiences. Sarah, who had been one of the first to speak, responds with sarcasm, insisting that the cute little princess better put up, as everyone else has had to: 'What makes you so special?' A heated discussion begins. In such a situation, the leader would be advised to talk about the differing rates at which people develop a sense of safety and trust within groups and to explore the possibility of making participation voluntary. If agreement is reached, it is then appropriate to add voluntary participation as an item on the group guidelines.

Taking time to cover guidelines for giving constructive feedback is a worthwhile part of the discussion of group rules. Providing information to other group members about the effect of their behaviour in the group is difficult and often a source of anxiety for many group members. The use of 'I' statements is particularly helpful at these times. Bundey et al. (1989) list the following guidelines for giving and receiving feedback:

- Describe rather than judge or interpret the behaviour that was observed.
- Be specific rather than general.
- Take into account the needs of the receiver of the feedback (considering their emotional state and ability to receive the information) as well as the needs of the giver (by considering motives in providing feedback).
- Direct the feedback at behaviour that is controllable; otherwise it is counterproductive and increases frustration.
- Check if the feedback is welcomed rather than merely imposing it.
- Consider the timing of the feedback (most appropriate at the earliest opportunity), readiness for the feedback, and the context—for example, presence of others.
- Check that the receiver has correctly understood the feedback.
- Give feedback in a tentative and non-dogmatic manner.
- Check that others concur with what has been said.

It is generally accepted that it is best to focus on the positives first when giving feedback. As this is widely anticipated, many receivers of feedback listen only half-heartedly until they hear the word 'but', which usually signals the impending negative aspects of feedback. It is therefore helpful to repeat the positive components as a way of concluding the feedback, in case the receiver failed to hear it the first time.

## Activity 13.2  Giving feedback

Consider a situation in which you were given (or gave) feedback that resulted in a negative or counterproductive outcome. Identify which of the guidelines in the list above were not followed, and formulate a more appropriate version of the feedback according to the guidelines.

# Group goals

Facilitating the development of group goals on which group members agree (Garvin 1981) and for which they feel a sense of ownership is of particular importance. It is never appropriate for the leader to assume that the 'working' goal that they had in mind when setting up the group will suffice for the group. A particular focus at the first session of the group needs to be the clarification of the group goal(s). It is only through the exploration of each of the members' hopes or needs (the individual goals that brought them to the group) that group goals will emerge with genuine ownership by the group.

The manner and extent of goal clarification has long-term consequences for the group. Clear and agreed-upon goals not only determine the manner in which group members respond to each other and the way the leader works with the group (Garvin 1981), but also significantly contribute to the overall quality of the group experience. Personal social needs may be met through involvement in a collective or group goal, and self-esteem will be boosted if the goal is successfully attained and the individual's involvement recognized (Dick 1991). Inexperienced group leaders sometimes allow groups to begin the 'work' of the group very quickly, prior to the group achieving a workable level of cohesion, and with insufficient clarification of the group goal. This may result in the more vocal members of the group hijacking the group's activity, such that dissent only becomes apparent later. By this time a great deal of work has probably already taken place and it may appear impossible to shift direction to accommodate an alternative interpretation of the group goal. This is more likely in groups that have come together to focus on quite concrete tasks, such as particular projects in work or community groups, and is less likely in groups where social-emotional relationships are a key feature, such as in support groups.

It is also important to realize that besides the publicly stated goals, group members sometimes have hidden agendas that are not recognized by the group or the leader at the outset. These underlying agendas do not necessarily need to be a cause for concern as the group is often able to work on both surface/public and underlying/private agendas (Bradford 1978) if they are not in conflict. Group leader strategies that assist in dealing with underlying agendas are covered in chapter 14, 'Intervention Strategies for Working with Groups'.

## Practice example 13.2

## Hidden agendas in groups

Mary joins a local environmental group because she is deeply committed to improving the state of parks and gardens in her municipality (public, personal goal). She has recently ended a long-term relationship and is hoping to meet like-minded young people, perhaps even an eligible young man with whom she may develop a romantic relationship (private, hidden agenda). The existence of both agendas may be no problem at all, unless of course Mary focuses solely on her desire to find a partner and engages in annoying flirtatious behaviour that interferes with the work of the group.

*continued*

> ## Questions for reflection
>
> Think about your past experiences as a group member.
>
> 1. Were you aware of interactions or behaviours that seemed to be at odds with what was expected?
> 2. How were these behaviours dealt with?
> 3. Could they have been connected with a group member's hidden agenda?

# Styles of leadership

Since the 1950s, the focus in regard to leadership styles has frequently been on task orientation versus interpersonal orientation of the leader. Although leadership is important, it is generally considered less important compared to the group membership. Bales (Sivasubramaniam et al. 2002) was the first to differentiate task and relational or social-emotional leadership roles. Hersley and Blanchard (cited in Napier & Gershenfeld 1993) incorporated these aspects into a situational leadership framework that also considers group members' maturity as a means of determining appropriate leadership style (Napier & Gershenfeld 1993). According to this model, as the level of group members' maturity increases, leaders should generally respond by reducing their involvement regarding both task and relationships. However, the situational leadership model also accommodates the reality that task and social-emotional maturity are not necessarily gained simultaneously. It does so by assessing group member maturity on both ability and motivation:

- mature ability–immature motivation (M4)
- mature ability–mature motivation (M3)
- immature ability–mature motivation (M2)
- immature ability–immature motivation (M1)

These four combinations are incorporated into a four-quadrant representation of leader style (Hersey & Blanchard 1988):

- low relationship–low task (S4)
- high relationship–low task (S3)
- low relationship–high task (S2)
- high relationship–high task (S1).

The model, though quite complex, predicts that effective combinations of leader-style and group member maturity are M4-S4, M3-S3, M2-S2, and M1-S1. Although, in theory, this appears to be a reasonable approach, the assessment of social-emotional maturity will necessarily be rather subjective. Considering it merely on the basis of motivation may be overly simplistic as it ignores various other factors also connected with social-emotional maturity such as group cohesion, trust (engaging in trusting and trustworthy behaviour), empathy, and anxiety.

## Practice example 13.3

### Applying the model of situational leadership

Working with a group of patients who are recovering from head injury, the leader is very aware of their cognitive difficulties and the likelihood of their reduced self-confidence. The group will require considerable assistance in formulating goals and strategies to work towards their achievement. At the same time, the leader will also need to focus on creating a safe and welcoming environment by offering acceptance, support, and encouragement (a group situation that corresponds to an S1-M1 combination). Over time, as the group members get used to being with each other, they are more likely to be supportive of each other, engaging in many of the relational, social-emotional behaviours previously offered by the group leader. Despite this development in their relational maturity, their cognitive impairment may prevent significant advances with regard to task functions. In this situation the leader would reduce their relationship focus while maintaining high task involvement (a group situation that corresponds to an S2-M2 combination).

### Questions for reflection

Think about one of the groups in which you have been a member and apply the situational model of leadership to analyze the leader style during the life of the group.

1. Can you identify changes in the way the leader responded to the group?
2. Can you identify changes in the maturity of the group?
3. Were the changes in leadership style appropriate to the development of the group?

## Participative dimensions of leadership style

An alternative framework for analyzing leadership style focuses on the extent of group member decision-making allowed by the leader, referred to as the *democratic versus autocratic* or *participative versus directive* dimension of leadership (Eagly et al. 2003). On a continuum of 'control', autocratic or directive leaders are at one end as they assume major responsibility for all leadership actions connected with decision-making, task organization, and the social-emotional well-being of group members (Benson 2001). At the other end of the continuum are laissez-faire or permissive leaders who allow the group to determine its own strategies and refrain from intervening. They choose to be non-directive leaders and assume the group can achieve its goal. There are advantages and disadvantages associated with each of these styles of leadership, depending on the goals and composition of the group. Perhaps one disadvantage that may not necessarily be anticipated relates to a permissive style of leadership. If it results in the leader avoiding dealing with group problems, then group members may view the leader as uncaring, incompetent, or disinterested. Consequently the group may be less motivated and their performance may fall below expectations (Sivasubramaniam et al. 2002). Participative or democratic leaders are somewhere in the middle of the 'control' continuum. They see their role as that of supporter and encourager. They remain involved in the group and offer their expertise as required.

Although adherence to one of the above styles of leadership may be appropriate for the entire life of some groups (Benson 2001), generally, as groups develop, leaders are able and should be encouraged to diminish their involvement in providing structure and direction for the group. It is therefore preferable for leaders to be sufficiently flexible in their style of leadership to be able to adapt to the changing needs of the group. Of course the type of group and the particular group's goals should also determine the style of leadership adopted. Such flexibility in style of leading needs to be compatible with the leader's personality and consonant with their theoretical knowledge of group behaviour (Benson 2001; Douglas 2000). Some leaders are less able to adopt certain styles of leadership and will therefore choose to work only with groups that respond to their preferred style of leading.

## Practice point 13.1

- Group leaders who generally work with community groups and have a preference for and have become accustomed to a facilitative, non-directive involvement with their groups, may find it difficult and frustrating to work with a group of young children who require a more hands-on, interventionist, and directive approach throughout the life of the group.

## Transformational leadership

It is now recognized that viewing leadership simply according to the autocratic–democratic–laissez-faire continuum is too restrictive as it ignores various key aspects of group-leader dynamics. A contemporary model of group leadership (frequently associated with organizational psychology) focuses on the nature of interactions between the leader and group members, differentiating between transactional and transformational leadership (Eagly et al. 2003; Sivasubramaniam et al. 2002; Avolio 1995). Transactional leadership exists in two forms: corrective and constructive. The former is significantly less effective, and involves the leader interacting with the group by either passively (responding when errors have occurred) or actively (looking for errors or mistakes) correcting group members' behaviour (Avolio 1995). Such a focus on mistakes is counterproductive to group members' development and minimizes the likelihood of members using their initiative (Avolio 1995). Constructive transactions are a little more effective as the leader also recognizes and rewards group members' accomplishments.

Transformational leadership, on the other hand, is far more effective as it involves a great deal more than positive transactions. It is characterized by the leader:

- communicating values and conveying a sense of purpose,
- intellectually stimulating the group by modelling means of challenging the status quo and offering new perspectives for problem solving,
- inspiring the group by demonstrating excitement and optimism regarding the group goal,
- acting as a mentor, considering the individual needs of group members, offering support, encouragement, learning opportunities, and appreciation of potential (Eagly et al. 2003; Avolio 1995).

Transformational leadership creates a highly motivated, cohesive, and inspired group that is able to achieve its individual and group potential and a high level of performance.

## Trait approach to leadership

The extent of control or direction a leader offers and the nature of interactions between the leader and group are significantly influenced by personal qualities of the leader. The trait approach to leadership is a traditional one and focuses on particular personal qualities that determine leader effectiveness (Gladding 2003).

 ### Activity 13.3  Reflecting on leader characteristics

Think about group situations in which you have been involved over the years.

1. Do any of the leaders of these groups stand out (in a positive sense) in your memory?
2. What was it about these leaders that differentiated them from the others?
3. What characteristics or behaviours did these leaders exhibit?

Many lists of effective leader characteristics have been developed. Their content is well represented by the lists to follow. Reid (1997, p. 98) suggests eight leader characteristics as indicative of effective group leading:

- courage
- honesty
- creativity
- self-knowledge
- empathy
- an action orientation

- enthusiasm
- humility

Corey (2004, pp. 26–8) believes that group members are greatly influenced by the behaviours leaders model for the group. His list of leader attributes is clearly consonant with those of transformational leaders:

- presence
- personal power
- courage
- willingness to confront self
- sincerity and authenticity
- sense of identity
- belief in group process
- inventiveness and creativity

Bundey (1980) raises the importance of being a well-functioning person as well as possessing good communication skills, and being appropriately assertive and self-aware regarding deficits in knowledge and biases that may negatively affect the group. She also highlights the importance of facilitating emotional stimulation and assisting group members to make sense of the processes in which they have participated (meaning attribution) as necessary for a positive group experience.

Benson (2001) refers to *three Cs*—competency, compassion, and commitment—as the basis for effective group leadership. The demonstration of credibility by knowing what you are doing regarding both content (particularly input) and group process engenders confidence in the group. Introducing strategies or structures such as developing a contract and clarifying expectations, as well as showing care and concern for members who may be struggling (Benson 2001), assist in the development of safety and trust in the group. However, each of these is insufficient if the leader does not appear to be committed to the group and its goals. If the leader is ambivalent or has reservations about the viability of the group or even the particular exercises to be used (Benson 2001), then the group will also be likely to respond with ambivalence, doubt, and perhaps even anxiety.

## Activity 13.4  Reflecting on negative group experiences

Think about your experiences in groups.

1. Were any of them less than satisfactory due either to a poor outcome regarding task or a lack of bonding among the group members?
2. Can you identify a lack in any of the leader characteristics (given in the text above) that may have contributed to your negative experience?

# Group process and dynamics

As group leaders observe their group in action and attempt to make sense of what they see, they are assisted in determining how, when, and where to intervene by having a framework of knowledge against which their observations can be checked. This can be likened to a nurse taking a patient's temperature. In isolation, a particular reading has no significance or meaning; however, when compared to scales within a medical framework, which reflect a normal or healthy range of readings, it is possible to determine if there is a need for intervention. Group process models/frameworks offer such a structure for analyzing group events, often referred to as group processes and group dynamics. Although it is difficult to simply describe what *group processes* are (Douglas 2000; Garvin 1981), they represent changes in group functioning or patterns of group behaviour, over time. In effective groups, the changes assist a group to utilize individual resources and create a new entity that is more effective than group members were individually (Douglas 2000). Group dynamics, on the other hand, refers to the forces, energies, and influences that fuel group processes. Bundey (1980) offers a group process model that identifies the following components:

- decision-making process (goal formulation and attainment, problem solving)
- maintenance process (related to socio-emotional needs of group members)
- role-differentiation process (including leadership)
- stage of group development (related to the changing needs of the group)
- communication–interaction process (shifting from member-to-leader to member-to-members)
- normative process (development of rules)

Incorporating these components into a 'mental map' and relating observations to it 'can lead to purposeful action' (Bundey et al. 1989, p. B30) by the group leader. Douglas (2000) identifies a different nomenclature for group processes (structural, operational, and regulating processes) but the sub-components are similar to those of Bundey (1980).

A valid criticism of group leaders is that many frequently attend to the content of interactions between group members (that is, what is being said or the task on which the group is working) rather than identifying underlying group processes that are responsible for the interaction (Hanson 1972), whether positive or negative. This fact is one of the reasons why it is often recommended to have two group facilitators available, in order to track both content and process issues.

## Practice example 13.4

### Focusing on group processes

Working with a group of children whose parents have recently divorced, the leader asks the group to take some time to draw a picture that represents how they are feeling. Melanie and Anne, who

*continued*

are sisters, begin arguing and the leader overhears the following:

*Anne:*    That's mine. I saw it first.

*Melanie:*    Give it back. You always get what you want.

*Anne:*    No I don't, and anyway your drawing will be silly so you don't need so many colours. Daddy says I'm a really good drawer and he always puts my drawings up at work.

If the leader responds by asking the girls to share and not raise their voices because it disturbs the rest of the group, they would be missing an opportunity to work with the dynamic that exists between them. Focusing only on the content of their interactions would be ignoring the fact that the sisters frequently compete with each other in the group and that it is quite likely this behaviour relates to their feelings about their family break-up. Providing information to the sisters (and the others in the group) that normalizes the many feelings (for example, anger, insecurity, wanting to seem special, jealousy) that are frequently experienced by young people in their situation, will assist all of them in relating to each other and their families.

Group leader strategies that assist in responding to both surface and underlying issues are covered in chapter 14, 'Intervention Strategies for Working with Groups'.

## Questions for reflection

1. Considering recent group experiences, can you think of opportunities for process observation that were not utilized?
2. Devise an appropriate response that would facilitate the interaction between the sisters discussed above.

To assist leaders in focusing on group process, Hanson (1972) provides guidelines for observing and analyzing groups, suggesting that when trying to understand the behaviours and interactions of group members, leaders look for:

- differences in participation among group members,
- the styles of influence and rivalry among group members,
- decision-making procedures,
- management of task and maintenance needs of the group,
- group membership and the development of sub-groups,
- feelings generated in the group (for example, excitement, boredom, anger, frustration, affection),
- group atmosphere,
- development of group norms (that may be both positive and negative).

# Group development

Different types of groups inevitably develop over time. Although variations due to type, goal, structure, and membership exist, general development patterns can be anticipated to occur in most groups. Benson (2001) highlights the intentionality of groups, suggesting that development is not a random process but dependent upon the social relationships that form in the group. It is crucial for group leaders to understand group development if they are to respond appropriately to members' needs. They also need to recognize that their own expectations of groups and their development are significantly influenced by the theoretical frameworks to which they adhere (Schiller 1997). Group needs change over time, due to the personal development or maturation of group members and the development of the group overall in its ability to respond to its internal and external environment. Such developments need to be considered by the group leader when interventions are being planned (see chapter 14, 'Intervention Strategies for Working with Groups', for a detailed discussion of leader interventions). Although it is possible to discuss group development in very broad terms such as the beginning, middle, and later stages of a group (Benson 2001), many group leaders are assisted in their understanding of groups by considering more detailed models of group development. A great many researchers/practitioners have devised theories, models, and frameworks outlining group development. It will not be possible in this chapter to cover all of these in detail. The focus therefore will be on earlier models—for example, Tuckman (1965), Hartford (1972), and Lang (1972), from which many later models have evolved—and specfic later models of group development such as Schiller (1997) that offer novel insights to aid our understanding of group processes. Tables 13.1 and 13.2 summarize the stages of development according to various early and more recent models of group development. It is possible to see recurring themes symbolized by the names by which stages are labelled in the various models:

- Several highlight an initial coming together that represents an immature connection in which group members are seen as dependent or passive—that is, being governed from outside themselves, generally by the leader (Lang 1972).
- The majority highlight a stage in which friction or tension emerges (counter-dependence, storming, power and control, disintegration, precipitating event, counterdependency and flight, challenge, and change). Maples (1988) explains this by suggesting that conflict develops as evidence of dissimilarity emerges and members begin to criticize or challenge each other. This is particularly likely when group members perceive a 'lack of progress of the group . . . or the perception by one member of "game playing" by another' (Maples 1988, p. 20).
- The majority of models refer to a mature coexistence prior to the group ending (interdependence, differentiation, autonomy, reintegration, trust and structure, and mutuality and interpersonal empathy).
- A closure or ending to the life of the group occurs in most models.

These commonly agreed upon developments imply a changing role for the leader. Appropriate changes in leader functioning can be easily demonstrated by considering group development from Lang's (1972) allonomous–autonomous framework. The more allonomous (unable to function independently) a group is, the more the leader will need to be actively involved in the group, offering a great deal of direction and support. The extent of direction and active involvement will need to diminish as the group moves towards maturity and

**Table 13.1** Early models of group development

| Bion (1961) | Tuckman (1965) | Garland et al. (1965, cited in Northen 1988) | Lang (1972) | Hartford (1972) | Schutz (1973) |
|---|---|---|---|---|---|
| Dependence | Forming | Pre-affiliation | Allonomous | Pre-group | Inclusion |
| Counter-dependence | Storming | Power and control | Transitional | Formation | Control |
| | Norming | | Autonomous | Integration | Affection |
| Inter-dependence | Performing | Intimacy | | Disintegration | |
| | (Adjourning) (added in 1977, see Maples 1988) | Differentiation | | Reintegration | |
| | | Separation | | Functioning and mainte-nance | |
| | | | | Termination | |

**Table 13.2** Later models of group development

| Northen (1988) | Worchel (1994, cited in Garvin 2001) | Whelan and Hochberger (1996) | Schiller (1997) |
|---|---|---|---|
| Orientation-inclusion | Discontent stage | Dependency and inclusion | Pre-affiliation |
| Dissatisfaction and power conflict | Precipitating event | Counterdependency and flight | Establishing a rela-tional base |
| Mutuality-work | Identity | Trust and structure | Mutuality and inter-personal empathy |
| Separation-termina-tion | Group productivity | Work | Challenge and change |
| | Individuation | Termination | Termination |
| | Decay | | |

autonomy. Remaining overly directive will cause frustration and even hostility for a group that is ready to determine their own functioning. Similarly, prematurely withdrawing support and direction from a group while it is still largely allonomous will be counterproductive and will potentially create fear and insecurity in the group. Although the majority of leaders will see their role as facilitating the movement towards autonomy for their group, this process cannot be forced or pushed by the leader. Groups will move to autonomy with varying speed, depending on the nature of the group and its members, and the previous group experiences of the members. It is helpful to recognize that many groups revert to an allonomous state at the very beginning of each session (Bundey 1980) but regain their previous state of autonomy as the session progresses, unless particularly challenging events occur, which require a different level of intervention from the leader.

## Activity 13.5  Groups that remain allonomous

Although most groups develop with appropriate leading, and progress along the allonomous–autonomous continuum, can you think of any groups in which such development would be unlikely? Give reasons why.

Despite the many similarities, there are several differences between the above-mentioned group development models and these can be summarized as:

- the implied structure of the model, whether it is linear or represents a cycle of development
- the order in which some of the stages occur
- the identification of a pre-group stage (Schiller 1997; Hartford 1972; Garland 1965, cited in Northern 1988)

## Group structure

Johnson and Johnson (1997) identify distinctions between 'sequential stage theories' that highlight the changing focus of the group (and the accompanying changes in members' behaviour) and the 'recurring phase theories' that specify the recurring 'issues that dominate group interaction' (Johnson & Johnson 1997, p. 24). Although some authors specifically raise the issue of development progressing through cycles, such that stages do not represent linear progression (Worchel, cited in Garvin 2001), others do not. This does not imply that the stages in any of the models should necessarily be viewed linearly. For example, whether referred to as storming or counterdependency, the stage of dissension at which issues of power, control, and challenge are raised is often followed by a brief return to an earlier stage in which the leader becomes more directive, offering substantial guidance and support. Depending on the nature and extent of the 'storm', the leader may need to reassert her authority as a means of recreating a sense of safety and containment for the group.

Whether the group experiences a major challenge or disruption, due to power and control issues, or merely a 'storm in a tea cup', group leaders should view such challenging dynamics positively. They indicate group development and a perceived level of safety in the group such that group members are able to voice dissent and explore reactions to interpersonal connections that have developed. Many group members express relief at being able to be 'real' with each other rather than what is often referred to as 'walking on eggshells' prior to the airing of differences in the 'storm'.

In a simple way, group development can be seen to parallel the natural progression of human development in a family context (Reid 1997; Lang 1972). Babies and children are generally seen to be dependent, requiring and accepting a great deal of guidance and support from family leaders. Adolescents generally become less tolerant of the 'guidance' offered by their parents. They begin to question the authority of family leaders, and create family tension when challenging family power relations. They are also focused on clarifying their identity and their place in the world, as much as within the family. As time goes on and all going well, young (and older) adults are able to co-create a more mature, interdependent family dynamic with other family members, one that recognizes the ability of the young adult to be responsible for him- or herself. The proviso 'all going well' is an important one. Just as family tensions during the adolescent years can result in major conflicts and long-term rifts if not handled with sensitivity and understanding, 'storming' in groups, if inappropriately handled by the group leader, may result in groups terminating prematurely, or not being able to function to their full potential. It is not suggested that individuals joining groups revert to childlike states per se, but it does recognize that group participation is quite daunting for many group members, as previously discussed. This may be due to a myriad of factors such as previous group experiences, the nature of the current group, individual personality factors, or social immaturity. It is the leader's role to facilitate individual development so that group members are able to take responsibility and deal with challenges that emerge. The leader needs to gauge the changing needs and abilities of the group, relinquishing and taking control and providing direction as required. It is also imperative that leaders are sufficiently mature psychologically, so that they do not respond to a challenge to their authority with counterproductive defensiveness or attempts to 'consciously suppress anger and hostility within their groups' (Reid 1997, p. 129).

## Practice example 13.5

## A defensive response to challenge

Let us return to the group of adolescents who are attending a voluntary support group for people recovering from excessive drug use. It's the second session and the group leader is discussing strategies for dealing with cravings and the temptation to 'use' again. One of the members, George, looks directly at the leader and says, 'Do you seriously believe what you're saying? When

*continued*

you're desperate, such strategies are the last thing you think about. If you'd ever been a user you'd know. So I guess you really don't know what you're talking about.' Responding to this challenge with, 'Well George, I'd really appreciate it if you could stop interrupting my presentation. I am the leader and obviously my employer believes I am qualified to be your group leader', would be inappropriate and sound defensive, further eroding the credibility of the leader. It is also likely to result in more challenges, possibly from other group members as well as George.

### Question for reflection

1. Consider the above interactions and devise a response to George's challenge that acknowledges his perspective and validates his needs and concerns.

# Group development and gender

The majority of models place the stage of dissension or 'storm' relatively early in the life of the group, generally as the second or third stage. Schiller (1997), in analyzing women's groups, suggests that in such groups normative development differs from those found in other groups. This, according to Schiller (1997, p. 4), is due to women's focus on connection and affiliation and a 'different relationship to power and conflict'. As a result, the stage in which conflicts arise occurs only after significant connections have been made and group members feel safe enough to explore their differences, while trusting the extent of their empathic connection and previously established respect for each other (Schiller 1997). Schiller (1997, p. 10) suggests that 'for men the arena of empathic self-disclosure and connection, and for women, the arena of engaging in productive conflict and maintaining connection during conflict, will likely be the respective areas of difficulty or challenge'. Therefore, recognizing the differing needs and development of groups with varying composition, whether all women, all men, or mixed, ensures group leaders respond with appropriate interventions to the different challenges facing groups.

## Pre-group stage

Of the few models of group development that include a pre-group stage, Hartford's (1972) model is the most detailed. She identifies the private, public, and convening components of the pre-group stage. The convening stage corresponds to the pre-affiliation stage during which members come together for the first time and are still wary of each other, with trust yet to develop. However, the group really begins with one person (privately) thinking about its possibility before publicly discussing the idea with others who may become involved in the planning and running of the group (or as future participants). Planning for a group needs to involve at the very least the formulation of a response to the following questions (Bundey 1980):

- What members' needs will the group meet?
- What will be the purpose of the group?
- What will need to be done to achieve the group's goals?
- What structure will be required for the group (for example, size of the group; number, duration, location of sessions)?

Decisions regarding group membership—finding the appropriate balance between heterogeneity and homogeneity with respect to gender, age, educational level, and so on— is also of particular importance and will be influenced by the nature of the group and its goals. Bundey et al. (1989) developed a planning checklist that expands on the above questions and is a very helpful reminder of the many issues that require attention when planning a group. A simple yet powerful concept that also assists in this planning process is to consider it with the image of an iceberg in mind (Morris 1989). The visible component, or the tip, represents the actions or activities of the group. This rather minimal part of the iceberg is supported by the much larger structure beneath the surface that represents (1) the group purpose/aim/goal as it is initially envisaged, and (2) the planning involved in devising the means by which the purpose will be achieved. Inadequate planning is unfortunately a common reason why many groups fail to thrive or even collapse. Group leaders who have previously experienced the benefits of a particular group as a group member, or perhaps observed the activities of other successful leaders, are often strongly motivated to recreate a similarly positive experience for others. If they merely copy the activities in which they were involved (the visible tip of the iceberg) without carefully considering their purpose and the possible strategies available, they are likely to find that there is insufficient foundation on which to build their group, and therefore may see their dream crumbling.

Despite apparent differences among the various models of group development, they offer a useful means of understanding the changes in group behaviour over time. It is helpful to see them as complementary rather than contradictory: 'A group may move through various stages while dealing with basic themes that surface as they become relevant to the group's work. Because the issues underlying the themes are never completely resolved, they can reoccur later.' (Johnson & Johnson 1997, p. 24) The length of time a group is together does not appear to determine the stages of group development. It is possible for groups to progress through each of the stages and deal with similar underlying themes whether together for six, ten, or twenty sessions, or only for a weekend. It is the actual length of time that the group is in each of the stages that will vary according to the group's total duration.

# Sample session agenda

Another aspect of planning relates to the individual group sessions. Group members generally appreciate knowing what they can expect of their time in the group. Whenever possible, offering a brief agenda for the session, whether verbally or in writing, assists members' feelings of trust and safety. Although the following list will not be relevant to all types of groups, it may assist as a general guideline for the content of group sessions and the items that may be included in an agenda:

- goal for the session
- focusing exercise or icebreaker
- review of/unfinished business from previous session
- body of session (content, structured exercises, and opportunity for participation)
- summary of learning (recap, meaning attribution)
- evaluation
- homework/preparation for following session

# Structured exercises

Structured exercises are 'game-like activities' (Watson et al. 1981, p. 1) and often referred to as icebreakers or focusing exercises, indicating the various purposes they serve. They facilitate communication between group members and provide opportunities to get to know each other, hence the term 'icebreaker'. Use of structured exercises can be particularly beneficial in the early stages of the group. Including an exercise that enables group members (and the leader) to learn each other's names is strongly recommended.

## Practice example 13.6

### Name game

The name–fruit (or food) game is simple and quite popular. Participants sit in a circle and say a fruit or food item that starts with the same letter of the alphabet as their given name, after repeating the previous members' name–fruit combinations around a circle. A typical sentence might be:

'Molly eats marshmallow, George eats grapefruit, Harry eats honey, Fran eats figs and Jane (the person speaking) eats jam.'

This type of chain learning can be successfully used with as many as twenty group members, as long as everyone in the group is reminded to repeat each name–food combination to themselves as the game progresses around the group. Variations on this game require group members to say an adjective that begins with the same letter of the alphabet, before their name—for example, 'happy Harry', 'tall Tammy' and so on. It is advisable to remind group members to choose a positive descriptor as their adjective–name combination as they occasionally become part of the person's identity during the life of the group. The long-term association of Wendy as 'whiny', for example, is likely to be counterproductive. Similarly, apparently humorous though potentially embarrassing combinations such as 'randy Robert' are also best avoided.

There are many books detailing hundreds of structured exercises, some as simple as asking couples or small groups to introduce themselves to each other, identifying their reason for joining the group, then reporting back to the whole group about what they learned about each other. Other structured exercises are more complex and, if carefully chosen, can achieve a great deal more than social connection. Depending on the type of group and the content or focus of a particular session, they can be designed to assist group members to become fully present in the group, letting go of thoughts or problems associated with work or other contexts they were in prior to arriving at the group venue. Structured exercises can also shift group processes—for example, they can change communication patterns, engender empathy for other group members, or facilitate personal insight through experiential learning.

It is important to critically consider the appropriateness of exercises before using them. Various versions of trust exercises have been around since the 1960s. They generally involve physical contact between group members—for example, being led by a partner while walking around blindfolded or allowing yourself to fall backwards into the arms of a partner. While such exercises were previously very popular and may have seemed appropriate in groups that had been together for a long time, it is now recognized that physical contact between group members can be traumatic for some group members. This is particularly the case if voluntary participation has not been discussed in the group and group members feel unable to decline to participate. When using structured exercises it is suggested that leaders prepare by considering:

- their purpose in using the exercise,
- the appropriateness of the exercise for that particular group,
- the consequences of using the exercise, anticipating potential problems for the group,
- the timing of the exercise, ensuring sufficient time has been allocated to process the outcome, and learning from the exercise,
- the manner in which to introduce the exercise.

Appropriate preparation of the group, no matter how simple the exercise, is crucial.

## Practice example 13.7

## Preparing the group for an icebreaker

Quite early in the first session the leader asks the group to think about how they are feeling at that moment and to write down on a piece of paper a few words that represent their feelings. Many, if not all, group members are reluctant to record their honest feelings (for example, of anxiety or concern about fitting in), fearing that they would be asked to either read their responses aloud or perhaps hand them in to the leader. However, if the leader was to have followed the original instruction with the comment, 'These words are for your use only, so that you can occasionally refer to them as a means of monitoring changes in your feelings about being in the group', then the exercise would have been a beneficial one.

*continued*

## Questions for reflection

1. As a group member, have you been reluctant to participate in a group activity?
2. What could the leader have said or done to facilitate your participation?

Many new leaders remember exercises that have been successfully used by other leaders and introduce them in their own groups assuming a similarly successful outcome. Without thinking through the factors listed above, they will likely not be prepared to deal with unpredicted outcomes. The 'iceberg' model referred to within the context of planning a group is equally relevant to planning the inclusion of structured activities.

## Activity 13.6   Reluctant participation as a group member

Think about the various group exercises in which you have been asked to participate.

1. Can you recall any that you particularly wished not to have been part of?
2. What were the features of the exercise that you found aversive?
3. Did you consider declining to participate? If yes, what was the outcome of your decision? If no, what prevented you from voicing your reluctance?

# Evaluation

The use of formal evaluations is generally at the discretion of the group leader, unless the agencies or organizations for whom the groups are run have specific requirements in this regard. Although evaluations provide quality control for the leader and can facilitate group responsibility and commitment when members are willing to give honest feedback, over-evaluation can be as damaging as no evaluation. Group members may become frustrated by the need to frequently respond in writing to forms that are time-consuming and often repetitive. Written evaluations that are simple to follow and clearly written can be very effective, but only when used infrequently. The key to effective evaluation is appropriate timing and creativity in the types of evaluations used. There are numerous quick, yet meaningful means of identifying how group members are feeling about being in the group and whether the group is on track with regard to group goals.

Leaders need to be clear of their intentions when devising evaluations. Evaluations can serve the purpose of providing feedback to the leader on their performance as leader, or providing feedback to the leader on the experiences of group members. The former can be achieved not only by group members' feedback but also by the group leader evaluating his or her own behaviour in the group, using checklists that monitor leader skills at various

## Practice point 13.2

■  A simple and effective means of quickly evaluating group members' experiences is
to ask the group to respond to questions in one of the following open-ended ways:

I learned . . .
I liked (or disliked) . . .
Right now I feel . . .
The session helped me . . .

stages in group sessions (Merritt & Walley 1977). Group members can also benefit from evaluating their group experience with regard to personal goal attainment and learning (Nelson-Jones 1991).

## Activity 13.7  Using evaluations

Consider the various forms of evaluation that you have had to complete over the years.

1. Do any stand out as a means of recording your thoughts and accurately representing
your experiences?
2. What were the features of this form of assessment that differentiate it from another
that you found less effective?

# Closure/termination

Groups end for many reasons. A particular number of sessions may have been planned, the group tasks may have been completed, or negative group processes may have led to a break-down of the group. Just as planning the first sessions is crucial, particular attention also needs to be paid to the ending of groups. It is important to provide opportunity for group members to remember significant group events and experiences, to complete any unfinished business that may still exist between members of the group, and to express feelings about the group ending (Johnson & Johnson 1997). The final stage also provides an opportunity to deepen connections between members as exploration of feelings regarding the group ending sometimes trigger 'issues of intimacy and loss in other areas' of group members' lives (Shulman 1999, p. 596). This is due to the features common to all losses such as the need to withdraw emotional investment when the connection is no longer available, after previously participating in 'an ongoing experience' (Garvin 1981).

Even when groups have a clearly defined ending time from their very beginning, group members sometimes ignore or deny the impending group closure. Planning is therefore required to prepare group members for the time when they will no longer be together. Group members may become critical and negative towards the group or leader just prior to group termination, creating dissatisfaction and a lowered group morale through increased lateness, absenteeism, and reduced involvement in the group (Hartford 1972). Such negative behaviours can be interpreted as unconscious strategies for eliminating or reducing separation anxiety, and may be avoided if sufficient preparation has taken place. Group members also frequently view closure with ambivalence. Positive experiences resulting from emotional intimacy and/or successful goal achievement lead to feelings of sadness in anticipation of the impending loss of contact with the group and the leader. This is frequently coupled with recognition of progress made, the desire to move forward, and a reluctance to remain dependent on the group and/or leader. Although the nature and purpose of the group will determine the closure strategy developed by the leader, preparation for termination sometimes involves group members individually processing their experiences and feelings about the group, in readiness for the final session when sharing of such insights is encouraged. It is through the processing of specific focus questions that a group is able to recognize and value the importance of their group experience, resolve any unfinished business, deal positively with the group ending, and transfer their learning to outside the group. Such questions include:

- What have been the most significant experiences of the group?
- What have you gained from being a member of this group?
- Is there anything that needs to be resolved, discussed, dealt with?
- How do you feel about the group ending?

A key for successful group closure is to 'create an end for the group which celebrates, synthesizes and symbolizes for members what the group was all about' (Benson 2001, p. 149).

## Activity 13.8  Facilitating closure

Think about the ending of groups in which you were a participant, and compare your feelings in a few of these situations.

1. What strategies did the leader employ to facilitate the process of closure?
2. Did the strategies work?
3. What could you now suggest as a means of improving the process?

## Questions for Review

1. What are five different types of groups that may be located within the social service sector?
2. What are Tuckman's (1977) stages of group development?
3. What are the different leadership styles?

4. What are the benefits of group versus individual intervention?
5. What are some ways in which feedback may be effectively shared with group members?

## Further Reading on Structured Exercises

Ashton, M., & Varga, L. (1991). *101 Games for Groups*. Adelaide: Hyde Park Press.

Canfield, J., & Wells, H.C. (1976). *100 Ways to Enhance Self-Concept in the Classroom: A Handbook for Teachers and Parents*. Englewood Cliffs, NJ: Prentice-Hall.

Dossick, J., & Shea, E. (1988). *Creative Therapy: 52 Exercises for Groups*. Florida: Professional Resource Exchange (Open Leaves Bookshop, Carlton, Victoria).

Johnson, D.W., & Johnson, F.P. (1997). *Joining Together: Group Theory and Group Skills* (6th edn). Boston: Allyn & Bacon.

Kroehnert, G. (1991). *100 Training Games*. Sydney: McGraw-Hill.

Kroehnert, G. (1999). *101 More Training Games*. Sydney: McGraw-Hill.

Merritt, R.E., & Walley, D.D. (1977). *The Group Leader's Handbook: Resources, Techniques and Survival Skills*. Champaign, IL: Research Press.

Nelson-Jones, R. (1991). *Leading Training Groups: A Manual of Practical Group Skills for Trainers*. Sydney: Holt, Rinehart & Winston.

Newstrom, J.W., & Scannell, E.E. (1980). *Games Trainers Play*. New York: McGraw-Hill.

Nilson, C. (1993). *Team Games for Trainers*. New York: McGraw-Hill.

Pfeiffer, J.W., & Jones, J.E. (eds) (1973). *A Handbook of Structured Experiences for Human Relations Training*. La Jolla: University Associates.

Silberman, M. (1995). *101 Ways to Make Training Active*. San Diego: Pfeiffer & Co.

Watson, H.J., Vallee, J.M., & Mulford, W.R. (1981). *Structured Experiences and Group Development*. Canberra: Curriculum Development Centre.

Williamson, B. (1993). *Playful Activities for Powerful Presentations*. Duluth: Whole Person Associates.

## References

Avolio, B. (1995). *The Full Range of Individual, Team and Organizational Leadership Development—Workshop Manual*. Paper presented at the Inaugural Industrial and Organisational Psychology Conference, Sydney.

Benson, J.F. (2001). *Working More Creatively with Groups* (2nd edn). London: Routledge.

Bion, W.R. (1961). *Experience in Groups*. London: Tavistock.

Birnbaum, M. (1986). The use of group process in the integrative seminar. In M. Parnes (ed.), *Innovations in Social Group Work: Feedback from Practice to Theory*. New York: The Haworth Press.

Bradford, L.P. (1978). The case of the hidden agenda. In L.P. Bradford (ed.), *Group development* (2nd edn). La Jolla: University Associates.

Bundey, C. (1980). Small group learning. In D. Armstrong & P. Boas (eds), *Experiential Psychotherapies in Australia*. Bundoora: Pit Press.

Bundey, C., Cullen, J., Denshire, L., Grant, J., Norfor, J., & Nove, T. (1989). *A Manual About Group Leadership and a Resource for Group Leaders*. Sydney: NSW Department of Health.

Corey, G. (2004). *Theory and Practice of Group Counseling* (6th edn). Belmont, CA: Brooks/Cole.

Dick, B. (1991). *Helping Groups to be Effective: Skills, Processes and Concepts for Group Facilitation* (2nd edn). Chapel Hill: Interchange.

Dickson, G. (2000). Aboriginal grandmothers' experience with health promotion and participatory action research. *Qualitative Health Research*, 10, 188–213.

Douglas, T. (2000). *Basic Groupwork*. London: Routledge.

Eagly, A., Johannesen-Schmidt, M., & van Engen, M. (2003). Transformational, transactional, and laissez-faire leadership styles: A meta-analysis comparing women and men. *Psychological Bulletin*, 129(4), 569–91.

Garvin, C. (1981). *Contemporary Group Work*. Englewood Cliffs, NJ: Prentice Hall.

Garvin, C. (2001). The potential impact of small-group research on social group work practice. In T. Kelly (ed.), *Group Work: Strategies for Strengthening Resiliency*. New York: The Haworth Press.

Gladding, S.T. (2003). *Group Work: A Counselling Specialty* (4th edn). Upper Saddle River, NJ: Merril Prentice Hall.

Greif, G.L., & Ephross, P.H. (1997). *Group Work with Populations at Risk*. Oxford: Oxford University Press.

Hanson, P. (1972). What to look for in groups. In J. W. Pfeiffer & J. E. Jones (eds), *The 1972 Annual Handbook for Group Facilitators*. San Diego: University Associates.

Hartford, M. (1972). *Groups in Social Work: Application of Small Group Theory and Research to Social Work Practice*. New York: Columbia University Press.

Healy, D. (1992). *On Team Leadership*. Sydney: Trilogy Group.

Hersey, P., & Blanchard, K.H. (1988). *Management of Organizational Behavior:* Utilizing Human Resources (5th edn). Englewood Cliffs, NJ: Prentice Hall.

Ivey, A.E., & Bradford Ivey, M. (2003). *Intentional Interviewing and Counseling: Facilitating Client Development in a Multicultural Society* (5th edn). Pacific Grove, CA: Thomson Brooks/Cole.

Johnson, D.W., & Johnson, F.P. (eds) (1997). *Joining Together: Group Theory and Group Skills* (6th edn). Boston: Allyn & Bacon.

Lang, N. (1972). A broad-range model of practice in the social work group. *Social Service Review*, 46(1), 76–89.

Maples, M.F. (1988). Group development: Extending Tuckman's theory. *Journal for Specialists in Groupwork*, March.

Merritt, R.E., & Walley, D.D. (1977). *The Group Leader's Handbook: Resources, Techniques and Survival Skills*. Champaign, IL: Research Press.

Morris, R. (1989). Personal communication whilst a participant in a groupwork training workshop run by the chapter author. Sydney.

Napier, R.W., & Gershenfeld, M.K. (1993). *Groups: Theory and Experience* (5th edn). Boston: Houghton Mifflin.

Nelson-Jones, R. (1991). *Leading Training Groups: A Manual of Practical Group Skills for Trainers*. Sydney: Holt, Rinehart & Winston.

Northen, H. (1988). *Social Work with Groups* (2nd edn). New York: Columbia University Press.

Reid, K. (1997). *Social Work Practice with Groups: A Clinical Perspective*. Pacific Grove, CA: Brooks/Cole.

Schiller, L.Y. (1997). Rethinking stages of development in women's groups: Implications for practice. *Social Work with Groups*, 20(3), 3–19.

Schutz, W.C. (1973). *Elements of Encounter: A Body-mind Approach*. Big Sur, CA: Joy Press.

Shulman, L. (1999). *The Skills of Helping Individuals, Families, Groups, and Communities*. Itasca, IL: Peacock.

Sivasubramaniam, N., Murry, W., Avolio, B., & Jung, D. (2002). A longitudinal model of the effects of team leadership and group potency on group performance. *Group and Organization Management*, 27(1), 66–96.

Tuckman, B. (1965). Developmental sequence in small groups. *Psychological Bulletin*, 63, 384–99.

Watson, H.J., Vallee, J.M., & Mulford, W.R. (1981). *Structured Experiences and Group Development*. Canberra: Curriculum Development Centre.

Whelan, S., & Hochberger, J. (1996). Validation studies of the group development questionnaire. *Small Group Research*, 27(1), 143–70.

# 14 Intervention Strategies for Working with Groups
## Agi O'Hara

Before deciding how to intervene in any group situation, group leaders need to have an awareness of many aspects of the group's functioning. At the most basic level, knowing how the group is progressing towards its goal and ascertaining whether the group is cohesive will be essential in beginning to make sense of what is happening in the group.

From a professional standpoint, it is important to acknowledge that group facilitation skills are generally developed through specialized training programs. Group leaders require knowledge in group theory and dynamics, leadership styles, counselling methods, ethical standards, approaches needed for different kinds of group work, and relevant research (Furr & Barrett 2000). The Canadian Group Psychotherapy Association (CGPA) is a multidisciplinary association of group psychotherapists who work together to foster and provide education and training for mental health professionals in group psychotherapy across Canada. Furthermore, the CGPA aims to encourage research in group psychotherapy; to set national standards for quality in training, practice and research; and to provide professional development opportunities for clinicians.

It may not be possible to understand all of the factors responsible for any particular group dynamic, but being aware of the group features described in this chapter will facilitate effective and appropriate intervention.

## Interventions and types of groups

People come together in groups for many reasons and, consequently, there are many different types of groups, each operating from a different theoretical and practice framework. For example, psycho-educational groups are designed to inform, educate, and provide supportive interventions for targeted groups of people regarding specific issues. Examples of these include groups for women who have experienced intimate partner violence and groups for family members of adolescents who are misusing drugs or alcohol. The general intent of psycho-educational groups is to assist individuals, within a group context, to cope and appropriately respond to the changes generated by a particular stressor. In contrast, psycho-therapeutic groups are less focused on a specific agenda, and change is grounded within the nature of the transference and counter-transference relationships between the group leader and group members. An example of this type of group may be a mothering group where issues are explored using Jungian analysis. Self-help groups bring together people with common issues. Through sharing their personal experiences, members are able to provide emotional support and assist others in developing new coping skills. Although some self-help groups may follow a particular format (for example, the 12-step model of Alcoholics Anonymous), they are run by and for group members, and are defined by the notable absence of a professional in the group leader role, which is typically assumed by a member of the group itself. Professional service providers may participate in the self-help process, but only at the request of group members.

As with all helping relationships, the group facilitator needs to remain sensitive to the dynamics of culture and gender. Within a cultural context, group work can be very effective and research is beginning to emerge identifying how groups may be used to address mental health issues and general well-being. Group healing has always been part of Aboriginal learning. However, clinicians need to be aware that the imposition of particular models into different contexts may not be effective and, at times, may result in further harm. For example, in self-help groups such as Alcoholics Anonymous, the traditional Western format has not been successful with Indigenous populations. However, transformations of the model including the use of traditional healing circles, a less formalized agenda, and the inclusion of family members have contributed to greater effectiveness of the model within some communities (Jilek 1994). Another example is the Change of Season group intervention model for Aboriginal men who have been violent towards their intimate partners. This model specifically incorporates a cultural and spiritual focus with the view towards providing meaningful, culturally competent service for Aboriginal men through the use of talking circles, smudging, and sweat lodge ceremonies as a means of addressing the cultural and spiritual needs of participants (Kiyoshk 2003).

Research on the effectiveness of group interventions indicates generally positive impact in a wide range of clinical situations. Canadian research suggests that groups provide support, facilitate coping, increase confidence, and contribute towards a more positive outlook in primary health settings (Marziali 2006; Stewart, Davidson, Meaded, & Weld-Viscount 2001); in addition, groups contribute to a reduction in women's aggressive behaviours (Tutty, Babins-Wagner, & Rothery 2006), pathological gambling (Ladouceur, Sylvain, Boutin, Lachance, Doucet, & Lablond 2002), obsessive thoughts and compulsive behaviours (Whital, Robichaud, Thordarson, & McLean 2008), and parenting stress (Levac, McCay, Merka, & Reddon-D'Arcy 2008).

# Group goals and needs

Although individual needs may differ in some respects, there is generally an assumption that the group will be able to achieve a particular goal, in a way that is not possible by any member individually. Johnson & Johnson (1997, p. 75) refer to a group goal as 'a future state of affairs desired by enough members of the group to motivate the group to work towards its achievement'. Such a general definition leaves open the possibility that individuals will differ at times in their priorities with regard to goal achievement. However, it is the overall movement towards goal achievement and experiencing a sense of inclusion, influence, and affection (Schutz 1973) that are essential for effective group functioning.

# Level of cohesiveness

Group cohesiveness refers to the forces of attraction and/or repulsion that are experienced by group members. Group cohesiveness is expressed in the feelings members have about being together. Feelings such as pride, loyalty, satisfaction, commitment, and a sense of belonging are frequently mentioned, as is the idea of group identity or group spirit (Johnson & Johnson 1997). Groups stand in opposition to isolation and transform individual problems into common concerns. It is the group bond that enables the group to weather challenges that arise from within the group and from forces external to the group. Yalom (1995) noted that although it is the group leader's role to facilitate a group culture that contributes toward therapeutic change, it is ultimately the group members whose interactions contribute to the positive outcomes.

Many factors assist or hinder the development of group cohesiveness. The level of trust in the group is a major consideration. The group leader plays a significant part in this regard. Initiating discussions around confidentiality and respect, modelling trusting and trustworthy behaviours, and offering protection to group members by monitoring the manner in which they respond and provide feedback to each other, help to develop a climate of trust (Heap 1977). For example, in a group intervention for children who had been sexually abused, it was critical to address issues of trust, cohesiveness, and safety in the first two group sessions (De Luca, Boyes, Furer, Grayston, & Hiebert-Murphy 1992). Other factors affecting group cohesiveness include:

- nature and purpose of the group (for example, survivors of sexual assault may achieve a more intense level of group cohesiveness based on the common experience compared to groups that are designed to advocate for animal rights)
- adherence to group rules by individual members
- group membership (whether closed or open—for example, permitting changes in membership over time)
- homogeneity or heterogeneity of group
- style of leadership (democratic, autocratic, or laissez-faire)
- clarity of the group goal
- ownership of the group goal by group members
- strategies adopted by the leader for dealing with conflict and other challenging behaviours within the group

As well, it is important to acknowledge cultural dynamics. Although the essence of group intervention is the opportunity to learn from each others' experiences, heterogeneous groups that replicate the social, cultural, racial, and class structures of Euro-Canadian society will likely not be helpful for Indigenous participants (Waldrum & Wong 1995).

Group cohesiveness is also facilitated if group members value the time spent in the group and if they have a sense of personal and emotional connection with what is taking place in the group. This is most likely if members are learning and developing in some meaningful way and are also being encouraged to reflect on their experiences. This process of constructing meaning, sometimes referred to as 'meaning attribution', helps members to understand processes that they have been part of. For example, Indigenous participants of a traditional mental health healing circle found that relationships, spirituality and connectedness, empowerment, and self-awareness, as well as the overall experience they gained from participating in the healing circle, both strengthened them on an individual basis and contributed towards group cohesion (Thomas & Bellefeuille 2006). Meaning attribution is sometimes quite difficult, and Northern (1969) reminds group leaders to be wary of mistaking frustration and floundering for genuine learning. Opportunity for members to reflect on their experiences can easily be incorporated into the lead-up to closure of a particular session by simply saying:

> Let's draw together what we might take away from our time together today. Perhaps each of you could tell us one thing that you have observed or learned in this session, or something that you could take away and apply elsewhere?

The recognition that aspects of group experiences can also be applied to members' life experiences outside of the group often enhances the perceived value of the group.

## Stages of group development

As stated in chapter 13, needs of individuals in groups change over time due to their own development and maturation, as well as the development of the group in its ability to respond to changes in its internal and external environment. Such development needs to be considered by the group leader when devising interventions. Tuckman's (1965) model remains relevant for the beginning group facilitator. He proposed that the majority of groups follow a pattern of forming, storming, norming, and performing. Forming refers to the initial stage of the group process in which members begin to assess their positions in the group, the group culture, and the rules. The second stage, storming, refers to the period in which conflict may arise as members begin to feel more comfortable in the group, and start to challenge other members and/or the group leader. The norming stage begins when the group establishes cohesiveness and commitment to the group process and sets norms for appropriate behaviours. The final stage, performing, occurs when the group demonstrates its abilities to work towards successful achievement of the group goals. Although these stages may not progress in a linear manner, it is helpful to remember that groups and group relationships are developmental in nature, and will shift, grow, and regress, depending on the individual needs of group members.

## The balance of task and maintenance

Leadership actions can be classified as either task or maintenance actions (Johnson and Johnson 1997; Napier & Gershenfeld 1993). Maintenance actions refer to actions that promote or facilitate the social–emotional relations between group members—for example, providing support and praise, encouraging participation, and facilitating interpersonal problem solving. Task actions refer to actions that assist the group to work on or complete a task related to the group goal—for example, giving opinions, providing information, and summarizing. A leader needs to be aware of the range of each of these types of actions, striking the appropriate balance between them. At any moment in time, a leader has a choice of attending to one of four task/maintenance alternatives (Bundey 1983):

- group task
- group maintenance
- an individual's task
- an individual's need for maintenance

It would not be appropriate to remain overly focused on an individual's needs with regard to either task or maintenance at the expense of the group, and similarly it would be inappropriate to ignore individual task and maintenance needs, focusing only on the group's task and maintenance needs. For these reasons, group leaders may also wish to consider a co-therapy, or co-facilitator, model that will ensure both task and maintenance functions are appropriately addressed. Co-facilitator models are particularly useful if the subject matter of the group is sensitive, as the leaders can ensure that both content and process issues are addressed. The co-therapy model is also useful if the group content, such as in programs for couples in which there has been partner violence, may be best addressed by the leaders modelling respectful, collaborative, male–female relationships.

Johnson and Johnson (1997) provide an inventory to assist group leaders in determining their typical leadership actions. The authors include a series of task/maintenance pattern descriptors (Johnson & Johnson 1997, pp. 194–5), ranging from one version in which the leader is only minimally involved in both task and maintenance, to the opposite version in which a great deal of leader commitment and effort is evident in both. When considering these descriptors, it needs to be remembered that there is no ideal balance between a leader's task and maintenance actions. The appropriateness of a leader's actions will be determined by:

- the type of group they are leading,
- the stage of group development,
- particular dynamics that may have developed in the group,
- the ability of group members to fulfill some or all of the leadership actions necessary for optimal group functioning.

As a group develops, the leader needs to recognize and encourage the ability of individual members to take on leadership actions eventually resulting in a situation of distributed leadership (Tyson 1989). What may appear to be an inappropriate pattern of task/maintenance actions due to the leader's minimal involvement may in fact be ideal if several group members are taking on many, if not all, of the leadership actions. This would be quite common in groups that have been together for some time and have developed a reasonable degree of autonomy. This clearly relates to the issue of group member maturity as discussed in chapter 13.

# Role differentiation

Not only do group members vary in the roles they have in a group; group leaders also take on various roles. At the beginning of the group process, effective leadership is integral to sustainability and the recruitment and retention of attendees (Oliffe, Halpin, Bottorff, Hislop, McKenzie, & Mroz 2008). Initially a leader's role is most likely to be a blend of expert and helper (Northen 1969). However, as the group matures and becomes more autonomous (Lang 1972), the leader's role takes on a facilitative function and may, in time, depending on the nature of the group, become closer to one of group member. Understanding and responding to the needs of the group enables leaders to be flexible with regard to their role and choice of interventions during the life of the group.

# Models of intervention

Numerous models and protocols have been devised to assist in developing and applying intervention strategies when leading groups. The intervention cube, as part of the Critical Incident Model (Cohen & Smith 1976), and the Focal Conflict Model (Heap 1977) are particularly helpful and will be discussed in detail below. Conflict mapping and mediation strategies offer specialized interventions for handling conflict in groups, and are covered in chapter 12, 'Understanding and Managing Conflict'. However, even without consideration of specific models of intervention it needs to be recognized that many actions that are simple and subtle are in fact interventions, with potentially significant consequences. For example, a group leader is already intervening by merely being present at the group. Similarly, staying silent while considering how to respond to a particular behaviour or interaction that has just taken place also needs to be seen as a leader intervention. This brief silence may have powerful consequences as individuals within the group may interpret the leader's silence in different ways.

## Activity 14.1  Interpreting silence

List at least three possible interpretations that group members may have if a group leader remains silent after a particular behaviour or interaction has taken place in the group.

# The Intervention Cube

The intervention cube as devised by Cohen and Smith (1976, p. 87), focuses on group behaviour and provides a framework 'that can be used to observe, categorize, analyze', and plan group interventions regardless of the leader's theoretical or practice orientation. The cube schema helps group leaders to monitor their awareness of the range of interventions available, to analyze the interventions they have already made, and to select an appropriate intervention according to the stage of development of their group. Within the framework of the intervention cube, interventions can be classified according to three response dimensions or categories each with three sub-categories, hence offering twenty-seven combinations of these intervention dimensions. The dimensions are:

- level of intervention,
- type of intervention,
- intensity of intervention.

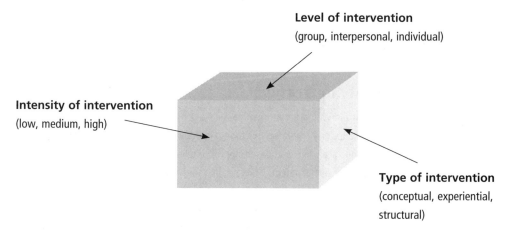

**Level of intervention**
(group, interpersonal, individual)

**Intensity of intervention**
(low, medium, high)

**Type of intervention**
(conceptual, experiential, structural)

## Level of intervention

The *level* of intervention refers to the focus of the intervention, whether it is aimed at group (all members of the group), interpersonal (a subgroup of two or more members of the group), or individual behaviour. Although those involved in the intervention-causing behaviour will often be the focus of the intervention, this is not always the case.

### Practice example 14.1

### Group level intervention

Group members Bob and John are involved in a fairly heated discussion about helping around the house and the expectations of their partners. The group leader, wanting to involve the group in the discussion, responds by asking, 'I wonder what the group thinks about the issues that have been raised?' This intervention would be at the group level. It could be followed by an individual intervention such as 'Mary, you seemed particularly interested in what was being said. Would you like to go first?'

## Type of intervention

The *type* of intervention refers to the nature of the intervention, whether it is (1) conceptual, (2) experiential, or (3) structural.

## Conceptual intervention

Intervention that is *conceptual* is one in which the group leader provides information to the group. It may be a spontaneous response to a group situation, a planned response related to the group's goal/purpose, or perhaps information related to a previously observed dynamic that the leader has been considering. It may therefore be either content-related (theoretical input) or process-related (observations of group behaviours), or a combination of the two. The stage of group development may be helpful in determining which is more appropriate.

## Practice example 14.2

# Handling anxiety in a group

Consider an anxious group in which group members are asking a lot of questions. The leader could choose to patiently answer each of the questions, thereby providing valuable information. This may alleviate the group's anxiety and be an appropriately non-threatening response for a group in a very early stage of development. However, it could lead to a never-ending series of questions, which may be time-consuming and possibly fulfil the members' motivation to avoid the real task at hand. It may be more helpful to provide a response that comments on the group process that is occurring. The nature of such a process-observation response can still be tailored to the stage of the group's development.

For a fairly new group, the following process observation from the leader may be very helpful in alleviating the group members' anxiety:

I can see that there are a lot of things you would like clarified. You may be interested to know that the sorts of questions you are asking are very common in new groups as they're about to begin an exercise. It's very natural to be a little anxious in such a situation. It becomes easier once we begin. Why don't we start and see how things work out?

However, if the group has been together for quite some time, the following intervention by the group leader may be more confronting:

We seem to frequently get into these lengthy question–answer interactions, just before beginning an exercise. I wonder if you're feeling anxious, perhaps asking questions as a means of avoiding the interactions that are about to take place?

Although such a response may appear to be a reasonable comment on the group process, it does not reflect on the reason for the implied reluctance, and puts the responsibility on the group members to behave differently. The leader also needs to consider her role and how she may have contributed to the situation. Adding the following suggestion can offer a shared solution:

*continued*

Such reluctance sometimes indicates that group members are not yet feeling comfortable enough to share their experiences. Why don't we take some time to talk about this and see what we could do to create greater trust in the group?

## Questions for reflection

1. Can you recall any experiences as a group member when you were confused by group events or behaviours?
2. Can you now think of a process observation that would have clarified what was happening?

## Experiential intervention

Intervention that is *experiential* is one that involves a behavioural response from group members. This may be the expression of feelings or thoughts related to an experience in the group (Cohen & Smith 1976). Although not strictly in accordance with Cohen and Smith's original formulation, physical behaviour such as taking part in a group exercise (for example, role-play) could also be considered to be experiential. Such an exercise creates a new experience for the group member(s) while engaged in the exercise and also, if processed appropriately, will inevitably lead to an expression of feelings or thoughts related to the experience.

## Practice example 14.3

## Experiential intervention in a group

The leader of a support group for people recovering from major heart surgery suggests that they form groups of three to role-play an interaction with their family members. This intervention has been devised as several group members expressed difficulties regarding the over-protectiveness of their families and their inability to speak about this.

Being involved in the role-play will assist the group members to experience how such an interaction might proceed. It will be beneficial to process their feelings while in role to facilitate the learning related to the pseudo-family interaction. It will also be important to provide an opportunity for group members to express how they felt about doing the exercise itself, thereby reflecting on their experience in the group.

## Questions for reflection

Consider recent role-plays in which you have participated.

1. How was the exercise processed by yourself and other group members? At a content level? At a feeling level?

*continued*

2. Did you have sufficient opportunity to reflect on your learning? Was there anything about the exercise that was noted by the group members of which you had not been aware? Were you surprised about your personal reactions (or absence of) to the exercise?

### Structural intervention

Intervention that is *structural* is, in a broad sense, anything that deliberately changes the physicality or manner in which the group is interacting. It may involve structured exercises, such as the role-play discussed above, focusing on tasks and reflection of feelings, or asking group members to close their eyes for a guided meditation. Asking the group to remove the chairs and sit on the floor, to move outside, or to meet at a new venue are also structural interventions.

## Intensity of intervention

The *intensity* of intervention refers to the intended impact of the intervention. It is generally the force with which awareness regarding a particular situation is offered to an individual, subgroup, or the group overall (Cohen & Smith 1976). The intensity ranges from (1) low, to (2) medium, to (3) high. The degree to which the intervention is diffused among the group may determine its intensity. Remarks aimed at the whole group will generally be less confronting than those directed at a particular individual. However, it is not simply the level (group, subgroup, individual) that determines intensity, but the total degree of confrontation involved. There are many factors to be considered in this regard—for example, the directness with which an issue may be raised or the language used. The intensity with which an intervention is received by the group or individual(s) may also be determined by individual factors that may or may not be apparent to the group leader.

### Practice example 14.4

### Intensity of interventions

Asking a group member, Jane, to move her chair to make room for another who arrived late may be considered as an intervention of low intensity. The aim of the intervention is to accommodate the latecomer. However, what the group leader also needs to consider is the effect on all persons involved. What is the relationship between Jane and the latecomer? What is the relationship between Jane and the person who was sitting next to her before moving her chair? Is the lateness a pattern of behaviour that has begun to irritate the group? If this is the case, the

*continued*

accommodation of the latecomer without confronting the lateness itself may create hostility or negativity in the group.

## Questions for reflection

1. Can you recall a group situation when a leader's apparently simple and non-threatening statement created an unusually strong response in one or more group members?
2. Do you now understand a potential reason for this?

Keeping track of the apparently complex interplay of factors can be quite daunting for new group leaders. Cohen and Smith (1976, p. 103) liken this process to the running of data through a 'personal intervention computer'. Experience in groups will assist with the ease and speed with which this personal intervention computer functions.

Although, at any moment in time, it is only possible to direct an intervention at a particular *level* (individual, subgroup, or group) with a particular *intensity* (low, medium, or high), it is possible to devise interventions for which *type* may be classified as conceptual and/or experiential and/or structural, all at the one time. The use of structured exercises is a good example of this. When analyzing group leader interventions it is not uncommon to observe consecutive interventions that encompass various levels, intensities, and types.

## Practice example 14.5

## Analyzing group interventions

Returning to the situation in which a group member arrives late to the group, the following group interactions and leader interventions may occur.

John enters the room fifteen minutes late as George is speaking about a difficult encounter with his boss earlier that day. Everyone looks up and the leader asks Jane to move her chair to make room for John, who has picked up a chair from the corner. Jane looks flustered as she moves her chair, not making eye contact with John. Mary and Betty begin quietly talking to each other and George is looking decidedly irritated.

(i) *Leader:*  George, could you please continue telling us what happened this afternoon with your boss?

(ii) *George:*  No, I've lost my train of thought and it's obvious not everyone wants to hear it.

(iii) *Leader:*  It can be very disruptive to the group when one member arrives late. This was

*continued*

the reason we talked about punctuality when we were drawing up our group contract.

(iv) *Leader:*    As I look around the room, I have the impression that the mood has changed since John arrived.

(v) *Leader:*    John, I know things can come up unexpectedly for all of us, but you have been late several times and have not offered any explanations. I wonder if you could tell the group why you're late?

(vi) *John:*    I'm sorry. I was trying not to make a fuss and take even more of the group's time. It's a bit of a long story but I'm now relying on public transport to get here and the bus is not always on time.

(vii) *Leader:*    Thank you, John. Perhaps we can catch up with you on this a little later, but for now let's try to return to our checking-in with everyone. George, would you like to continue?

## Question for reflection

1. Analyze interventions (i), (iii), (iv), (v), and (vii) according to the three response dimensions of the intervention cube.

## General guidelines for choosing interventions

At the beginning stages, when the group is in the process of forming, interventions would more frequently be of a structural or conceptual type, at the group level, and of low intensity. The leader is likely to be focusing on creating a safe, non-threatening environment and perhaps, depending on the size of the group, breaking into small subgroups to facilitate the members' interactions and group cohesion. Once a group has been together for sufficient time to become more cohesive, and is working well on its task, interventions may more frequently be of an experiential type, at an individual or interpersonal level, and of medium or high intensity if circumstances require it. Of course, it is not merely stage of development that determines the appropriateness of an intervention. The type of group, individual member needs, and previous group interventions, for example, also need to be considered. The Critical Incident Model (Cohen & Smith 1976), incorporating the intervention cube, assists in focusing on the various aspects that need to be evaluated when devising an intervention. The Critical Incident Model will be described in detail later in this chapter.

# Focal Conflict Model

Communication in groups can be rather complex. Many factors such as the group context, cultures represented in the group, verbal ability of group members, emotional obstacles due to prejudices, past interactions, or concerns regarding acceptance by other group members

(Heap 1977) will impact on both the content and manner of communication between group members. The apparent, overt (manifest) content of discussions may in fact be masking meanings and feelings that group members are unwilling or unable to express. Such hidden meanings may not even be apparent to the group members themselves. It may become necessary for group leaders to interpret the apparent unexpressed, perhaps unconscious (latent), communication of group members. Heap (1977) cautions group leaders to be tentative in the hypotheses and interpretations they make in such situations, to use these only as guides to assist in developing appropriate intervention, and to do so 'with care and humility' (Heap 1977, p. 88).

Particular aims and problems are sometimes a continuing preoccupation of members of a group and are a focus of their activity. It may be the group as a whole or an individual member who signals common concerns (Heap 1977). These concerns will relate either directly or indirectly to the goal(s) that brought the group together and may be expressed overtly or covertly. Group focal conflict theory (Heap 1977; Stock Whitaker 1985; Whitaker & Lieberman 1965) offers a means by which such preoccupations may be analyzed. Stock Whitaker (1985) describes a commonly-observed group process that serves to protect group members from the anxiety associated with fears or wishes. He suggests that pressures are experienced by many, if not all, group members and, although the fears or wishes may not be identical, they are sufficiently similar to cause the group to develop a 'group solution' to deal with them. Such solutions may become group norms and assist in the avoidance of behaviours that invoke fear, anxiety, or guilt. Within the Focal Conflict Model, the shared wish or impulse is referred to as the 'disturbing motive' and the accompanying fear or guilt, the 'reactive motive' (Stock Whitaker 1985).

Solutions to anxiety-provoking situations emerge from the group and vary in their ability to alleviate the anticipated anxiety associated with the expression of the disturbing wish. The solution may be directed purely at the fear, thereby preventing any expression of the shared wish (Stock Whitaker 1985). This is called a 'restrictive solution'.

**Table 14.1** Focal conflict example (adapted from Heap 1977)

| Disturbing motive | in conflict with | Reactive motive | Restrictive solution |
|---|---|---|---|
| Wish to be seen by the group leader as special and not just one of the group | | Fear of negative judgment by the leader or group members | All decide to be alike, so an unspoken group norm develops |

Other solutions may actually deal with the fear and allow the 'expression of the wish' (Stock Whitaker 1985, p. 53) to a lesser or greater extent. Such solutions are called 'enabling solutions' as they potentially facilitate the exploration of the wishes and associated fears. Enabling solutions vary in their appropriateness in that they may only partially address the issues involved and are, at times, at the expense of one or more of the group members. Scapegoating in a group is likely to be the result of this type of dynamic.

## Practice example 14.6

### Disturbing motives in a group

Consider the group in Practice example 14.5 and assume that the disturbing motive is the same as in Table 14.1. One group member decides to arrive early to help the group leader set up the chairs in the room (an alternative/enabling solution). As the rest of the group members arrive, they find the non-conforming group member enjoying a conversation with the group leader. This behaviour may result in the other group members punishing the non-conforming group member for daring to be different, by excluding him or her from discussions during the breaks.

When a group leader encounters behaviours in a group that appear to be counter-productive or irrelevant to the group goal (for example, discussions about trivial subject matter, excessive blaming of others, engaging in avoidant behaviour, or directing all of the group's focus toward themselves), it is beneficial to consider if there might be something that members want to say or do but are afraid to do so. Initiating a discussion around group norms and feelings of safety in the group is likely to assist in revealing any disturbing motives that may be present.

## Activity 14.2  Focal conflict in a school setting

Students in classrooms are also members of a group and some of their challenging or difficult behaviours can be analyzed according to the Focal Conflict Model.

Jenny is in primary school and frequently initiates interesting topics of conversation, particularly when the teacher is beginning to take out the reading books.

Gregory is in high school and always seems to begin talking/fighting/making jokes when it comes to correcting the previous day's homework.

1. Identify potential disturbing motives in each of these situations.
2. Identify potential reactive motives in each of these situations.

The work of the group leader in sessions where a focal conflict exists is to assist the group to find an appropriate 'enabling solution' to the conflict, which optimally satisfies the wish and at the same time alleviates the reactive fears (Heap 1977). This is made possible by the group leader's awareness of the latent or covert messages that group members are giving and the leader's ability to provide the group with an understanding of these messages. Offering tentative interpretations, modelling alternative behaviours (Yalom 1995), and demonstrating supportive acceptance of the feelings latently communicated normalize the group's feelings and reduce the associated anxiety. By sensitively facilitating a discussion of group members' fears, the group leader also promotes a greater sense of safety in the group and helps to enhance group cohesion.

## Practice example 14.7

## Focal conflict in a support group

The following is an abbreviated and adapted version of a case study discussed by Heap (1977, pp. 92–3).

An adoption agency initiated the formation of groups for future adoptive parents. The purpose of the groups was to discuss general questions that prospective parents may have about child and family development, to alert parents to the special circumstances of adopting older or special needs children, and to have a forum in which to discuss their decision to adopt. It was common knowledge that some of the groups had been waiting for six or more years without receiving their child and that they had little or no contact with the agency during that time. This agency operated privately, alongside the provincial system that also facilitated adoptions for infants, special needs and older children.

One of these groups appeared to be rather formal and the social worker who was leading the group assumed it was due to their anxieties about being in the group and the prospect of becoming parents. At the third meeting of the group the leader was delayed and upon arriving found the group in a heated discussion about the new policies that had recently been introduced regarding adoptions. These new policies required prospective adoptive parents to undergo further scrutiny from the adoption agency, which in turn was accompanied by an increase in service fees. The group was angry with the possessors of the power (the private adoption agency) to both dispense and withhold their services, and the implication that parents who could afford the fees were placed with children far more quickly than those who chose to remain within the provincial system. The prolonged and angry discussion involved all of the group despite its indirect association with the group's common aims and problems, which was to adopt through the provincial system.

An analysis of the group's behaviour suggests that the expressed anger was disproportionate to the situation being discussed. It is likely that the anger was latent communication of the group's feeling towards the adoption agency, which was perceived to be in a similar position of power as the provincial agency. The agency was arbitrarily making decisions and withholding their longed-for children. The group would have assumed that an overt expression of their anger would be counterproductive, as such behaviour would inevitably jeopardize their prospects for adoption. The group leader in

*continued*

this situation needed to offer a tentative interpretation of their behaviour, in a sensitive manner, that normalized their anxieties, frustrations, and anger. It would be imperative for the leader to also clarify his role as a support person for the group, rather than being an agency 'mole', and therefore offer the group members an opportunity to discuss their feelings in a safe environment.

## Questions for reflection

1. How would you intervene if you were the leader of this group?
2. What would you say to address the group's concerns?

# Critical Incident Model

A critical incident, within the context of group work, is any behaviour of group members that is important enough to warrant leader intervention (Cohen & Smith 1976). Although the name suggests otherwise, the 'incident' may not be particularly dramatic but nevertheless requires a response by the group leader, as ignoring the incident may have negative consequences for the group.

The Critical Incident Model as devised by Cohen and Smith (1976) offers a framework for considering group events in a logical sequence. It may be used to analyze previous group processes or, time permitting, be used to develop appropriate and effective interventions in the moment. It incorporates five aspects of group process:

1. context of behaviour
2. actual behaviour
3. choice point
4. intervention
5. intervention result

The intervention cube (detailed earlier in the chapter) is the means by which an intervention (4) is devised. Although not intended by Whitaker and Lieberman (1965), the Focal Conflict Model can be successfully incorporated into the Critical Incident Model at (3) when group leaders are considering potential underlying issues at the intervention choice point. Choice point refers to the recognition that many interactions can be considered from both surface and underlying perspectives. The former refers to the overt or expressed aspects of an interaction, whereas the latter refers to latent or hidden meanings that may be masked. There are not always hidden aspects to group interventions, but it is important to consider the possibility of their existence and whether it may be beneficial to focus on these. The Focal Conflict Model assists in this analysis.

The following is a summary of the Critical Incident Model as outlined by Cohen and Smith (1976).

**Step 1** involves specifying the context within which the 'critical incident' occurred:

a) Specify the session number and the phase of the group: beginning, middle, or end.
b) Specify the climate or mood of the group as it relates to the critical incident—for example, dependent, counterdependent, unified, silent, hostile, or depressed.
c) Give a brief description of the person(s) involved in the interaction with the leader and/or other group members. Specify both past and current behaviours.

**Step 2** involves specifying the behaviour and/or conversation that led up to and immediately preceded the 'choice point'. For example:

> *Leader:*  George, could you please continue telling us what happened this afternoon with your boss?
>
> *George:*  No, I've lost my train of thought and it's obvious not everyone wants to hear it.

**Step 3** involves describing the critical incident choice-point situation, specifying both the surface issue(s) and the underlying issue(s):

a) Surface issue(s)—for example, George's reluctance to continue could be due to the fact that several members of the group have begun talking to each other and are apparently ignoring him.
b) Underlying issue(s)—for example, George's reluctance to continue could also be due to irritation and anger with the group leader. John's frequent lateness has until now been accepted without comment by the group leader. George perceives this as unfair and not in keeping with the group contract.

A decision regarding the level of focus needs to be made at this point. Identifying the stage of group development may assist in this regard. In the very early stages of a group's development, and depending on the issues involved, it may be too confronting to respond to underlying issues. In the example provided, this would not be the case. It is also possible to respond to both surface and underlying issues.

**Step 4** involves specifying the intervention according to the three response categories of the intervention cube as previously described:

a) Level of intervention (group, interpersonal, individual)
b) Type of intervention (conceptual, experiential, structural)
c) Intensity of intervention (low, medium, high)

(See Practice example 14.5 for a possible intervention.)

**Step 5** involves specifying the results of the intervention on the group:

a) The intended directional movement of the group—for example, the leader recognized the importance of addressing the issue of lateness, but wanted to do so in a fairly low key manner so as not to appear too confronting towards John. This was assumed to be the best way of validating individual needs and at the same time demonstrating fairness and caring.

b) The actual group response to the intervention—for example, silence, agreement, hostility, further developing critical incidents.

# The advantage in considering models of intervention

Confidence in group leading is largely determined by the ability to devise interventions that are appropriate and facilitative of individual and group development and goal achievement. The Critical Incident Model (Cohen & Smith 1976) incorporating the Focal Conflict Model (Heap 1977) provides a clear structure for analyzing one's own interventions as well as those made by other group leaders. Taking time to analyze the results of previous interventions and the manner in which these were determined by the particular intervention components chosen, assists leaders to more accurately anticipate the outcome of their future interventions. This increases confidence and diminishes the fear of many new leaders that they are at the mercy of the group. It is not always possible to take a lot of time to consider interventions in the moment. However, spontaneity based on frequent and disciplined analysis of previous group interventions offers a greater chance of success than merely 'flying by the seat of one's pants'.

## Activity 14.3  Critical incident in a support group

A family support agency had set up a long-term support group for women who were managing multiple roles in their lives. The group was scheduled to meet once a week for an eight-month period. At the beginning of the group, the leaders were impressed by how quickly the group became cohesive, and the level of the interaction quickly moved beyond superficiality to an affective (emotional) level.

Two months after the group began, one group member stopped attending. When the leaders followed up with her, she indicated that approximately three weeks prior, the group members had begun meeting outside of the group for coffee. Although all other members were included, she had not been included, and, in fact, had only learned about the coffee meetings accidentally from another member. Although she had expressed a desire to meet with the other members, they did not invite her. As a result of her exclusion, she stopped attending the group.

1. Develop an appropriate group leader intervention according to the Critical Incident Model. Use the summary of the five steps in the table below to assist you.

2. Remember to use the Focal Conflict Model to identify potential disturbing motives, potential reactive motives, and the type of solution being adopted by the group.

*continued*

| Step 1 | Step 2 | Step 3 | Step 4 | Step 5 |
|--------|--------|--------|--------|--------|
| Specify context of the critical incident | Specify behaviours/ conversations leading up to the 'choice point' | Specify (a) surface issues and (b) underlying issues | Specify response categories of the intervention (level, type, intensity) | Specify (a) intended and (b) assumed result of the intervention |

## Activity Answers

### Activity 14.1

1. Condoning the behaviour or interaction, therefore not requiring a response.
2. Providing opportunity for a group member to respond.
3. Seemingly not knowing how to respond, thereby resulting in a loss of confidence in the leader.

### Practice example 14.5

  (i) Individual, experiential/structural, low intensity

(iii) Group, conceptual, low intensity

(iv) Group, conceptual, medium intensity

  (v) Individual, experiential, medium/high intensity

(vii) Shifting from individual/conceptual/low to group/conceptual/low to individual/experiential/low-medium

### Activity 14.2

1. Disturbing motive: wanting the teacher to protect them from failing at the task
2. Reactive motive: fear of looking like a sycophant, being unmasked as stupid or incompetentjoking to side-step difficult emotions, filtered listening, and evaluative listening.

## Questions for Review

1. What are some roles of the group leader(s)?
2. Name and describe Tuckman's stages of group development.
3. What may be the rationale for having a co-leader system?

# References

Bundey, C. (1983). Group Leader Training Course. Sydney: Unpublished workshop handouts..

Cohen, A.M., & Smith, R.D. (1976). *The Critical Incident in Growth Groups: Theory and Technique.* La Jolla, CA: University Associates.

De Luca, R., Boyes, D., Furer, P., Grayston, A., & Hiebert-Murphy, D. (1992). Group treatment for sexually abused children. *Canadian Psychology*, 33, 168–79.

Furr, S., & Barret, R. (2000). Teaching group counseling skills: Problems and solutions. *Counselor Education and Supervision*, 40, 94–105.

Heap, K. (1977). *Group Theory for Social Workers: An Introduction.* Oxford: Pergamon Press.

Jilek, W.G. (1994). Traditional healing in the prevention and treatment of alcohol and drug abuse. *Transcultural Psychiatric Research Review*, 31, 219–58.

Johnson, D.W., & Johnson, F.P. (eds) (1997). *Joining Together: Group Theory and Group Skills* (6th edn). Boston: Allyn & Bacon.

Kiyoshk, R. (2003). Integrating spirituality and domestic violence treatment. *Journal of Aggression, Maltreatment, and Trauma*, 7, 237–256.

Ladouceur, R., Sylvain, C., Boutin, C., Lachance, S., Doucet, C., & Lablond, J. (2002). Group therapy for pathological gamblers: a cognitive approach. *Behavior Research and Therapy*, 41, 587–96.

Lang, N. (1972). A broad-range model of practice in the social work group. *Social Service Review*, 46(1), 76–89.

Levac, A.M., McCay, E., Merka, P., & Reddon-D'Arcy, M. (2008). Exploring parent participation in a parent training program for children's aggression: Understanding and illuminating mechanisms of change. *Journal of Child & Adolescent Psychiatric Nursing*, 21, 78–88.

Marziali, E. (2006). Developing evidence for an Internet-based psychotherapeutic group intervention. *Journal of Evidence-based Social Work*, 3, 149–66.

Northen, H. (1969). *Social Work with Groups.* New York: Columbia University Press.

Oliffe, J., Halpin, M., Bottorff, J., Hislop, T., McKenzie, M., & Mroz, L. (2008). How prostate cancer support groups do and do not survive: British Columbian perspectives. *American Journal of Men's Health*, 2, 143–55.

Schutz, W.C. (1973). *Elements of Encounter: A Body-mind Approach.* Big Sur, CA: Joy Press.

Stewart, M., Davidson, K., Meaded., H.A., & Weld-Viscount, P. (2001). Group support for couples coping with a cardiac condition. *Journal of Advanced Nursing*, 33, 190–99.

Stock Whitaker, D. (1985). *Using Groups to Help People.* London: Routledge.

Thomas, W., & Bellefeuille, G. (2006). An evidence-based formative evaluation of a cross cultural Aboriginal mental health program in Canada. *Australian e-Journal for the Advancement of Mental Health (AEJAMH)*, 5, 1–14.

Tuckman, B.W. (1965). Development sequence in small groups. *Psychological Bulletin* 63, 348–99.

Tutty, L., Babins-Wagner, R., & Rothery, M. (2006). Group treatment for aggressive women: an initial evaluation. *Journal of Family Violence*, 21, 341–49.

Tyson, T. (1989). *Working with Groups.* Melbourne: Macmillan.

Waldrum, J.B., & Wong, S. (1995). Group therapy of aboriginal offenders in a Canadian forensic psychiatric facility. *American Indian and Alaska native mental health research* (Monographic series), 34–56.

Whitaker, D., & Lieberman, M. (1965). *Psychotherapy Through the Group Process.* London: Tavistock.

Whital, M., Robichaud, M., Thordarson, D., & McLean, P. (2008). Group and individual treatment of obsessive-compulsive disorder using cognitive therapy and exposure plus response prevention: A 2-year follow-up of two randomized trials. *Journal of Consulting and Clinical Psychology*, 76, 1003–14.

Yalom, I.D. (1995). *The Theory and Practice of Group Psychotherapy* (4th edn). New York: Basic Books.

# Working Effectively in Teams
## Zita Weber

*The real benefit from teams comes not just from co-ordinating separate professions' activities but from melding them in new and creative ways and hence producing a sum which is greater than the parts.*

Ovretveit 1995, pp. 41–2.

During the latter part of the twentieth century and the beginning of the twenty-first century the words 'team' and 'teamwork' have liberally peppered discussions about service delivery to clients. Practitioners in the health and welfare arenas are constantly being encouraged to collaborate and work within teams. An important skill of practice is the capacity to operate as an effective and productive member of a team. The critical practitioner should look beyond some of the rhetoric and recognize that the reality of teams and teamwork means challenging assumptions and reflecting on the very nature of teams, their internal functioning, and the promise of a better organized and efficient delivery of services to clients. Nevertheless, before any deconstruction can take place, it is worthwhile to take the time to explore the contemporary realities of the teamwork phenomenon.

## What is a team? What is teamwork?

Being a practitioner in an organization means that you will find yourself working jointly as a member of several different types of teams. These may be (1) single-discipline teams within your agency, the social work team, for example; (2) multidisciplinary and interdisciplinary teams, where you will work collaboratively, to some extent, with other professionals from different disciplines within your organization; and (3) interagency teams where you will work with a variety of professionals from other agencies. Multidisciplinary teamwork is one way of addressing complex cross-cutting social issues as members of different professional groups work together to address common concerns. When working within a team, the following questions need to be addressed:

1. What services are provided?
2. Who is service directed towards?
3. Where is the service provided?
4. How is the service provided?
5. What is the purpose of the service?

## Practice example 15.1

### A multidisciplinary interagency team

A multidisciplinary interagency team was formed in a regional area with a high concentration of young families who migrated from the city to secure low-cost housing. Over time, there has been a significant increase in reports of family breakdown and family violence. It has become apparent that there is a strong need for early intervention approaches that address the tensions impacting on local families. Human service workers from local government, provincial health, child protection, disability support, and a range of non-governmental organizations meet on a monthly basis to plan a coordinated response to the issues that have been identified by individual service providers.

Courtesy of Deborah Hart.

In the health and social welfare context, a key defining word in teams is *collaboration*. The following definitions highlight this quality:

*Teams are collections of people who must rely on group collaboration if each member is to experience the optimum of success and goal achievement* (Dyer 1987, p. 4).

*Ideally, teamwork involves the definition of common goals and the development of a plan to which each member makes a different but complementary contribution towards the achievement of the team's aims* (Hunt 1979, p. 13).

*Teamwork is individuals working together to accomplish more than they could alone* (Woodcock 1979, p. 3).

*Ideally, team members collaborate and value one another's different contributions* (Finlay 2000, p. 165).

It is widely believed that strengthening teamwork improves the organization's services and the quality of help given to the public (Payne 1982). Compher (1987) points out that without effective teamwork and collaboration, clients are caught in a system that fragments their care and leads to confusion. Effective teamwork, on the other hand, helps to reconcile incongruities and deal with any contradictory information.

## Activity 15.1  Thinking about teams

Reflect on your biography and identify at least one occasion in which you believe you were part of a team. What was the nature of the team? What qualities identified the collective of people as a team? What implications can you draw from that experience for future use in teams?

When talking about teams, helping professionals often use the terms 'interdisciplinary teams' or 'multidisciplinary teams' interchangeably. But is there a difference? If so, what is the difference? Many argue that the difference between 'inter' and 'multi' is largely numerical. 'Inter' appears to involve two professions only (Carpenter 1995), and becomes 'multi' if more than two groups are involved.

Finlay suggests that there are many different ways of organizing teams; however, one defining difference centres around the 'different degrees of co-operation and collaboration' (2000, p. 166). She gives the example of a multidisciplinary team in a hospital setting where generally the consultant medical professional takes responsibility for key decisions and 'treatments are carried out in parallel manner rather than being co-ordinated' (Finlay 2000, p. 167). In such a team, although weekly management meetings might allow the voices of other professionals to be heard, clients' voices remain very limited. Finlay points out that the term 'team' might be more appropriate in this context if the consultant medical officer listened to and welcomed the input of other team professionals, if clients' voices were more influential, and if the whole team actively participated in decision-making.

In terms of the interdisciplinary team, Finlay (2000) gives the example of a community mental health team where team members work closely together and collaborate on cases and projects. She comments that when regular, collaborative team meetings are held and each professional has a sense of participating and decision-making, a good sense of team identity can result. Generally speaking, individual members of a coordinated team are more likely to be bound by what Finlay (2000, p. 168) calls 'the policies and priorities of their own profession or agency', whereas the members of a collective responsibility team are likely to be more accountable to their team in the way they use their time and resources. Of course, there will inevitably be a number of conflicts and tensions in any team, and these will be discussed more fully later.

In a similar vein, Ovretveit (1997a) distinguishes between the multidisciplinary, or 'coordinated profession team', and the interdisciplinary, or 'collective responsibility team'. Essentially, the multidisciplinary team comprises a network of professionals who deliver separately organized services, whereas the interdisciplinary team consists of a group of professionals who work closely together and take shared responsibility for their work.

## Practice example 15.2

## Social work in different teams

Consider the difference in a social work service being provided by referral in a general surgical unit, and one being provided as a 'blanket' service in a brain injury rehabilitation unit (BIRU). Social workers working in the surgical unit would receive referrals from the nursing staff to see patients or their families, conduct their assessments, formulate their plans, write in the medical file, and perhaps speak to the physician as needed. They may liaise with other allied health staff such as

*continued*

physiotherapists, again as needed. These social workers may work in several wards, and cover other wards in colleagues' absences.

In contrast, the social workers in the BIRU would see all patients and their families, conduct detailed assessments, provide ongoing support and counselling as required, and take part in weekly team meetings with all members of the team, including medical specialists, to discuss patients' progress and plans for their ongoing treatment. They may be involved in providing in-service professional development sessions for other team members, in some research projects, or with a wider network of social workers working in similar units elsewhere. The positions of these social workers would probably be funded separately from the main hospital social work department, and as such would not be required to cover absences of other social workers. Their own absences, likewise, would be covered from within the unit.

Courtesy of Annette Riley.

# Models of teamwork

Nowadays, teams in many health and welfare contexts have a multi-professional profile, and traditional professional boundaries are often set aside to create a team of people who can manage and coordinate clients' care irrespective of their traditional roles and professional backgrounds. Defining roles and professional boundaries is critical to effective teamwork.

Many helping professionals in community mental health practice, including social workers, have articulated the challenges inherent for them in today's interpretation of team-work. In interviews conducted by the author with case managers in community mental health teams, many respondents expressed the tension between the freedom and anxiety they experience when working from a generalist practice base. One social worker commented, 'I believe there is an undervaluing of my professional knowledge on this team and as a gener-alist worker. I feel my professional identity is not as strong as it might be' (Weber 2004). Another case manager, a psychologist, on the same team, said, 'The challenge of using my specialist knowledge and skill base, and letting others know what that is, is a daily one when working in a team where "common" knowledge and skills and "general" approaches to work are fundamental to the philosophy and practice' (Weber 2004). Another social worker in the same study spoke about the tension between 'de-skilling' and 'multi-skilling', stating, 'Role diffusion is at the core of teamwork, with everyone doing much the same work, but really, we all have our separate skills as well, and sometimes, some of us use these' (Weber 2004). Role clarity refers to the extent to which professionals are aware of what is required of them by the organization and team, including the goals and tasks, and whether they have the authority to carry out their responsibilities.

While in practice, the work of teams may be too complex to be classified neatly, it is useful to understand some identified models of teamwork in order to gain more insight into patterns of team behaviour and their implications for practice.

Three models of teamwork have emerged as characterizing the differences between the way teams operate: the 'hierarchical team', the 'collaborative team', and the 'parallel team' (Finlay 2000; Pritchard 1995). Teams that function in a hierarchical manner are not necessarily negative as they can allow for greater democratization in service planning. Although the responsibility for decision-making may reside with one individual as a function of role, hierarchical teams can invite all participants' knowledge and ideas, provide skill development opportunities for team members, and, ultimately, the case decision will reflect the culmination of a range of suggestions. Conversely, collaborative teams are not inherently preferable, as educational, professional, social, and cultural backgrounds, norms, and organizational and disciplinary affiliations can all challenge effective team collaboration. In the parallel team, a loose network of professionals liaise pragmatically where necessary, but each professional works autonomously with little collaboration.

## Practice example 15.3

## Parallel teams in the public hospital system

There is an emerging emphasis in the public health system on interdisciplinary strategic planning approaches designed to meet managerial goals of optimal efficiency. A *clinical pathways model* brings medical and allied health professionals together to devise efficient and cost-effective systems for patient care. Clinical pathways team members represent all clinical disciplines within the hospital and draw on real case scenarios to devise best practice patient care plans and referral processes. This time-limited team comes together for a specific planning purpose, but individual team members return to work in their own clinical or disciplinary teams for the majority of the time.

Courtesy of Deborah Hart.

Finlay (2000) points out that, 'In practice, teams operate a combination of these models as members work both in parallel and in collaboration, whilst simultaneously being a part of a hierarchy' (p. 169). It is also worth keeping in mind that the composition of team members may determine how the team works, as well as the task at hand. In reviewing a community mental health team, Ovretveit (1997b) found a range of practices. Although the day centre staff collaborated as a sub-team, they also operated as parallel teams, with contact with other services and professionals being essentially ad hoc and sometimes dependent on personalities.

The structure and process points in Table 15.1 have been adapted from Pritchard's (1995) analysis of the differences between teams. Remember that this table represents a paradigm. In reality, there might be variations within a particular model of teamwork.

As Finlay (2000) states, what is at issue in teamwork is not whether the style of working is 'good' or 'bad', but whether the way of working as a team is appropriate to the purpose and function of the services delivered and the decisions that need to be made. The real challenge for teams is to organize ways of working that achieve these recognized aims.

**Table 15.1**  Three models of teamwork (adapted from Pritchard 1995, p. 208)

| Team behaviour | Parallel team | Hierarchical team | Collaborative team |
|---|---|---|---|
| Team decision-making | Decisions made by autonomous individual professionals | Team leader sets the agenda and prescribes action after considering other team members' input | Team shares responsibility for goal setting and negotiates team decisions |
| Referral of clients | To individual team members as relevant | Formal system where senior professional delegates tasks | Referrals negotiated at both a formal and an informal level |
| Service delivery | Specialist professionals work in parallel | Practitioners work in parallel under the senior professional | Joint work |
| Perception of roles | Both understanding and perhaps misunderstanding

Some stereotyping may occur | Understanding and misunderstanding occur | Roles are clearly understood, but role diffusion and boundary blurring may cause tensions |
| Professional status | Differences are seen as less relevant and professional contributions are valued | Cooperation may be impeded by inequalities and differences between professionals | Little attention to differences. Negative use of power or status is challenged |
| Interaction in the team | Irregular and mostly of a pragmatic nature between some members | Regular, mostly formal but closer collaboration | Regular, close interaction and collaboration between members |

## Activity 15.2  Values and limitations of models of teamwork

Study Table 15.1 and reflect on each model.

1. Draw out two values underlying each model. (For example, in the parallel team, professionals have autonomy; in the hierarchical team, efficient use of resources can

*continued*

minimize duplication; and in the collaborative team, the coordinated division of labour enables holistic, integrated care.)

2. Identify two limitations of each model. (For example, in the parallel team, clients can become confused when contradictory approaches are adopted; in the hierarchical team, tensions and inequalities can impede co-operation; and in the collaborative team, collaboration may be time-consuming and take time away from actual service delivery.)

The model of teamwork that ultimately results may be influenced by such things as:

- working effectively within tight time constraints, such as hospital in-patient settings with short lengths of stay;
- the presence of part-time staff, who need to spend time in service delivery rather than in collaboration, such as in community health settings;
- the dispersed nature of the service delivery, such as in community mental health teams where many home visits are done;
- the legislative context of practice, where protocols have to be strongly adhered to, such as in child protection. (courtesy of Annette Riley)

# Some obstacles to effective teamwork

For a team to function effectively, all the members must be active players. Essentially, our sense of satisfaction with what we do, as well as our frustrations, will be influenced by how well we are able to participate. It might be argued that a practitioner's participation in helping other practitioners to deliver services is just as important as any direct contact with clients. In fact, it is not an overstatement to suggest that any direct work with clients will be helpful only if the practitioner can effectively use teamwork. Good communication is only one aspect of multidisciplinary interaction. Staff who work together develop an awareness of each other, begin opening up boundaries, and develop and recognize the strengths and learning edges of team members.

# Understanding and dealing with difficulties and divisions

## The myth of co-operation

First, there is a myth that all that is required of the practitioner for teamwork is a spirit of co-operation. This, of course, raises the question: does anyone see themselves as uncooperative? The practitioner must move beyond the naïve assumption identified by Compton and Galaway (1994, p. 501) that 'since we are friendly, outgoing, and thoughtful of others that good interdisciplinary collaboration will follow us all the days of our lives and that we will dwell in peaceful work situations the rest of our professional lives.'

This unrealistic view rests on two erroneous assumptions. The first assumption is that getting along with others on a team is an inherent gift and not a professional skill. The second assumption is that all collaborative processes can be reduced to psychological dimensions. Although personality factors are important, teamwork does not rest on personality traits alone. Frustrations in teamwork cannot be reduced simply by assigning malevolent intentions to others and whitewashing oneself. Differences will inevitably emerge between people and 'personalities'. From a critical perspective, the practitioner would welcome differences of view and opinion, respond to the challenges inherent in conflictual situations, enter into negotiations to resolve differences, explore the range of possible alternatives, and accept the innate legitimacy of differences. The critical practitioner would resist the tendency to evaluate differences in binary terms of right and wrong and the assumption that if something is different from something else, one must be more preferable than the other.

Nevertheless, as Payne (1982, p. 74) points out, the phenomena of liking and conflict in teams is a reality, stating, 'Teamwork promotes close relationships and so liking or conflict can easily arise, with helpful and unhelpful consequences.' He maintains that liking one another in a team will mean that people will be more motivated to work together productively. He recommends that where dislike and conflict arise between team members, two approaches to conflict might be considered. The first approach, *control strategies*, aims to prevent conflict flaring or to hold things steady while attempts are made to resolve the conflict. The second approach, *confrontation strategies*, aims to 'directly engage each other and focus on the conflict between them' (Walton 1969, p. 95). Lawrence and Lorsch (1967) in their research found that the most successful teams, in terms of results, used more confrontation than control strategies. Apart from these two approaches, which have been called 'smoothing' (Payne 1982), Filley (1975) identifies three other approaches: *withdrawal* (avoiding conflict); *forcing* (the use of power to impose a resolution); and *compromise* (seeking a midway point).

## Practice example 15.4

### Tensions within a team

Consider yourself part of a team of social workers who work in a specialist team, a child protection counselling service, which offers counselling and therapy to abused children and non-offending parents. This team meets weekly for administrative reasons, and bi-weekly for case reviews. The team leader, Ryan, has recently divorced, and has had considerable time off work. One of your colleagues, Fleur, had been acting in his position.

*continued*

On returning to work, Ryan insists on resuming his position full-time, even though a staggered return to work was suggested by the human resources department. It soon becomes clear that Ryan is not managing the demands of the position very well. He is often late, is disorganized, misses meetings, has not completed tasks, and has had a number of angry outbursts in front of staff. He has resumed his full counselling caseload. Fleur is appalled at Ryan's performance, and is scathing about him behind his back. She has become quite sarcastic in meetings, and seems to argue with Ryan about every issue. Other team members are concerned about Ryan's emotional state, and feel that they should take on more of the work to enable him to recover more of his equilibrium. Fleur refuses, and states that as Ryan gets paid for coordinating the team, he should pull his weight. She announces she will directly raise the issue in the next team meeting. Other team members are horrified, and believe that Ryan should be given some more time. In the next team meeting, everyone is on knife-edge.

## Questions for reflection

1. What are the issues for the team here?
2. What are the arguments for adopting a confrontational strategy? What could be the outcomes of this approach?
3. What are the arguments for adopting more of a control strategy? What could be the outcomes of this approach?
4. What other approaches may be employed here which meet personal needs, but preserve the professional responsibilities of this team?
5. To what extent can a team be expected to 'carry' a non-performing team member?
6. What are the limits to accepting diversity in teams? Can, for example, differences in professional standards of behaviour be tolerated by appealing to the argument that teams of people are heterogeneous, and not homogeneous?

Courtesy of Annette Riley.

## Power, authority, and competence

Inevitably, there will be conflict in teams from time to time: 'conflict is interwoven with interprofessional collaboration because there are deep-rooted social differences in the division of labour which has developed over the last two hundred years in the health and welfare service' (Loxley 1997, p. 1). Sometimes, as Loxley suggests, this conflict will be based in the differences inherent in the positions and power of team members. Conflicts between different professional values, team member positions and priorities occur when there is unequal status and power.

A second obstacle to effective collaboration is rooted in practitioners believing that they have limited power and their role is devoid of authority and influence. In settings where social work is in a secondary position to the 'primary' professions—for example, in a medical setting—social workers often complain that they can not influence the course of events. As a critical practitioner, it is essential that you reflect on power and authority issues, and challenge ideas around the authority of position, and re-conceptualize it as the authority of competence. The positive or negative stereotyping of the 'other' can lead to competition and division. A team in which some colleagues are labelled 'pill pushers' and others 'bleeding hearts' is unlikely to function effectively. Having respect for each others' perspectives and competencies, as well as the more shared, generic competencies is a prerequisite for effective teamwork.

For the critical practitioner, challenging power structures is vital. What is the distribution of power within the team? Are certain team members competing for control? Who feels marginalized? When team relationships are problematic and power becomes an issue, then the team should give itself time to reflect on what is happening and why, and what should be done about it. Inherent in the critical practitioner's role is the duty to confront practices that are destructive, disempowering, or discriminatory. As Payne (1982) points out, problems related to power in teams often arise in three areas: (1) dominance and submission, (2) power and responsibility, and (3) social structures.

Embedded in team relationships are patterns of *dominance and submission*. In order to understand this, Payne (1982, p. 72) suggests that the team 'look at whether a person's or group's dominance derives from personality (their push for their position, or the preference of others for submission), from the use of resources (rewards, sanctions, the ability to withdraw without disadvantage), or are reinforced by the structure and hierarchy of the agency'. In terms of *power and responsibility*, Payne argues that discontent, and even resentment, might grow from a situation in which a team member has responsibility without power or when a team member has power but does not accept the concomitant responsibilities. In practice, such misalignment needs to be redressed so that resources and rights match responsibilities. Power problems related to *social structure* cause frustration 'because things are difficult to change, or people may have the trappings of power and responsibility without sanctions or duties to back them' (Payne 1982, p. 72).

### Questions about the use of power in a team

Payne (1982, p. 73) developed a set of questions, adapted here, to help assess issues of power in teams:

1. What is the distribution of power within the multidisciplinary team?
2. Who is often, or always, dominant in team discussions?
3. Who is often, or always, submissive in team discussions?
4. Is the pattern of dominance or submission due to (a) personality or socialization, (b) resources, rewards, or sanctions, or (c) hierarchical powers and responsibilities?
5. Do people have competencies that they do not have the power or responsibility to use?

6. Do some people use their power to direct activities when other people think this is inappropriate?
7. Are important disagreements resolved by the use of unilateral power rather than by mutual agreement?
8. Do team members use a shared language or rely upon discipline-specific jargon?

## Activity 15.3  Reflecting on a recently-made decision

Think of a recently-made decision in which you, with others, were involved. Using the eight questions in the text above, can you identify aspects of team behaviour and the use of power in your example?

Practitioners should work on defining areas of special competence as well as areas of overlap. Working collaboratively and engaging in role negotiation are important aspects of daily practice. This means that critical practitioners, after close reflection on their role and its possibilities, are in a position to identify their role. The next step is to work towards broadening the sanction appropriately, along with bargaining for common areas of practice with other professionals who claim competence in that area. At these times, the role of the professional associations may provide guidance. The primary functions of a professional body are to safeguard professional standards and to ensure that education and training are appropriate to that purpose. Professional associations focus on professional standards through accreditation of professional competence.

## Practice example 15.5

## Collaboration for effective multidisciplinary practice

A large non-governmental community service runs programs for families in a high density public housing estate located in an inner-city area. The service is managed by a social worker and employs workers with backgrounds in nursing, psychology, social work, and community development. The service provides an innovative and successful home-visiting program for new parents, using trained volunteers as visitors.

The manager facilitates weekly meetings so that paid and volunteer team members can discuss their progress with individual families. These meetings provide an opportunity for team members to share ideas and to draw on a wide range of disciplinary knowledge and skills in order to provide the best possible interventions to families. The manager encourages a workplace

*continued*

culture in which every team member's input is valued, regardless of disciplinary background. Volunteer home visitors are highly regarded by the paid professionals for their personal experience and their ability to engage with struggling parents.

Courtesy of Deborah Hart.

## Practice example 15.6

# The role of the social worker in trauma

An emergency department of a large hospital used social work services only sporadically. The social work department decided to increase the resources, and hired an additional worker to provide a full-time service. As part of the coordinated response to trauma patients coming into the hospital, key team members in emergency carried a special pager that was activated when patients arrived. These team members included various medical specialists, junior medical personnel, nurses, radiographers, and a chaplain. The chaplain's role was to provide support and comfort to any relatives of the trauma patient. The social worker approached the medical director of emergency to request that the social worker also carry a trauma pager. The director replied that the chaplains provided a very good service in supporting relatives, and did not see the need of 'doubling up'. Several meetings were held with the director, the social worker, and the chaplain to try to resolve the issue.

Consider the following alternative responses:

A   The social worker was surprised that the medical director did not recognize the inherent worth of having a qualified social worker involved in responding to traumas. At the meetings, the social worker took the opportunity to demonstrate this inherent worth, and provided copies of studies that showed the effectiveness of social work intervention at a time of crisis. A list of key skills possessed by the worker was also furnished. The chaplain responded to this defensively, and considered it a 'fight for territory'. He likewise provided research evidence. The medical director was reluctant to change the present arrangements, stating that the chaplaincy had always provided a good service and that he did not want to send the message that they were not doing a 'good job'. Some time later, the director of emergency wrote to the director of social work services to say that the request for an additional trauma pager for the social worker had been denied.

*continued*

B    The meetings were approached by the social worker as information-gathering and orientation meetings, whereby the response to trauma in emergency was described by both the director and the chaplain. Discussion of the general nature of responding to trauma gave way to more detailed accounts of specific cases, and, through this means, the social worker was able to demonstrate empathy in acknowledging the difficult and challenging nature of the work. As a result of these discussions, further meetings of a more informal nature occurred between the social worker and the chaplain, whereby the chaplain spoke at length about feeling overwhelmed when involved in traumas, indicating that he needed support himself. The chaplain suggested that he page the social worker directly when his trauma pager went off, and that they approach the support of families as a team. They then had discussions about possible role divisions, which were refined through ongoing collaboration with families over the next couple of months. These were then formalized in the accident and emergency department's procedures and protocols, which were being rewritten at the time.

Courtesy of Annette Riley.

## Competition within the team

A third obstacle to effective teamwork is rivalrous behaviour within the team. Such behaviour can block people's ability to listen to and consider the perspectives of others. Rivalry is a great divider of teams. Team members who are not operating with individual agendas, not wedded to rigid discipline-specific boundaries, and are open to varying viewpoints are necessary for a successful multidisciplinary approach. Team members must work to maintain relationships that foster trust and mutual respect (Mouzakitis & Goldstein 1985). A team also should be focused on the reason for coming together and understand that competition and rivalry works against co-operation (Compton & Galaway 1994). All team members need to keep in mind their common goals. The expertise of individual members and co-operation between members are key elements to successful teamwork.

Co-operation is the goal but this is tested where different and often conflicting values and theoretical perspectives lead to divergence of opinion. Sands et al. (1990) discovered that interdisciplinary teams in conflict contained individual team members who saw themselves as primarily representatives of their discipline rather than as members of a team. The researchers suggest that team members need to identify their common value base, language, and conceptual framework.

Although practitioners from diverse backgrounds can bring different value systems, principles, and frames of reference to the team, Abramson (1984) points out it is of concern when these valuable differences create rivalry. Abramson (1984) provides some guidelines for enhancing collective responsibility in interdisciplinary collaboration. First, he suggests that team members need to establish shared meaning in terms of values and ethical principles such as confidentiality, as there are different professional boundaries around which information may be shared openly. Second, Abramson favours the idea of developing a regular process by which complex ethical dilemmas can be analyzed and give direction to team members. Third, he suggests that team members must be aware of their responsibility for group decisions.

## Practice example 15.7

## Competition and teamwork

A forty-eight-year-old man was admitted to a hospital palliative care unit for pain control of his advanced bowel cancer. The social worker had spent much time with him and his wife over a two-week period, providing support and assisting with some practical arrangements. She had several long interviews with the man, who appeared very despondent and talked at length about 'giving up'. His wife said that she felt he had 'dropped his bundle'. At the weekly team case conference where all of the patients' progress was discussed, this man's care came up for review by the team. The team was well-established, with the medical specialist, nursing staff, and allied health staff, including a social worker, being long-standing members.

A new intern (a specialist-in-training), who was on rotation, began the discussion about the man by giving a full medical history and a comprehensive update of his current treatment. All team members provided information, but it was not until the social worker's contribution that the issue of the man's possible depression was raised. The social worker provided her assessment, and suggested to the medical specialist that a psychiatric review be organized. The specialist agreed, and the meeting ended.

When the social worker returned to her office, she found the attending physician waiting for her. He was furious and berated her for her audacity to suggest a psychiatric review. He said this was a medical issue and added that if he had considered a psychiatric review necessary, he would have recommended it. He said she was out of her depth, and should leave medical matters to the medical staff. He claimed he had been made to look a fool in front of the specialist.

### Questions for reflection

1. What are the issues in this team?
2. What elements of teamwork contributed to this scenario?
3. What would have made the case conference different?
4. What responses could the social worker consider when faced with this scenario?

Courtesy of Annette Riley.

# Professional and agency culture

Teamwork presupposes effective collaboration in terms of team members demonstrating respect and trust towards each other, realistic expectations, and acceptance in their interactions. Within teams, professional subcultures often develop and these subcultures have their own value systems and ways of operating (Compton & Galaway 1994). For critical practitioners, reflecting on how these subcultures work is crucial if they are to avoid the risk of over-identification with a subculture within the team. It is worth asking: who and what are included? Who and what are excluded? Unless insights are developed and team members endeavour to act as collaboratively as possible, conflicts, and even bitter rivalry, can result.

Teamwork allows us an intimate view of our colleagues. Abramson (1984) reveals the sensitive issue of the questionable competence of a team member's performance, particularly if that person has authority and power within the team. It is important that all team members understand the basics of effective teamwork and be prepared to challenge ways of working that undermine the team's ability to effectively deliver services. Training can enhance group problem-solving, and team-building activities can help consolidate the 'team-ness' or 'teaming' of a group.

Team building can occur when a team carves out time and space to pursue a team endeavour. This can include such pursuits as a day of staff development, a common meal, or a bonding through an outdoors survival exercise. Fundamentally, the aim of such team pursuits is to develop and enhance a sense of team spirit through shared participation and collaboration.

Work teams usually exist within an institutional framework that may be supportive of multidisciplinary teamworking. The key question to consider is, 'What is the level of institutional support for multidisciplinary teamwork?' In some cases, traditional organizational structures may act as a barrier to multidisciplinary teaming.

# Towards effective collaboration

Because teams are made up of 'difference' in terms of professions, knowledge, perception, and skills, conflicts are inevitable and collaboration requires effort. As Loxley (1997, p. 1) puts it, 'There are differences of knowledge, of ways of working, of priorities. There is competition for resources and for power among professions. Collaboration is not experienced as easy. It is, however, recognized as sometimes necessary in meeting the complex needs of individual patients or clients, or responding to complex social situations.'

In her argument for greater collaboration between team members, Loxley (1997, pp. 49–50) continues, 'Collaboration requires communication across open boundaries, the willingness to take risks, [and] the reciprocity of costs and gains.' Nevertheless, it is a truism that difference can become a source of tension. In addressing this issue, Davies (1998, p. 51) proposes the concept of 'reflective solidarity': 'Each of us may arrive at a position we were not previously in—a position we could not have reached by dint of struggle on our own, or by dint of seeking support from those whose histories and perspectives are similar.'

Further, Davies (1998, p. 52) argues that the challenge of difference 'gives expression to some of the most powerful and energizing moments in social life'. She argues for strong collaboration and points out that adopting the assumption that each of us is bounded restricts our ability to be truly collaborative. Table 15.2 contrasts traditional team styles with more collaborative styles.

**Table 15.2** Two team styles (Davies 1998, p. 52)

|  | **Traditional** | **Collaborative** |
| --- | --- | --- |
| Concept of the individual | Bounded | Connected |
| Group process/style | Formal | Relaxed |
|  | Adversarial | Cooperative |
|  | 'Explaining' | 'Exploring' |
| Outcomes | Resolution is imposed | Agreement is tried |
|  | Assumption of finality | Expectation of change |
|  | Vindication and elation | Enhanced commitment |
|  | or | Stronger bonds |
|  | Defeat and despair | Personal renewal |

Models of professional development suggest that members of professions develop by reflecting on their practice (Schön, 1983). This can be encouraged by team members sharing insights with others, engaging in collaborative supervision, and willingness to share both successful and less successful outcomes.

The argument in favour of strengthening collaboration within the team is incontrovertible. Strong collaboration in a team means that members have the opportunity to connect with one another, be challenged by the differences between them, and be stimulated and complemented professionally.

# Critical practice and teamwork

Although teams and teamwork have many fine qualities, they also have limitations. Critical practitioners needs to reflect on how the teams in which they operate function and not automatically accept the assumption that teams are cost effective and efficient or the more dangerous assumption that teams offer a 'good experience' to all concerned, including professionals and clients. If you speak with any experienced practitioner, they will tell you that teams can be inefficient, filled with tension, and, sometimes, even damaging. It is the responsibility of team members to confront problematic situations and to work together to repair interpersonal and professional relationships, keeping in mind their purpose for being a team and their moral duty to deliver services to clients. Engaging in the team process is a challenge and requires the willingness to listen to others, to own our knowledge, and yet to also have the courage to value the contributions of others and be prepared to put aside cherished perspectives in the spirit of discovering new 'truths'.

## Practice example 15.8

## Teamwork in the new contract culture

A community-based mental health centre in an inner-city area employs eight workers from a number of different professional backgrounds to provide a broad range of crisis, urgent, and supportive programs for individuals who have been diagnosed with chronic mental health problems. As a result of their sometimes erratic behaviours, this population is often at risk for homelessness as they are often evicted for behaviours associated with their diagnoses.

The centre was recently granted a twelve-month contract to develop a supportive housing program with the view towards ensuring clients had access to safe, affordable housing that would not be lost as a result of their presenting symptoms. This pilot program will run in conjunction with a number of existing and innovative programs that are informed by harm-reduction principles. These include a drop-in support and living skills program, a mobile psychiatric service, and a support and counselling service. The centre is also active in advocacy campaigns to highlight discrepancies in government policies that impact persons with mental health issues.

The standard 'reconnect' contract stipulates that funding will be withdrawn if any of the workers engage in advocacy campaigns that publicly criticize government policy. The team supervisor is keen to get this program off the ground so agrees in writing to this funding condition without consulting members of her team.

The supervisor has become aware of escalating conflict between team members, but she is reluctant to address underlying tensions in case this jeopardizes the smooth running of the centre. It seems there has been a long-standing division between team members who adopt very different positions on implementing government policy. Some members of the team believe there is no use challenging government policy, while others wish to resist all changes unless they are consistent with social justice values. For example, some team members were pleased that the government recognized the need for safe, affordable housing, while other team members criticized the perceived 'forget and hide' approach, instead preferring to transition clients to the community. Some team members are beginning to openly attack colleagues who they label as 'troublemakers'. In response, others are accused of being uncritical government functionaries who are out of touch with the needs of service users.

Over the past month, there has been a sudden increase in unexplained staff absences, and the supervisor is coming under increasing pressure from her management committee to

*continued*

implement staff disciplinary action. Team members are feeling stressed and despondent and two of them are thinking about leaving the centre despite their passion for working with people with mental health issues.

## Questions for reflection

1. Working from a critical perspective, identify the sources of conflict within this team (think broadly).
2. What are the likely consequences for the mental health centre if this conflict is not resolved?
3. What strategies need to be put in place to address this issue?

Courtesy of Deborah Hart.

## Practice example 15.9

# Challenges in teamwork

You are working as a social worker in a large hospital. You work on a renal unit, where people with chronic kidney disease receive dialysis treatment. The patients are all long-term, and are very well known to the staff. Your team consists of specialist medical staff, nurses, a dietician, and yourself as the only social worker. The other team members have all worked on the unit for several years. You were appointed six months ago.

One of the patients, Mr Ross, who is seventy-four years old, has been admitted because he is unwell. Ten years ago, he had a failed kidney transplant and has been on dialysis three times a week ever since. He is very depressed and wants to stop treatment. If he stops dialysis, he will die.

The renal specialist is very upset at his request to stop treatment, and has asked you to set up a meeting with his wife, Mrs Ross, who is sixty-eight years old and in good health, and their two daughters, Linda, thirty-eight years old, and Sally, forty years old.

In the meeting, Mrs Ross is very emotional. She says that her husband is very difficult to live with, that he has significant mood swings, is very demanding, and often yells at her. She says she drives him to the hospital for treatment, but feels exhausted at the constant care she has to provide at home. As his condition has deteriorated, she has found it extremely difficult to care for him. Her husband will not allow community services to assist, insisting that his wife manage on her own. He was very angry at the failure of the kidney transplant, and has felt resentful of the need for dialysis since then. She feels she cannot continue looking after him. She said that her husband has been talking of stopping dialysis for a couple of months now, and has insisted that she tell the doctors that it is his wish to die. If the doctors insist on continuing treatment against her husband's wishes, she has been instructed by her husband to involve their lawyer.

*continued*

The two daughters, who both live out of town, have flown in for the meeting with the team. They are also very emotional, saying that they do not want their father to die, and that Mrs Ross is, as usual, overreacting. They accuse their mother of 'bringing this on herself', and say that she has always been resentful of their close relationship with their father. They, too, are threatening to involve lawyers if there is a move to have their father 'euthanized'.

The meeting ends without a clear plan. The specialist asks you to write up the meeting in the patient's medical file.

In the corridor, the nurse tells you that Mrs Ross has previously told her that Mr Ross has been a violent man throughout their marriage, and that she felt very sorry for her. She says that it would probably be 'best for everyone' if Mr Ross 'didn't continue dialysis', for what hope is there for him?

## Questions for reflection

1. As a relatively inexperienced social worker, what feelings do you imagine this case will bring up for you?
2. What roles do you have in this scenario? Think about your social work role with Mr Ross, his wife, and their daughters. What role do you have within the team?
3. Practise writing up the meeting in the medical file (filling in extra details as needed). What do you find difficult? What areas are you unsure about? What areas are you sure about?
4. What issues is this team facing? What are the possible strains or tensions between the team members? What underlies these issues (what are they due to)?
5. Consider roles and power in this team. What effect could these have on the process of the team reaching agreement on the plan for Mr Ross? What could be the effect on the outcome?
6. How will you decide what your obligations are?
7. Does the request of the patient take priority? Or do the obligations of the medical staff take priority?
8. Think about the possible outcomes and the impact on the treating team of these. How will you position yourself within the team in each of these outcomes?

Courtesy of Annette Riley.

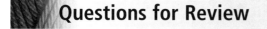 **Questions for Review**

1. What is the definition of a multi- or interdisciplinary team?
2. What are the benefits to a multidisciplinary team approach? What are some potential problems?

3. What factors enhance multidisciplinary team functioning? What factors impede team functioning?

4. What are the advantages of having services of separate disciplines embedded within the same team/environment?

5. What types of practice, techniques, or processes best translate into multidisciplinary team practice?

# References

Abramson, M. (1984). Collective responsibility in interdisciplinary collaboration: An ethical perspective for social workers. *Social Work in Health Care*, 10(1), 35–43.

Compher, J.V. (1987). The dance beyond the family system. *Social Work*, 32(2), 105–8.

Compton, B.R., & Galaway, B. (1994). *Social Work Processes*. Pacific Grove, CA: Brooks/Cole.

Davies, C. (1998). Care and the transformation of professionalism. In T. Knijn and S. Sevenhuijsen (eds), *Care, Citizenship and Social Cohesion: Towards a Gender Perspective*. Utrecht: Netherlands School for Social and Economic Policy Research.

Dyer, W.G. (1987). *Team Building: Issues and Alternatives*. Reading, MA: Addison-Wesley.

Filley, A.C. (1975). *Interpersonal Conflict Resolution*. Glenview, IL: Scott, Foresman and Co.

Finlay, L. (2000). The challenge of working in teams. In A. Brechin, H. Brown, & M.A. Eby (eds), *Critical Practice in Health and Social Care*. London: Sage.

Hunt, M. (1979). Possibilities and problems of interdisciplinary teamwork. In M. Marshall, M. Preston-Shoot, & E. Wincott (eds), *Teamwork: For and Against*. Birmingham: BASW Publications.

Lawrence, P.R., & Lorsch, J.W. (1967). *Organization and Environment: Managing Differentiation and Integration*. Homewood, IL: Irwin.

Loxley, A. (1997). *Collaboration in Health and Welfare: Working with Difference*. London: Jessica Kingsley.

Mouzakitis, C., & Goldstein, S. (1985). A multidisciplinary approach to treating child neglect. *Social Casework: The Journal of Contemporary Social Work*, 66(4), 218–24.

Ovretveit, J. (1995). Team decision making. *Journal of Interprofessional Care*, 9, 41–51.

Ovretveit, J. (1997a). How to describe interprofessional working. In J. Ovretveit, P. Mathias, & T. Thompson (eds), *Interprofessional Working for Health and Social Care*. Basingstoke: Macmillan.

Ovretveit, J. (1997b). Evaluating interprofessional working—a case example of a community mental health team. In J. Ovretveit, P. Mathias, & T. Thompson (eds), *Interprofessional Working for Health and Social Care*. Basingstoke: Macmillan.

Payne, M. (1982). *Working in Teams*. Basingstoke: Macmillan.

Pritchard, P. (1995). Learning how to work effectively in teams. In P. Owens, J. Carrier, & J. Horder (eds), *Interprofessional Issues in Community and Primary Health Care*. Basingstoke: Macmillan.

Sands, R.G., Stafford, T., & McClelland, M. (1990). I beg to differ: Conflict in the interdisciplinary team. *Social Work in Health Care*, 26(4), 55–72.

Walton, R.E. (1969). *Interpersonal Peacemaking: Confrontation and Third Party Consultation*. Reading, MA: Addison-Wesley.

Weber, Z. (2004). Case management in action. (Unpublished research project) School of Social Work and Policy Studies, Faculty of Education and Social Work, University of Sydney.

Woodcock, M. (1979). *Team Development Manual*. Farnborough: Gower Press.

# 16 Asset-based Community Development: Recognizing and Building on Community Strengths

Karen Healy

Community work refers to a range of methods used to work with groups of people who share a common identity or geographical location. Community development focuses on building community capacities, not only individual capacities. In this chapter, we will focus on asset-based community development, which is one of a range of approaches to community development. This model has been chosen because of its links to the strengths perspective, which is a popular contemporary approach to social casework, and also because of the growing popularity of asset-based community development in community service agencies (Green & Haines 2002).

In this chapter, we will:

- outline the relationship between human services professions and community work,
- consider the principles of asset-based community development,
- introduce the skill of conducting an asset audit, which is a core technique of asset-based community development,
- analyze the strengths and limitations of asset-based community development.

## Human service professions and community work: an uneasy alliance

According to Dixon et al. (2003, p. 5), 'community work' refers to 'the conscious application of principles, strategies and skills to build and maintain a sense of community, both as an end in itself and as a vehicle to achieve social, economic, political, and cultural change'. Community work involves building the capacity of community members to address the challenges facing their community and to facilitate increased control by local community members over decisions that affect their community. In the community work literature, the term 'community' is used to refer to communities of place—that is, people who inhabit a geographical location—or to communities of identity—that is, people who share a common and important identification such as membership of a cultural or ethnic minority group.

Communities of identity are usually developed around shared personal identifications such as communities of women, ethnic minorities, Indigenous groups, and shared experiences of mental illness (Crossley & Crossley 2001; Healy 2005, ch. 4). When communities of identity are formed around marginalized and oppressed identities, members can use their collective might to challenge the social oppressions they face (Campbell & Oliver 1996).

Community work practice has an ambivalent relationship to the formal helping professions, particularly social work. Social work pioneers, especially American social work pioneers Jane Addams and, later, Bertha Capen Reynolds, worked to build local communities. During the early twentieth century, when professional social work was first emerging, Jane Addams promoted 'neighbour to neighbour' helping networks via the settlement house movement and local neighbourhood-based research (Brieland 1990, p. 135; see also Addams 1938, pp. 125–6). Community work practice fell out of favour during the middle part of last century when psychodynamic perspectives dominated helping professions such as social work (for a discussion see Healy 2005, ch. 3). It was not until the 1960s with the re-emergence of systems perspectives in social work that community work came to the fore again as a practice method.

During the 1970s, a strong local community development movement emerged, drawing on authors, activists, and practitioners from a range of disciplines including, but certainly not limited to, social work. Indeed, many community developers sought to distance themselves from professional social work because of the profession's links to the social control functions of the state.

Jane Jacobs may be one of Canada's best known community developers. In 1968, Jacobs moved from New York with her family to Toronto, in opposition to the Vietnam War. In Toronto, she was an outspoken critic of top-down city planning. In the early 1970s, she helped lead the *Stop Spadina Campaign*, to prevent the construction of a major highway through some of Toronto's liveliest neighborhoods. She also advocated for greater autonomy for the City of Toronto, criticized the bloated electric company Ontario Hydro, supported broad revisions in Toronto's Official Plan and other planning policies, and opposed expansion of the Toronto Island Airport.

Today in Canada and many other countries, community work remains a popular method of practice in a range of social and community services. As governments across the English-speaking world 'rediscover' community, a range of new program initiatives have emerged aimed at building local community capacity (Healy et al. 2004). Asset-based community development is consistent with the renewed policy emphasis on building local social cohesion.

Community-building policy initiatives are supported by a growing body of evidence highlighting the critical role that local support networks can play in promoting individual and community resilience in the face of adversity. Strong local networks have been found to reduce isolation, increase personal and local pride, and increase access to the exchange of resources to meet needs such as child care or transport (Cattell 2001; Healy et al. 2004; Vinson et al. 1996). Of course, many proponents of local community development recognize the limits of these initiatives for addressing the effects of socio-economic disadvantage. As Cattell (2001, p. 52) warns: 'There is much evidence to suggest that even if networks can ameliorate the harsher health effects of poverty and deprivation, they are, nevertheless, no substitute for a more equitable distribution of resources nationally.' In summary, local community building has been demonstrated to play a useful role in ameliorating social adversity, but these measures cannot confront the macro-economic contributors to socio-economic disadvantage.

## Activity 16.1  Understanding the terms

1. How do you define the term 'community development'?
2. How do you define the term 'community capacity building'?

(Smith & Frank 1999)

## Activity 16.2  Focusing on community

The purpose of this activity is for you to reflect on your own experiences of geographical community and to use this as a basis for understanding the asset-based community development approach.

Consider, first, a geographical area that you have experience of: it could be the area you currently live or work in or an area where you grew up. Next, outline what you see as the relevance of the concept of 'community', either community of place or community of identity, for building the individual and collective capacities of people living in this geographical community. It would be ideal if you could explore these questions with people living in the geographical community you have identified, but, if you can not, you can use your own knowledge gained through previous work or research with them. Some questions that might be useful here include:

1. How important is geographical community, or a sense of place, to you and to others living in this area? Why is it important or unimportant?
2. To what extent do members of this community share a common identification? How is their shared identity expressed?
3. To what extent do members of this community have a shared identity attached to them by others?
4. What do they say are, or what do you see as being, the positive features of being part of the community?
5. What do they say are, or what do you see as being, the negative features of being part of the community?

# Asset-based community development

Asset-based community development, often referred to simply as ABCD, is linked to the strengths perspective in casework. John Kretzmann and John McKnight, from the US, are frequently credited as the founders of this approach. These community development authors sought to challenge what they viewed as the deficit orientation of traditional community development. Kretzmann and McKnight (1993) argue that common community development practices such as needs assessment and focusing on bringing outside resources into a community have obscured the capacities, skills, and resources that, in their view, exist in even the most disadvantaged communities. A primary goal of asset-based community development is revealing and capitalizing on the *gifts, skills, and assets within a community* (Green & Haines 2002, p. 9). Just as strengths-based case workers focus on the strengths and capacities of services users, in the ABCD model community workers prioritize recognition of the assets and capacities of communities. According to Kretzmann and McKnight (1993, p. 13), 'Strong communities are basically places where the capacities of local residents are identified, valued and used. Weak communities are places that fail, for whatever reason, to mobilize the skills, capacities and talents of their residents or members.' Building on the work of Kretzmann and McKnight, Mathie and Cunningham (2002) propose that ABCD can be understood as 'an approach, as a set of methods for community mobilization, and as a strategy for community-based development' (p. 5). The Coady International Institute, located within St. Francis Xavier University, extends ABCD within Canada and within the international context to create effective and practical solutions to reduce global poverty and injustice.

## Principles of ABCD

The asset-based model of community development proposed by Kretzmann and McKnight (1993) is founded on four key principles. The first of these is that *change must begin from inside the community*. Asset-based developers sometimes refer to their approach as 'inside-out' development (Kretzmann & McKnight 1993; Mathie & Cunningham 2002). In concert with most community development approaches, ABCD focuses on community members participating in decision-making and action in relation to their community. Community participation is important because community members are more likely to support initiatives which they have helped to develop rather than those that are imposed upon them. In addition, members' experiences of the process of creating and sustaining change will build pride and interdependence among community members, whereas change introduced from outside may contribute to the demoralization, disempowerment, and fragmentation of community members. Kretzmann and McKnight (1993, p. 5) also contend that for most socio-economically disadvantaged communities, it is futile to depend on outside help and so 'the hard truth is that development must start from within the community'. Their view is that outside help often does more harm than good, especially when it is short-term in nature and when the community's capacity for self-determination is compromised by the expectations of external sources of support.

A second principle is that *change must build on the capacities and assets that already exist within communities*. Asset-based developers assert that all communities possess capacities and assets, and these strengths must form the foundation of development practice. Asset-based community developers do not deny the realities of significant problems facing many communities, especially socio-economically disadvantaged communities, but they assert that we should resist making them the focus of our assessment and intervention. Indeed, they argue that many forms of community development inadvertently depower communities by focusing on needs and deficits rather than strengths and capacities. They argue that community needs assessment, a method often used in community development, is 'basically an effort to count up the emptiness in an individual or a neighbourhood' (Kretzmann & McKnight 1993, p. 14). Rather, we must primarily recognize the assets of communities because we can only build on strengths, not deficits. For example, in working with a community with high rates of crime, we must balance our focus on the negative effects of crime and the causes for it with recognition of those aspects of the community on which a relatively crime-free future might be built. As we shall see in our introduction to the asset audit, the ABCD model requires that we comprehensively consider a broad range of assets including those existing within individuals, informal networks such as neighbours who check on one's house when one is away on vacation, community kitchens or babysitting cooperatives, civic institutions such as sporting organizations and self-help groups, and formal institutions such as schools, non-profit institutions, businesses, and government agencies.

The third principle is that *change is relationship driven*. This approach assumes that relationships between members of disadvantaged communities and members of core institutions of government, business, and the non-profit sector are important for achieving sustainable change. The principle of relationship-driven change means community workers and members should reject donor-type relationships in favour of relationships based on mutual learning and exchange. This approach contrasts significantly with philanthropy, which is based on donor-type relationships, and also with critical community development (Craig et al. 1982), which points to fundamental oppositions between the core institutions, such as government and private enterprise, and the interests of community members.

The fourth principle of ABCD is that *change should be oriented towards sustainable community growth*. For asset-based community developers, the primary way to achieve sustainable development is by recognizing and building the community's own assets, and then using this as a foundation for mutual social and economic partnerships with external institutions (Green & Haines 2002, p. 11). Advocates of the asset-based approach are critical of community development practices that focus primarily on 'community maintenance', and on approaches that focus outside the community for resources to achieve change (Green & Haines 2002, pp. 9–11). Kretzmann and McKnight (1993) argue that asset-based community developers should be reluctant to rely on government funding as a source of financial aid for community development initiatives, for to do so can compromise the capacity of the community to develop its own direction and also to achieve long-term independence from welfare income and services (Pearson 2000).

Mathie & Cunningham (2002) add a fifth principle. They view ABCD as *a strategy* for sustainable community-driven development. Beyond the mobilization of a particular community, ABCD is concerned with how to link micro-assets to the macro environment (p. 6).

Asset-based developers share the concern of many proponents of community economic development (Shragge 1997) that all change activity must incorporate local economic capacity building. It is this economic strength that underpins local empowerment and forges the basis of mutual partnerships with external institutions. According to Kretzmann and

McKnight (1993, p. 354), 'Clearly, a community which has mobilized its internal assets is no longer content to be a recipient of charity. Rather, this mobilized community offers opportunities for real partnerships, for investors who are interested in effective action and in a return for their investment.' Thus, it is important that we understand the strengths of the community so that we incorporate these into economic, as well as social, development activities.

### Questions for reflection

1. What are the key conditions within your community that you believe will support (or have supported) a successful community development effort?
2. What are the key factors within your community that you believe might cause (or have caused) resistance to a community development approach?

(Smith & Frank 1999)

## Auditing the assets of the community

Asset-based community developers use a broad range of strategies to recognize and build the social and economic capacities of communities. Initially, ABCD practitioners focused on identifying the assets of a community as a strategy for engaging communities and for planning action. Asset-based developers use the terms 'asset audit' and 'community capacity inventory' to refer to the process of mapping the asset base of the community with which they are working. This involves working with community members to list the range of assets—economic, physical, environmental, as well as human assets—existing among them.

We now turn to the steps in conducting an asset audit, which are:

1. engaging the community,
2. constructing the inventory of community strengths,
3. gathering data and listening for strengths,
4. recognizing strengths to creating action,
5. achieving sustainable community-driven development through ABCD.

### Step 1: Engaging the community

1. How can you create commitment among various interests and organizations to work together for the benefit of the community?
2. What strategies can you employ to overcome resistance (by community members) to community development?

Asset-based community development aims to promote the participation of citizens in community planning and action. A vital first step of recognizing and building assets is engaging community members as partners in the community development process. It is essential that this occurs prior to data collection with, and about, the community, and certainly before planning community action. Asset-based community developers, like most community workers, use a range of methods for engaging community members, including low-key informal activities, such as picnics, through to more formal methods, such as public meetings. Rather than focus on the needs of the community, the initial engagement with the community should focus on what members identify as positive and strong about their community. Bradford (2005, p. 5) has described the importance of 'tapping local knowledge'. Effective problem-solving requires that governments tap local knowledge, bridging outdated divides between experts, citizens, and community-based organizations.

Community engagement begins from a position of mutual respect, and is founded upon a relationship of openness and transparency, as demonstrated by the following example. The graduation rate of First Nations students from post-secondary educational institutions in Canada is significantly lower than that of non–First Nations students. In order for a First Nations community to be receptive to participating in a post-secondary initiative, it is important for administrators and educators to recognize that the graduation rates are not a function of students' abilities, but of access and academic preparation. It is from this position of respect that post-secondary institutions are able to engage with First Nations communities. The role of the worker is then to identify, strengthen, and/or maintain community connections and facilitate community engagement by encouraging residents to connect with a variety of community resources, such as literacy programs, specialized post-secondary preparatory programs, study groups, and other forms of social resources.

## Practice example 16.1

### Community connection key to program success

The First Nations Partnership Programs are an excellent example of community development initiatives targeted towards post-secondary education. The programs highlight the importance of reciprocal partnerships both within the communities and between the communities and institutional partners. They are unique programs of training that strengthen capacity within cultural communities to create and operate services for children, youth, and families. One program provides child care training for community members that is delivered within First Nations communities, and incorporates the First Nations perspective on cultural practices, values, language, and spirituality. The program is asset-based, and was developed in partnership with the community in all phases of program planning and delivery, and features an open curriculum that depends upon community input, particularly the facilitation of cultural input through elder involvement (Ball 2004).

### Step 2: Constructing the inventory of community strengths

1. What are the key questions that you believe must be answered as part of a community assessment in order to better understand your community?
2. What do you see as a useful starting point for developing answers to the key questions you have identified?

3. What sources and approaches can be used to obtain this information?

(Smith & Frank 1999)

Asset-based community developers seek to build knowledge about the existing strengths of the community with which they are working. Some of the key asset-based texts provide a list of items to include in this inventory (Kretzmann & McKnight 1993). In practice, however, this process may begin inductively, that is, 'from the bottom up', by engaging small groups within the community. Possibilities include:

- *Focus groups*: Through these groups, community developers involve small and relatively homogeneous groups of community members in identifying what is strong and positive about their community. Homogeneity of groups is important so as to avoid, as far as possible, focusing on tensions and differences within the focus group and, instead, to turn members' attention to understanding their community as a whole.
- *Sharing circles:* The recovery of tradition at a collective level recognizes that mental health promotion within Indigenous communities is facilitated by community members' knowledge of living on the land, connectedness, and historical consciousness (Kirmayer, Simpson, & Cargo 2003).

From initial meetings with community members, the asset-based community developer should have enough information to work with community members to construct a beginning inventory for identifying the strengths in the community. The process of meeting with community members and listening to their strengths is also intended to motivate members to further participate in the asset-building process by highlighting their own capacities and by developing their interest in what else might be discovered about the capacities of their communities.

The community capacity inventory, or asset audit, is a comprehensive list of the forms of capital possessed by community members that can be used to promote community strengths. The inventory, which ideally is administered by community members, should include a broad range of headings, as well as room for community members to include more information on local capacities. The inventory would typically include a broad scope of headings and items of forms of capital that could potentially be used in the service of the community (Green & Haines 2002).

Let's turn now to a brief outline and illustrations of each of the forms of capital you may include in an asset audit. *Human capital* refers to the skills and capacities of individual community members and could include items such as local historical knowledge, cultural knowledge, and capacities such as home maintenance or cooking skills. *Social capital* refers to the norms and networks through which people collaborate to achieve common goals (Stone & Hughes 2002). Participation in local networks, such as neighbourhood gardens, volunteering groups, parent and citizen associations, and sporting clubs, are recognized as providing resources for change. *Financial capital* refers to money and potential credit sources for a community. In community economic development initiatives, data about financial capital may be linked to social capital. For example, we might investigate whether community members have contact with sources of financial assistance, such as start-up business loans. *Physical capital* refers primarily to the physical infrastructure of an area and may include such things as buildings, meeting halls, and housing that may be available for use in providing sites to build community capacity. For example, the building operated by the family daycare service may be available for other uses in the afternoon or the evening. The concept of *environmental capital* focuses our attention on the natural assets of a location and their potential use as a resource for the community. For example, the close proximity of an inner-city neighbourhood to city services, or the rural location of another community may provide tourism opportunities. This form of capital is primarily useful for analyzing the strengths of communities of place, rather than communities of identity.

## Activity 16.3  Identifying capital within a community

Returning to your community, as identified in Activity 16.2, note items that would appear under each of the forms of capital (social, economic, and so on).

1. List the forms of capital that you believe would be strong in this community.
2. What forms of capital, if any, are absent or very weak in this community?

### Step 3: Gathering data and listening for strengths

Consistent with the participatory ethos of asset-based development, it is important that the practitioner engages community members in gathering data about the strengths and assets of the community. Indeed, the process of data collection can itself contribute to the formation of forms of capital, particularly human and social capital in the community, by providing a forum for community members to develop skills in data collection and opportunities for meeting with other community members.

An important difference between gathering data from an asset-based perspective and a traditional needs-assessment process is that the data gatherer must be attuned to identifying strengths even when these are not apparent to informants. Thus, the process of asset discovery and recovery may involve challenging community members to recognize assets in those features that may previously have been seen as deficits. For example, some residents may perceive cultural diversity within a community as a source of deficit because of its assumed contributions to local tensions, but an asset-based community developer would identify the ways in which this feature could be a resource for the community in, for instance, local economic development initiatives.

As we listen for strengths and capacities in the community with which we are working, we may identify skills and capacities that do not quite match the needs of the community. For example, people may have lots of time on their hands and lots of enthusiasm but few financial resources. The asset-based developer would encourage community members to identify how their capacities could be used to help them achieve positive change.

Cunningham and Mathie (2002) describe 'collecting stories' as an effective means of gathering data. In contrast to traditional methods of assessment, 'informal discussions and interviews that draw out people's experience of successful activities and projects will help to uncover the gifts, skills, talents and assets people have. Not only does this uncover assets that people have not recognised before, but it also strengthens people's pride in their achievements. This celebration of achievement and realisation of what they have to contribute builds confidence in their abilities to be producers, not recipients, of development' (p. 1).

### Step 4: Recognizing strengths to creating action

As asset-based community developers, we can use the data we and others have gathered about the strengths of the community to plan action with community members. Like the strengths perspective, a popular method of social work practice, asset-based community developers aim to move beyond a focus on immediate problem-solving to create positive and sustainable futures with communities. For this reason, action planning is less about immediate solutions to current problems than about realizing the hopes and dreams of individuals and communities (Saleebey 2002). Because of this orientation, there is often a creative and even theatrical element to asset-based community initiatives.

Additionally, practical asset-based initiatives will usually focus on building a range of capital, especially financial capital, within a community rather than focusing on a narrow range of community capacities such as building local community networks only. Social enterprises such as community-based cafés, kitchens, laundries, catering services, and cleaning services are examples of the integration of social and economic capital building that characterizes many asset-based community development activities. Practice example 16.2 provides one example of asset-based development in action.

### Step 5: Achieving sustainable community-driven development through ABCD

The process continues as an ongoing mobilization of community assets for economic development and information sharing purposes, initiated by the associational base. Associations are encouraged to engage by appealing to community members' interests, finding common ground, and ensuring that they are contributing on their own terms. Eventually, an 'association of associations' will emerge (Cunningham & Mathie 2002).

## Practice example 16.2

## Identifying and building on assets

Let's consider the example of Point William*, an inner-city area in the core of a large city. The area was established by the public housing authority three decades ago and was originally intended to provide housing for 'unskilled' workers in the various manufacturing industries in the area. As most of the manufacturing work moved offshore, job opportunities for local residents

*continued*

disappeared and the suburb became characterized by high levels of unemployment. The area has long been known to government, police, and welfare agencies as a troubled location, with high rates of crime, low employment, and many social welfare problems. The proportion of single parent households, mostly female-headed households, is more than twice the national average. The area is home to two distinct population groups: a 'white' Anglo-Saxon majority and a minority group of immigrants, mostly from the African continent. The little interaction existing between these two populations has been characterized by tension. The area had minimal private business activity and this contributed further to poor employment opportunities. The only services in the area were provided by large government and non-profit agencies, which had a substantial presence there.

An assets audit, among other features, revealed that:

- Several people in the community were excellent cooks and many had good home maintenance skills associated with cleaning and basic home repairs.
- Some of the immigrant community members were growing vegetables and fruits in their backyards. These vegetables and fruits were indigenous to their homelands and were considered to be exotic in the city.
- Government agencies had offices in the area and they regularly purchased catering and cleaning services from non-local providers. Catering services were used for the purposes of agency meetings, and cleaning services were purchased primarily to clean vacated houses.

By identifying the community members' skills and assets, including the untapped asset of the service needs of large government offices located in the area, community members in collaboration with staff of a non-profit agency designed to help people start small businesses formed a business plan to establish two new businesses in the area. These businesses are a catering service and cleaning service; both are aimed primarily at the government and community service agencies in the local area. These small businesses are intended to provide some income for community members and also to provide experiences in a broad range of skills including delivery of catering and cleaning services and in running a small business. At the time of writing, the catering cooperative was established and bringing in a small income for its members, and the cleaning business was being developed.

* Note: Port William is a pseudonym for an actual suburb. The case study is based on community-based research with this location and identifying details have been altered to retain the anonymity of community members.

# Analysis of asset-based community development

Asset-based community development is a relatively new approach to community development with growing popularity in practice. However, there is little sustained analysis of the approach in community development research or social services literature. Let us now consider the strengths and limitations of asset-based community development as an approach for building the capacities of communities, particularly communities of place.

First, the approach can empower community members to use existing resources that might otherwise remain unrecognized and underdeveloped. Social enterprises developed from asset-based development have capitalized upon existing capacities within specific communities. For example, in Practice example 16.2, an asset audit revealed capacities in the community associated with catering and cleaning skills, thus enabling community members to tap into small business opportunities.

Second, the ethos of 'inside-out' development fosters community members' control over the direction of development. In asset-based community development, developers focus on using and creating the local assets of a community so that community members become partners with outsiders, rather than just recipients of outside help. This point is especially relevant given the increasing emphasis by governments on contract-based funding, which can tie community members to specific pre-defined outcomes and, in so doing, compromise their capacity to determine the nature and direction of community development initiatives.

The focus on inside-out development is consistent with the aim of some communities to reduce their reliance on government agencies. For example, in some communities, such as some Indigenous communities, there is a concern that an over-emphasis on government funding as the major source of income and infrastructure has limited the capacity of local community members to participate in mainstream economic exchange (Anderson, Kayseas, Dana, & Hindle 2004).

Third, proponents of asset-based development argue that the focus on relationship-driven development can lead to unique cross-sectoral partnerships. The emphasis here is on breaking down 'silos' between sectors to create opportunities for mutual understanding and to utilize cross-sectoral knowledge and capacities to create new options for action. For example, some Indigenous communities have formed collaborative partnerships with government, business, and third sector organizations to create a range of initiatives in business, tourism, and health care (Anderson, Kayseas, Dana, & Hindle 2004).

Despite the strengths of this approach, there are also concerns and limitations. While ABCD emphasizes the capacities of local communities to drive change, it tends to ignore the non-local origins of many of the challenges facing disadvantaged local communities. For example, the community of Point William, like many disadvantaged communities, is negatively affected by globalization. While there are examples of highly successful local economic development initiatives, for the most part, these initiatives are unlikely to promote substantial changes to the economic well-being of local communities. In addition, the emphasis on local community capacity and responsibility for change can lead to blame by governments and third sector services of those communities that fail to comply with the strengths-based outlook or for whom local enterprise initiatives fail. In short, the focus on creating 'can do' communities can lead us to ignore how factors outside the local community's control, especially structural and historical factors, constrain local capacities for change. This neglect of non-local factors can lead to blame and further marginalization of disadvantaged communities and can detract from the need for political action aimed at a more just distribution of economic resources nationally and internationally.

By focusing on the local capacities of communities, this approach can be used by governments and third sector agencies to withdraw support to communities. Seemingly resigned to the dominance of neo-classical economics in public policy, Kretzman and McKnight (1993, p. 5) argue that disadvantaged communities have 'no other choice' than to create change themselves (Weick et al. 1989, p. 354). Many social change advocates, such as anti-oppressive workers and members of consumer rights movements, would argue that there is another choice, that is, to transfer economic and social resources to disadvantaged communities as a way of minimizing the impact of global economic and technological change upon them (Dominelli & Hoogvelt 1996).

## Conclusion

This chapter has outlined the elements and application of asset-based community development. The key points of this approach are:

- We must look for the strengths and capacities in the community rather than focus on its weaknesses and deficits.
- We must build these capacities, that is, development must work from the 'inside out'.
- We must promote inter-sectoral collaboration.

The chapter has outlined some of the strengths and weaknesses of this approach. Notwithstanding the reservations outlined here, the approach is likely to remain popular as governments continue to focus on 'community-led' initiatives and as some community developers seek alternatives to 'needs-led' approaches to community building. In its focus on recognizing and building existing strengths within a community, ABCD challenges us to see the potential and capacities within even the most disadvantaged communities and to use this understanding to work for change.

## Questions for Review

1. What is asset-based community development (ABCD)?
2. What are the five principles of ABCD?
3. How does ABCD contrast with traditional models of community development?
4. What is a good example of a livable, viable community?
5. What are some consequences of adopting a needs and deficiency focus within communities?
6. What are the critical barriers to fulfilling a commitment to asset-based community development?

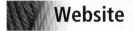 **Website**

### The Asset-Based Community Development Institute

If you want to learn more about asset-based community development, I recommend the website of the ABCD institute at <*http://www.abcdinstitute.org/*>. It includes a history of this mode of practice and related papers.

**References**

Addams, J. (1938). *Twenty Years at Hull-house*. New York: Macmillan.

Anderson, R., Kayseas, B., Dana, L., & Hindle, K. (2004). Indigenous land claims and economic development: The Canadian experience. *American Indian Quarterly, Summer/Fall*, 634–48.

Ball, J. (2004). As if Indigenous knowledge and communities mattered: Transformative education in First Nations communities in Canada. *American Indian Quarterly* 28, 454–79.

Brieland, D. (1990). The Hull-house tradition and the contemporary social worker: Was Jane Addams really a social worker? *Social Work*, 35(2), 134–8.

Campbell, J., & Oliver, M. (eds) (1996). *Disability Politics: Understanding Our Past, Changing Our Future*. London: Routledge.

Cattell, V. (2001). Poor people, poor places, and poor health: The mediating role of social networks and social capital. *Social Science and Medicine*, 52, 1501–16.

Craig, G., Derricourt, N., & Loney, M. (1982). *Community Work and the State*. London: Routledge, Kegan Paul.

Crossley, M., & Crossley, N. (2001). Patient voices, social movements, and the habitus: How psychiatric survivors 'speak out'. *Social Science and Medicine*, 52, 1477–89.

Dixon, J., Hoatson, L., & Weeks, W. (2003). Sharing theory and practice. In W. Weeks, L. Hoatson, & J. Dixon (eds), *Community Practices in Australia*. Melbourne: Pearson Education.

Dominelli, L., & Hoogvelt, A. (1996). Globalization and the technocratization of social work. *Critical Social Policy*, 16, 45–62.

Green, G., & Haines, A. (2002). *Asset Building and Community Development*. Thousand Oaks, CA: Sage.

Healy, K. (2005). *Social Work Theories in Context: Creating Frameworks for Practice*. Basingstoke: Palgrave.

Healy, K., Hampshire, A., & Ayres, L. (2004). Beyond the local: Extending the social capital discourse. *Australian Journal of Social Issues*, 39(3), 329–42.

Indigenous Business Australia. (2004). *Indigenous Australians in Business* (5th edn). Indigenous Business Australia, Australian Government. http://www.iba.gov.au, accessed 27 January 2005.

Kretzmann, J., & McKnight, J. (1993). *Building Communities from the Inside Out*. Chicago: Centre for Urban Affairs and Policy Research.

Mathie, A., & Cunningham, G. (2002). *From clients to citizens: Asset based community development as a strategy for community driven development*. <http://www.stfx.ca/academic/dev-studies/Devs200/Occ%20paper2002.htm>, accessed 1 November 2004.

Pearson, N. (2000). Passive welfare and the destruction of Indigenous society in Australia. In P. Saunders (ed.), *Reforming the Australian Welfare State*. Melbourne: Australian Institute of Family Studies.

Saleebey, D. (ed.) (2002). *The Strengths Perspective in Social Work*. New York: Longman.

Shragge, E. (1997). Community economic development: Conflicts and visions. In E. Shragge (ed.), *Community Economic Development: In Search of Empowerment* (pp. 1–18). Montreal: Black Rose Books.

Smith, A. & Frank, F. (1999). The community development facilitator's guide: A tool to support the community development handbook. Ottawa: Human Resources and Development Canada.

Stone, W., & Hughes, J. (2002). *Social Capital: Empirical Meaning and Measurement Validity*. Melbourne: Australian Institute of Family Studies.

Vinson, T., Baldry, E., & Hargreaves, J. (1996). Neighbourhoods, networks and child abuse. *British Journal of Social Work*, 26(4), 523–43.

Weick, A., Rapp, C., Sullivan, P., & Kisthart, W. (1989). A strengths perspective for social work practice. *Social Work*, 34(4), 350–4.

# Community Education
## Karen Healy

Community education aims to both recognize and build the knowledge of a community by engaging community members as peer learners and teachers. This method of community work practice, sometimes referred to as 'popular education', seeks to overcome the limitations of traditional modes of teaching and community service by engaging with the innate learning potential of all community members. The ancient saying, 'Give a man a fish and he eats for a day; teach a man to fish and he eats for a lifetime', reflects the credo of community educators—that is, community education should empower and transform rather than only respond to the immediate need at hand. While community education strategies are extensively used by community workers, the practice principles can also be applied to a range of social service practices.

In this chapter, we will:

- define community education and the influences on this approach, especially the influence of Paulo Freire's theory of education,
- outline the principles of community education and introduce practical strategies associated with this approach,
- analyze the strengths and limitations of this approach for practice in social service and community-building contexts.

## Definition and influences

Community education is a form of education and community-building practice aimed at radical personal and social transformation. This method is widely used by community work practitioners and, occasionally, by other helping professionals to engage individuals and community members in building knowledge useful for changing their personal and social circumstances (Lorenz 1994; Smith 1994). At the centre of community education is the ideal of community members as active learners and co-participants in knowledge production. This method rejects the division between teacher and student, helper and helped, on which traditional education and social services practices have depended. Community education practices are pre-figurative, which means that practitioners seek to promote the humane social values in their direct practice that they aim to achieve in the society at large. Community educators seek to contribute to a just society by enabling all community members to 'make their full contribution to the process of building a new society in which it is possible for all people to meet their fundamental human needs' (Hope & Timmel 1995, p. 16; see also McLaren & Leonard 1993).

Brazilian literacy educator Paulo Freire (1921–97) is widely recognized as providing the core intellectual foundation for community education practice. Freire's methods were initially developed in teaching basic literacy skills to illiterate farming workers and their families, who were among the most economically disadvantaged members of Brazilian society. Through this practice, Freire developed a theory of educational practice, which he referred to as a 'problem-posing' approach. This approach is fully outlined in his book *Pedagogy of the Oppressed*, first published in 1968, which is a core text not only for community educators but also for a range of education and community development practices aimed at social transformation (Freire 1997).

Freire (1997) presents the problem-posing method in opposition to the traditional banking model, in which the knowledge of the expert is transferred to the student. In Freire's view, the banking model dominates traditional education practice and separates teacher from student and academic knowledge from practical know-how. Freire (1997) argues that literacy education must instead engage with the knowledge and experience of students so that the words taught are relevant to building a critical understanding of the everyday life experiences of community members. For example, in traditional literacy education for infants, students might begin with basic and seemingly neutral words such as 'cat', 'dog', or 'apple'. By contrast, in problem-posing education, learning begins with words associated with the lived experience of disadvantage, such as 'hunger', and involves not only learning to spell the word but also to explore the experience and causes of hunger in the world.

Community educators aim to initiate learning conversations with community members. This involves forming learning groups within a community. The community educator prepares problem-solving materials to stimulate discussions about the 'why, how, who' of the phenomena impacting upon a group (Hope & Timmel 1995). For example, a community educator working with members of a geographical community to address the problem of a waste installation being located near them might present a series of images of waste installations and alternative waste solutions, and, use these images to stimulate conversations about 'why' the instalment is being located at a particular site, 'who' is responsible, and 'how' the community might develop effective resistance and alternative responses to the problem.

An example of a community education project in Canada is the Community Education program located at Simon Fraser University in British Columbia. The mandate of this program is to support positive social change for socially excluded individuals and communities by creating access to education and other resources. The program builds partnerships with multicultural communities who experience ongoing poverty, racism, gender bias, and low levels of literacy. The work is grounded in community-based projects that address critical needs identified by the community, and in which community members play active roles in decision-making, implementation, and evaluation. All projects provide opportunities for participants to develop the skills and knowledge necessary to carry out their community work (Simon Fraser University 2009).

# Principles of community education in health and social service settings

The primary roles of the community educator and the helping professional using community education strategies are to facilitate learning through identifying and using the knowledge that exists among community members and to assist them to further develop the knowledge they require. The community educator's role is to facilitate knowledge development rather than knowledge transfer. Consistent with the humanist values of equality, democracy, and social justice that underpin this approach, the educator and helping professional must work alongside community members rather than do for, or to, community members.

Community education is well established in social development practices, especially in developing countries (Hope & Timmel 1995). Increasingly too, community education strategies are used by mainstream health and social service professionals for engaging community members in a range of learning and community-building processes (Lorenz 1994; Smith 1994). Let us now outline and explore the relevance of community education to practice in health and social care services. We will use the example of parenting education with a young parents' group to illustrate these principles in practice.

## Practice example 17.1

### Applying community education principles

Imagine that you are employed as an adolescent mothers' support worker in a family support service. The adolescent mothers have identified that they would like to learn parenting skills. Some members of the group have previously attended parenting skills groups but complain that many of the people who attended were much older than them and also that it was too much like being at school, that is, they were talked at and were bored most of the time! Let us consider how we would apply community education principles to the task of creating a context for learning parenting skills.

### Activity 17.1  Reflections on community

1. What are some problems that your community is currently experiencing?
2. Who is most affected by these problems?
3. What do you believe to be the root causes of the problems identified?
4. What do you believe keeps the problems from being solved in a meaningful way?

The *first principle* of community education is respect for the lived experience of community members. Community educators challenge the separation of formal and informal knowledge by showing community members that they already possess some of the knowledge they require and the capacity to acquire the skills they need to access and create knowledge. In this process, community educators can assist community members to develop a more critical view of professional expertise—to view such expertise as *one* source of truth to be used in the service of the community rather than as a source of power over them.

*How?* The community educator can show respect for the lived knowledge of community members by exploring members' existing knowledge of the concern, rather than assuming the status of expert in relation to it. Referring to Practice example 17.1, we would engage in conversations with the young women, focusing on identifying the skills they already possess and look for opportunities for peer learning. For example, one mother may feel confident in handling toddler tantrums and we would encourage her to share this 'informal' knowledge with her peers.

The *second principle* is education through dialogue. Consistent with the principle of respecting the lived knowledge of community members, learning is based on dialogical conversations and, in this process, the traditional division between 'teachers' and 'students' is replaced with the common position of co-learner. As Freire (1997, p. 57) asserts, 'The teacher is no longer merely the-one-who-teaches, but one who is himself taught in dialogue with the students, who in turn while being taught, also teach.'

*How?* The process of exploration may begin with a series of 'unstructured conversations' with members of the community (Hope & Timmel 1995) aimed at identifying common learning needs among community members and strategies for meeting these learning needs. For example, the young mothers may agree that they find it difficult to manage their anger. In the spirit of critical reflection, we would first explore the range of factors that contribute to anger, such as discriminatory attitudes to young parents and the lack of support available for them. We might also engage a consultant for a specified number of group sessions to discuss anger management strategies. However, unlike the traditional banking model of education, group members are encouraged to critically analyze 'expert' knowledge—that is, to understand its uses and limitations in their life context. Finally, community educators often use action research strategies to engage community members in researching their concerns and in developing solutions (Healy 2001). In relation to the young mothers' desire for parenting skills education, we could use action research strategies to involve young parents in developing 'formal' knowledge about their experiences of parenting and in developing formal parenting skills approaches that are relevant to their needs.

The *third principle* is that education should be holistic. Community educators recognize that the learning needs of communities cannot be separated from their entire life context, and this can impact on the educational process in a number of ways. A holistic approach requires us to recognize that the community members' learning needs are related, often in complex ways, to other life needs. For example, the 'immediate' concern of addressing parenting skills cannot be separated from other skills the young parents may require, such as literacy skills. In addition, a holistic approach requires us to recognize the myriad of personal and practical barriers to participation in learning. For instance, it is likely that members of disadvantaged communities have prior negative experiences of learning environments and of social exclusion, which may contribute to a suspicion towards community education processes. This is particularly true for several communities in Canada, including Aboriginal and First Nations groups.

*How?* In practice, we can use the principle of holism to ensure that we recognize the whole-of-life context, rather than focus on single goals. In relation to working with young mothers to address their perceived need for parenting skills, it is important that we explore with them any experiential barriers to participation in learning, such as low levels of literacy, histories of abuse or neglect, or previous negative experiences of education and community participation processes. Consistent with the principle of holism, we should also address practical barriers to participation, such as access to child care and transportation. Finally, it is important that we examine with them how their presenting need—parenting education— may be transferred to learning in other areas in their life. For example, for young parents seeking to return to school, we could consider how the learning approach used to explore and develop parenting skills can be transferred to assist them achieve academic success.

The *fourth principle* is that education should be transformative. Community educators recognize that education is a political process on a range of levels. According to Freire (1997), members of disadvantaged communities are often excluded from formal knowledge-building processes by elitist educational institutions. Marginalization occurs as the lived knowledge of disadvantaged people is devalued in the education process in favour of abstract ways of knowing (McLaren & Leonard 1993). In the Freirian tradition, the practice of connecting people with their capacity to learn by using their lived experiences as a basis for learning is a politically-transformative act. Education is also transformative when it empowers community members to develop a critical understanding of their world, which in turn leads them to undertake change activity.

*How?* The community education process should enable members to critically explore the social context of their concerns and to consider opportunities for action. Returning to Practice example 17.1, in assisting young parents to address their desire for improved parenting skills, we could explore with them discriminatory public images of young mothers as irresponsible and welfare-dependent that deny the capacities of young mothers, such as the energy and enthusiasm some young parents bring to the role, and to understand how the effects of government policy, such as the lack of affordable child care and family support, contribute to the difficulties encountered by young parents. In this way, we shift our analysis from a focus on individual skill deficit to a critical analysis of the social context of young parents' needs and concerns.

## Activity 17.2 Community education in action

The purpose of this activity is for you to apply the community education principles to a practice scenario in health and social care services. Imagine that you are working in a community health service. A group of service users living with chronic illness would like to form a group aimed at improving services in their community. Their common concern is

*continued*

that their condition is often misunderstood and undervalued by health and social service professionals. They would like to develop more skills in asserting themselves with health and social service professionals and also in raising awareness of the issues of chronic illness among service providers.

1. Identify how you would use community education to assist these service users to form their group.
2. What kinds of practical activities would you, as a community educator, be likely to encourage and support?

## Activity 17.3  Assessing the strengths and weaknesses of community education

The purpose of this activity is for you to consider the strengths and weaknesses of community education in your context of practice.

1. Divide a sheet of paper into two.
2. On one side, write the heading 'Strengths' and on the other 'Issues and Concerns'.
3. Reflecting on both the context of practice presented in Activity 17.1 and a practice context that interests you, list the strengths and weaknesses of community education in those settings.
4. Try to provide an example of each strength and weakness.
5. Once you have completed this part of the exercise, see if you can identify the practice contexts in which community education is likely to be most useful and those in which it is likely to be limited.

# Critical commentary

Community education principles are consistent with the humanitarian and transformative values to which community workers and many helping professionals aspire. The practice principles provide practical pathways for workers to respect and build the knowledge of community members. Moreover, by connecting community members with their capacities to learn and to act, these strategies promote sustainable development among community members.

Community education strategies are applicable to a wide range of health and social service settings. For example, peer learning strategies are well established in some areas of health care, such as women's and men's health (Sherwin 1998). Yet, these strategies can be extended to more traditional areas of service provision and education. For instance, in cancer care and support, peers can provide core knowledge about living with a life-threatening condition and may provide critical insights for improving professional care, which might otherwise remain unknown to service providers.

Community education strategies can also enable service providers to link 'private' concerns with public issues (Smith 1994). The dual focus on personal and social transformation means that the immediate needs of community members are respected while also working towards recognizing the broader context of service users' concerns. The focus on political action can facilitate service users' participation in creating sustainable and just solutions to the problems facing them. The process of community education can assist in transforming community members from the position of recipients of policy processes and community services to becoming actors and activists within them (Lorenz 1994).

Notwithstanding the usefulness of community education in a range of health, social service, and community development contexts, limitations and concerns also exist regarding this practice method. A key problem is that community educators may frustrate and confuse community members. The banking model of education and professional service delivery, in which the professional transfers knowledge to the service user, dominates mainstream institutions of education, health, and welfare. Hence, our peers and many service users will expect that, as helping professionals, we will have the expertise required to help them with the issues they face. The problem-posing approach at the centre of community education requires that we challenge this expectation. Tensions can emerge between the community educators' desire to facilitate knowledge development and community members' or peers' desire to receive knowledge. To use Freire's terminology, community members may seek a banking education process rather than a problem-posing one. For example, the young parents seeking parenting skills may want exposure to the formal knowledge (banking education) of parenting experts rather than participating in uncovering and developing their knowledge of parenting (problem-posing approach). Other situations in which the banking model is likely to be especially attractive include those where a high level of formal expertise is involved and, thus, where there is substantial cost involved in developing the skills within the community. For instance, in undertaking a piece of community research, it may be more effective to engage a statistical consultant to access and interpret complex demographic data rather than encouraging community members to develop these skills themselves. Indeed, community educators must acknowledge the balance between learning outcomes and the costs of acquiring knowledge if we are to sustain community engagement.

The potential mismatch between the community educator's approach and community members' expectations can lead to frustration on both sides. This mismatch can also damage the credibility of the helping professional, who community members may perceive as withholding knowledge or manipulating community members to conform to a specific world view, which we as community educators define as being 'critically reflective' (for discussion, see Healy 2001). We can prevent this problem by being willing from the outset to share our perceptions as perceptions, rather than as truths, and by negotiating the appropriate balance of banking and problem-posing methods for addressing the concern at hand with community members. Our willingness to negotiate this balance is consistent with the respectful and democratic ethos of community education.

The time demands of community education processes can reduce the attractiveness of this approach to education for community members with substantial calls on their time, such as people with heavy informal caregiving responsibilities. Rather than adopt the entire community education framework, from collaborative problem identification through to peer learning and reflection, it may be necessary for health and social service professionals to adopt only some elements of the approach. For example, in educating fellow service providers about the needs of service users with chronic illness, one could use community education strategies such as critical reflection on the causes of the neglect of these needs, without also having to adopt other elements of the community education model, such as building formal knowledge.

In summary, community education is a method of education and community building originally developed in the field of adult literacy. The method aims to achieve social transformation through recognizing and building community members' capacity for critical social action. Community education provides practical strategies for achieving greater equality and democracy in learning and community building. The method is well established in social development, and in this chapter we have argued that these elements are highly relevant to learning and action in health and social service fields. We have reviewed the strengths of, and key concerns about, this method in the hope that you may use this method critically and effectively in your practice context.

## Questions for Review

1. What is the working definition of community education?
2. What are the aims of a community education model?
3. How may community educators reach out to the community with the goal of empowering community members?

## References

Freire, P. (1997). *Pedagogy of the Oppressed*. New York: Continuum.

Healy, K. (2001). Participatory action research and social work: A critical appraisal. *International Social Work*, 44(1), 93–105.

Hope, A., & Timmel, S. (1995). *Training for Transformation: A Handbook for Community Workers*. London: Intermediate Technologies Publications.

Lorenz, W. (1994). *Social Work in a Changing Europe*. London: Routledge.

McLaren, P., & Leonard, P. (eds) (1993). *Paulo Freire: A Critical Encounter*. London: Routledge.

Sherwin, S. (1998). *The Politics of Women's Health: Exploring Agency and Autonomy*. Philadelphia: Temple University Press.

Simon Fraser University (2009). Community Education Program.

Smith, M.K. (1994). *Location Education: Community, Conversation and Action*. Buckingham: Open University Press.

# Bibliography

AASW (2000). *Code of Ethics*. Kingston, ACT: Australian Association of Social Workers.

Abella, I. (2008). Refugees. *The Canadian Encyclopedia*, Online edition. http://www.thecanadianencyclopedia.com/index.cfm?PgNm=TCE&Params=A1ARTA0006738

Abramson, A. (1996). Reflections on knowing oneself ethically: Toward a working framework for social work practice. *Families in Society: The Journal of Contemporary Human Services*, April, 195–201.

Abramson, M. (1984). Collective responsibility in interdisciplinary collaboration: An ethical perspective for social workers. *Social Work in Health Care*, 10(1), 35–43.

Adams, M., Bell, L.A., & Griffin, P. (1997). *Teachings for diversity and social justice: A sourcebook*. New York, NY: Routledge.

Addams, J. (1938). *Twenty Years at Hull-house*. New York: Macmillan.

Agger, B. (1991). Critical theory, poststructuralism, postmodernism: Their sociological relevance. *Annual Review of Sociology*, 17, 105–31.

Agger, B. (1998). *Critical Social Theories*. Boulder, CO: Westview Press.

Alaszewski, A. (1998). Risk in modern society. In A. Alaszewski, L. Harrison & J. Manthorpe (eds), *Risk, Health and Welfare* (pp. 3–23). Buckingham, PA: Open University Press.

Alaszewski, A., Alaszewski, H., & Harrison, L. (1998). Professionals, accountability and risk. In A. Alaszewski, L. Harrison & J. Manthorpe (eds), *Risk, Health and Welfare* (pp. 89–103). Buckingham, PA: Open University Press.

Anderson, I. (1999). Aboriginal well-being. In C. Grbich (ed.), *Health in Australia, Sociological Concepts and Issues*. Sydney: Prentice Hall.

Anderson, R., Kayseas, B., Dana, L., & Hindle, K. (2004). Indigenous land claims and economic development: The Canadian experience. *American Indian Quarterly, Summer/Fall,* 634–48.

Argyris, C., & Schön, D. (1976). *Theory in Practice: Increasing Professional Effectiveness*. San Francisco: Jossey-Bass.

Ashton, M., & Varga, L. (1991). *101 Games for Groups*. Adelaide: Hyde Park Press.

Attlee, C. (1920). *The Social Worker*. London: G. Bell and Sons.

Avolio, B. (1995). *The Full Range of Individual, Team and Organizational Leadership Development—Workshop Manual*. Paper presented at the Inaugural Industrial and Organisational Psychology Conference, Sydney.

Baird, B.N. (1999). *The Internship, Practicum, and Field Placement Handbook: A Guide for the Helping Professions* (2nd edn). Upper Saddle River, NJ: Prentice Hall.

Baird, C., Wagner, D., Healy, T., & Johnson, K. (1999). Risk assessment in child protective services: Consensus and acturial model reliability. *Child Welfare*, 78(6), 723–48.

Baird, C., & Wagner, D. (2000). The relative validity of actuarial- and consensus-based Risk Assessment Systems. *Children and Youth Services Review*, (11/12), 839–71.

Ball, J. (2004). As if Indigenous knowledge and communities mattered: Transformative education in First Nations communities in Canada. *American Indian Quarterly* 28, 454–79.

Banks, S. (2001). *Ethics and Values in Social Work* (2nd edn). Basingstoke: Palgrave.

Barker, R. (1991). *The Social Work Dictionary*. Washington: NASW Press.

Barnes, R., Josefowitz, N., & Cole, E. (2006). Residential schools: Impact on Aboriginal students' academic and cognitive development. *Canadian Journal of School Psychology*, 21, 18–32.

Baruch, V. (2004). Self-care for therapists: prevention of compassion fatigue and burnout. *Psychotherapy in Australia*, 18(4), 64–8.

Bateman, N. (2000). *Advocacy Skills for Health and Social Care Professionals*. London: Jessica Kingsley.

Baumann, D., & Fluke, J. (2004). *Steps to a Decision Making Ecology for Child Protective Services: A Multi-National Research Perspective*. Paper presented at the 15th International Congress on Child Abuse and Neglect, Brisbane.

Baumann, D.J., Law, J.R., Sheets, J., Reid, G., & Graham, J.C. (2005). Evaluating the effectiveness of actuarial risk assessment models. *Children and Youth Services Review*, 27, 465–90.

Beauchamp, T.L., & Childress, J.F. (1994). *Principles of Biomedical Ethics*. New York: Oxford University Press.

Bennet, M., & Blackstock, C. (2002). A literature review and annotated bibliography focusing on aspects of aboriginal child welfare in Canada. Winnipeg, MB: First Nations Research Site of the Centre of Excellence for Child Welfare.

Benson, J.F. (2001). *Working More Creatively with Groups* (2nd edn). London: Routledge.

Beresford, P., & Croft, S. (1993). *Citizen Involvement: A Practical Guide for Change*. London: Macmillan.

Berg, I., & Kelly, S. (2000). *Building Solutions in Child Protective Services*. New York: Bytheway.

Biestek, F.P. (1957). *The Casework Relationship*. London: Allen & Unwin.

Bion, W.R. (1961). *Experience in Groups*. London: Tavistock.

Birnbaum, M. (1986). The use of group process in the integrative seminar. In M. Parnes (ed.), *Innovations in Social Group Work: Feedback from Practice to Theory*. New York: The Haworth Press.

Bishop, A. (2002). *On becoming an ally: Breaking the cycle of oppression in people*. Toronto: ON: Zed Books.

Bloom, M. (1975). *The Paradox of Helping: Introduction to the Philosophy of Scientific Helping*. New York: John Wiley & Sons.

Bourgeault, R. (1991). Race, class and gender: Colonial domination of Indian women. In O. McKague (ed.), *Racism in Canada* (129–50). Saskatoon, SK: Fifth House.

Bowlby, J. (1980). *Attachment and Loss: Loss, Sadness and Depression*. Harmondsworth: Penguin.

Brach, C., & Fraser, I. (2000). Can cultural competency reduce racial and ethnic health disparities? A review and conceptual model. *Medical Care Research and Review*, 57(1), 181–217.

Bracken, D., Deane, L., & Morrisette, L. (2009). Desistance and social marginalization: The case of Canadian Aboriginal offenders. *Theoretical Criminology*, 13, 61–78.

Bradford, L.P. (1978). The case of the hidden agenda. In L.P. Bradford (ed.), *Group development* (2nd edn). La Jolla: University Associates.

Brearley, J. (1995). *Counselling and Social Work*. Buckingham, PA: Open University Press.

Brechin, A. (2000). Introducing critical practice. In A. Brechin, H. Brown & M.A. Eby (eds), *Critical Practice in Health and Social Care*. London: Sage.

Brieland, D. (1990). The Hull-house tradition and the contemporary social worker: Was Jane Addams really a social worker? *Social Work*, 35(2), 134–8.

Brookfield, S. (1991). Using critical incidents to explore learners' assumptions. In J. Mezirow & Associates, *Fostering Critical Reflection in Adulthood. A Guide to Transformative and Emancipatory Learning*. San Francisco: Jossey-Bass.

Brown, A., & Bourne, I. (1996). *The Social Work Supervisor*. Buckingham, PA: Open University Press.

Brownridge, D. (2008). Understanding the elevated risk of partner violence against Aboriginal women: A comparison of two nationally representative surveys of Canada. *Journal of Family Violence*, 23, 353–67.

Bucharski, D., Reutter, L., & Ogilvie, L. (2006). 'You need to know where we're coming from': Canadian Aboriginal women's perspectives on culturally appropriate HIV counseling and testing. *Health Care for Women International*, 27, 723–37.

Bundey, C. (1980). Small group learning. In D. Armstrong & P. Boas (eds), *Experiential Psychotherapies in Australia*. Bundoora: Pit Press.

Bundey, C. (1983). Group Leader Training Course. Sydney: Unpublished workshop handouts.

Bundey, C., Cullen, J., Denshire, L., Grant, J., Norfor, J., & Nove, T. (1989). *A Manual About Group Leadership and a Resource for Group Leaders*. Sydney: NSW Department of Health.

Campbell, J., & Oliver, M. (eds) (1996). *Disability Politics: Understanding Our Past, Changing Our Future*. London: Routledge.

Canadian Association of Schools of Social Workers (2008). *Educational Policy Statement*. Ottawa, Ontario: Canadian Association of Social Workers.

Canadian Association of Social Workers (2005). *Code of Ethics*. Ottawa, Ontario: Canadian Association of Social Workers.

Canadian Association of Social Workers (2005). *Guidelines for ethical practice*. Ottawa, Ontario: Canadian Association of Social Workers.

Canadian Institutes of Health Research (2007). CIHR *guidelines for health research involving Indigenous people*. Ottawa, Ontario: Canadian Institutes for Health Research.

*Canadian Multiculturalism Act* (1988). Government of Canada, Ottawa, Ontario: Department of Justice.

Canfield, J., & Wells, H.C. (1976). *100 Ways to Enhance Self Concept in the Classroom: A Handbook for Teachers and Parents*. Englewood Cliffs, NJ: Prentice-Hall.

Campbell, L. (1997). Family involvement in decision-making in child protection and care: Four types of case conferences. *Child and Family Social Work*, 2, 1–11.

Cattell, V. (2001). Poor people, poor places, and poor health: The mediating role of social networks and social capital. *Social Science and Medicine*, 52, 1501–16.

Chapman, V., & Sork, T. (2001). Confessing regulation or telling secrets? Opening up the conversation on graduate supervision. *Adult Education Quarterly*, 51, 94–108.

Clark, C.L. (2000). *Social Work Ethics: Politics, Principles and Practice*. London: Macmillan.

Cleak, H., & Wilson, J. (2004). *Making the Most of Field Placement*. Southbank, Victoria: Thomson.

Coates, T., & Hayward, C. (2005). The costs of legal limbo for refugees: A preliminary study. *Refuge*, 22, 77–87.

Cohen, A.M., & Smith, R.D. (1976). *The Critical Incident in Growth Groups: Theory and Technique*. La Jolla, CA: University Associates.

Collins, D., Jordan, C., & Coleman, H. (1999). *An Introduction to Family Social Work*. Itasca, IL: Peacock.

Compher, J.V. (1987). The dance beyond the family system. *Social Work*, 32(2), 105–8.

Compton, B.R., & Galaway, B. (1994). *Social Work Processes*. Pacific Grove, CA: Brooks/Cole.

Corby, B. (1996). Risk assessment in child protection work. In H. Kemshall & J. Pritchard (eds), *Good Practice in Risk Assessment and Risk Management* (pp. 13–30). London: Jessica Kingsley.

Corey, G. (2004). *Theory and Practice of Group Counseling* (6th edn). Belmont, CA: Brooks/Cole.

Corey, G. (2005). *Theory and Practice of Counselling and Psychotherapy* (7th edn). Belmont, CA: Thomson Brooks/Cole.

Cormier, S., & Nurius, P.S. (2003). *Interviewing and Change Strategies for Helpers*. Pacific Grove, CA: Thomson Brooks/Cole.

Cowger, C.D. (1992). Assessment of Client Strengths. In D. Saleebey (ed.), *The Strengths Perspective in Social Work Practice*. New York: Longman.

Craig, G., Derricourt, N., & Loney, M. (1982). *Community Work and the State*. London: Routledge, Kegan Paul.

Cross, T., Bazron, K., & Isaacs, M. (1989). *Towards a Culturally Competent System of Care, Volume I*. Washington, DC: Georgetown University Child Development Center, CASSP Technical Assistance Center.

Crossley, M., & Crossley, N. (2001). Patient voices, social movements, and the habitus: How psychiatric survivors 'speak out'. *Social Science and Medicine*, 52, 1477–89.

D'Cruz, H. (2004). *Constructing Meanings and Identities in Child Protection Practice*. Melbourne: Tertiary Press.

Dalgleish, L. (2004). *Steps to a Decision Making Ecology for Child Protective Services: A Multi-National Research Perspective*. Paper presented at the 15th International Congress on Child Abuse and Neglect, Brisbane.

Dane, E. (1985). *Professional and Lay Advocacy in the Education of Handicapped Children*. New York: Routledge and Kegan Paul.

Danso, R., & Grant, M. (2000). Access to housing as an adaptive strategy for immigrant groups: Africans in Calgary, *Canadian Ethnic Studies*, 32, 19–43.

Davies, C. (1998). Care and the transformation of professionalism. In T. Knijn & S. Sevenhuijsen (eds), *Care, Citizenship and Social Cohesion: Towards a Gender Perspective*. Utrecht: Netherlands School for Social and Economic Policy Research.

Davies, M. (1994). *The Essential Social Worker*. Aldershot: Arena.

Davies, M. (2000). *The Blackwell Encyclopaedia of Social Work*. Oxford: Blackwell.

Davies, M., & Webb, E. (2000). Promoting the psychological well-being of refugee children. *Clinical Child Psychology and Psychiatry*, 5(4), 541–54.

de Bono, E. (1985). *Conflicts: A Better Way to Resolve Them*. London: Harrap.

De Luca, R., Boyes, D., Furer, P., Grayston, A., &

Hiebert-Murphy, D. (1992). Group treatment for sexually abused children. *Canadian Psychology,* 33, 168–79.

Department of Human Services (1998). *The Victorian Risk Assessment Framework, Version One.* Melbourne: DHS.

Dick, B. (1991). *Helping Groups to be Effective: Skills, Processes and Concepts for Group Facilitation* (2nd edn). Chapel Hill: Interchange.

Dickson, G. (2000). Aboriginal grandmothers' experience with health promotion and participatory action research. *Qualitative Health Research,* 10, 188–213.

Dillon, C. (2003). *Learning from Mistakes in Clinical Practice.* Pacific Grove, CA: Brooks/Cole Thomson Learning.

Dixon, J., Hoatson, L., & Weeks, W. (2003). Sharing theory and practice. In W. Weeks, L. Hoatson & J. Dixon (eds), *Community Practices in Australia.* Melbourne: Pearson Education.

Dlugos, R.F., & Friedlander, M.L. (2001). Passionately committed psychotherapists: A qualitative study of their experiences. *Professional Psychology: Research and Practice,* 32(3), 298–304.

Doel, M., & Shardlow, S. (1998). *The New Social Work Practice.* Aldershot: Ashgate.

Dominelli, L. (2000). Tackling racism in everyday realities. A task for social workers. In S. Hessle & S. Strega (Eds.) *Valuing the field: Child welfare in an international context,* 141–56. Burlington, VT: Ashgate Publishing.

Dominelli, L. (2002). Values in social work: Contested entities with enduring qualities. In R. Adams, L. Dominelli & M. Payne (eds), *Critical Practice in Social Work.* Hampshire: Palgrave.

Dominelli, L., & Hoogvelt, A. (1996). Globalization and the technocratization of social work. *Critical Social Policy,* 16, 45–62.

Donnison, D. (1991). *A Radical Agenda—After the New Rights and the Old Left.* London: Rivers Oram Press.

Dossick, J., & Shea, E. (1988). *Creative Therapy: 52 Exercises for Groups.* Florida: Professional Resource Exchange (Open Leaves Bookshop, Carlton, Victoria).

Douglas, T. (2000). *Basic Groupwork.* London: Routledge.

Drew, N. (2004). *A Leader's Guide to The Kid's Guide to Working Out Conflicts: How to Keep Cool, Stay Safe, and Get Along.* Minneapolis: Free Spirit Publishing.

Dunn, J., & Dyck, I. (2000). Social determinants of health in Canada's immigrant population: Results from the National Population Health Survey. *Social Science and Medicine,* 51, 1573–93.

Dyer, W.G. (1987). *Team Building: Issues and Alternatives.* Reading, MA: Addison-Wesley.

Eagly, A., Johannesen-Schmidt, M., & van Engen, M. (2003). Transformational, transactional, and laissez-faire leadership styles: A meta-analysis comparing women and men. *Psychological Bulletin,* 129(4), 569–91.

Eby, M. (2000). The challenge of values and ethics in practice. In A. Brechin, H. Brown & M. Eby (eds), *Critical Practice in Health and Social Care.* London: Sage.

Eckermann, A., Dowd, T., Martin, M., Nixon, L., Gray, R., & Chong, E. (1992). *Binan Goonj, Bridging Cultures in Aboriginal Health.* Armidale: University of New England Press.

Egan, G. (2002). *The Skilled Helper* (7th edn). Pacific Grove, CA: Brooks/Cole.

Eisenbruch, M. (1991). From post-traumatic stress disorder to cultural bereavement: Diagnosis of South East Asian refugees. *Social Science Medical,* 33(6), 673–80.

Ellis, K. (1993). *Squaring the Circle: User and Carer Participation in Need Assessment.* York: Joseph Rowntree Foundation.

Evans, D.R., Hearn, M.T., Uhleman, M.R., & Ivey, A.E. (2004). *Essential Interviewing: A Programmed Approach to Effective Communication* (6th edn). Toronto: Thomson Brooks/Cole.

Everitt, A., Hardiker, P., & Littlewood, J. (1992). *Applied Research for Better Practice.* London: Palgrave Macmillan.

Falicov, C. (2003). Immigrant family processes. In F. Walsh (Ed.), *Normal Family Processes* (3rd edn). New York: The Guilford Press.

Fawcett, B., Featherstone, B., Fook, J., & Rossiter, A. (eds) (2000). *Practice and Research in Social Work.* London: Routledge.

Fazel, M., & Stein, A. (2002). The mental health of refugee children. *Archives of Disease in Childhood,* 87, 366–70.

Fernandez, E. (1996). *Significant Harm.* Aldershot: Ashgate.

Fiedler, R., Schuurman, N., & Hyndman, J. (2006). Hidden homelessness: An indicator-based approach for examining the geographies of recent immigrants at-risk of homelessness in Greater Vancouver. *Cities,* 23, 205–16.

Filley, A.C. (1975). *Interpersonal Conflict Resolution.* Glenview, IL: Scott, Foresman and Co.

Finlay, L. (2000). The challenge of working in teams. In A. Brechin, H. Brown & M.A. Eby (eds), *Critical Practice in Health and Social Care.* London: Sage.

Fisher, R., & Ury, W. (1999). *Getting to Yes: Negotiating an Agreement Without Giving In.* London: Random House.

Fitzpatrick, T., & Freed, A. (2000). Older Russian immigrants to the USA, their utilization of health services. *International Social Work*, 43(3), 305–23.

Flood, M., & Lawrence, A. (1987). *The Community Action Book* (2nd edn). Sydney: Maxwell.

Fook, J. (1993). *Radical Casework.* Sydney: Allen and Unwin.

Fook, J. (2002). *Social work: Critical Theory and Practice.* London: Sage.

Forder, A. (1976). Social Work and System Theory. *British Journal of Social Work,* 6(1), 23–42.

Fournier, S., & Crey, E. (1997). *Stolen from our embrace: The abduction of First Nations children and the restoration of Indigenous communities.* Vancouver, BC: Douglas & McIntyre.

Fowler, M., & Levine-Ariff (1987). *Ethics at the Bedside.* Philadelphia: J.B. Lippincott.

Freedberg, S. (1989). Self-determination: Historical perspectives and effects on current practice. *Social Work*, 34, 33–8.

Freire, P. (1997). *Pedagogy of the Oppressed.* New York: Continuum.

Friedlander, W.A. (1958). *Concepts and Methods of Social Work.* Englewood Cliffs, N.J: Prentice-Hall.

Funk-Unrau, N. & Snyder, A. (2007). Indian residential school survivors and state-designed ADR: A strategy for co-optation? *Conflict Resolution Quarterly,* 24, 285–304.

Furr, S., & Barret, R. (2000). Teaching group counseling skills: Problems and solutions. *Counselor Education and Supervision*, 40, 94–105.

Gabb, D. (2000). Development of transcultural mental health education by the Victorian Transcultural Psychiatry Unit. *Synergy*, Summer, 5–30.

Gambrill, E. (1997). *Social Work Practice: A Critical Thinker's Guide.* New York: Oxford University Press.

Garvin, C. (1981). *Contemporary Group Work.* Englewood Cliffs, NJ: Prentice Hall.

Garvin, C. (2001). The potential impact of small-group research on social group work practice. In T. Kelly (ed.), *Group Work: Strategies for Strengthening Resiliency.* New York: The Haworth Press.

George, U., & Ramkissoon, S. (1998). Race, gender, and class: Interlocking oppressions in the lives of South Asian women in Canada. *Affilia*, 13, 102–19.

Gibbs, L., & Gambrill, E. (1999). *Critical Thinking for Social Workers.* Thousand Oaks, CA: Sage.

Gilligan, C. (1982). *In a Different Voice: Psychological Theory and Women's Development.* Cambridge, MA: Harvard University Press.

Gilmour, H., Gibson, F., & Campbell, J. (2003). Living alone with dementia: A case study approach to understanding risk. *Dementia*, 2(3), 403–20.

Gladding, S.T. (2003). *Group Work: A Counselling Specialty* (4th edn). Upper Saddle River, NJ: Merril Prentice Hall.

Goddard, C., Saunders, B., Stanley, J., & Tucci, J. (1999). Structured risk assessment procedures: Instruments of abuse? *Child Abuse and Review*, 8, 251–63.

Goldberg, G. (1974). Structural approach to practice: a new model. *Social Work*, 150–55.

Goldberg, M. (2000). Conflicting principles in multicultural social work. *Families in Society: The Journal of Contemporary Human Services*, 81(1), 12–21.

Goldstein, E.G. (1984). *Ego Psychology and Social Work Practice.* London: Collier Macmillan.

Graham, J., Brownlee, K., Shier, M., & Doucette, E. (2008). Localization of social work knowledge through practitioner adaptations in Northern Ontario and the Northwest Territories, Canada. *Arctic*, 61, 399–406.

Green, G., & Haines, A. (2002). *Asset Building and Community Development.* Thousand Oaks, CA: Sage.

Greif, G.L., & Ephross, P.H. (1997). *Group Work with Populations at Risk.* Oxford: Oxford University Press.

Hall, K., & Dixon, J. (2001). *The RARM: A strengths based and collaborative approach to risk assessment.* Paper presented at the 8th Australasian Conference on Child Abuse and Neglect, Melbourne.

Halpern, N. (1995). Who is helping the helper? Self-care for therapists working with traumatized and abused clients. Paper presented at the Australian Association of Trauma and Dissociation 4th Annual Conference, Melbourne.

Hanson, P. (1972). What to look for in groups. In J.W. Pfeiffer & J.E. Jones (eds), *The 1972 Annual Handbook for Group Facilitators*. San Diego: University Associates.

Hanvey, C. & Philpot, T. (1994). *Practising Social Work*. London: Routledge.

Harding, R. (2006). Historical representations of aboriginal people in the Canadian news media. *Discourse & Society*, 17, 205–35.

Harris, P., & Williams, V. (2003). Social inclusion, national identity and the moral imagination. *The Drawing Board: An Australian Review of Public Affairs*, 3(3), 205–22.

Hartel, C.J., & Trumble, R.B. (1995). IDADA: The individual difference approach to cultural-awareness. Paper presented at the Inaugural Industrial and Organisational Psychology Conference, Sydney.

Hartford, M. (1972). *Groups in Social Work: Application of Small Group Theory and Research to Social Work Practice*. New York: Columbia University Press.

Hawkins, P., & Shohet, A.R. (2000). *Supervision and the Helping Professions*. Buckingham, PA: Open University Press.

Health Canada (2007). Continuing Care in First Nations and Inuit Communities: Evidence from the Research. H34-182/2007. Ottawa, Ontario: Ministry of Health.

Healy, D. (1992). *On Team Leadership*. Sydney: Trilogy Group.

Healy, K. (1998). Participation and child protection: The importance of context. *British Journal of Social Work*, 28, 897–914.

Healy, K. (2000). *Social Work Practices: Contemporary Perspectives on Change*. London: Sage.

Healy, K. (2001). Participatory action research and social work: A critical appraisal. *International Social Work*, 44(1), 93–105.

Healy, K. (2001). Reinventing critical social work: Challenges from practice, context and postmodernism. *Critical Social Work*, 2(1). Online at <http://www.criticalsocialwork.com>, accessed 9 June 2005.

Healy, K. (2005). *Social Work Theories in Context: Creating Frameworks for Practice*. Basingstoke: Palgrave.

Healy, K. (2005). Under reconstruction: Renewing critical social work practices. In S. Hick, J. Fook & R. Pozzuto (eds), *Social Work: A Critical Turn*. Toronto: Thompson Educational.

Healy, K., Hampshire, A., & Ayres, L. (2004). Beyond the local: Extending the social capital discourse. *Australian Journal of Social Issues*, 39(3), 329–42.

Heap, K. (1977). *Group Theory for Social Workers: An Introduction*. Oxford: Pergamon Press.

Hepworth, D.H., & Larsen, J.A. (1993). *Direct Social Work Practice*. Pacific Grove, CA: Brooks/Cole.

Hersey, P., & Blanchard, K.H. (1988). *Management of Organizational Behavior: Utilizing Human Resources* (5th edn). Englewood Cliffs, NJ: Prentice Hall.

Hick, S., Fook, J., & Pozzuto, R. (eds) (2005). *Social Work: A Critical Turn*. Toronto: Thompson Educational.

Hollier, F., Murray, K., & Cornelius, H. (1993). *Conflict Resolution Trainers' Manual; 12 Skills*. Sydney: The Conflict Resolution Network.

Hollis, F. (1972). *Casework: a psychosocial therapy* (2nd edn). New York: Random House.

Holmes, K. (1981). Services for victims of rape: A dualistic practice model. *Social Casework*, 62, 30–9.

Honey, P., & Mumford, A. (1986). *The Manual of Learning Styles*. St Leonards: Allen & Unwin.

Hope, A., & Timmel, S. (1995). *Training for Transformation: A Handbook for Community Workers*. London: Intermediate Technologies Publications.

Hugman, R. (2003). Professional ethics in social work: Living with the legacy. *Australian Social Work*, 56(1), 5–15.

Hunt, M. (1979). Possibilities and problems of interdisciplinary teamwork. In M. Marshall, M. Preston-Shoot & E. Wincott (eds), *Teamwork: For and Against*. Birmingham: BASW Publications.

Husband, C. (2000). Recognising diversity and developing skills: The proper role of transcultural communication. *European Journal of Social Work*, 3(3), 225–34.

Ibrahim, F.A., & Kahn, H. (1987). Assessment of worldviews. *Psychological Reports*, 60, 163–76.

Ife, J. (1997). *Rethinking Social Work: Towards Critical Practice*. South Melbourne: Longman.

Isaacs, M., & Benjamin, M. (1991). *Towards a Culturally Competent System of Care, Volume 2, Programs Which Utilise Culturally Competent Principles*. Washington, DC: Georgetown University Child Development Center, CASSP Technical Assistance Center.

Ivey, A.E., & Bradford Ivey, M. (2003). *Intentional Interviewing and Counseling: Facilitating Client Development in a Multicultural Society* (5th edn). Pacific Grove, CA: Brooks/Cole.

Ivey, A.E., Rathman, D., & Colbert, R.D. (2000). Culturally-relevant microcounselling: Australian Aborigines and the Eurocentric tradition. *Australian Journal of Counselling Psychology*, 2(1), 14–21.

Jack, R. (1995). *Empowerment in Community Care*. London: Chapman and Hall.

Jamrozik, A., Boland, C., & Urquhart, R. (1995). *Social Change and Cultural Transformation in Australia*. Cambridge: Cambridge University Press.

Jarvis, M. (1995). *Adult and Continuing Education*. London: Routledge.

Jilek, W.G. (1994). Traditional healing in the prevention and treatment of alcohol and drug abuse. *Transcultural Psychiatric Research Review*, 31, 219 -58.

Johnson, D.W., & Johnson, F.P. (1997). *Joining Together: Group Theory and Group Skills* (6th edn). Boston: Allyn & Bacon.

Johnson, M., & Rattan, R. (1992). Traditional environmental knowledge of the Dene: A pilot project. *Lore: Capturing traditional environmental knowledge*. Yellowknife, NWT: International Development Research Centre (Canada).

Johnstone, M.-J. (1989). *Bioethics: A Nursing Perspective*. Sydney: Harcourt Brace Jovanovich.

Jordan, B. (1987). Counselling, advocacy and negotiation. *British Journal of Social Work*, 17, 135–46.

Jordan, J. (1991). Catching slips from lips. *Sydney Morning Herald*, 18 April, p. 10.

Kadushin, A. (1976). *Supervision in Social Work*. New York: Columbia University Press.

Kadushin, A. (1990). *The Social Work Interview* (3rd edn). New York: Columbia University Press.

Kaplan, B.J. (1997). *A Nurse's Guide to Public Speaking*. New York: Springer.

Kazemipur, A., & Halli, S. (2001). Immigrants and 'New Poverty:' The case of Canada. *International Migration Review*, 35, 1128-56.

Kendall-Tackett, K. (2003). *Treating the Lifetime Health Effects of Childhood Victimization: A Guide for Mental Health, Medical and Social Service Professionals*. New York: Civic Research Institute.

Kennedy, R., & Richards, J. (2004). *Integrating Human Service Law and Practice*. Melbourne: Oxford University Press.

Kiyoshk, R. (2003). Integrating spirituality and domestic violence treatment. *Journal of Aggression, Maltreatment, and Trauma*, 7, 237–256.

Kluckhohn, F., & Strodtbeck, F. (1961). *Variations in value orientations*. Evanston, IL: Row Peterson and Co.

Kolb, D. (1984). *Experiential Learning: Experience as the Source of Learning and Development*. Englewood Cliffs, NJ: Prentice Hall.

Konrad, G. (1987). *The Caseworker*. Harmondsworth: Penguin.

Kramen-Kahn, B., & Downing Hansen, N. (1998). Rafting the rapids: Occupational hazards, rewards, and coping strategies of psychotherapists. *Professional Psychology: Research and Practice*, 29(2), 130–4.

Kretzmann, J., & McKnight, J. (1993). *Building Communities from the Inside Out*. Chicago: Centre for Urban Affairs and Policy Research.

Kroehnert, G. (1991). *100 Training Games*. Sydney: McGraw-Hill.

Kroehnert, G. (1999). *101 More Training Games*. Sydney: McGraw-Hill.

Kuo, B.C., Chong, V., & Joseph, J. (2008). Depression and its psychosocial correlates among older Asian immigrants in North America: A critical review of two decades research. *Journal of Aging and Health*, 20, 615–52.

Lacroix, M. (2006). Social work with asylum seekers in Canada: The case for social justice. *International Social Work*, 29, 19–28.

Ladouceur, R., Sylvain, C., Boutin, C., Lachance, S., Doucet, C., & Lablond, J. (2002). Group therapy for pathological gamblers: a cognitive approach. *Behavior Research and Therapy*, 41, 587–96.

Lai, D., & Chau, S. (2007). Predictors of health service barriers for older Chinese immigrants in Canada. *Health and Social Work*, 32, 57–65.

Lang, N. (1972). A broad-range model of practice in the social work group. *Social Service Review*, 46(1), 76–89.

La Prairie, C. (2002). Aboriginal over-representation in the criminal justice system: A tale of nine cities. *Canadian Journal of Criminology*, 4, 181–208.

Larocque, E. (2006). The colonization of a Native woman scholar. In M.E. Kelm & L. Townsend (Eds) *In the days of our grandmothers: A reader in Aboriginal women's history in Canada*, 397–406. Toronto, ON: University of Toronto Press.

Lawrence, P.R., & Lorsch, J.W. (1967). *Organization and Environment: Managing Differentiation and Integration*. Homewood, IL: Irwin.

Le Clair, M., & Fortune, P. (1986). *A Lazy Man's Guide to Public Speaking*. Sydney: Fortune.

Leavey, G., Sembhi, S., & Livingston, G. (2004). Older Irish migrants living in London: Identity, loss and return. *Journal of Ethnic and Migration Studies*, 30(4), 763–79.

Levac, A.M., McCay, E., Merka, P., & Reddon-D'Arcy, M. (2008). Exploring parent participation in a parent training program for children's aggression: Understanding and illuminating mechanisms of change. *Journal of Child & Adolescent Psychiatric Nursing*, 21, 78–88.

Lishman, J. (1994). *Communication in Social Work*. Basingstoke: Macmillan/BASW.

Loewenberg, F.M., & Dolgoff, R. (1996). *Ethical Decisions for Social Work Practice*. Itasca, IL: Peacock.

Lorenz, W. (1994). *Social Work in a Changing Europe*. London: Routledge.

Loxley, A. (1997). *Collaboration in Health and Welfare: Working with Difference*. London: Jessica Kingsley.

Lum, D. (1999). *Culturally Competent Practice: A Framework for Growth and Action*. Pacific Grove, CA: Brooks/Cole.

Lynch, D. (2004). The protection, care and adjustment of refugee children in Australia. Paper presented at the 15th International Conference on Child Abuse and Neglect, Brisbane.

Maidment, J. & Egan, R. (2004). *Practice Skills in Social Work and Welfare*. Crows Nest, N.S.W.: Allen & Unwin.

Maluccio, A. (1979). The influence of the agency environment on clinical practice. *Journal of Sociology and Social Welfare*, 6, 734–55.

Maples, M.F. (1988). Group development: Extending Tuckman's theory. *Journal for Specialists in Groupwork*, March.

Marshall, T.H. (1975). *Social Policy*. London: Hutchinson Educational.

Martin, J. (2000). Social workers as mediators. *Australian Social Work*, 53(4), 33–9.

Martinez, C. (1986). Hispanic psychiatric issues. In C. Wilkinson (ed.), *Ethnic psychiatry*. New York: Plenum.

Marziali, E. (2006). Developing evidence for an Internet-based psychotherapeutic group intervention. *Journal of Evidence-based Social Work*, 3, 149–66.

Mathie, A., & Cunningham, G. (2002). From clients to citizens: Asset based community development as a strategy for community driven development. <http://www.stfx.ca/academic/dev-studies/ Devs200/Occ%20paper2002.htm>, accessed 1 November 2004.

McCarthy, P., & Hatcher, C. (2002). *Speaking Persuasively*. Sydney: Allen & Unwin.

McGibbon, E. (2000). The 'situated knowledge' of helpers. In C.E. James (ed.), *Experiencing difference*, 185–99. Halifax, NS: Fernwood Publishing.

McGoldrick, M. (2003). Culture: A challenge to concepts of normality. In F. Walsh (Ed.), *Normal Family Processes* (3rd edn). New York: The Guilford Press.

McKenzie, B., & Morrisette, V. (2003). Social work practice with Canadians of Aboriginal background: Guidelines for respectful social work. *Envision: The Manitoba Journal of Child Welfare*, 2, 13–39.

McKenzie, B., & Morrissette, V. (2003). Social work practice with Canadians of Aboriginal background: Guidelines for respectful social work. In A. Al-Krenawi and J.R. Graham (eds.) *Multicultural social work in Canada: Working with diverse ethno-racial communities*, 251–82. Don Mills, ON: Oxford University Press.

McLaren, P., & Leonard, P. (eds) (1993). *Paulo Freire: A Critical Encounter*. London: Routledge.

McMahon, M., & Patton, W. (2002). *Supervision in the Helping Professions A Practical Approach*. Sydney: Prentice Hall.

Merritt, R.E., & Walley, D.D. (1977). *The Group Leader's Handbook: Resources, Techniques and Survival Skills*. Champaign, IL: Research Press.

Meyer, C.H. (1983). The search for coherence. In C.H. Meyer (ed.), *Clinical social work in the ecosystems perspective*. New York: Columbia University Press.

Mezirow, J., & Associates (1991). *Fostering Critical Reflection in Adulthood. A Guide to Transformative and Emancipatory Learning*. San Francisco: Jossey-Bass.

Miller, M.N., & McGowen, K.R. (2000). The painful truth: Physicians are not invincible. *Southern Medical Journal*, 93(10), 966–73.

Milner, J. & O'Byrne, P. (2002). *Assessment in Social Work* (2nd edn). Basingstoke: Palgrave Macmillan.

Mitchell, P. (2000). *Valuing Young Lives: Evaluation of the National Youth Suicide Prevention Strategy*. Melbourne: Australian Institute of Family Studies.

Moffitt, P. (2004). Colonialization: A health determinant for pregnant Dogrib women. *Journal of Transcultural Nursing*, 15, 323–30.

Moore, C.W. (1996). *The Mediation Process: Practical Strategies for Resolving Conflict*. San Francisco: Jossey-Bass.

Moreau, M.J. (1990). Empowerment through advocacy and consciousness-raising: Implications of a structural approach to social work. *Journal of Sociology and Social Welfare*, 17(2), 53–68.

Morrison, T. (1993). *Supervision in Social Care*. London: Macmillan.

Morrison, T. (2001). *Staff Supervision in Social Care: Making a Real Difference for Staff and Service Users*. Brighton: Pavilion.

Morris, R. (1989). Personal communication whilst a participant in a groupwork training workshop run by the chapter author. Sydney.

Mouzakitis, C., & Goldstein, S. (1985). A multidisciplinary approach to treating child neglect. *Social Casework: The Journal of Contemporary Social Work*, 66(4), 218–24.

Najavits, L.M. (2000). Researching therapist emotions and countertransference. *Cognitive and Behavioral Practice*, 7, 322–8.

Napier, L., & Fook, J. (2000). *Breakthroughs in Practice: Theorising Critical Moments in Social Work*. London: Whiting and Birch.

Napier, R.W., & Gershenfeld, M.K. (1993). *Groups: Theory and Experience* (5th edn). Boston: Houghton Mifflin.

Naylor, L. (1998). *American Culture: Myth and Reality of a Culture of Diversity*. Westport, CN: Bergin and Garver.

Nelson-Jones, R. (1991). *Leading Training Groups: A Manual of Practical Group Skills for Trainers*. Sydney: Holt, Rinehart & Winston.

Nelson, S.E. (2000). A new paradigm for teaching counseling theory and practice. *Counselor Education & Supervision*, 39, 254-70.

Newstrom, J.W., & Scannell, E.E. (1980). *Games Trainers Play*. New York: McGraw-Hill.

Nguyen, T., & Bowles, R. (1998). Counselling Vietnamese refugee survivors of trauma: Points of entry for developing trust and rapport. *Australian Social Work*, 51(2), 41–7.

Nierenberg, G.I. (1981). *The Art of Negotiating*. New York: Simon & Schuster.

Nilson, C. (1993). *Team Games for Trainers*. New York: McGraw-Hill.

Noddings, N. (1984). *Caring: A Feminine Approach to Ethics and Moral Education*. Berkeley: University of California Press.

Norcross, J.C. (2000). Psychotherapist self-care: Practitioner-tested, research-informed strategies. *Professional Psychology: Research and Practice*, 31(6), 710–13.

Northen, H. (1969). *Social Work with Groups*. New York: Columbia University Press.

Northen, H. (1988). *Social Work with Groups* (2nd edn). New York: Columbia University Press.

Nugent, P., & Zamble, E. (2001). Affecting detention referrals through proper selection. *Forum on Corrections Research*, 13.

O'Connor, I., Wilson, J., & Setterlund, D. (1995). *Social Work and Welfare Practice* (2nd edn). Melbourne: Longman.

O'Connor, I., Wilson, J., & Setterlund, D. (2003). *Social Work and Welfare Practice* (4th edn). Melbourne: Pearson Education.

Oh, J., Segal, R., Gordon, J., Boal, J., & Jotkowitz, A. (2001). Retention and use of patient-centred interviewing skills after intensive training. *Academic Medicine*, 76(6), 647–50.

Oliffe, J., Halpin, M., Bottorff, J., Hislop, T., McKenzie, M., & Mroz, L. (2008). How prostate cancer support groups do and do not survive: British Columbian perspectives. *American Journal of Men's Health*, 2, 143–55.

Omidvar, R., & Richmond, T. (2003). Immigrant settlement and social inclusion in Canada. Laidlaw Foundation's Working Paper Series, Perspectives on Social Inclusion. Toronto, Ontario: Laidlaw Foundation.

Osher, D.M., & Osher, T.W. (1995). Comprehensive and collaborative systems that work: A national agenda. In C.M. Nelson, R. Rutherford & B.I. Wolford (eds), *Developing Comprehensive Systems that Work for Troubled Youth*. Richmond, KY: National Coalition for Juvenile Justice Services.

Ovretveit, J. (1995). Team decision making. *Journal of Interprofessional Care*, 9, 41–51.

Ovretveit, J. (1997a). How to describe interprofessional working. In J. Ovretveit, P. Mathias & T. Thompson (eds), *Interprofessional Working for Health and Social Care*. Basingstoke: Macmillan.

Ovretveit, J. (1997b). Evaluating interprofessional working—a case example of a community mental health team. In J. Ovretveit, P. Mathias & T. Thompson (eds), *Interprofessional Working for Health and Social Care*. Basingstoke: Macmillan.

Pack-Brown, S.P., & Williams, C.B. (2003). *Ethics in a Multicultural Context*. Thousand Oaks, CA: Sage.

Papadopoulos, R. (1999). Working with Bosnian medical evacuees and their families: Therapeutic dilemmas. *Clinical Child Psychology and Psychiatry*, 4(1), 107–20.

Pare, A., & Allen, H.S. (1995). Social work writing: Learning by doing. In G. Rogers (ed.), *Social Work Education: Views and Visions*. Dubuque, IA: Kendall/Hunt.

Parton, N., & O'Bryne, P. (2000). *Constructive Social Work*. Basingstoke: Palgrave Macmillan.

Payne, M. (1982). *Working in Teams*. Basingstoke: Macmillan.

Payne, M. (1997). *Modern Social Work Theory*. Basingstoke: Macmillan.

Pearson, N. (2000). Passive welfare and the destruction of Indigenous society in Australia. In P. Saunders (ed.), *Reforming the Australian Welfare State*. Melbourne: Australian Institute of Family Studies.

Pedersen, P.B. (2000). *A handbook for developing multicultural awareness* (3rd edn). Alexandria, VA: American Counseling Association.

Pellegrino, E., & Thomasma, D. (1993). *The Virtues in Medical Practice*. Oxford: Oxford University Press.

Peoples' Experience of Colonization (2008). http://web2.uvcs.uvic.ca/courses/csafety/mod1/resource.htm, accessed 12 January 2009.

Perlman, H. (1957). *Social casework: A problem-solving process*. Chicago: University of Chicago Press.

Perlman, H. (1976). Believing and doing: Values in social work education. *Social Casework*, 57(6), 381–90.

Pfeiffer, J.W., & Jones, J.E. (eds) (1973). *A Handbook of Structured Experiences for Human Relations Training*. La Jolla: University Associates.

PIAC (2008). Comments of the Public Interest Advocacy Centre (PIAC) and the National Anti-Poverty Organization (NAPO) to the maximum total cost of borrowing advisory board.

Picot, G., Hou, F., & Coulombe, S. (2008). Poverty dynamics among recent immigrants to Canada. *International Migration Review*, 42, 393–424.

Pincus, A., & Minahan, A. (1973). *Social Work Practice: Model and Method*. Itasca, IL: Peacock.

Porter, S. (1998). *Social Theory and Nursing Practice*. Basingstoke: Macmillan.

Preston, V., Murdie, R., & Murnaghan, A.M. (2007). The housing situation and needs of recent immigrants in the Toronto Census metropolitan area. CERIS Working Paper No. 56. The Ontario Metropolis Centre, Toronto, Ontario: CERIS.

Prince, K. (1996). *Boring records? Communication, Speech and Writing in Social Work*. London: Jessica Kingsley.

Pritchard, P. (1995). Learning how to work effectively in teams. In P. Owens, J. Carrier & J. Horder (eds), *Interprofessional Issues in Community and Primary Health Care*. Basingstoke: Macmillan.

Proctor, B. (1988). Supervision: A co-operative exercise in accountability. In M. Maren & M. Payne (eds), *Enabling and Ensuring*. Leicester: National Youth Bureau and Council for Education and Training in Youth and Community Work.

Ramsden, I. (2000). Cultural safety/Kawa whakaruhau ten years on: A personal overview. *Nursing Praxis in New Zealand*, 15(1), 4–12.

Reamer, F.G. (1999). *Social Work Values and Ethics*. New York: Columbia University Press.

Rechtman, R. (2000). Stories of trauma and idioms of distress: From cultural narratives to clinical assessment. *Transcultural Psychiatry*, 37(3), 403–15.

Reed, H., Cameron, D., & Spinks, D. (1985). *Stepping Stones: A Management Training Manual for Community Groups*. Hurstville: Community Management Training Scheme.

Reid, K. (1997). *Social Work Practice with Groups: A Clinical Perspective*. Pacific Grove, CA: Brooks/Cole.

Reynolds, B. (1965). *Teaching and Learning in the Practice of Social Work*. New York: Russell & Russell.

Rhodes, M.L. (1991). *Ethical Dilemmas in Social Work Practice*. New York: Routledge, Chapman and Hall.

Richmond, M. (1917). *Social Diagnosis*. New York: Russell Sage Foundation.

Rose, S.M., & Black, B. (1985). *Advocacy and Empowerment: Mental Health Care in the Community*. New York: Routledge and Kegan Paul.

Rose, S.M., & Black, B. (1990). Advocacy/empowerment: An approach to clinical practice for social work. *Journal of Sociology and Social Welfare*, 17(2), 41–52.

Rossiter, A. (1996). A perspective on critical social work. *Journal of Progressive Human Services*, 7(2), pp. 23–41.

Rowland, A., & McDonald, L. (2009). Evaluation of social work communication skills to allow people with aphasia to be part of the decision making process in healthcare. *Social Work Education*, 28, 128–44.

Sakamoto, I. (2007). A critical examination of immigrant acculturation: Toward an anti-oppressive social work model with immigrant adults in a pluralistic society. *British Journal of Social Work*, 37, 515–35.

Saleebey, D. (1996). The strengths perspective in social work practice. Extensions and cautions. *Social Work*, 41, 296–305.

Saleebey, D. (1997). Introduction: Power in people. In Saleebey, D. (ed.), *The Strengths Perspective in Social Work*. New York: Longman.

Saleebey, D. (ed.) (2002). *The Strengths Perspective in Social Work*. New York: Longman.

Sambono, A. (2004). Indigenous Australian history and health (lecture notes). Sydney: Koori Centre, University of Sydney.

Sands, R.G., Stafford, T., & McClelland, M. (1990). I beg to differ: Conflict in the interdisciplinary team. *Social Work in Health Care*, 26(4), 55–72.

Sattler, J.M. (1998). *Clinical and Forensic Interviewing of Children and Families: Guidelines for the Mental Health, Education, Pediatric, and Child Maltreatment Fields*. San Diego, CA: Jerome M. Sattler.

Schiller, L.Y. (1997). Rethinking stages of development in women's groups: Implications for practice. *Social Work with Groups*, 20(3), 3–19.

Schneider Corey, M., & Corey, G. (1997). *Groups: Process and Practice*. Pacific Grove, CA: Brooks/Cole.

Schön, D. (1983). *The Reflective Practitioner*. London: Temple Smith.

Schön, D. (1987). *Educating the Reflective Practitioner*. San Francisco: Jossey-Bass.

Schutz, W.C. (1973). *Elements of Encounter: A Bodymind Approach*. Big Sur, CA: Joy Press.

Scott, D. (1998). A Qualitative Study of Social Work Assessment in Cases of Alleged Child Abuse. *British Journal of Social Work*, 28, 73–88.

Seden, J. (1999). *Counselling Skills in Social Work Practice*. Philadelphia, PA: Open University Press.

Shardlow, S., & Doel, M. (1996). *Practice Learning and Teaching*. London: Macmillan.

Sheldon, B. (1995). *Cognitive-Behavioural Therapy, Research, Practice and Philosophy*. London and New York: Routledge.

Sheppard, M. (1995). *Care Management and the New Social Work: A Critical Analysis*. London: Whiting and Birch.

Sherwin, S. (1998). *The Politics of Women's Health: Exploring Agency and Autonomy*. Philadelphia: Temple University Press.

Shragge, E. (1997). Community economic development: Conflicts and visions. In E. Shragge (ed.), *Community Economic Development: In Search of Empowerment* (pp. 1–18). Montreal: Black Rose Books.

Shulman, L. (1992). *The Skills of Helping: Individuals, Families and Groups*. Itasca, IL: Peacock.

Shulman, L. (1999). *The Skills of Helping Individuals, Families, Groups, and Communities* (4th edn). Itasca, IL: Peacock.

Silberman, M. (1995). *101 Ways to Make Training Active*. San Diego: Pfeiffer & Co.

Simon Fraser University (2009). Community Education Program.

Siporin, M. (1975). *Introduction to social work practice*. New York: Macmillan.

Sivasubramaniam, N., Murry, W., Avolio, B., & Jung, D. (2002). A longitudinal model of the effects of team leadership and group potency on group performance. *Group and Organization Management*, 27(1), 66–96.

Skovholt, T.M., Grier, T.L., & Hanson, M.R. (2001). Career counseling for longevity: Self-care and burnout prevention strategies for counselor resilience. *Journal of Career Development*, 27(3), 167–76.

Smith, A. & Frank, F. (1999). The community development facilitator's guide: A tool to support the community development handbook. Ottawa: Human Resources and Development Canada.

Smith, B. (1999). Community consultation: It's essential. In R. Craven (ed.), *Teaching Indigenous Studies*. Sydney: Allen & Unwin.

Smith, E., & Jackson, A. (2002). Does a rising tide lift all boats? The labour market experiences and incomes of recent immigrants 1995–98. Canadian Council on Social Development, Ottawa, Ontario; Canadian Council on Social Development.

Smith, M.K. (1994). *Location Education: Community, Conversation and Action*. Buckingham, PA: Open University Press.

Smith, R. (1984). Teaching interviewing skills to medical students: The issue of 'countertransference'. *Journal of Medical Education*, 59(7), 582–8.

Sosin, M., & Caulum, S. (1983). Advocacy: A conceptualization for social work practice. *Social Work*, 28, 12–17.

Stanley, J., & Goddard, C. (2002). *In the Firing Line: Violence and Power in Child Protection Work*. New York: John Wiley & Sons.

Statistics Canada (2003). Longitudinal survey of immigrants to Canada: Process, progress and prospects. Statistics Canada, Social and Aboriginal Policy Division. Catalogue no. 89-615-XIE. Ottawa, Ontario: Statistics Canada.

Statistics Canada (2008). Aboriginal identity population by age groups, median age and sex, percentage distribution for Canada. Release number 5, 15 January 2008.

Stewart, M., Davidson, K., Meaded., H.A., & Weld-Viscount, P. ( 2001). Group support for couples coping with a cardiac condition. *Journal of Advanced Nursing, 33*, 190–99.

Stitt, A.J. (1998). *Alternative Dispute Resolution for Organizations.* Toronto: John Wiley & Sons.

Stock Whitaker, D. (1985). *Using Groups to Help People.* London: Routledge.

Stone, W., & Hughes, J. (2002). *Social Capital: Empirical Meaning and Measurement Validity.* Melbourne: Australian Institute of Family Studies.

Strom-Gottfried, K. (1999). *Social Work Practice.* Thousand Oaks, CA: Pine Forge Press.

Sue, D.W., & Sue, D. (2003). *Counseling the Culturally Diverse.* New York: John Wiley and Sons.

Sullivan, E.L. (1999). Discrimination and 'meta-discrimination': Issues for reflective practice. *Australian Social Work, 52*(3), 3–8.

Sullivan, W.P. (1992). Reconsidering the Environment as a Helping Resource. In D. Saleebey (ed.), *The Strengths Perspective in Social Work Practice.* New York: Longman.

Swain, P. (2002). Why social work and law? In P. Swain (ed.), *In the Shadow of the Law: The Legal Context of Social Work Practice* (pp. 2–6) Annandale, NSW: Federation Press.

Thomas, W., & Bellefeuille, G. (2006). An evidence-based formative evaluation of a cross cultural Aboriginal mental health program in Canada. *Australian e-Journal for the Advancement of Mental Health* (AEJAMH), 5, 1–14.

Thompson, N. (1997). *Anti-Discriminatory Practice* (2nd edn). Basingstoke: Palgrave Macmillan.

Thompson, N. (2002). *People Skills* (2nd edn). Hampshire: Palgrave Macmillan.

Thurston, W. (2006). Immigrant women, family violence, and pathways out of homelessness. Report prepared for the National Secretariat on Homelessness. Calgary, Alberta: National Secretariat on Homelessness.

Thursz, D., Nusberg, C., & Prather, J. (1995).

*Empowering Older People: An International Approach.* London: Cassell.

Tillett, G. (1991). *Resolving Conflict: A Practical Approach.* Sydney: Sydney University Press.

Timms, N. (1983). *Social Work Values: An Enquiry.* London: Routledge and Kegan Paul.

Trevithick, P. (2000). *Social Work Skills: A Practice Handbook.* Buckingham, PA: Open University Press.

Trocmé, N., Knoke, D., & Blackstock, C. (2004). Pathways to the over-representation of Aboriginal children in Canada's child welfare system. *Social Service Review, 78*, 577–600.

Troper, H. (2008). Immigration. *The Canadian Encyclopedia,* Online edition. http://www.the-canadianencyclopedia.com/index.cfm?PgNm=TCE&Params=A1ARTA0003960

Trotter, C. (1999). *Working with Involuntary Clients.* Sydney: Allen & Unwin.

Tschudin, V., & Marks-Maran, D. (1993). *Ethics: A Primer for Nurses.* London: Bailliere Tindall.

Tuckman, B.W. (1965). Developmental sequence in small groups. *Psychological Bulletin, 63*, 384–99.

Turnell, A., & Edwards, S. (1999). *Signs of Safety. A Solution and Safety Oriented Approach to Child Protection Casework.* New York: Bytheway.

Tutty, L., Babins-Wagner, R., & Rothery, M. (2006). Group treatment for aggressive women: an initial evaluation. *Journal of Family Violence, 21*, 341–49.

Tyson, T. (1989). *Working with Groups.* Melbourne: Macmillan.

Vallence, K. (1987). Speaking in a group. In K. Vallence & T. McWilliam (eds), *Communication That Works.* Melbourne: Thomas Nelson.

Vasta, E. (2004). Community, the state and the deserving citizen: Pacific Islanders in Australia. *Journal of Ethnic and Migration Studies, 30*(1), 195–214.

Vicary, D., & Andrews, H. (2000). Developing a culturally appropriate psychotherapeutic approach with Indigenous Australians. *Australian Psychologist, 35*(3), 181–5.

Vickery, A. (1976). A Unitary Approach to Social Work with the Mentally Disordered. In M.R. Olsen (ed.), *Differential Approaches in Social Work with the Mentally Disordered.* Birmingham: British Association of Social Workers.

Vigilante, J. (1974). Between values and science: Education for the professional during a moral crisis or is proof truth? *Journal of Education for Social Work,* 10, 107–15.

Vigilante, J. (1983). Professional values. In A. Rosenblatt & D. Waldfogel (eds), *Handbook of Clinical Social Work*. San Francisco: Jossey-Bass.

Vinson, T., Baldry, E., & Hargreaves, J. (1996). Neighbourhoods, networks and child abuse. *British Journal of Social Work*, 26(4), 523–43.

Vonk, E.M., & Zucrow, E. (1996). Female MSW students' satisfaction with practicum supervision: The effect of supervisor gender. *Journal of Social Work Education*, 32, 415–20.

Waldram, J., Herring, A., & Young, K. (2006). *Aboriginal health in Canada: Historical, cultural, and epidemiological perspective*. Toronto, ON: University of Toronto Press.

Waldrum, J.B., & Wong, S. (1995). Group therapy of aboriginal offenders in a Canadian forensic psychiatric facility. American Indian and Alaska native mental health research (Monographic series), 34–56.

Walton, R.E. (1969). *Interpersonal Peacemaking: Confrontation and Third Party Consultation*. Reading, MA: Addison-Wesley.

Ward, C., & Styles, I. (2003). Lost and found, reinvention of the self following migration. *Journal of Applied Psychoanalytic Studies*, 5(3), 349–67.

Wasserstrom, R. (ed.) (1975). *Today's Moral Problems*. New York: Macmillan.

Watson, H.J., Vallee, J.M., & Mulford, W.R. (1981). *Structured Experiences and Group Development*. Canberra: Curriculum Development Centre.

Waugh, F. (2000). Initial assessment: A key stage in social work intervention. *Australian Social Work*, 53(1), 57–63.

Webb, N.B. (2003). *Social Work Practice with Children*. New York: Guilford Press.

Weber, Z. (2004). Case management in action. (Unpublished research project.) School of Social Work and Policy Studies, Faculty of Education and Social Work, University of Sydney.

Weick, A., Rapp, C., Sullivan, P., & Kisthart, W. (1989). A strengths perspective for social work practice. *Social Work*, 34(4), 350–4.

Whelan, S., & Hochberger, J. (1996). Validation studies of the group development questionnaire. *Small Group Research*, 27(1), 143–70.

Whitaker, D., & Lieberman, M. (1965). *Psychotherapy Through the Group Process*. London: Tavistock.

Whital, M., Robichaud, M., Thordarson, D., & McLean, P. (2008). Group and individual treatment of obsessive-compulsive disorder using cognitive therapy and exposure plus response prevention: A 2-year follow-up of two randomized trials. *Journal of Consulting and Clinical Psychology*, 76, 1003–14.

White, F.A. (1996). Sources of influence in moral thought: The new moral authority scale (MAS). *Journal of Moral Education*, 25(4), 421–39.

Williamson, B. (1993). *Playful Activities for Powerful Presentations*. Duluth: Whole Person Associates.

Wilson, C., & Powell, M. (2001). *A Guide to Interviewing Children: Essential Skills for Counsellors, Police, Lawyers and Social Workers*. Sydney: Allen & Unwin.

Wilson, J. (1995). *How to Work with Self-help Groups: Guidelines for Professionals*. Aldershot: Arena.

Windschuttle, K., & Elliott, E. (2002). *Writing, Researching, Communicating: Communication Skills for the Information Age*. Sydney: Irwin/McGraw-Hill.

Wolfensberger, W. (1972). *The Principle of Normalisation in Human Services*. Toronto: National Institute on Mental Retardation.

Wolfensberger, W. (1984). A reconceptualization of normalization as social role valorization. *Mental Retardation*, 32, 22–5.

Woodcock, M. (1979). *Team Development Manual*. Farnborough: Gower Press.

Yalom, I.D. (1995). *The Theory and Practice of Group Psychotherapy* (4th edn). New York: Basic Books.

Zellerer, E. (2003). Culturally competent programs: The first family violence program for Aboriginal men in prison. *The Prison Journal*, 83, 171–90.

# Index